MW01628532

People Among the People

THE PUBLIC ART OF SUSAN POINT

niʔ xʷc̓əθət tə šxʷtəhims
ʔə tə xʷən̓aʔəl̓məxʷ ʔi ʔə
tə n̓a təməxʷ, ʔiʔ ƛ̓əw
tə n̓əcə́wməxʷ

ʔi swiw̓əl̓ tə sya:ys ʔə ƛ̓ ʔəy̓xʷatiye

ROBERT D. WATT

People Among the People

THE PUBLIC ART OF SUSAN POINT

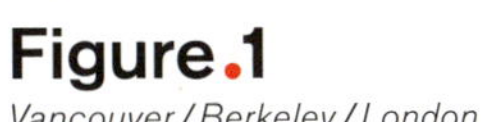

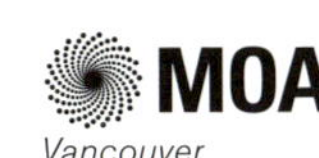

SPONSORS

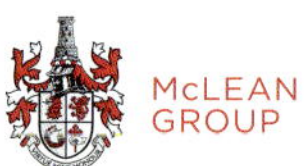

LEAD SPONSOR

THE MCLEAN FAMILY, VANCOUVER, BC
Brenda and David
Andrea and Jason
Melanie and Sacha

"We gratefully acknowledge the beautiful work of Susan Point. She makes us all richer for having experienced her amazing artistic talent."

FOUNDATIONS AND CORPORATIONS

The Audain Foundation

London Drugs

The W. Garfield Weston Foundation

The Fei and Milton Wong Family Foundation

The Salish Weave Foundation of Christiane and George Smyth

The Martha Lou Henley Charitable Foundation

Urban Accessories, Tacoma, WA

Vancouver Fraser Port Authority

INDIVIDUALS

Gift of Dr. Joseph Segal, C.M., O.B.C. and Mrs. Rosalie Segal

Yosef Wosk, O.B.C.

Victoria J. Huntington

Doreen Braverman

For Susan and Alison

19 20 21 22 23 5 4 3 2 1

Cataloguing data is available from Library and Archives Canada
ISBN 978-1-77327-042-5 (hbk.)

Series design by Jessica Sullivan
Design by Naomi MacDougall
Editing by Michael Leyne
Proofreading by Melanie Little

Jacket images: Front: *Four Corners* (detail), 1999. Courtesy of Archives of Coast Salish Arts. Photo: Bob Mathison.
Back: *Salmon Spawning Run*, 2012. Collection of The Mint Museum, Charlotte, North Carolina. Art © Susan Point 2012

Every effort has been made to identify the photographer of each piece; please contact Figure 1 with inquiries or information about outstanding credits.

Measurements of artworks are given as height × width × depth.

Printed and bound in China by
C&C Offset Printing Co., Ltd.
Distributed in the U.S. by Publishers Group West

Figure 1 Publishing Inc.
Vancouver BC Canada
www.figure1publishing.com

Museum of Anthropology at UBC
6393 N.W. Marine Drive
Vancouver BC Canada V6T 1Z2
www.moa.ca

Contents

A Note on the Use of hən̓q̓əmin̓əm̓

THIS BOOK INCLUDES a number of names for people, places, and things in hən̓q̓əmin̓əm̓, the Downriver dialect of halq̓emeylem (Halkomelem), the Central Coast Salish language of many First Nations Peoples on southern Vancouver Island and in the Lower Mainland region of British Columbia, including the xʷməθkʷəy̓əm (Musqueam). If available, an English translation follows in parentheses (or, for names of individuals, after a dash); non-hən̓q̓əmin̓əm̓ First Nations words are followed by their hən̓q̓əmin̓əm̓ (if available) and English translations in parentheses. On page 239 there is a pronunciation guide to hən̓q̓əmin̓əm̓ orthography.

We are deeply grateful to have had the expert help of Musqueam Elder sʔəyəɬəq—Larry Grant in compiling these words. His personal commitment over many decades to strengthening the use of his ancestral language means that in a special way, as Susan has remarked, this book on her art introduces a wider public to the riches of the language of her forebears.

Artist's Statement

SUSAN A. POINT, O.C.

SINCE I WAS a young child I have always been interested in art, especially drawing to my heart's content, and this passion will stay with me forever. But when I began making art very few people were aware of the history of Coast Salish art and its connection to the community. Northern art was the predominant style, probably because northern communities were less impacted by early contact, and few people would even acknowledge that different styles existed. It wasn't until I was in my late twenties, when I took a jewellery course at Vancouver Community College in January of 1981, that I discovered that we, as Coast Salish people, have our own unique art style. This discovery marked the beginning of my career, and for the past thirty-seven years I have truly dedicated myself to reviving Coast Salish art.

I feel that it is important to re-establish our Salish footprint upon our lands, to create a visual expression of the link between the past and present that is both accessible and people-friendly. Whether it's public sculptures or prints on paper, I create unique, "original" artwork that honours both my people and the diverse group of peoples from around the world who have come to live upon our lands on the Northwest Coast. My hope is that my art leaves a lasting impression on visitors, locals, and the surrounding communities.

When I began, very little information or documentation could be found on the art style of the Coast Salish people, due to early and extensive European contact in our territory. Many of our traditional artifacts, such as houseposts and other utilitarian pieces created by my ancestors, were collected by eastern Canadian and European museums, or destroyed because of their ceremonial significance in an attempt to assimilate our First Nations Peoples. It was almost a lost art form.

Through extensive research I tried to educate not only myself but also the public about Coast Salish art. There was none of today's modern technology available to assist me, so this entailed endless legwork, going to various libraries and museums to gather up as much information as I could. I was determined to learn everything I could about the art of my people.

In hindsight, one of the most important things I learned is that although our ancestors shared a common visual language, they each had their own unique art style. This is what separated Coast Salish art from all other art forms on the Northwest Coast. I have worked strictly in our Coast Salish art style, incorporating the main distinctive elements (crescents, wedges, V-cuts) found in our traditional pieces that are housed in various museums around the world.

At the same time, because I found so little information on our Salish Peoples' art and culture, and at first I did not yet truly understand the unique significance of our art, I went beyond the traditions of my people to develop my own style. I re-designed and re-created traditional imagery in my own "original" way, and developed a unique contemporary art style that created a movement.

Susan Point carves the "Grandchildren" upright, part of *People Amongst the People* (2008; see page 66), in her studio at Celtic Shipyards in Vancouver, August 2007.

The late Bud Mintz, who owned the Potlatch Arts gallery in Vancouver, was my number one supporter—he believed in me and promoted me as a Coast Salish artist right from the start. He was very knowledgeable and aware of the art and culture of the Coast Salish. Soon other galleries began to show my work, in B.C., Montreal, and Washington State.

Over the years I have worked with a wide range of materials, from the traditional carved red and yellow cedar to contemporary mediums such as precious metals, paper, glass, cast iron, stainless steel, aluminum, bronze, concrete, and polymers, depending on the requirements and context of each project. Working with each new medium for the first time is an exciting challenge. All of these were experimental in the beginning and I approached every medium differently. I spent much of my time learning these processes hands-on so as to understand each medium and to ensure that my artwork was done to my satisfaction.

As shown in this book, I have completed many large-scale site-specific public art commissions in Canada and the U.S. These works involved combining my fine-art and design abilities with actual architectural finishes and embellishments, which always presents new challenges in terms of the site, the budget, and the unique community inhabitants. I always work very closely with the professional people involved in each project so that I understand the whole process, and can ensure that my artwork tells the whole story of my vision for it.

All my designs for public art are site-specific, based on the history of the area. This requires research, and often community input from certain tribes for insight into their distinct legends and local preferences towards proposed artworks. This is a time-honoured protocol that was shared as Salish people, and a protocol that I abide by as taught by my Elders. From there, I consider the medium, and design my imagery for that specific medium, revising as required by the limitations of the material.

In all of my works, regardless of medium, my imagery is very important to me. Every piece has a special meaning behind it, whether it's accompanied by a story or not. Re-creating traditional imagery in my own style honours and shows respect to my artisan ancestors, the creators of imagery found on tools, houseposts, basketry, blankets, jewellery, and other objects, while my contemporary imagery reflects experiences in my family life, and our love of the outdoors. I am mostly inspired by nature and our connected "human spirit"—I try to illustrate our need to protect and restore our natural treasures and bring reflection and awareness to issues of concern in all our lives.

As a contemporary Coast Salish artist, I have encountered many pre-conceived ideas of what Salish artwork is. I try to create art that honours my heritage while embracing new techniques and subject matter. My art is my voice—made visible by marrying colour with positive and negative space. I am always happy to surprise and, I hope, connect

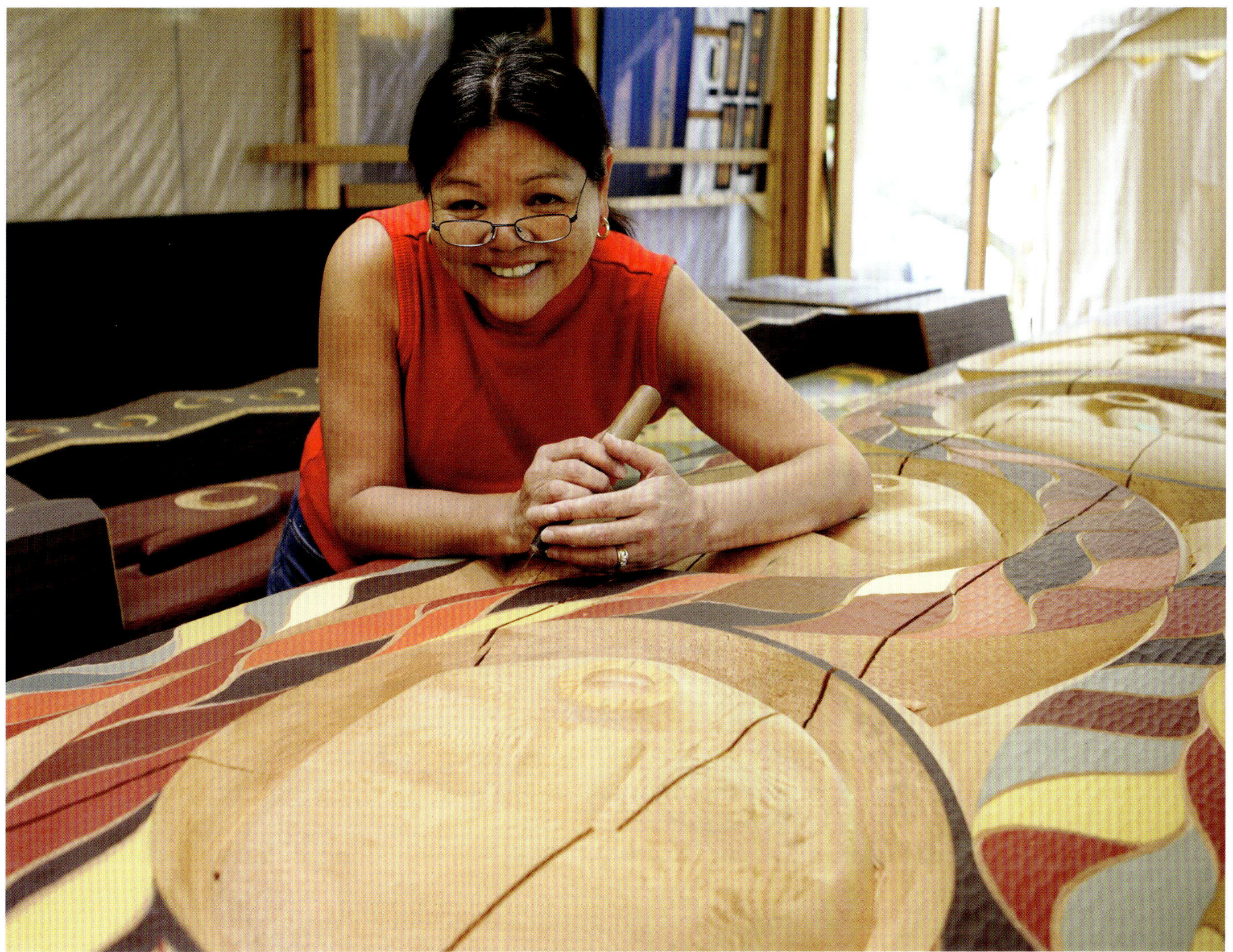

people with a visual language that is universal in its appeal.

In closing, I would truly like to thank my long-time friend Robert Watt and his wife, Alison, for putting this book together. Their work has taken many years. Thank you to the many donors who contributed to this project, and to Figure 1 Publishing for bringing this book to fruition. Thank you to my four children, ʔəy̓xʷatələq—Brent Sparrow, ʔəy̓xʷatəma:tiye—Rhea Point, ʔəy̓xʷacəlenəxʷ—Thomas Cannell, and ʔəy̓xʷatəna:t—Kelly Cannell, and my husband Jeff Cannell, for their assistance on many of these projects. Thank you to my fabricators, who have patiently worked with me in realizing my vision, and to the numerous people who have contributed to my artistic journey over the years. A special thank you to my carving teacher John Livingston, and to Ron Denessen, who has been with me for eighteen years. So many other people have worked with me over the years, too many to list individually. I am eternally grateful to all of them!

Director's Foreword

ANTHONY ALAN SHELTON

PEOPLE AMONG THE PEOPLE: The Public Art of Susan Point provides a crucial source to help us better appreciate her wider oeuvre and its unique importance in contemporary Canadian art. Her first solo exhibition was *Art of the Northwest Coast*, organized by the London Regional Art Gallery in Ontario (1982), followed by *New Visions: Serigraphs by Susan A. Point, Coast Salish Artist* (1986), curated by Karen Duffek at the University of British Columbia's Museum of Anthropology. More recently, the Vancouver Art Gallery organized *Susan Point: Spindle Whorl* (2017), and the Deer Lake Gallery in Burnaby, B.C., presented *Vue Point* (2018). Between these landmark exhibitions, she has held numerous shows in commercial galleries and her work has been featured in over sixty group exhibitions in North America and Europe.

The majority of these, however, focus on her serigraphs and smaller carvings, leaving a lacuna over many of her most important works: her massive sculptures that grace our streets, churches, hospitals, airports, museums, and colleges and universities.

Susan Point D. Litt., OC, RCA, a recipient of many achievement awards and no less than four honorary doctorates, is the daughter of Edna Grant and Anthony Point; like her parents, she was raised embedded in the strong social and cultural fabric of the Musqueam ("People of the River Grass"), a Halkomelem community at the mouth of the Fraser River, close to UBC and the Museum of Anthropology. Her mother, Edna, the daughter of Mary Charlie Grant, was an accomplished basketmaker who encouraged her daughter's creativity, just as Susan, in turn, has encouraged her own children and grandchildren to take up art.

When Point began her career In the early 1980s she was part of a group—including Stan Greene, Rod Modeste, and Floyd Joseph—dedicated to reviving Coast Salish art styles, which had been eclipsed by a renaissance in northern sculptural styles that were popularly believed to represent all Northwest Coast communities. It is telling that at this time some Coast Salish artists were themselves accepting commissions to carve totem poles, even though these were northern in both form and style. In an attempt to rediscover the Coast Salish vernacular style, which had all but disappeared locally, Point conducted research in museums across North America and Europe. These works—which included Salish spindle whorls and archaeological collections held by the Vancouver Museum, the Museum of Anthropology, and the Royal British Columbia Museum; massive carved houseposts in the American Museum of Natural History; and carved mortuary boxes in what is now the Canadian Museum of History—revealed a naturalistic style depicting animals such as dogs and fishers. Like the funerary monuments engraved by the nineteenth- and early-twentieth-century artist Edward Whymper, they are intricately carved to impart a plasticity that makes them appear almost alive. Boxes and weavings revealed startlingly modern-looking abstract designs completely different from those found in northern British Columbia and Alaska.

Like other Musqueam artists, Point has never been content to imitate or copy historical styles and forms, but has always striven to abstract their formal conventions and set them in motion to reinvigorate an Indigenous canon; to adopt the formal aesthetics of her ancestors to new conditions, concerns, and issues relevant to the contemporary world. In her catalogue to the 1986 exhibition, Karen Duffek characterizes the principal elements in Point's work as "crescents, wedges, V-cuts." In her works on paper, Point adapted spindle whorl designs to the medium of print, creating one of her recurring stylistic motifs—the circular foregrounds, which she has identified with the circle of life, the moon, salmon eggs, and the ripples that spread out in pools of water. In more recent work she has embedded the circle in intricate geometrical grids, quadrupling it to represent what the Musqueam and other First Nations Peoples believe to be an essential quality of worldly existence: the four peoples; the four elements; the four winds; the four moons; the four directions; the four seasons; the four cycles of salmon. In works like *Salish Footprint*, animals have become more abstract. A growing number of her most stunning works, many made of wood or polymer, are carved in low relief, recalling the abstract fish design on the mortuary box surmounting a human figure displayed at the Museum of Anthropology. Her concern with the interconnectedness of life and respect for the environment, waterways, and the creatures around us are recurring themes.

It is not only her style, but her use and mastery of different mediums that distinguish her work. Printmaker, drawer, painter, mosaic maker, carver, mason, smith, and glassmaker, she seemingly effortlessly makes works in different mediums, depending on the intended theme, aesthetic effect, and purpose. "My art is my voice," she insists, a voice alive with the teachings of her ancestors and the innovations in subject and materials that intone such vigour in her massive carvings and murals.

Susan Point's public works provide an alternative translation and understanding of the urban ecology of British Columbia and Washington. These lands, colonized for little over a century and a half, remain part of a millennia-old Indigenous civilization that has never accepted the unjust disposition and calculated destruction of its lands and culture. Susan Point's public works, each one site-specific and nurtured from the history of a place, reassert an Indigenous voice and significance to the land that surrounds us. They re-inscribe a different history and significance and, for those with open minds, generously open a portal to alternative views of the world—to the marvellous real of an animate and active nature that cradles Indigenous and settler societies and demands the respect of both. This re-inscription of our ecology—whether it's conducted by Susan Point and other contemporary First Nations artists such as Lawrence Paul Yuxweluptun, Michael Nicoll Yahgulanaas, and Edgar Heap of Birds, whose works directly intervene in our everyday life and vision, or by the canvases of Alex Janvier and Norval Morrisseau, protected away in galleries—provides a glimpse into a world that beckons a coming transformation, one that will affect us all.

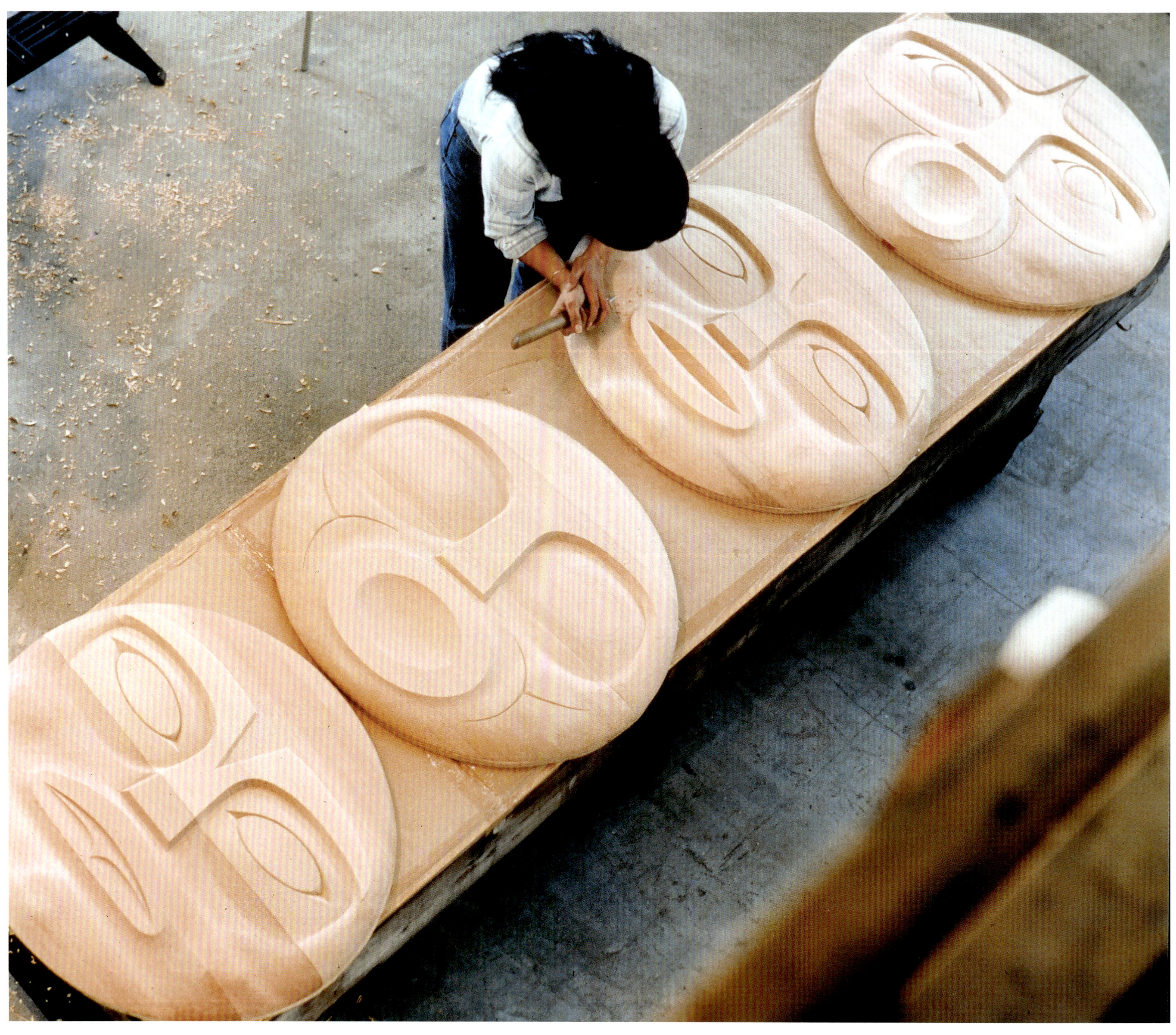

Susan Point and the Complexities of Culture

DR. MICHAEL KEW

WHEN I FIRST met Susan she was a child living with her parents, Tony and Edna, in the house that Tony had built. It was in an old section of Musqueam called Mali, close to the north arm of the Fraser River. My wife, Della, and I were there to invite Tony and Edna to a smilha, a traditional gathering we were preparing to call for naming our sons. At such events in winter, which it was, spirit dancing takes place, and Susan's parents were invited because they were dancers. But more than that, they were Siiyem: high-born, important people. We wanted them to witness the names we intended to confer. This act of making announcements to the community, and calling special people to hear, is a traditional, important process in maintaining the formal structure of Coast Salish society. But our invitation and meeting, formal though it was, meant more to us, for Edna and Della were "cousins," and Tony was also kin to Della.

I relate this meeting to show how fully and completely Susan Point is grounded in the culture and society of the hən̓q̓əmin̓əm̓-speaking Musqueam. She left her home daily to attend nearby Southlands Elementary, and after a few years she was sent to the Roman Catholic residential school at Sechelt, which she attended until age thirteen. But in summer months she returned to her home, to Musqueam, to her parents and her kinfolk.

Both parents had made previous marriages, and Susan had many siblings. The hən̓q̓əmin̓əm̓ kinship system gives firm standing to one's blood relatives, and keeps them distinct by generation, so Susan grew up among a multitude of classificatory siblings (cousins), and as many or more aunts and uncles. For Susan and others like her, Musqueam is more than a place to live. It is a home in the fullest sense: it is where her ancestors were born, where many of them lie at rest.

Susan married and began her own family. She put her schooling to work and took employment as a secretary for Musqueam First Nation, and then with the Alliance Tribal Council (an association of representatives from Musqueam and other Coast Salish groups) in its office at Musqueam. It was there that we renewed acquaintance with Susan.

My own interest in Coast Salish art stemmed from assisting Wilson Duff as curator of anthropology at the Royal British Columbia Museum in Victoria. Within its collection were old Salish rattles and spindle whorls. These rattles were familiar to Della and other Coast Salish people, for they continued to be used in ceremonies as part of contemporary Coast Salish life. Pursuing my interest and preparing for an exhibition at the Museum of Anthropology (MOA) at the University of British Columbia, I visited other museums known to have Coast Salish material. One of them was the American Museum of Natural History in New York City, which held several Musqueam houseposts collected in the nineteenth century. We knew them from photographs, but seeing them standing against a bare wall, stark, weathered, and browned with age, they had a presence beyond the power of photography to convey—I found them

Susan applies finishing touches to the four faces she carved in yellow cedar to use as moulds for *Four Corners* (1999; see page 173).

special and moving, perhaps because we knew where they had originally stood.

At this time, Della was assisting staff at the Vancouver Museum (since renamed the Museum of Vancouver) with a program for schoolchildren, and revisiting her own knowledge and her parents' teaching about basketry, rush matting, and artwork. My own formal, academic knowledge was extended and enriched by her direct and personal understanding.

As we accumulated photos and information in preparation for the MOA exhibition, Della and I shared them with people at Musqueam, including Susan, who was beginning to be known as the "niece who can draw." One result of my research was a large collection of photographs taken in various museums. This collection, and a full visual record of material to be borrowed for the exhibition, were made available at MOA for research and duplication by Coast Salish bands for their own archives. Susan had access to this material. But she did her own research as well, and also visited the American Museum of Natural History, among other places. I do not know what her thoughts were on such direct experiences, for in her own way she pursued and developed her understanding of Coast Salish art.

Many of the sculpted objects in the collection—hammers, adze handles, mat creasers, spindle whorls—were tools shaped or decorated to have simple objective meanings. A viewer sees a duck, owl, eagle, snake, fish, or four-footed animal. The housepost representing the renowned Musqueam leader qeypəlenəxʷ (Capilano) is simply a stylized man. The complex sχʷəyχʷəy masks are human head forms, with additional features of birds or other beings. Origin stories exist that relate to and explain the features. However, many of the wonderful sculpted objects do not represent things in recorded stories or events, or anything in what we know as the real world.

Some have suggested that many ideas and meanings in this art come from Coast Salish spiritual experience in the complex called syəwən, or spirit dancing. But I do not think this a reasonable explanation, for the experiences of an individual involved in this complex, whether in dream or altered consciousness, are private. Syəwən is meant, and understood, to be private. Participants—that is, dancers and those who assist them—are taught that it is improper, unhealthy, even dangerous, to share or talk about a dancer's dream experience. Protracted questioning of a dancer is likely to elicit an answer such as, "If you want to know what a dancer sees, you must become a dancer!"

I think it unlikely that Coast Salish material art that comes down to us from ancient times represents vision experiences. That was expressed, properly and formally, in dance and song. Expressive, artistic performances in their own right, but contained within the field of their own informed, understanding community.

This is not to say that Coast Salish material art has no connection to spiritual activity or other mystical experiences. But, for myself, I am content to let such questions stand. Accepting and understanding this, questions about meaning and inspiration are best answered by the artist, and by the art itself.

Where does the inspiration and ability of Susan Point come from? I have no hesitation in saying that it comes from her preparation—from the strength of her family, her social system, her community; and from her desire to learn, and her wish to share something with us.

Susan working on *Kneeling Stool* (1993; see page 161) in her home studio at the Musqueam settlement, 1993.

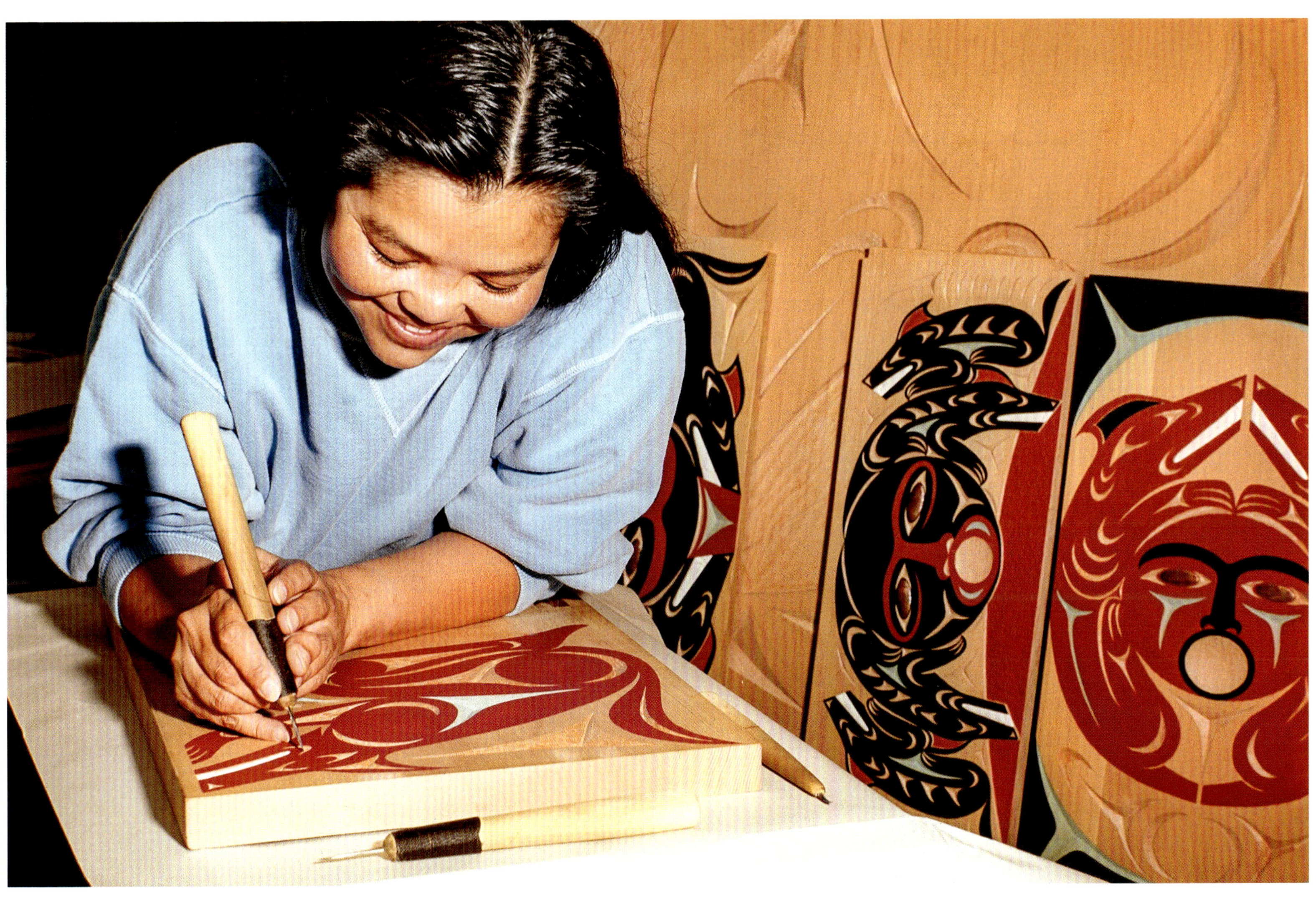

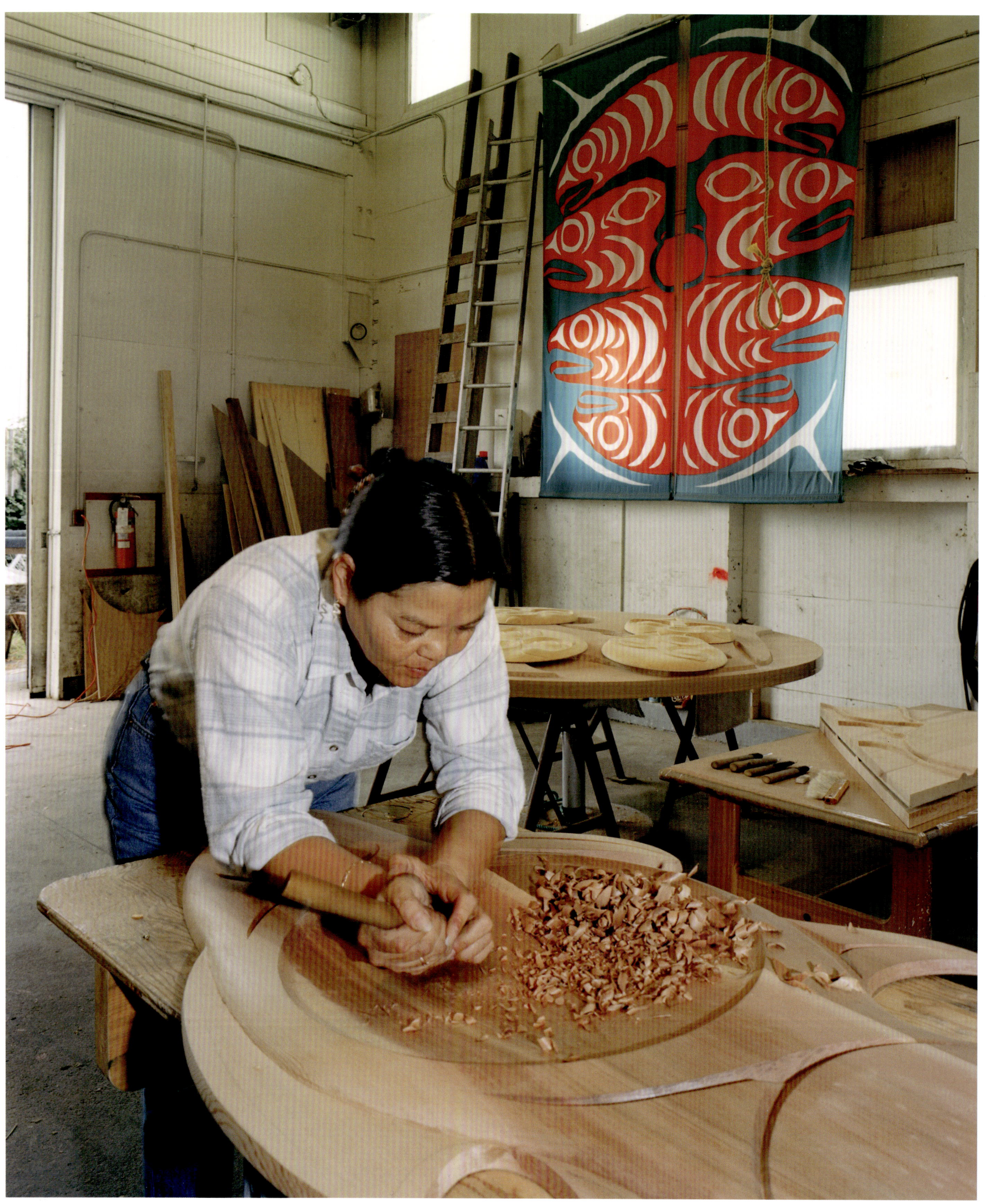

Introduction

ROBERT D. WATT

THIS BOOK CELEBRATES the public art of one of Canada's most accomplished artists and designers. ʔəy̓xʷatiyə—Susan Point is endlessly creative and astonishingly prolific. She is a demanding perfectionist, so her work is meticulous and detailed, but she's also adventurous: she shows great artistic courage in her embrace of opportunities to explore and master new mediums like fused and hot glass, copper, aluminium, bronze, concrete, and synthetic polymers, and new skills like drafting, wood carving, print making, and engraving. She is a generous artist, a lifelong learner, a quick study, and a cultural ambassador.

She has honoured the art of her ancestors and the sniw̓ (teachings) of her parents, relations and xʷməθkʷəy̓əm (Musqueam) Elders, while at the same time developing a personal style rooted in her research into surviving early Salish artworks. This has ensured that she is recognized not as a copyist, but as a transformer: a female artistic Raven, with her own contemporary tool kit of elegant designs and bright colour palettes, which she's able to deploy in diverse mediums with her varied skill set.

Susan Point has played perhaps a larger role than any other artist in reinvigorating traditional Coast Salish art, which for years had languished in the collections of a limited number of museums. Her expressions and explorations of the Salish aesthetic have given it new life. And by serving as a mentor to her artistic colleagues and partners—including her own children who, guided by her example, have become recognized figures in Salish art—she has helped ensure the next generation of artists will be creating works in a Salish idiom.

She has many fans, including myself, and a reputation that extends far beyond the kitchen table in her home, where she began her career as an artist in January 1981. In 2006 she was invested as an Officer of the Order of Canada. She has been recognized with honorary degrees by four British Columbia universities: the University of Victoria, Emily Carr University of Art and Design, Simon Fraser University, and the University of British Columbia, and has regularly received other important honours and awards. I hope that this volume will be seen as another tribute to her unique qualities as an artist, student, teacher, family member, and team leader, and as a creator of works that consistently challenge artistic conventions by employing new materials in new directions.

I HAVE long been an admirer of Susan's creativity and dazzling public art. I first met her in the spring of 1981—just a few months after she had started to produce prints in her kitchen—while I was helping the City of North Vancouver develop an official coat of arms for its seventy-fifth birthday.

I had suggested to the committee overseeing the process that of course the City would be eager to include something to honour the local Coast Salish Peoples, for example a səl̓səl̓tən (spindle whorl), the traditional instrument for spinning wool into yarn for weaving. The idea was well received, especially by the Skwxwú7mesh Úxwumixw (Squamish

At her Celtic Shipyard studio, Susan works in red cedar to create the original pattern for *Salmon People* (1998; see page 110).

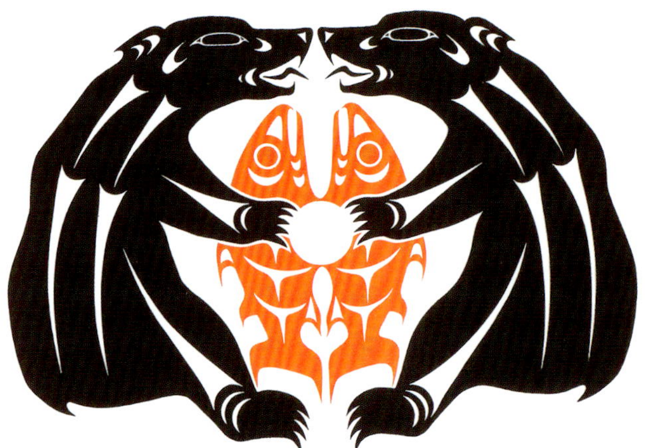

Grizzly Bears with Sockeye (1981), print no. 12 of 60. This spindle whorl design was commissioned for use in the City of North Vancouver's armorial bearings.

Nation) Elder on the committee. He proposed that the whorl feature a salmon, because of its central importance to First Nations, and a bear, as a symbol of the splendour of the natural environment. He asked me to return to the committee in a few weeks with photos of a whorl showing bears and salmon. I remember thinking that this should not be too difficult; the Museum of Anthropology at UBC or the Royal British Columbia Museum in Victoria should have such a whorl in their collections of historic Salish objects. But after weeks of searching I could not find one. Lots with bird figures, some with humans, some with more abstract designs—but none with bears and salmon.

Della Kew, a Musqueam Elder and one of the star docents at the Vancouver Museum, where I was director, came to my rescue one morning over coffee. She was a cousin of Susan's mother, Edna Grant-Point, and when she understood what I was searching for she said, "I think I know somebody who can help." I will never forget her next words: "I have a niece who draws."

Soon we were on our way to the Musqueam settlement. We pulled up in front of a house on West 51st Avenue and Della got out and called upstairs, "Susan, we're here." Up we went into a kitchen and she introduced me to her niece, Susan Point, then twenty-nine years old. I explained the committee's request. Susan thought for a few moments and said, "I think I can do something to help you and the City."

The result was her first public art commission: a beautiful limited-edition print, *Grizzly Bears with Sockeye* (1981), a powerful arrangement of two black grizzly bears holding bright red sce:łtən (salmon), backs arched to follow the circumference of a spindle whorl. Even in this first year of her printmaking, the work reflected her deepening understanding of the nature of Salish art, the styling of the main elements, and the use of crescents and V- and U- forms. A styling of Susan's speʔəθ (bears) and salmon were included, with her blessing, in the coat of arms of the City of North Vancouver.

I did not appreciate at that time how different this print was from almost everything else being done by Indigenous artists on the coast. And there was no way I could have known that I was looking at a print that was part of the beginning of

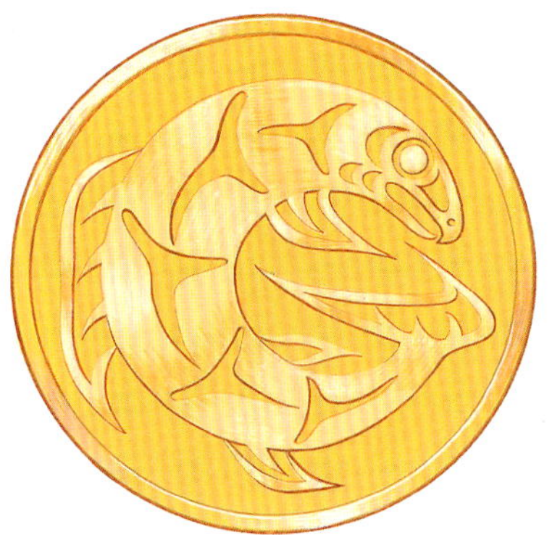

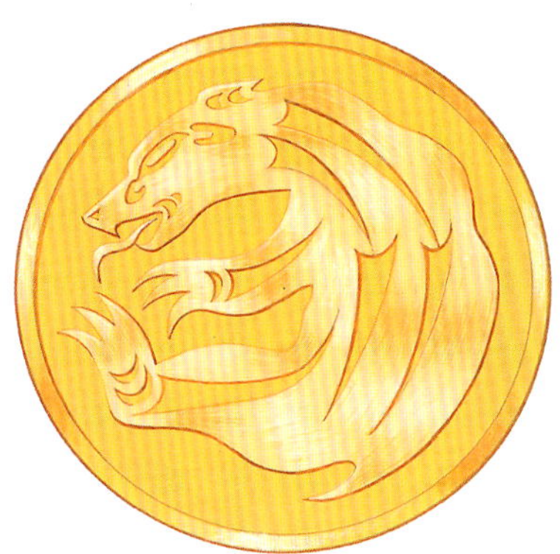

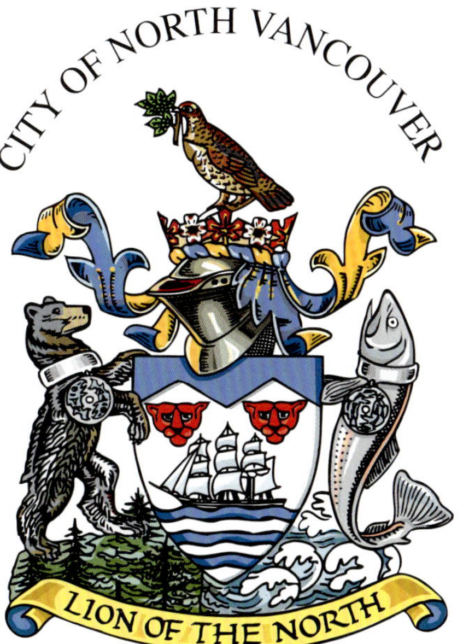

The spindle-whorl medallions (left), which are modelled on Susan's *Grizzly Bears with Sockeye* (facing), were designed by Ottawa artist Karen Bailey (1982, gouache on board) and then crafted in silver by R.S. Jacoby Jewellers of Vancouver for use in North Vancouver's mayoral chain of office. Versions of the medallions also appear on the bear and salmon in the city's coat of arms (right), designed by Irene Alexander and then painted by John Bainbridge, herald painter at the College of Arms in London, U.K.

a phenomenon: the rebirth of art that would evoke and honour the traditional art forms of the First Nations Peoples who have lived near the Salish Sea for thousands of years.

FOR SUSAN POINT, art is at the centre of her being. As she told me several years ago,

> I've always been interested in art. Throughout my schooling, art was my best subject—always straight A's. I always helped other people along with their artwork, right from the time I can remember, Grade I. But not necessarily Salish native art—I love drawing life, animals... So right from childhood I did enjoy drawing and creating things.[1]

To explore the arc of Susan Point's public art is to engage with every phase of her development as an artist, which allows us to highlight a number of themes that have grown increasingly important to her: her curiosity and respect for Musqueam practices and early Salish art; her eagerness to try new mediums; and her mission to ensure there is a prominent "Salish footprint" in the traditional territories of the Salish Peoples, and that their message of environmental stewardship is embraced by all who now share this land.

She has been determined to apply what she has learned about Salish art from closely studying historic Salish art pieces in museum collections and drawing on the sχʷəy̓em̓ (Oral Traditions) and syəθ (Traditional Knowledge) of the Musqueam, learned from parents and relatives. She integrates this understanding into her new art at every opportunity.

Rather than reproduce the traditional pieces, she has deftly balanced her respect for Traditional Knowledge with a constant desire to try new things, to develop new skills. "I didn't think of myself as an artist at the beginning. First of all, I was a jewellery maker. Then I tried prints and I was a printmaker. Then a painter, not necessarily an artist. Experimenting—enjoying everything I tried."[2] Her developing talent led to a growing number of opportunities, which she discovered with the help of her husband, Jeff Cannell; other family members; and friends and supporters like the late Bud Mintz, owner of the Potlatch Arts gallery. It was Mintz who convinced Susan to try sχt̓ek̓ʷ (carving):

> He said why not try carving and I said no, that's not a woman thing. I think I was afraid of getting flack, and I think I was actually more afraid of getting slapped on the hand than actually trying it, and he said I will get John Livingston to teach you. He came over, helped me, taught me the basics. My first carving project was a four-by-eight-foot panel, *The Seal and the Raven*, which I carved for the Sechelt Nation Raven's Cry Theatre. It was based on a local Salish legend.... From there it was non-stop. I love working in wood—it was amazing. I thought to myself you can't do this... but I kept on doing what I was doing and it was fun, and every time I had big projects I would bring John over; he was my teacher. I can't use a chainsaw but he would take off the bulk of the wood and I would finish the rest, and I would do that for years.[3]

Experimentation with the help of mentors has been a constant element in Susan's career, especially in her printmaking. In Vancouver she studied with Bill Watson of Behnsen Graphics in 1981, and later with Walter de Jong of Prism Graphics; she learned woodblock and intaglio printing from Peter Braune of New Leaf Editions; and she studied handmade papermaking with Sharon Yuen of Kakali Papers. She has worked with Eric Bourquin of Seacoast Screen Printing in Victoria for over fifteen years.

As her reputation grew and her Salish style became more widely accepted, Susan pursued opportunities to work in different mediums. She was the first Indigenous artist in Canada to work with glass in a variety of forms. She created her first glass artwork in 1986 with the help of David Montpetit, who at the time worked with Yves Trudeau at Studio One Glass Art in Vancouver. She returned to glass in the early 1990s and, through a close working relationship with Trudeau—as well as back-to-back residencies at the Pilchuk School in Stanwood, Washington in 2002—soon learned to work with engraved, sandblasted, fused, kiln-cast, and stained glass.

As Susan deepened her knowledge of traditional Salish art, it became increasingly important to her that members of Musqueam, other Salish Peoples, and the wider community understand that Northwest Coast art from the Nuu-chah-nulth, Kwakwa̲ka̲'wakw, X̱aayda/X̱aad (haytə, Haida), and other nations north of the Lower Mainland—which was the dominant style of First Nations art in B.C. when she began her career—was not the only form of art present on the coast. She came to feel strongly that her art helped to re-establish the Coast Salish imprint on their land.

Directly linked to this is a view of the world that arises from the recognition that the earth and its creatures are precious and must be respected and protected. One of her frequent and most important themes is the interconnectedness of all life. She is not unrealistic; she understands deeply that the settlement of her childhood is not the settlement of today. She remembers walking with her mother and her siblings from their home in maləy̓ (Mali, an area of the Musqueam settlement) northwards through the forest to visit an aunt and other relations, while her mother named the plants and commented on their usefulness. Much of the area that supported these plants has now been developed into homes or golf courses. The clock cannot be turned back, but through her art she can make strong environmental and in some cases political statements.

> As a family of artists, these lands (which includes the whole surrounding Lower Mainland as well)

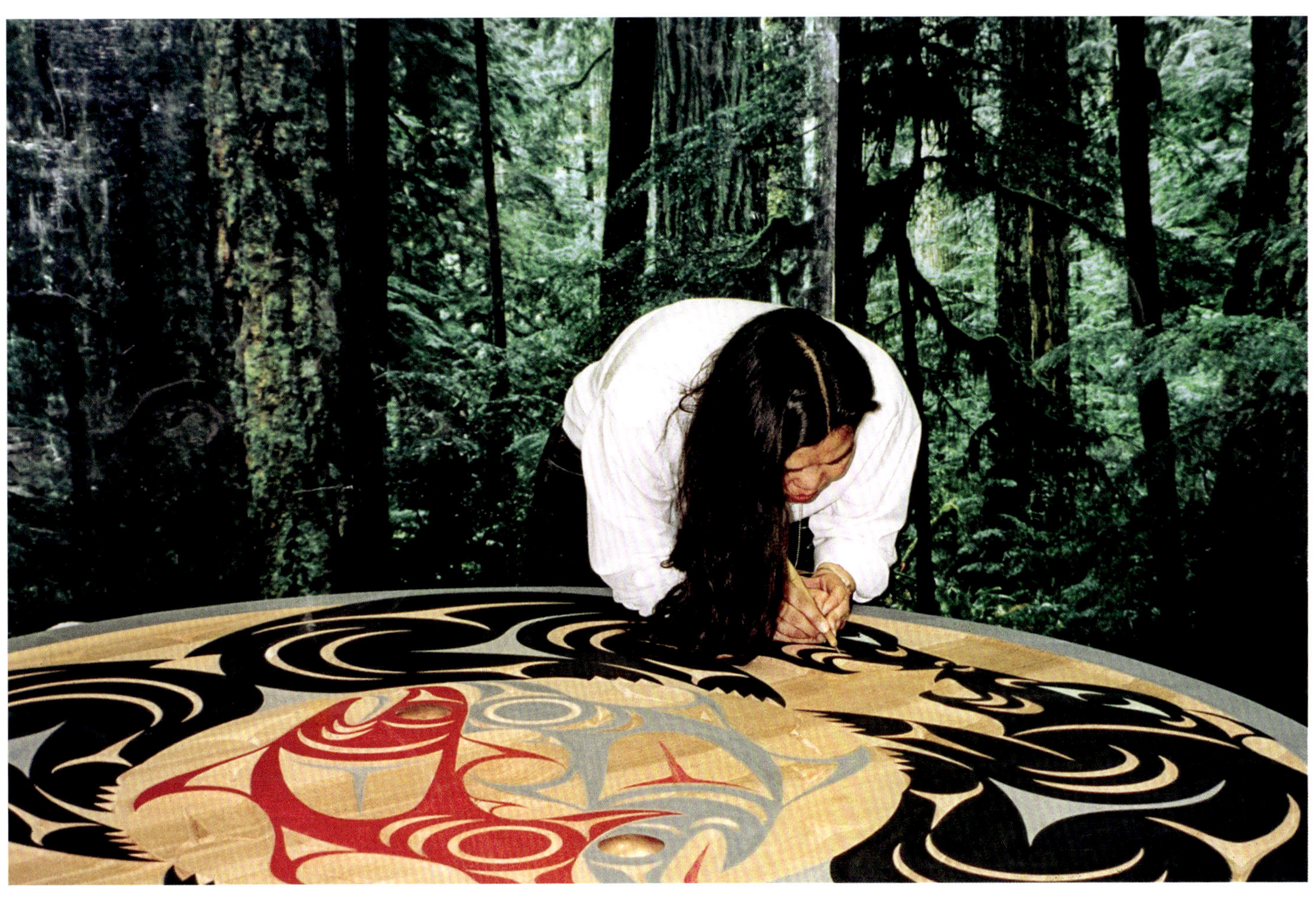

Susan works in Seattle on the details of *Black Bear Children* (c. 1995), a carving that sold into a private collection.

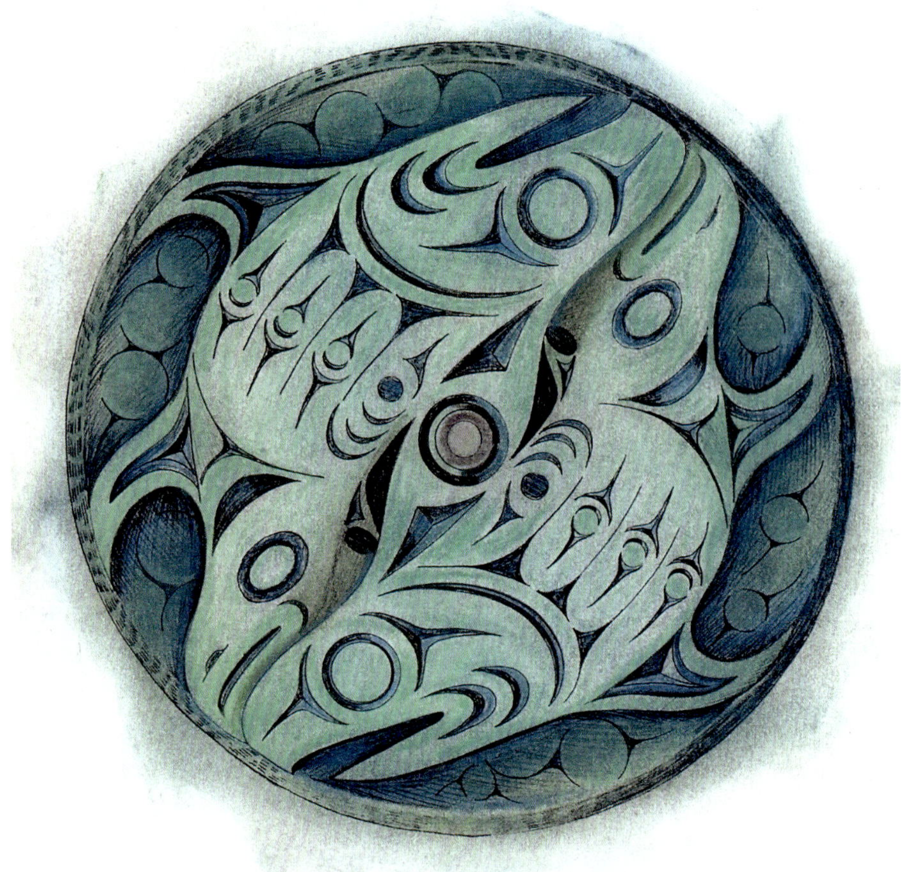

A colour rendering for *The River—Giver of Life* (1998; see page 84).

which our ancestors once lived upon, is where we get our inspiration from when creating a work of art... stories told to me by my family of elders (parents, grandparents, uncles and aunts) who have all since passed on... I am still learning and trying to understand the ways of my ancestors whose number one priority was to take care of and protect what Mother Earth gave us. In some way, I guess I am trying to do this through my art.[4]

Her Salish roots are clear and never far from her mind, but it is the challenge of creating something new and lasting that is the ultimate driving force behind her work. As she told me recently, "I do not like the separation between 'Non-Native Art Galleries (fine art) v. Indian Art Galleries (ethnic/craft).' There's a point where the art speaks for itself and is accepted as thus."[5]

WHEN WE LOOK at the public and monumental art of Susan Point, certain works stand out. Some dramatize the breadth of her vision: they show the marriage of an idea to a place using a particular material, or they synthesize important truths about the land, sea, air, and the creatures we share them with, or they fascinate us by reshaping forms Susan has seen on historic ʔeləw̓k̓ʷ (belongings) into a contemporary work of art. Others mark an important stage in the development of her ability to work to a large scale. Still others dazzle us with their sheer beauty. All of the works included in this book speak to one or more of these facets, but the following are especially noteworthy.

In her first public commission in an architectural setting, in 1982 for St. Paul's Church near ƛ̓əɬəməɬqəʔ (Mackay Creek) in North Vancouver (see page 126), Susan used the Salish elements of wedges and crescents in a non-traditional setting,

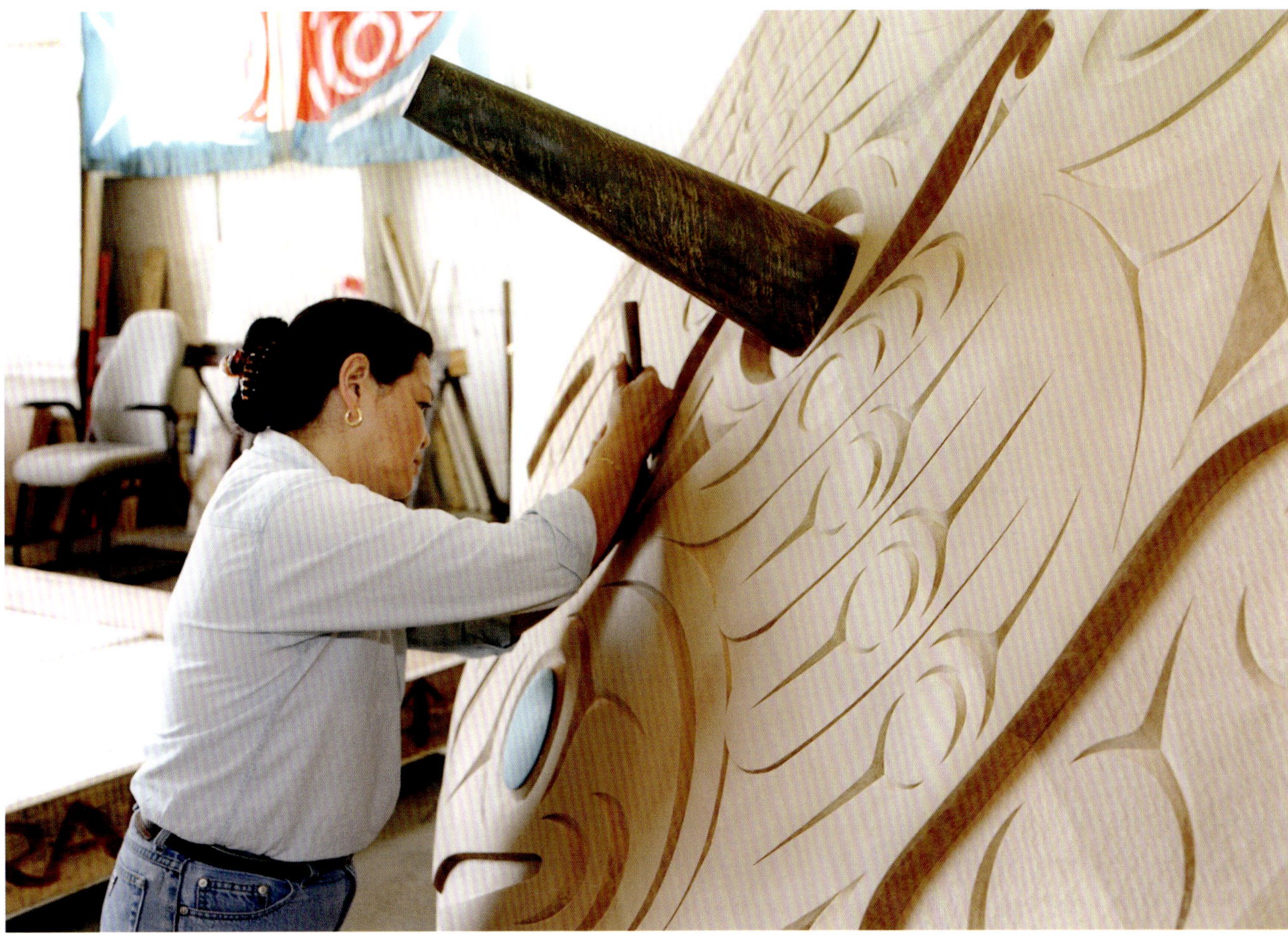

Susan carves *Good Luck* (1998; see page 163) in her Celtic Shipyards studio.

in non-traditional colours, as a decorative element in the church. From the beginning of her career she found ways to successfully reintroduce these simple, subtle, but very clear signals of a Salish presence in the region.

Her next public commission, in Seattle in 1986 (see page 170), was a landmark on her long road as an artist—it began the development of her ability to adhere to the exacting technical standards required for urban infrastructure projects while working with architects, engineers, casting craftspeople, and iron and bronze metalworkers. She designed and fabricated a striking set of iron tree grates, a complex pattern of generic birds and red-oak leaves and acorns. With her husband Jeff and her brother Bill Point, she fabricated a pattern for casting from various materials like art board, balsam wood, tacks, and gesso. The late David Gulassa, then of Urban Accessories, Inc. in Seattle, made a mould from this pattern, which was then cast in iron. Susan's practice of carving in wood and then casting in metal or a synthetic material became her signature approach to many public art commissions, on both sides of the international border, for the next thirty-plus years.

Not only was the material of the grates a new medium to Susan, the grates themselves were a new object, unknown to her ancestors. In her hands, however, iron tree grates were fully worthy of being the canvas on which to celebrate some of their ideas, using forms and shapes that would have been familiar to them. This marked the first time that Susan was able, through her art, to share First Nations art and thinking in an area outside of traditional Musqueam territory: in this case, in an area traditionally occupied by Salish "cousins" of her own people.

Her technical ability was honed and tested again in 1990 when she was commissioned to create a mural for a government and cultural complex for the shíshálh (sxəxeʔɬ, Sechelt) Nation, on the Sunshine Coast northwest of Vancouver (see page 117). Susan designed a grid of spawning salmon that was created from only two unique panels that were cast in reinforced concrete and repeated to cover nearly 929 square metres—at the time, the largest display of Salish art in the world.

After three years of training and working with John Livingston, Susan had two opportunities to fully test her new carving skills. The First Nations House of Learning at UBC commissioned her to create a housepost as one of four supports for the roof beams in the great hall of the House (see page 30). This was her first full carving in the round. Using Salish elements, she developed two interpretations of Raven: one that formed the central figure of the post with wings wrapped around the sides, and the second set in a circular frame at the feet of the larger raven. The second raven was shaped like a spindle whorl and carved into the body of the post in low relief.

During this same period, 1994–96, Susan earned important commissions from the Vancouver International Airport Authority as part of an effort to introduce First Nations art to YVR. It was vital to feature art created by an artist from Musqueam, the First Nation on whose traditional territory the airport stands. The most dramatic result of this invitation was *Flight*, the world's largest spindle whorl, which is installed in front of a waterfall in the airport's international terminal (see page 103). It is the the centrepiece of a space recognized as the Musqueam Welcome Area.

The whorl is carved in laminated red cedar and is nearly five metres in diameter. It is not just the scale of the work that is arresting, it is the beauty of the carving and the wonderful way that Susan has combined eagle and human figures. Jeff Cannell and John Livingston helped her with the execution of this huge piece, but the design itself is entirely her creation. It is a breathtaking example of her ability to take Salish forms and ideas and dramatize their essence on a large scale.

Susan's public art commissions during the 1990s took her back and forth across the Canada–U.S. border. In today's post-contact world the border is of course significant, but from her cultural perspective it arbitrarily divides the land of Salish sisters and brothers. When she was a young girl she often travelled with her parents to Washington State, especially to xʷɬəməỷ (Lummi) territory for winter ceremonial dancing and canoe races. Salish cultural practices—including, as Susan Point has shown with her work, the reinvigoration of traditional Salish art forms—continue to reach across the border from Salish nations in both countries.

Beginning with the tree grates in 1986, Susan established good working relationships with officials in both the King County and Washington State art commissions. For the latter she created a decorative mural made from laser-cut stainless steel backed with coloured Plexiglas; she installed *Sea to Sky* on a government building in Olympia in 1993 (see page 196). As on many other occasions, Susan drew on her research skills and her careful approach to exploring and honouring local traditions: the design featured motifs from traditional basketry styles of the local sq̓ʷali'abš (Nisqually) people.

This careful approach was also evident in a major installation two years later at the West Seattle Pump Station, where she transformed a mundane structure into a gallery of Salish forms, honouring the dxʷdəwʔabš (Duwamish) Tribe, the original first inhabitants of the sbaqWábaqs (Alki Point) area. *Water—The Essence of Life* (page 185) used a variant of the grid approach that she had first developed in Sechelt to cover the facade and wing walls of the pump station with human faces, fish, and birds, blended together in a powerful design.

A couple years later, and much nearer to home, she created her first large-scale public work for the Museum of Anthropology (MOA) at UBC. Her uncle by marriage, Michael Kew, worked at MOA, and it housed some early Salish objects, spindle whorls especially, that had sparked her appreciation for the difference between Salish art and more northern styles. MOA also stands on territory traditionally occupied by the Musqueam, near an area called q̓ew̓əm; including art by Susan was an important political as well as aesthetic statement.

Her first piece, completed in 1997 (see page 36), was a tall, imposing sculpture, in painted red cedar, of a male welcome figure holding a šxʷəməcən (fisher); interested visitors can compare her fisher with those carved in the traditional objects on display near the main entrance. The U-shape at the figure's head was to be fitted with a crossbeam supporting the roof of a Salish sθe:w̓tx (longhouse), and the base featured a spindle whorl as a symbol of welcome to people from all over the world. As always, Susan was conscious of the context of her work.

That same year, Susan completed two traditional-style Salish houseposts for the museum (see page 38). These were based on original posts from Musqueam that were now at the American Museum of Natural History, which she and Jeff had travelled to New York to see. Her deeply carved and brilliantly coloured interpretations of these posts were important examples of how Susan could channel the inspiration of the originals, while avoiding any trespass on their cultural meaning, to create something dramatically new and quintessentially Salish. The posts were shown for several months in the museum's Great Hall and then moved outside to welcome visitors.

As she moved into the new century, Susan had completed an impressive list of public and monumental artworks in Vancouver, Sechelt, Victoria, Seattle, and Olympia; many in carved and painted wood, others in cast concrete, bronze, or synthetic polymers. Many more commissions would follow, including some of the most important of her career. *Cedar Connection* (2009; page 113), at the Vancouver International Airport, is a complex carving that revisits some of Susan's early themes and reinforces the presence of the land's original inhabitants; *ts'u-hey-us* (2011; see page 140) is a stunning female welcome figure carved in red cedar for the campus of Douglas College; *Salish Gifts* (2016; see page 89) echoes traditional woven Musqueam baskets, but in concrete, bronze, and stone. Three other monumental works demand recognition as perhaps her finest achievements.

The Beaver and The Mink (2004; page 228) was a gift from Canada to mark the official opening of the National Museum of the American Indian in Washington, D.C. The cedar sculpture, inspired by the whorl shape and by a story of the same name from the Oral Traditions of the Musqueam people, features a human face, an incised whorl with four salmon, and four animals carved in the round so that they are visible from either side. Even though this sculpture has important traditional aesthetic and cultural references, and the quality of the carving and the piercing and the painting is superb, I think what impresses us most is the sheer artistry of Susan's composition—how the eye easily follows and understands the elements of the piece on both sides. This piece established Susan as an artist of the first rank.

Susan was commissioned to create a design (left) that was included on the reverse of the Governor General's Academic Medal (right), which was presented during the mandate of the Right Honourable Adrienne Clarkson (1999–2005).

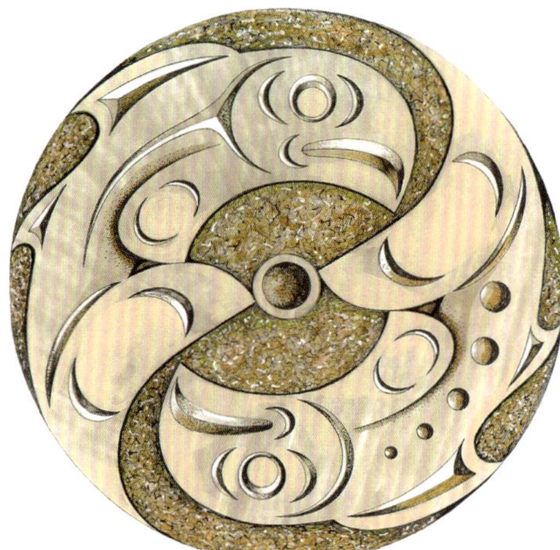

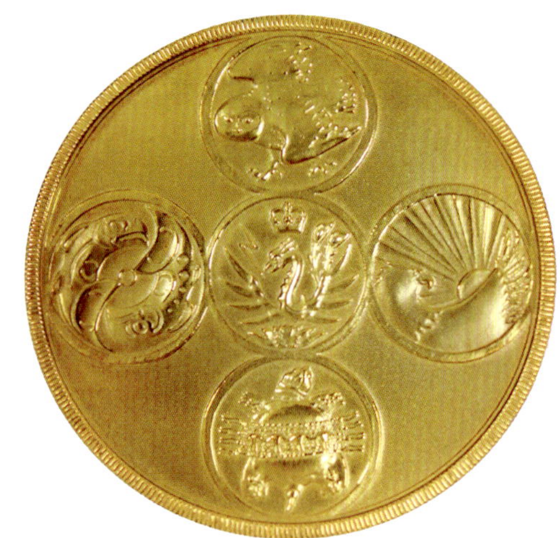

Arguably the most important public art in Vancouver is Susan's masterpiece at spapəỷəq (Brockton Point), *People Amongst the People*—the first artwork in Stanley Park by a Coast Salish artist. This opportunity to place in such a visible setting art that reflected pre-contact culture of the area, art that used Salish aesthetics and spoke about Salish beliefs, was supremely important, and Susan was the ideal artist for the task. The thematic richness of the three portals and the symbols and figures they show, carved with such vigour and painted with such an appropriate and distinctive palette, is simply breathtaking. The process and results of *People Amongst the People* (2009; see page 67) are described in much greater detail below—as Susan says, "you could write a book just on this project alone!"[6]

Before that work was finished, Susan teamed with Yves Trudeau in the creation of *The Tree of Life* (2009; see page 52), a huge five-light antique-glass window in the south wall of Christ Church Cathedral in downtown Vancouver. Susan had previously worked with hand-blown glass for a private commission (*The Mahli*, 2000), but this opportunity was in a far more prominent setting, and on a much larger scale. Yves Trudeau was a strong ally here; he helped Susan modify her dramatically contemporary design to ensure the weight of the glass was appropriately distributed across the large area, and together they supervised the production of the glass in Seattle. The *Tree of Life* was the first large-scale stained glass work by a First Nations artist—and the latest example of how Susan never stops learning new means of realizing her vision.

In the pages that follow are photographs and descriptions of all the public and monumental art that Susan has created since 1982: every work, whatever the medium, that was created to be publicly accessible, whether in parks or institutional buildings or in more unexpected places such as police vehicle decals and storm sewer covers.

The majority of these works were created by Susan alone, but on rare occasions she has shared the artistic stage with several other artists. One notable example occurred in 2000, when she was invited by then–Governor General Adrienne Clarkson to submit a design for part of the Governor General's Academic Medal. The medal also features designs by Inuk, Mi'kmaq, and Kanien'kehá:ka (Mohawk) artists. Susan's contribution was a spindle whorl design featuring a female and a male salmon, symbols of good fortune and sustenance. The drawing Susan prepared is an excellent example of the vigour of her designs and the meticulous character of her drawing.

Over nearly forty years, Susan has produced a huge body of artwork, tremendously varied in scale, medium, and location. She has not only enriched the metropolitan Vancouver community with marvellous works in wood, glass, concrete, iron, and synthetic materials, but has created art for locations far from her home settlement on staľəẁ (the Fraser River), from Victoria to Fort McMurray to Toronto to North Carolina. To date, the public art farthest from her home is found in a museum in Zurich. Some are well-known locally, but many are not. I have felt for a long time that Susan's work deserves to be more widely known, even in the area where she lives.

Each of the works featured here is described as much as possible in Susan's own words, from interviews we held in her studio and from written submissions to juries and committees. The aim is to give a clear sense of the art itself, its scale, location, and special features; and, through photography, a sense of how it looks and, in many cases, the context around it.

The procession of artworks begins with the one that is nearest Susan's own studio in Musqueam, and then expands out from there to nearby works in Vancouver and Richmond, and then to places farther afield in Coast Salish territories, and ultimately to places thousands of kilometres away, far beyond the Musqueam settlement. As a historian I initially organized the book in chronological order; this new arrangement is the brainchild of the book's editor, Michael Leyne, and I am indebted to him for suggesting a geographical approach. It is an arrangement that emphasizes the deep roots of Susan's creative spirit, her debt to family, Elders, and ancestors, and her success in taking Salish forms and reshaping them in her own way to re-establish a Salish footprint in the ancestral lands of her people, as well as delighting more distant publics with her creations.

These public and large-scale works were created while Susan and her fabricators were creating hundreds of new works—on paper, wood, glass, metal, and synthetic materials—that were privately acquired, thus disappearing from public view. We have made every effort to locate and document all the public work, but she has gently reminded me that we may have missed a few pieces. These would not be numerous, and certainly none of them would alter the portrait that is painted in this volume of her style and the breadth of her achievement as an artist.

What is described here gives a full and rich flavour of the scale of what she conceived and produced over nearly four decades. The earliest work is those simple decorations in St. Paul's Church (1982; see page 126), one of the oldest churches in Greater Vancouver. The most recent is *Salish Girl* (2017; see page 42), a small carving that represented a Salish contribution to *Reconciliation Pole* by 7idansuu (Edenshaw) James Hart, which was raised at UBC in April 2017. In between were more than eighty public commissions in wood, stone, bronze, glass, and synthetic materials, each a new essay in taking ancient Salish art forms and ideas and responding to a contemporary opportunity with a personal vision.

Since Susan's early days as a child who loved to draw, she has mastered so much—and she carries on exploring new opportunities. She is a brilliant artist, a consummate designer, a fearless explorer of new methods and materials, and a national treasure. She has a unique point of view that arises from her talent, her vision, and her roots. Her career-long quest to re-establish a Salish footprint in the Pacific Northwest, and to share her work with a wider audience, has been a resounding success—and we are all richer for it.

Part One

Close to xʷməθkʷəy̓əm (Musqueam)

Raven with Spindle Whorl

LOCATION: First Nations House of Learning
1985 West Mall, ʔəlqsən (Point Grey), Vancouver

The First Nations House of Learning, near an area called ʼtθəcəliʔqʷ, is a special place on the campus of the University of British Columbia. Its home, the First Nations Longhouse, opened on 25 May 1993, the culmination of years of planning, by First Nations Elders, students, teachers, and friends, to realize the vision first put forth by Verna Kirkness. It was conceived as a home-away-from-home for Indigenous students at UBC. Kirkness was the first director of the House.

The ceremonial and spiritual heart of the Longhouse is the Sty-Wet-Tan Great Hall. The name is from the Musqueam people and was first given to Jack Bell, the initial major donor to the project, and then applied to the ceremonial space. As Dominic Point, a Musqueam Elder, explains in a book by Kirkness and Jo-Ann Archibald,

> from the beginning of time, the Musqueam have acknowledged and respected spiritual powers. Sty-Wet-Tan is the west wind spiritual power, which introduces and recognizes the people of the West. The name Sty-Wet-Tan conferred on Dr. Jack Bell is most fitting as he has made it possible for the West to host people from all of British Columbia, Canada, and other countries in a Coast Salish longhouse where all can experience the spiritual powers of our Ancestors.[1]

The hall was designed as a contemporary structure built around four qeqən (houseposts) and two roof beams, with plenty of light entering from the south. Four is an important figure not only in Coast Salish cultures but in many other cultures both ancient and modern, and appears frequently in Susan's work. To define the character of the great hall and reinforce the essential purpose of the House of Learning, First Nations artists would create the posts, each telling a story.

Selecting the artists for such an important building was a challenging task. A committee of Elders was created to guide the selection process; they researched various styles of houseposts and solicited sketches from many artists. The committee was supported in their work by one of MOA's curators, Bill McLennan.

> With all those drawings I met with the elders and First Nations people who were involved in the project. They sat down; it was a long process... everybody was positive about all the choices that are in the building. I think some people were pleasantly surprised by Susan's submission because although they had lived here all their life they had no idea what a Salish housepost would look like. And so when they saw it, they were very positive about it.[2]

Susan's design for one of the houseposts became her first in-the-round carving in wood. Galleries, collectors, and museums were still focused on northern-style formline work, so the choice to offer her a commission was a recognition of the growing appreciation for Salish art as a distinctive aesthetic on the West Coast. In Sty-Wet-Tan, Susan's work is featured alongside compositions carved and painted in cedar by Lyle Wilson (Haisla), Stan Bevan (Tahltan, Tlingit, Tsimshian), Ken McNeil (Tahltan, Tlingit, Nisga'a), Don Yeomans (Haida, Métis), and Bradley Hunt (Heiltsuk).

In a statement made after the housepost was unveiled, Susan described the nature of Salish houseposts and her thinking behind her design.

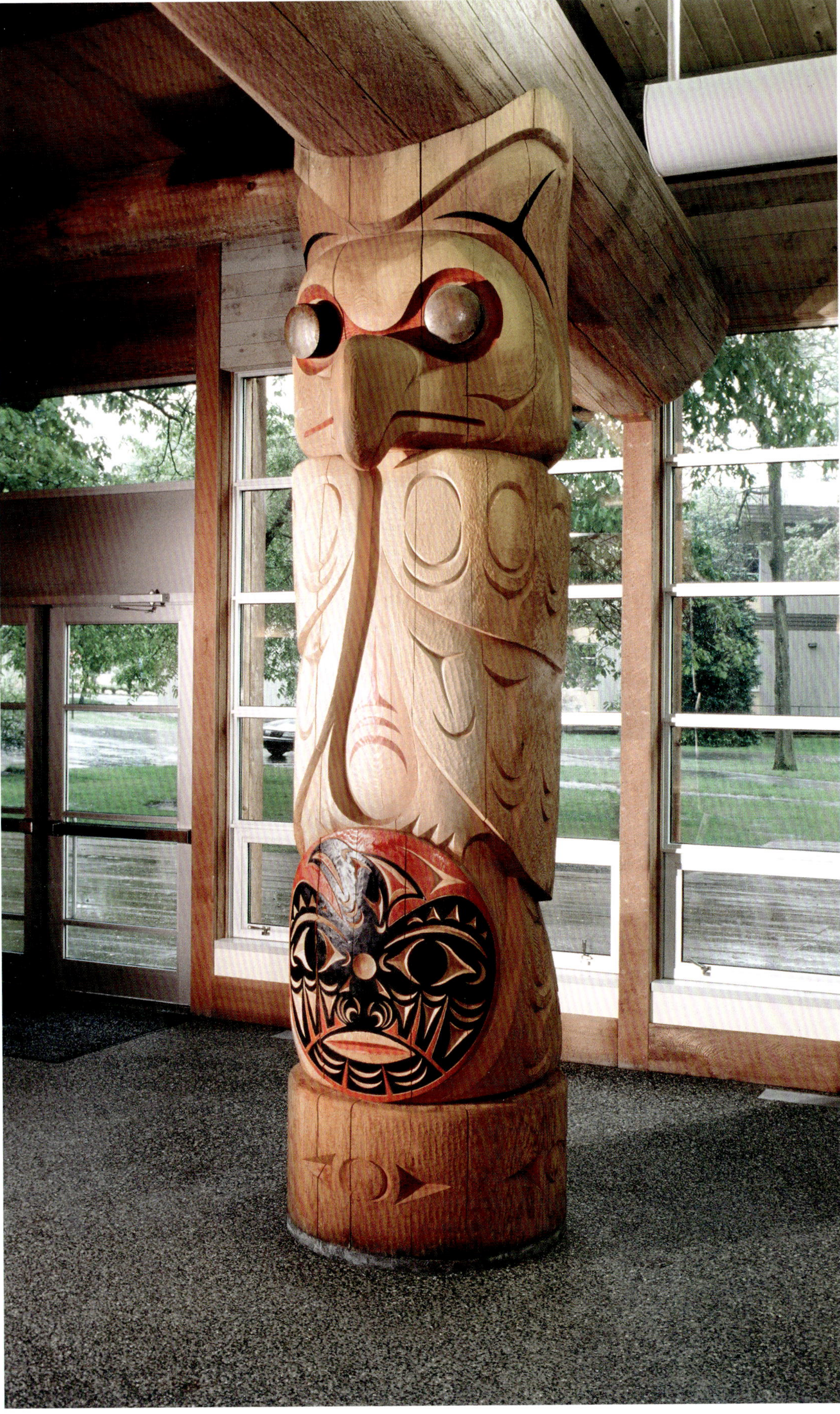

Raven with Spindle Whorl, 1993
Carved and painted red cedar with copper features
3.66 × 1.22 m

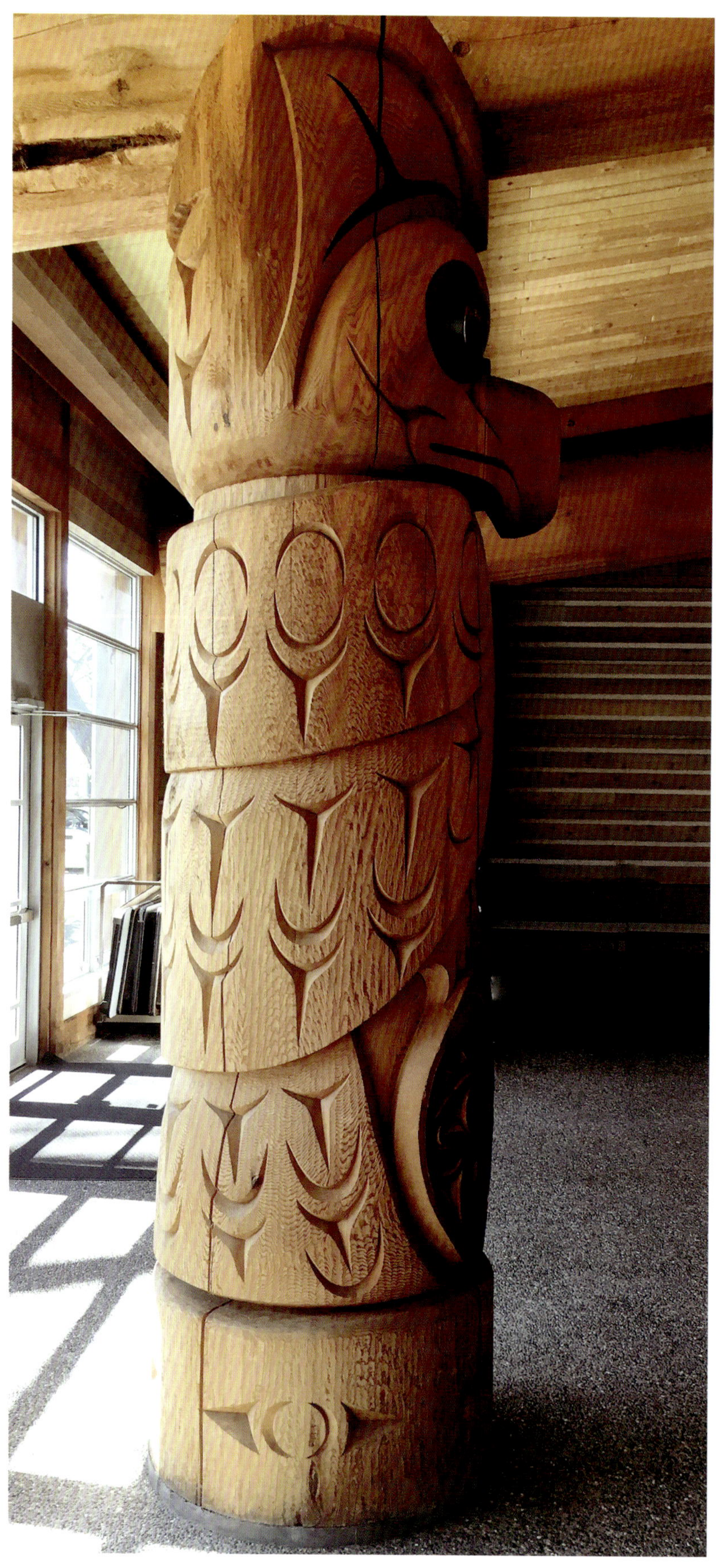

> Traditionally, the backs of Salish houseposts were not carved in any detail as they were meant to butt up against walls. However, for the purposes of this project and the fact that this post was meant to be free standing, I carved this piece in the round and carved traditional Coast Salish elements into the back.
>
> Many Coast Salish houseposts reflected spiritual and healing elements ... which were associated with cleansing ceremonies and were private and sacred rites. For this particular project, I felt that I would do something with a little more of a contemporary theme so as not to conflict with the other houseposts from the three other tribes. What I was looking to achieve was a housepost which would not offend any of the Salish peoples but having it still come across as looking traditionally Salish.
>
> The imagery in the Coast Salish housepost consists of a somewhat traditional bird image which represents a raven; and within its claws I incorporated an enlarged version of an original Coast Salish spindle whorl. The image in the spindle whorl depicts a raven with a human face incorporated within its body—the human face representing the raven's ability to transform itself into human form as depicted in several Coast Salish legends.
>
> The purpose for my having incorporated the spindle whorl is because it has been a key element in my quest to revive Coast Salish art and in so doing making everyone aware of this beautiful and almost lost art form.[3]

This work is a excellent example of how, from early in her career, Susan was able to not only understand what makes Salish art distinctive, but reshape it to give it fresh life. To understand this central theme of her work we can begin by asking, What was traditional Salish art? Dr. Wayne Suttles, an American anthropologist and linguist who devoted his career to learning about Coast Salish Peoples, said of ceremonial paraphernalia that

> discovering what this art meant to the people who made it and used it is now very difficult. But perhaps we can make a start by sorting it out by its associations with some Native concepts. It seems to me that, while some Central Coast Salish art may have been purely decorative, much of it can be related to four sources of power and prestige—the vision, the ritual word, the ancestors, and wealth.[4]

Shortly before Susan began making art, Michael Kew addressed the survival of this art in the context of the local culture and history.

> Of the many Northwest Coast tribes in British Columbia the Central Coast Salish are among the least familiar to the general public, and their art is almost completely unknown. At first glance this is remarkable, for they were one of the most numerous indigenous groups and their art was vigorous and powerful in subject and form. Massive wood sculptures adorned their houses; tiny figures and delicate engravings embellished ritual implements and personal ornaments.
>
> This apparent neglect has been partly a consequence of Central Coast Salish history. Their aboriginal territory, The Lower Mainland and Southeastern portion of Vancouver Island, was subject to early settlement by Europeans, and is today the most heavily populated part of the province. The impact of colonization

> was severe and ensuing culture change saw complete disappearance of some forms of art.
>
> Central Coast Salish art was probably always less abundant than art among northern coastal tribes, for it was closely associated with private religious expression and used less in secular display."[5]

Dr. Kew goes on to distinguish between Central Coast Salish sculpture and engraving, two art forms that both use wood, horn, or bone to create forms or images, but differ in their treatment of depth. Engravings sacrifice some detail to work primarily with two dimensions, using "incised lines or cuts." Sculpted works have different degrees of depth—be they low-relief, high-relief, fully rounded, or some combination of the three—but all employ the third dimension to add detail, which "enabled artists to achieve dynamic and realistic association of figures—animals chasing one another, birds being held by a human, man and animals confronting one another."[6]

In 1986, Karen Duffek, now curator of Contemporary Visual Arts and Pacific Northwest at MOA, prepared an exhibition of some of Susan's early serigraphs. Susan had been studying surviving examples of traditional Salish art and making prints for less than a decade. Duffek noted the distinctive crescents, U-forms, and wedges or V-forms common in two-dimensional Salish designs, and called attention to the careful thought that goes into shallow engravings. "The Salish artist must be aware of the integral relationship between positive and negative space in the overall design,"[7] says Duffek, comparing the process to that of creating woodblocks for printing. On the continued relevance of these traditional elements and techniques, Duffek predicts that "by reinterpreting the ancient designs, contemporary artists will undoubtedly contribute to a further understanding of two-dimensional forms. At the same time they are drawing upon their Salish heritage to create art with new meanings relevant to the present day."[8]

Even so early in her career Susan was undoubtedly doing just that, as Duffek observes: "Point approaches the old designs from a primarily aesthetic point of view—she wishes to present them accurately, but has begun to feel more freedom in using Salish art as personal expression." Susan confirmed this, telling Duffek, "I won't make drastic changes, I'll use the same forms, but I'll experiment with different techniques and put a lot more movement and life into my designs."[9]

SUSAN RECALLS that one of the challenges in carving this housepost was to take care not to carve too deeply, three inches at the most, because the architects had made careful measurements to ensure that the posts could support the weight of the beams and roof, and to meet seismic requirements. Nonetheless, the vigour of her design is readily apparent. Kirkness and Archibald describe the richness of the symbols that Susan carved:

> [Raven] faces toward the hall with gleaming eyes of copper, denoting the wealth and the nobility of the coastal people .... Two dark, pointed crescents arch over the eyes, giving Raven the transformational look of another form or of a mask to be worn at ceremonies.
>
> Raven has two rows of wing feathers carved gracefully around the pole, with tail feathers extending downward at the back. He seems to hold his wings close like a blanket to keep warm, the way grandmothers sit at the winter potlatches. His beak is mortised on, giving

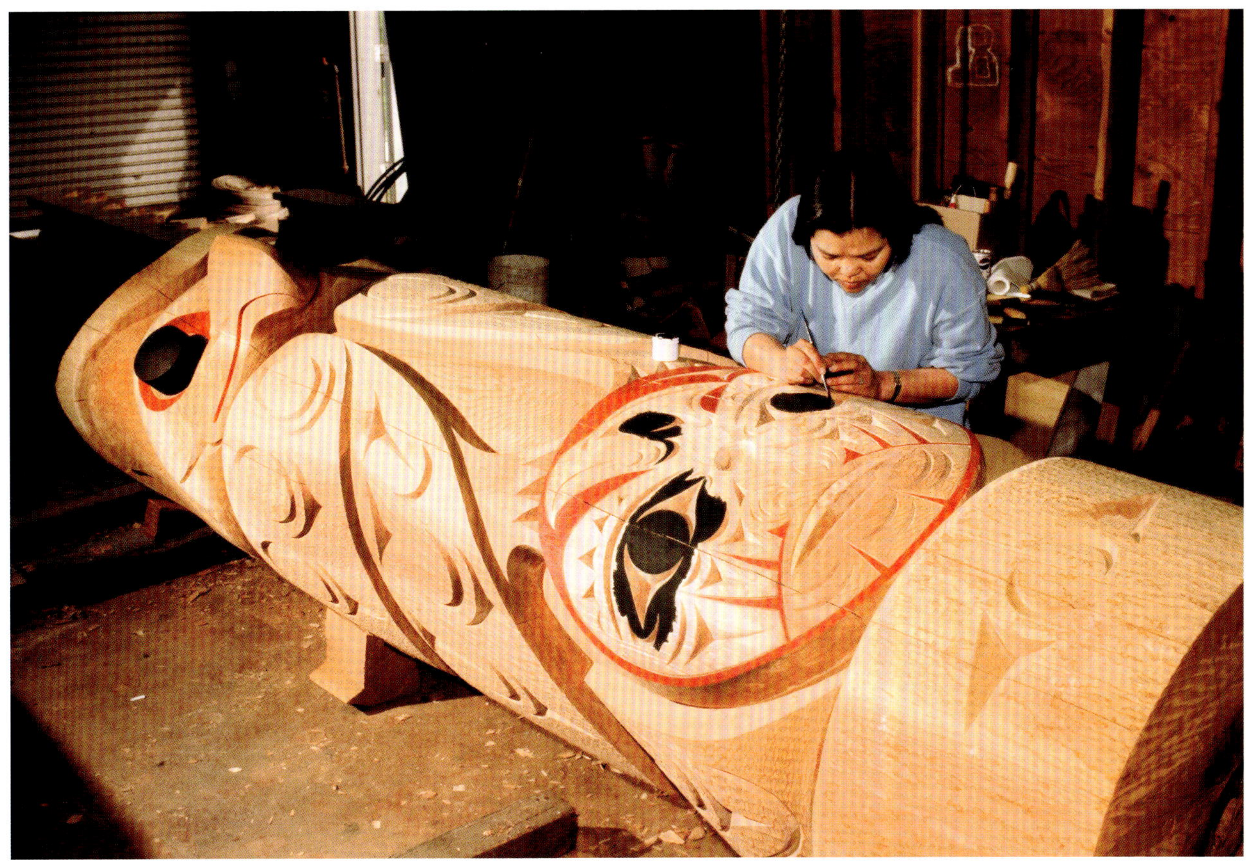

Susan works on *Raven and Spindle Whorl* in 1993.

Raven's face more dimension. His feet rest on a spindle whorl, the symbol of the powerful place of women in Northwest culture.

...The spindle whorl in the carving is a large circle with a Raven design in black and a reddish brown and natural cedar background. Raven is looking up to the left with wings outspread as if to fly away. Inside his wings, two large eyes look out at the viewer, revealing the human spirit that lives within.[10]

Susan's housepost joins the work of her fellow artists, working in various northern styles, to create a ceremonial space for Indigenous students on UBC's campus, a space where diverse styles come together to make a rich and harmonious whole.

UNIVERSITY OF BRITISH COLUMBIA MUSEUM OF ANTHROPOLOGY

Those wishing to see examples of Susan's monumental art will naturally plan a visit to the Museum of Anthropology, one of Canada's leading museums, walking distance from the Musqueam settlement. The museum is built on traditional Musqueam territory high above the beach at ʔəlqsən (Point Grey), and has in recent years worked closely with the Musqueam. Susan has long recognized that the museum's mission and territory includes much of the world, and the collections reflect that diversity. Nevertheless, she would like to see more Coast Salish works on display at MOA and hopes that this goal can be achieved in coming years.

Susan's involvement with MOA began in 1981 when Dr. Michael Kew showed her traditional Salish art and photos of Salish belongings that he had found in his own research. She recently described a later MOA exhibit of her framed prints and a Museum Note by Karen Duffek as "a pivotal point for me early in my career."[11] The museum precinct has since been enriched by four examples of Susan's interpretation of Salish aesthetics and traditions.

Welcome Figure

LOCATION: Museum of Anthropology
6393 NW Marine Dr, ʔəlqsən (Point Grey), Vancouver

The label for this impressive figure reads "Imich Siiyem—Welcome Good People." The Royal Bank commissioned this and the two houseposts to mark the centennial of its banking operations in B.C.; they were unveiled on 3 March 1997. In announcing the unveiling MOA noted that the works "stand as an acknowledgement of the traditional territory of the Musqueam, upon which the Museum of Anthropology stands."

Susan had been carving large-scale pieces in cedar for nearly seven years at this point while she continued to study surviving Salish art (frequently guided by Dr. Michael Kew) and incorporate her growing understanding of it into her work. As Kew noted in 1980, humans were the most common sculpture subjects for Central Coast Salish carvers, and were generally depicted in a realistic style, with bodies and limbs in proportion, and even buttons or other details of clothing included. Faces are recognizably of a Northwest Coast style, but with some distinctive Central Coast Salish features that are also visible in Susan's welcome figure:

> Eyebrows are prominent, arched, and often join above or are attached to, a long, thin nose which has tiny pinched nostrils. Eyes, usually oval and proportionately smaller than in other Northwest Coast styles, are surrounded by clearly marked eyelid forms.[12]

The figure shows Susan's development as both an artist and as an interpreter of traditional Salish forms. It is modelled after a traditional Salish housepost, but rather than outstretched arms with palms facing up in the classic sign of welcome, the figure holds a fisher, a creature that, as noted in the sculpture's label, "has the ability to carry power in a positive or negative form." In a statement around the time of the work's installation, Susan commented on several important elements of the figure.

> He is wearing a hat adorned with celestial images which represents the moon, the stars and the sun . . . It [the fisher] is also associated with cleansing and in this case, I have used the fisher within this Welcome Figure to wish all visitors good health. As you can all see, I have included the male organs which is something you wouldn't see in old slides or photographs of houseposts. Originally the old houseposts had their male organs intact but when the missionaries were sent into the communities, they had them all chopped off. On the base is a circular motif depicting two Thunderbirds; the Thunderbird, living high in the mountains, being the most powerful of the spirits. Here I have one of their wings transforming into hands in a raised fashion (with symbolic heads in each of their palms) welcoming all peoples from around the world.[13]

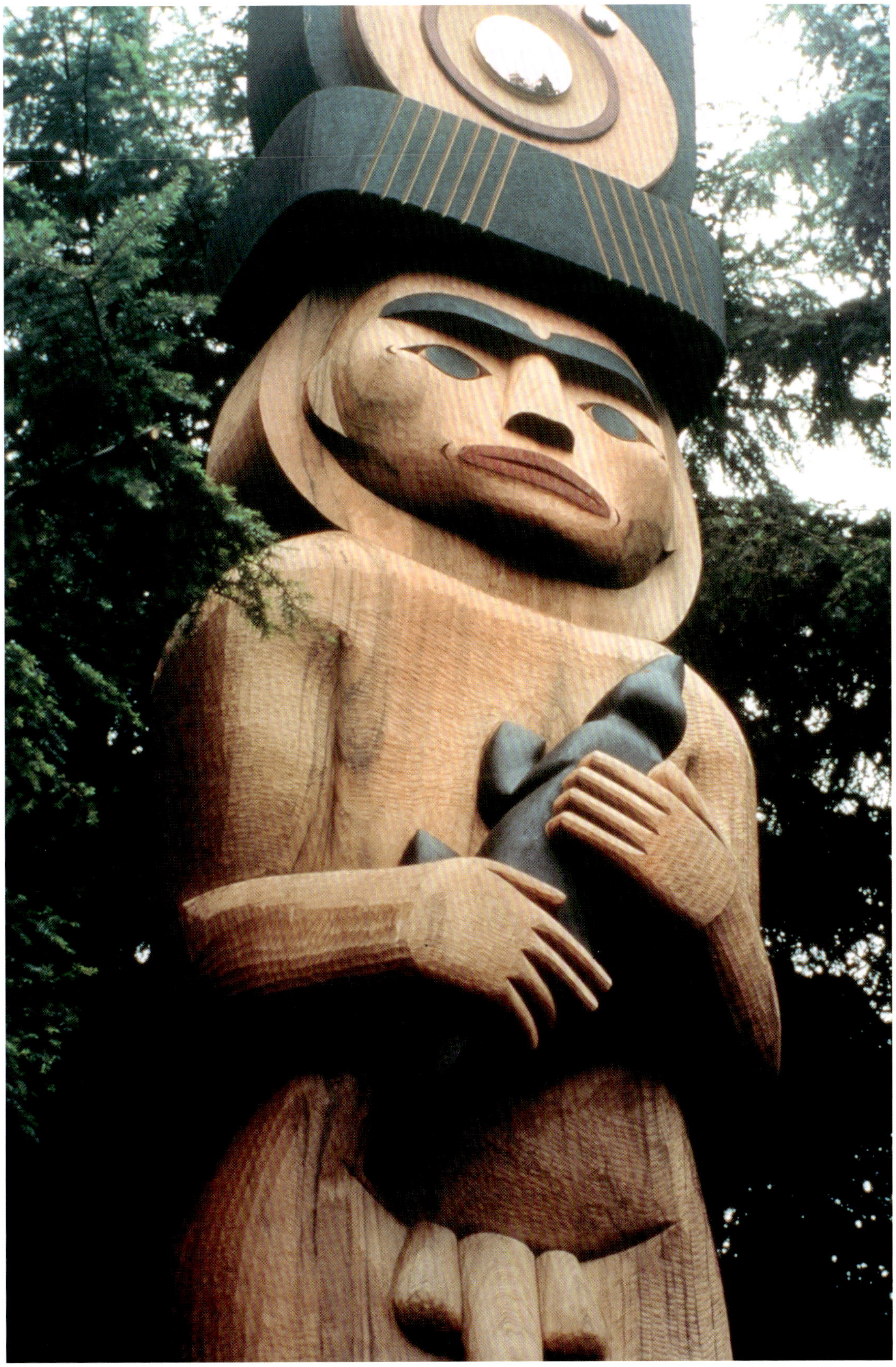

Welcome Figure, 1997
Carved and painted western red cedar
with copper features
7.8 × 1.03 × .57 m

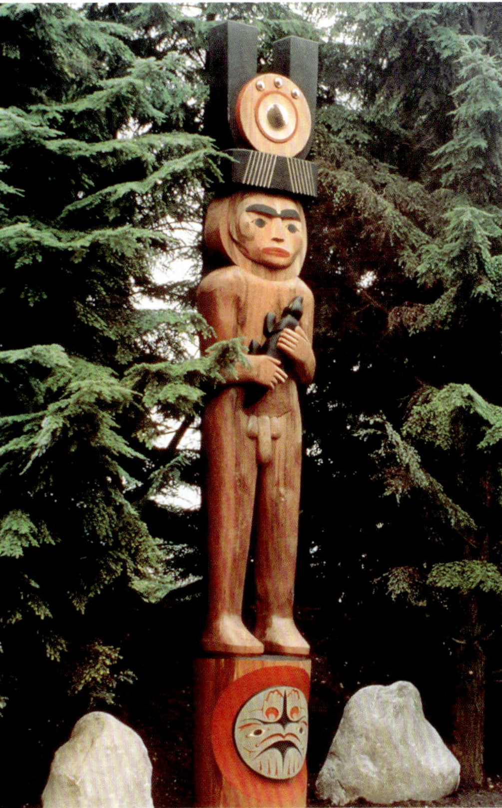

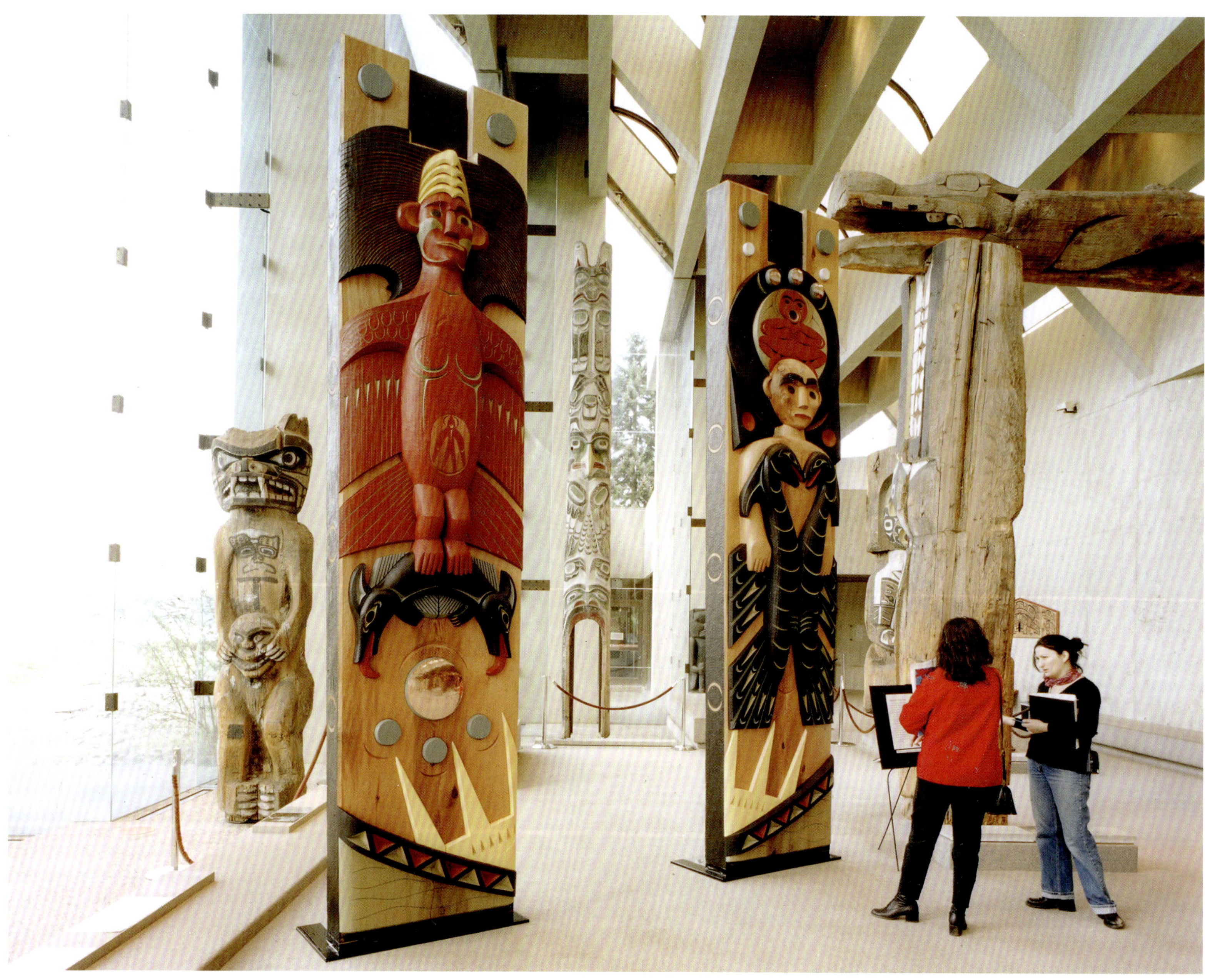

Houseposts

LOCATION: Museum of Anthropology
6393 NW Marine Dr, ʔəlqsən (Point Grey), Vancouver

The other two works from this commission, the Musqueam houseposts, were briefly displayed in the Great Hall at MOA and are now situated outside, on the path south and west of the museum, which leads to the open-air complex of housefronts and totems in various northern styles. Visitors to MOA must orient themselves carefully and leave time to locate these singular carvings.

During her study of Salish belongings Susan had seen images of two nineteenth-century Musqueam houseposts held by the American Museum of Natural History in New York. Always respectful of the mostly private manner in which Musqueam and other Salish Peoples treated objects and ceremonies, Susan never considered copying these earlier works. Nevertheless, she was excited to have the opportunity to be inspired by them, and to be able to design and carve new versions, in her own style, of these precious relics of Musqueam life. She described the design elements and how they developed in an extended artist's statement.

> As the slides and photographs did not do justice to these original houseposts—losing a lot of minute detail within each of them—I had the

Houseposts, 1997
Carved and painted western red cedar with copper features
4.3 × .93 × .39 m (left)
4.3 × .93 × .34 m (right)

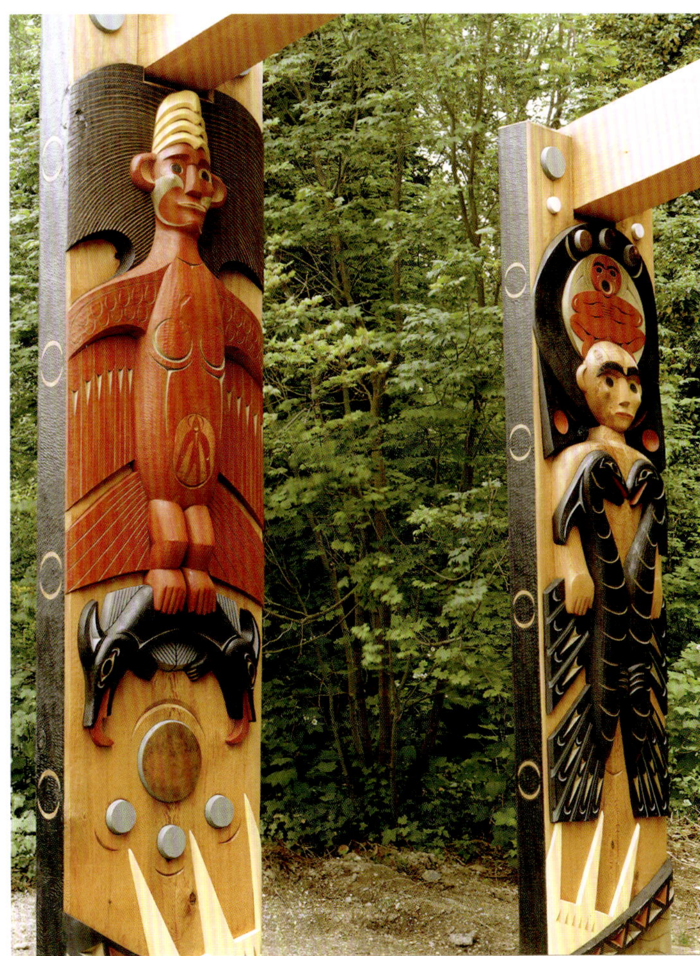

pleasure of travelling to New York to see these original pieces in their purest form ... It was very exciting to see these original houseposts but it's unfortunate that I had to travel thousands of miles just to study them, when in all reality, they should be here at home in their traditional territory.

As a tribute to the original artist or artists ... I used the same format and main figures from each of them—mind you, I made considerable changes in both pieces. One can only guess as to what these traditional figures meant; I am not about to make my own interpretation. Throughout these houseposts I added traditional Salish elements as you can see on the bodies and wings of the animal figures. On the tops of the houseposts are celestial images representing the moon, the stars and the sun.

On the contemporary side, I have incorporated personal imagery which has a story of its own. Because I had to go to New York, on the bottom left housepost I incorporated the East River; and naturally, on the right housepost I incorporated the Fraser River. I also incorporated the mountain [sme:nt] and valley motif—the triangular patterns—which represent the mountains on the North Shore and the fact that this whole area, which is now called Vancouver, was once a flourishing rain forest. I have the sun rising in New York and setting in British Columbia. Coincidentally, the sun in the east somewhat resembles the crown of the Statue of Liberty.[14]

Susan recently explained that after checking with Michael Kew and Musqueam Elder Dominic Point, she found neither could be certain what the central figures on the original posts might be or represent. Susan has her own theories, however: on the left, this may be a human transforming into a bird, the head fitted with a cap of eagle beaks, with perhaps a water wolf of some sort in its claws. On the right she sees a closed-mouth human sʔaθəs (face), with two snakes facing inward, meeting over the person's chest. The snakes seem to have wings as well as small feet, representing a composite mythic being.[15] All we can know for sure is that, as symbols of wealth and status, they are somehow associated with the story and the vision of the families for which they were made. There can be no doubt, however, of the visual impact of Susan's interpretation. Through this permanent display at MOA, Susan is showcasing the sculptural traditions of her ancestors and reaffirming the ongoing presence of these traditions on this territory.

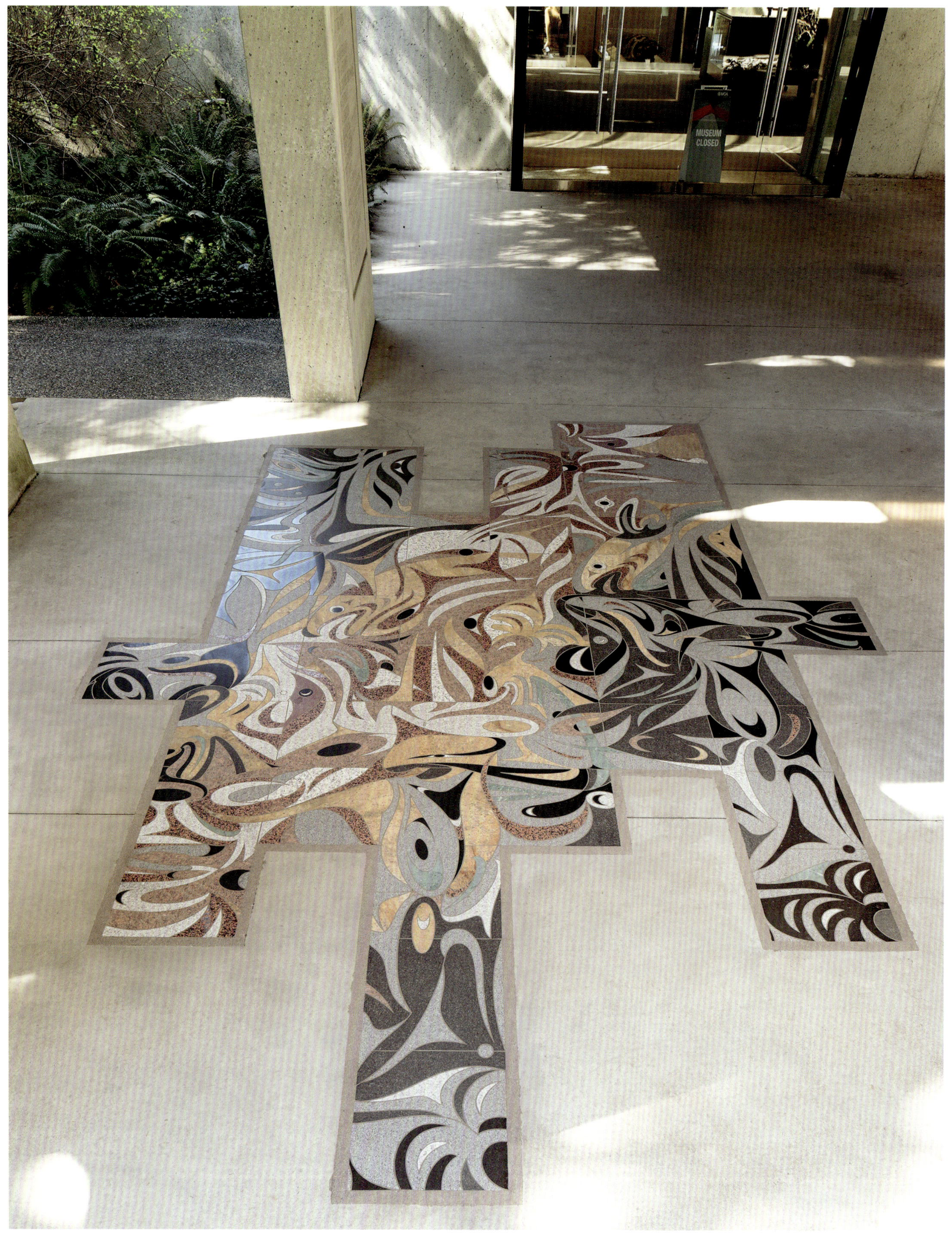
MUSEUM
CLOSED

Salish Footprint, 2010
Granite
5.59 x 3.69 m

Salish Footprint

LOCATION: Museum of Anthropology
6393 NW Marine Dr, ʔəlqsən (Point Grey), Vancouver

The most recent of Susan's works at MOA is *Salish Footprint,* a stone mosaic laid in the floor of the museum's outdoor welcome plaza. It grew out of a call for new Musqueam art, jointly issued by the museum and the Musqueam in July 2006, that expressed a commitment "to visually represent Musqueam to all visitors to the UBC Museum of Anthropology and to offer a clear message that the Museum sits on Musqueam traditional territory."[16] This call was open only to individuals or groups of artists who were Musqueam band members. The proposals were to take into account a number of themes: traditions of welcoming; welcome in the language of the Musqueam; ancestors as people of the community; journeys on the river, and its relationship to the Musqueam; representation of community history and relationships; and community wealth in the form of resources, baskets, weavings, and carvings.

In a message to a staff member at MOA in January 2010, Susan described the work as

> a crop of a print I did in 2006 called "Peripheral Visions–Salish Footprint," however, over time it has been revised quite a bit in order to make the overall design work in stone. The imagery is based on the whorls and lines of a thumb or toe print, transformed using distinctive Salish elements, and incorporating many of the life forms found in the land, sea and skies surrounding the Museum of Anthropology. The artwork emphasizes the Salish connection to the site—a reminder that the surrounding land is Musqueam territory and a welcome from the Musqueam people to this territory.
>
> The imagery in this design, although done in my own contemporary style, is created

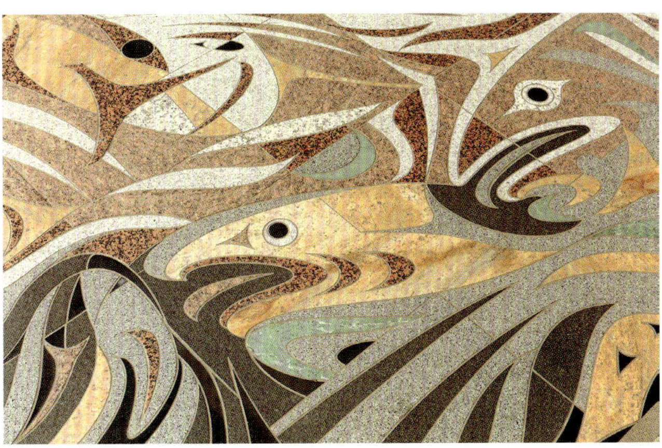

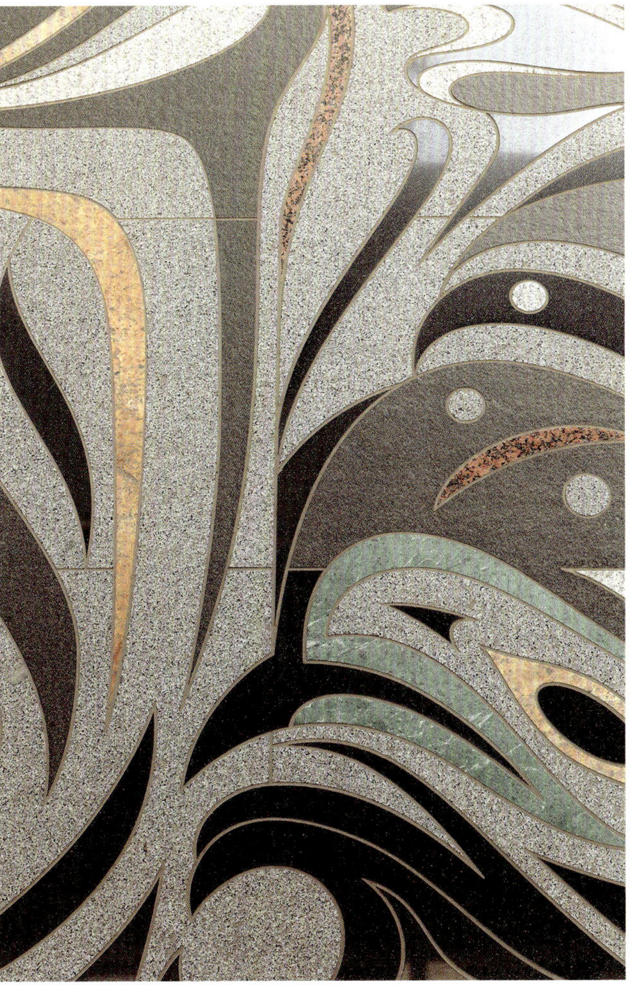

> incorporating traditional Salish elements (basically reflecting the Salish vocabulary/alphabet in my artistic style). The imagery within reflects salmon and birds; upon a closer look other subtle images can be seen (left to the viewer's creativity)...
>
> In laying out the colours of the stonework... the red running through the centre represents the blood of the people (all peoples). Artwork is laid out haphazardly to make the point that no one's print is the same. The layout also complements the architecture. As well, it relates to Musqueam houseposts and cross beam architecture."[17]

Susan's long experience working with architects and her legendary meticulousness came fully into play on this occasion: the selection of the stone, the method of cutting it, and the surface treatment given to the pieces were all important issues. Each of the fifty-four 50-centimetre-square pieces required precision measurements. The bed for the stones needed to be prepared with care. And the final result had to be pedestrian-friendly, low-maintenance, and watertight so that the seams wouldn't freeze, expand, and crack the stone. Susan was at the centre of the entire process, encouraging all the players—the museum architects, the stone suppliers and cutters, and her family members who were part of the production team—to carefully consider all these questions.

In a celebration in 2011 of *Salish Footprint* and Joe Becker's *Transformation*, another artwork commissioned at the same time, the plaza was officially renamed xʷəńiwən ce:p kʷθəθ nəw̓eyəɬ ("remember your teachings"). The mosaic is an important reminder of Musqueam teachings, as well as a worthy complement to the Arthur Erickson–designed museum building. The whole composition is a tribute to Susan's ability to create an exciting mix of traditional elements using a non-traditional material. Visitors should take the time to stop and read her introduction to the piece, and then turn to find the salmon, birds, and other life forms hidden in the curves and crescents of this masterful celebration of ownership of the land through art.

Salish Girl

LOCATION: *Reconciliation Pole*
2373–2425 Main Mall, near q̓ələχən,
ʔəlqsən (Point Grey), Vancouver

In November 2016, 7idansuu (Edenshaw), also known as James Hart, hereditary chief and master carver of the Haida, invited Susan to carve a child's face on the pole that he and members of his family had spent two years carving and painting. Hart explained in a message to Susan that he was

> carving a totem to help with Reconciliation, to create a platform to speak from and help bring continued attention to what had gone on in native communities all across Canada... the whole program that was designed to hurt our peoples.... I am inviting different First Nations artists/carvers from across Canada to carve a child's face in their area's style to have representation on the Pole... I know you to be a well known Artist/Carver from this area, Musqueam's Unceded Territory. We talked yesterday [November 2, 2016] about carving a Child's Face on one of the Children and you agreed, this shall represent your people and your area.[18]

Reconciliation Pole, 2017
7idansuu (Edenshaw) James Hart
Carved and painted western red cedar with copper elements
Approx. 16.76 × 1.8 × 1.5 m

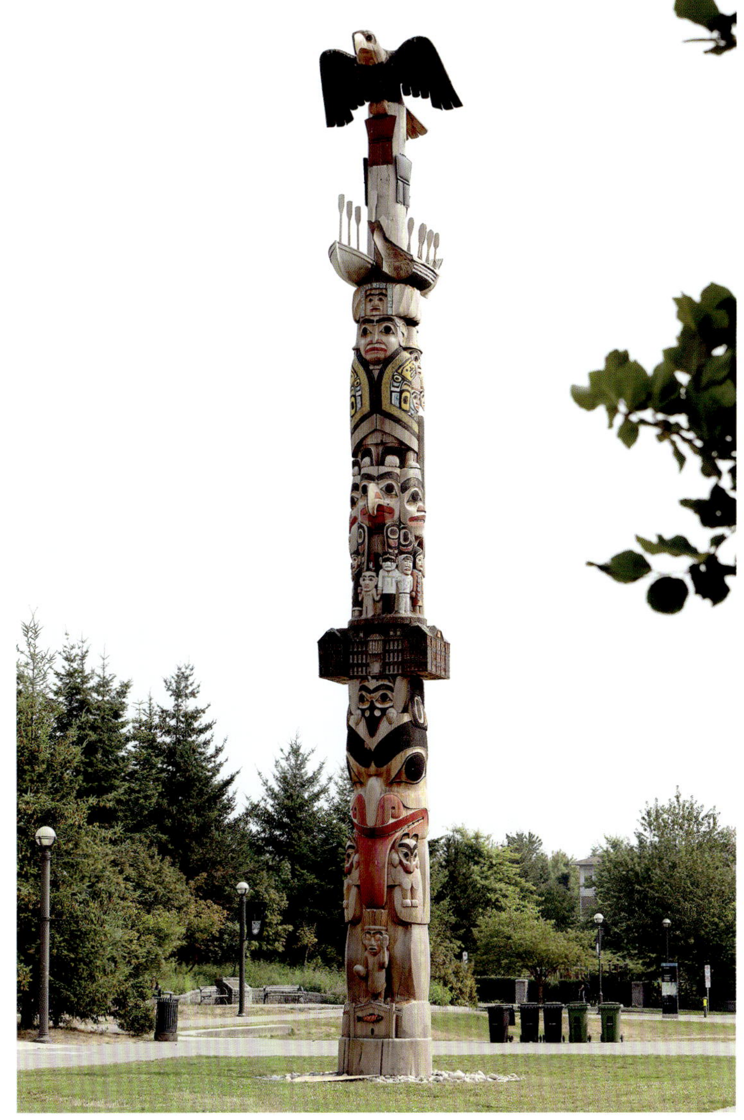

Reconciliation Pole honours the children who attended Indian residential schools, and especially the thousands who died there. It tells the story of how First Nations Peoples lived before the schools, and what they suffered and lost there. And it honours the First Peoples who survived and are moving forward.

Susan designed a solemn-faced girl in Salish style. At the carving site north of the Museum of Anthropology, about six kilometres from her home, Jim Hart and his team were finishing their huge project. Susan worked with her children Thomas and Kelly, her long-time collaborator Ron Denessen, and her husband Jeff Cannell to carve a figure with large black eyes and a closed mouth, wearing a red coat decorated with green patinated stylized paddles from a traditional Salish ceremonial robe. Susan's grandchildren also contributed, hammering in some of the more than 6,800 copper nails that cover various parts of the pole, each of which represents a child who died in the residential school system.

Salish Girl is one of several figures above a carved schoolhouse that represents the actual residential school in the Lower Mainland that Hart's grandfather and other family members attended. The feet of all the children are hidden because, as Jim Hart's son Gwaliga Hart explained, "they weren't grounded in family and culture."[19]

The seventeen-metre pole was raised on the Main Mall at UBC on 1 April 2017, in a special ceremony attended by thousands. In his remarks, James Hart acknowledged and thanked Susan and her family for their help and for enshrining a Musqueam presence in the pole.

Susan is herself a survivor of the residential school system; she was forced to attend Sechelt Indian Residential school until the age of thirteen. This project was an emotional and important experience for her. In the spirit of the conception of the pole, we can hope that the presence of this great work on campus contributes to long-term healing, through both its viewing and creation. Though the work speaks to horrific events, the experience of working on it was positive for Susan and her "Coast Salish Family."

> All I can say is how proud I am to have had the opportunity to work with Jim Hart, one of THE best carvers and artists.... I think Jim was impressed watching five people working on this small figure that was less than 4 feet tall. It was fun! I believe we brought an energy that he seemed to love, me and my kids and husband. My children learned a lot at this time by just watching Jim carve and listening to his inspirations. It was a chance to get to know such an awesome artist.[20]

Salish Girl, 2017
Carved and painted western red cedar with patinated green copper decoration
Approx. 114 × 40 × 20 cm

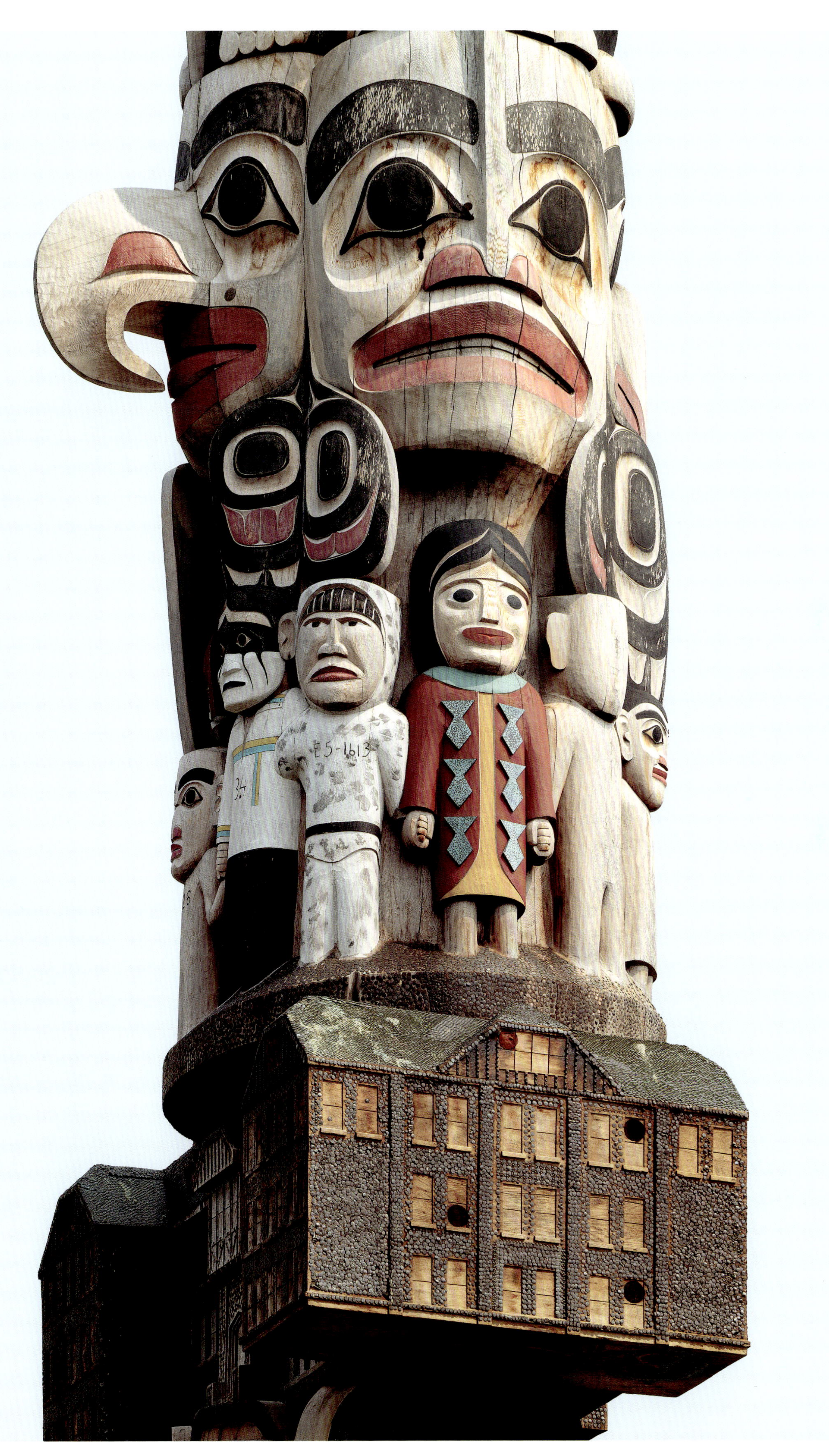
E5-1613
34

The Coming Together of Two Ancient Cultures

LOCATION: West Broadway Avenue
2800–3000 blocks, W Broadway Ave, Vancouver

In January 2007, Mary Stewart of the West Broadway Business Association contacted Susan with an interesting proposal. They planned to install sidewalk medallions along three blocks of West Broadway Avenue in the Kitsilano neighbourhood (partially to occupy the space left by recently removed trees), and wished to feature the work of local artists. The area has long had a strong Greek presence, and several Greek artists had contributed designs featuring octopi, fish, and Greek aphorisms; now the committee was hoping that Susan would contribute works to represent the presence of the Coast Salish Peoples.[21]

Mary Stewart, who introduced herself as a "long-time admirer" of Susan's work, made it clear that she was not certain that her group could offer appropriate compensation, but that they were engaged in fundraising, and she hoped Susan could be involved. Susan agreed to provide older, as-yet-unused designs, which would be sandblasted onto granite medallions by Century Monuments.

Susan initially offered two designs: a whorl showing two eagles, and another featuring four salmon. They were both well-received, so much so that the committee requested seven more, so Susan invited her daughter, Kelly Cannell, to join her for their part of the project. The committee continued fundraising through 2007 and into 2008, and the city made the necessary alterations to the sidewalks.

These designs were all modelled on the classic Salish spindle whorl that Susan had used as a structure for many of her creations over the past twenty-five years. Several of the designs are relatively simple, featuring variations of four salmon; others show human faces and figures, frogs, birds of several types, or fishers. Susan's titles hint at the meaning and inspiration: *Salish Vision*, *Salish Spirit*, *Swanisit*, *Four Salmon*. Kelly's design, *Connecting Generations* (bottom-right on facing page), was also whorl-inspired, comprising six female figures, each kneeling and holding a symbolic book in her hands.

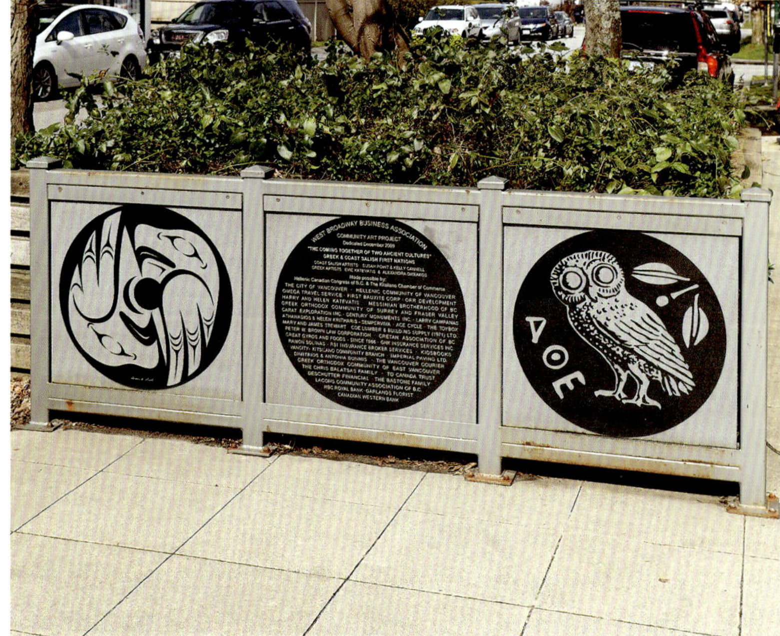

The project was formally dedicated in December of 2009. The sponsors had raised enough funds for thirty-six medallions of sandblasted black granite, which were set into the sidewalks on both sides of Broadway on the three blocks west of Macdonald, and three sandblasted medallions mounted in a frame at Bayswater Street and Broadway: one by Susan showing two eagles; one by Evie Katevatis and Alexandra Dikeakos depicting the owl of the goddess Athena and the Greek letters alpha, theta,

The Coming Together of Two Ancient Cultures, 2009
Susan Point and Kelly Cannell
Sandblasted black granite
66 cm (diameter; each)

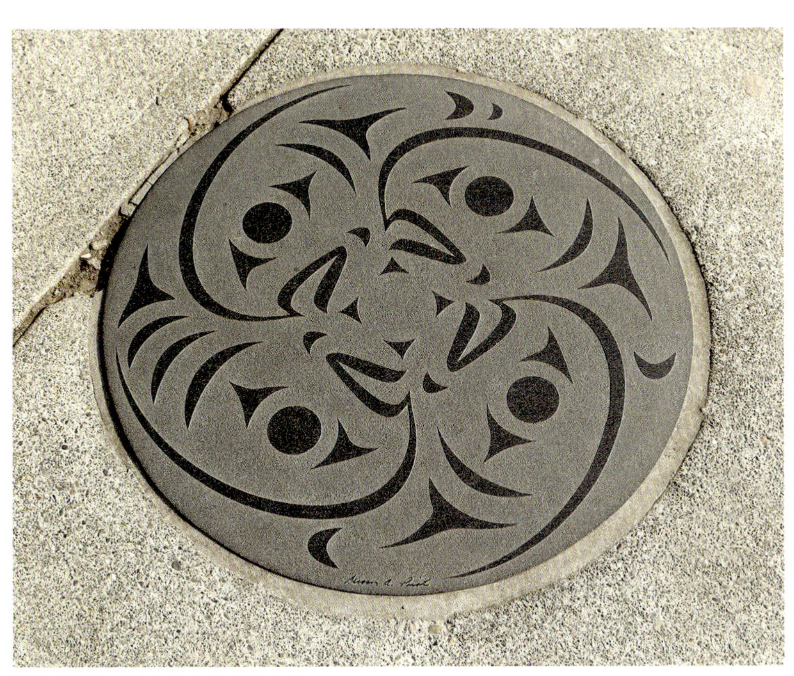

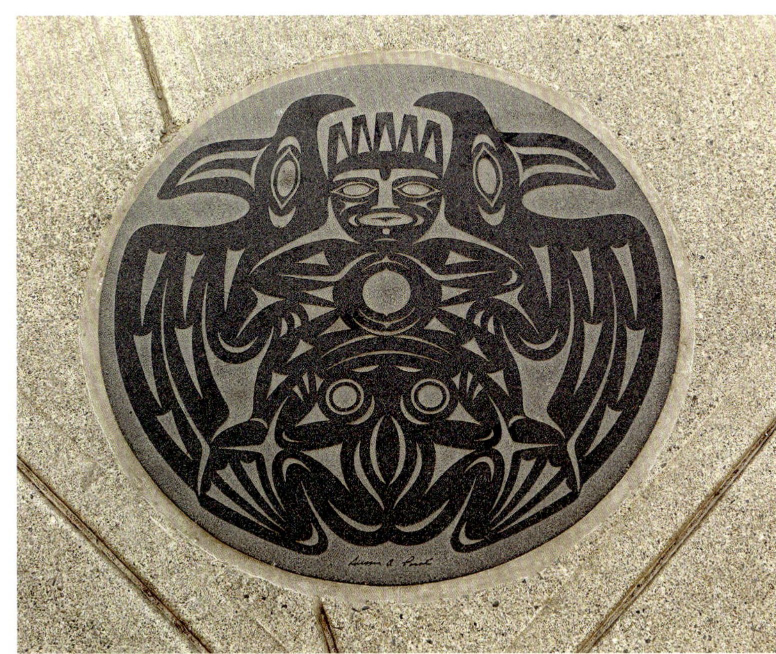

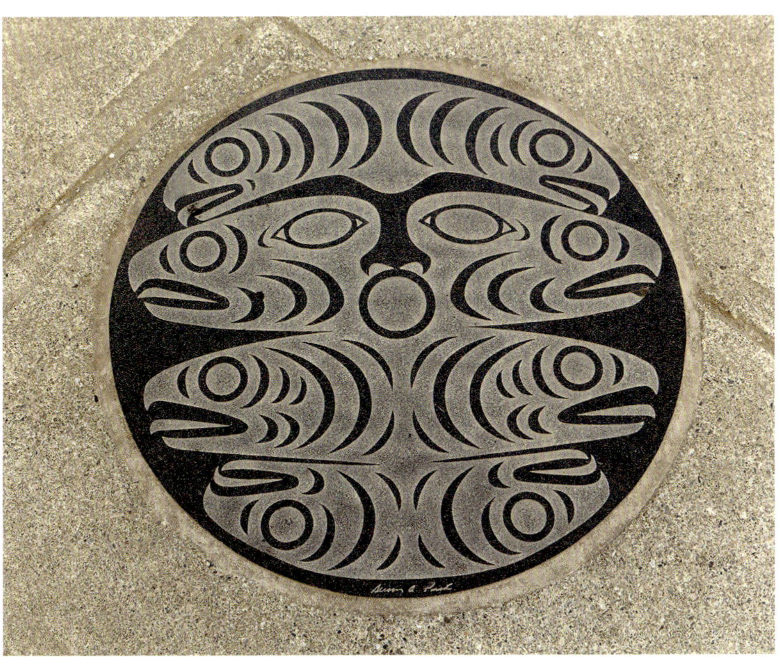

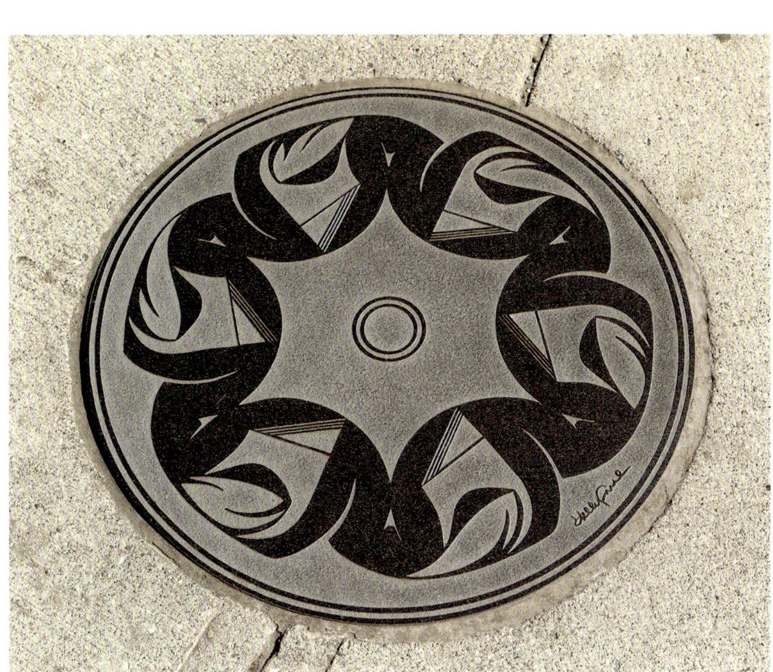

Man and Salmon, 2009
Carved and painted western red cedar
1.22 m (diameter)

and epsilon; and one that lists the title, artists, and sponsors of the project.

Many of the Greek images would be familiar to students following a standard high school curriculum, but for many the Salish whorls might be more of a discovery, a pleasant and intriguing surprise. Once again, Susan and her family are re-establishing the Salish imprint on the lands of their ancestors through their art, in this case, a few blocks from where a creek called t̓θəmt̓θaməls once ran. Mary Stewart and her committee not only linked two ancient cultures, but ensured an ongoing educational and artistic opportunity for the whole community.

Man and Salmon

LOCATION: Vancouver School Board
1580 W Broadway Ave, Vancouver

In the lead-up to the 2010 Olympics, Vancouver schools increased their efforts to introduce students to First Nations art. This beautifully sculpted whorl was installed at the school board's administrative headquarters in 2009, some ten years after the building was first opened.

Susan returns here to themes and ideas she has explored in various mediums from the beginning of her career. The human face dominates the whorl with its forceful expression that engages the viewer. Four sce:ɬtən (salmon) circle the face, "swimming" clockwise. The strong black outline of each fish is a distinctive interpretation of traditional Salish forms, with crescents and wedges adding emphasis to the various parts of the fish. No line is wasted; each element contributes to the character of Susan's representation of salmon.

The whorl is mounted on a wall above a staircase so that those entering the building from the north need to pause at the top of the stairs, turn around, and take a few moments to appreciate the artwork. In the foyer hangs a framed label (by an unidentified author) that describes the meaning and significance of the whorl.

> In First Nations tradition, the salmon, once so abundant off the West Coast, is believed to be the giver of life. Salmon in the Central Coast Salish tradition are usually depicted in pairs, which is also a symbol of good luck. The salmon is an indicator of wealth and an important symbol at the heart of Salish existence, used as a food source and for bartering. The piece honours the central role of the salmon in West Coast existence, and celebrates the connections between all living beings. The reflection of four also runs through much of Susan Point's work. It carries many important meanings to all aboriginal peoples; there are four seasons, four winds, four directions and four elements (earth, fire, water and air), each of which must be respected for their gift of life.

This whorl enshrines ideas that Susan has often expressed herself, ideas that are central to many of her compositions. It depicts a Salish view of the world that is a perfect point of departure for teachers and students whose work and learning is shaped by the board that commissioned this art.

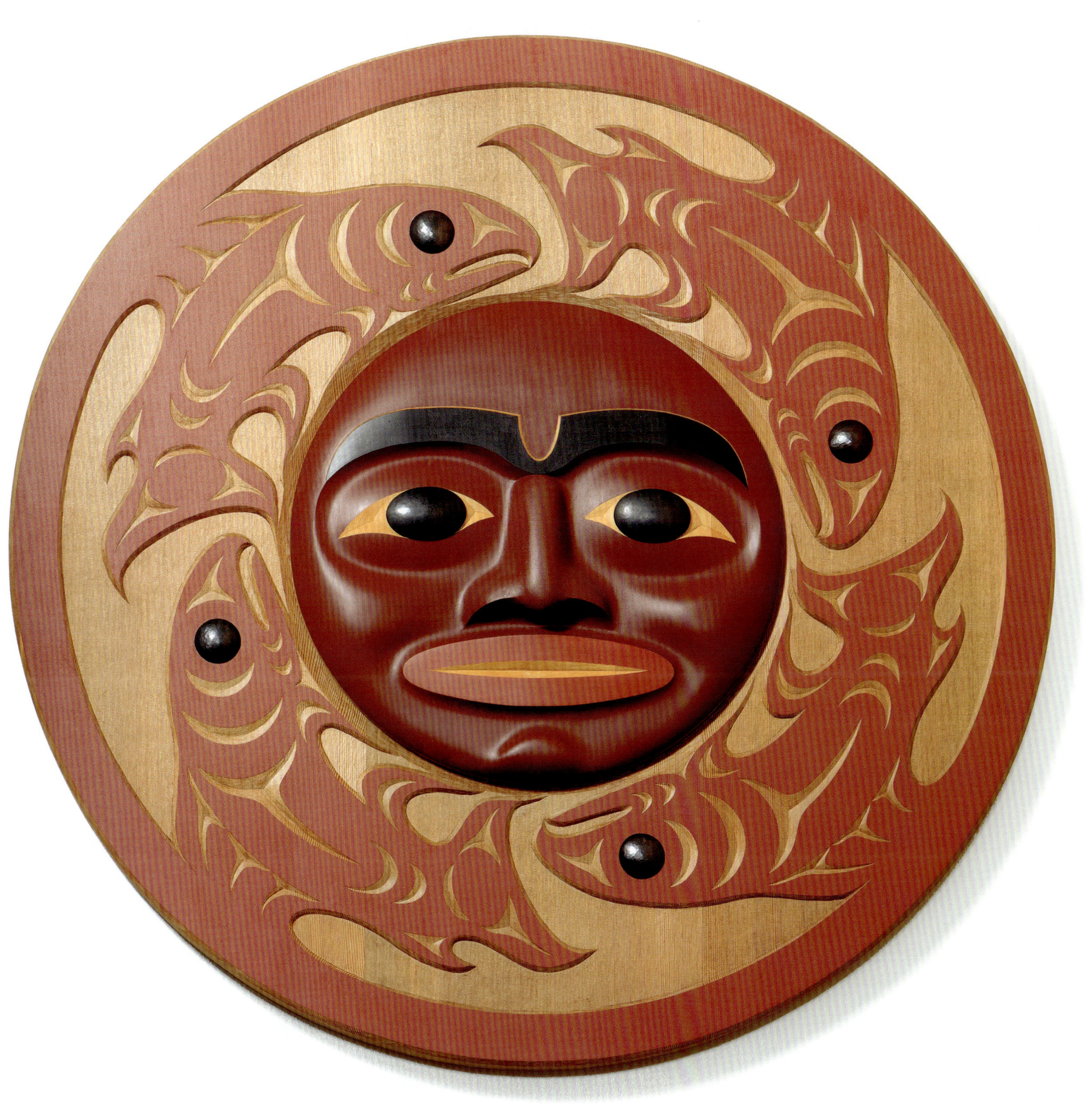

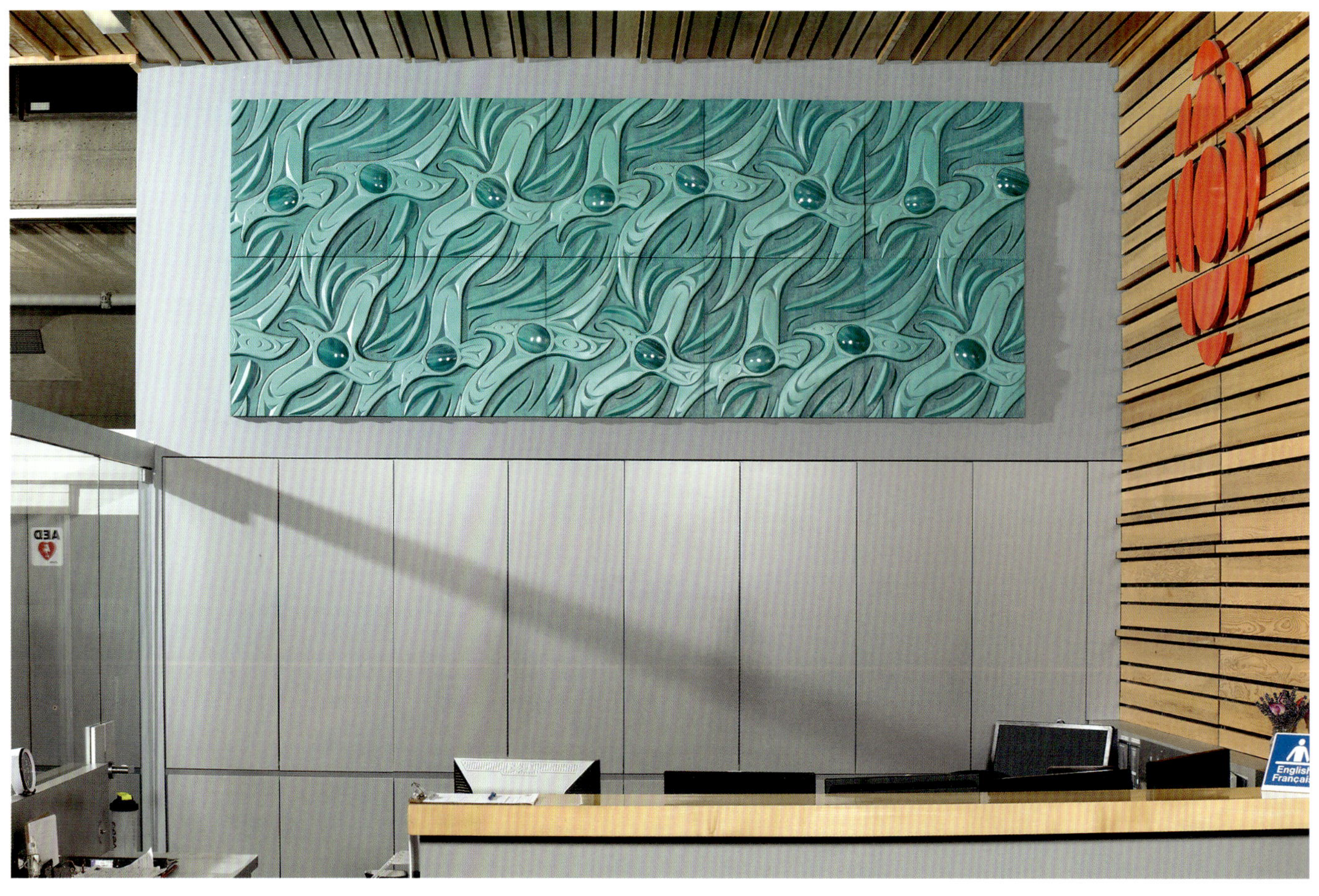

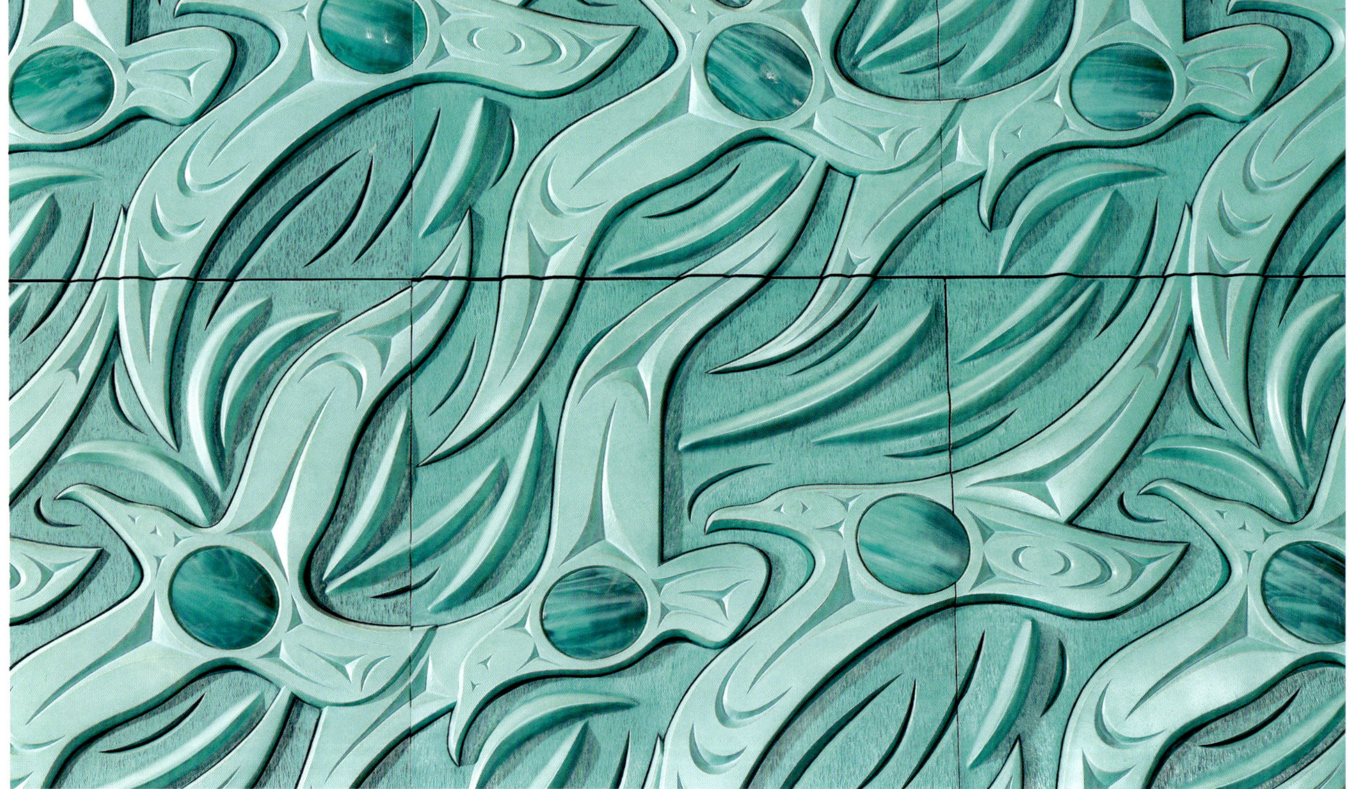

Salish Sky, 2008
Forton, fused glass, oil paint
1.2 × 3.3 m

Salish Sky

LOCATION: CBC Vancouver Broadcast Centre
700 Hamilton St, Vancouver

In January 2008, CBC Vancouver decided to commission works from local artists to furnish its newly renovated facility with works that would celebrate the culture of the Musqueam people. Susan proposed a mural featuring bird forms, to fit on a wall behind the main reception desk. The tight timeline did not permit Susan to carve a completely new design, so she took advantage of part of an existing mould that she had originally created in 1993 for the West Seattle Pump Station.

Bird forms are a frequent element in early Salish objects in museum collections. The proximity of the Musqueam settlement to the north arms of stal̓əw̓ (the Fraser River) and the delta lands immediately south, which are a popular resting spot on the Pacific Flyway, attracts a widely varied and extensive migratory bird population. Many local species abound on Musqueam territory as well: eagles, herons, ducks and geese, gulls, and smaller birds; all would have been familiar to Susan's ancestors, and to Susan herself from a young age.

For the CBC building, Susan created birds flying across a dynamic background in a powerful expression of the natural environment. Each of the ten mural components was cast in Forton (a polymer-modified gypsum often used on building facades, where durability and weather resistance are key requirements) with suspended green bronze powder, then patinated and remarked with oil paint. The colour is intriguing: another artist might have felt that the sky called for blue, but the greens give a cool, fresh reference to the land and environment. Fitted together, the panels show birds in three different flight positions, the heads and wings embellished with classic Salish elements: crescents, V-forms, and elongated and shorter wedges, all within lively, curving outlines. In the centre of each bird are ovals of green fused glass that catch the light and sparkle like jewels, drawing fresh attention to each bird. The overall effect is of elegant movement, the birds swooping and diving through the moving air.

This mural celebrates Musqueam culture, but also seems especially appropriate for a broadcast centre. The Salish birds can perhaps represent messengers, bearing the stories that flow from this place every day on radio and television, moving through the air to the wider world. Once more, Susan has used her fresh interpretations of Salish art to shape a larger message for people of all backgrounds: the earth is precious, and the sky, filled with life forms, is a highway for our thoughts.

The Tree of Life

LOCATION: Christ Church Cathedral
690 Burrard St, Vancouver

A short walk northwest of the CBC building, Christ Church Cathedral has stood at the corner of Georgia and Burrard for 125 years. Sharp-eyed pedestrians passing the south end of the cathedral may find their gaze drawn to the elegant lines of the windows in the old stone wall facing Georgia Street. If they venture inside they will find a surprising treasure—*The Tree of Life*, an elegant θqet (tree) sweeping across five windows, or lights—the first large-scale stained glass window designed by a First Nations artist.

The Tree of Life grew from the gift of Jean MacMillan Southam, a legendary philanthropist in Vancouver, and found its ideal fruition through the creative vision of Susan Point. By the time work began in 2006, Susan had established a reputation regionally, nationally, and internationally as the person most responsible for the rebirth of Salish art forms. Her work had gained admiration for many reasons, including her willingness to embrace opportunities for large-scale art in a variety of locations. The five lancet windows at Christ Church Cathedral offered an opportunity that Susan was keen to explore. As Nancy Southam described it, the result of her mother's donation is "this blazing, transcendent, luminous and final gift."[22]

Jean Southam's benefactions had already enriched many parts of the restoration of this historic neo-Gothic cathedral when, in early 2006, her donation enabled the replacement of the unremarkable coloured glass in the windows. Her deed of gift specified that the theme of these new windows was to be "the tree of life." The dean of the cathedral, the Very Reverend Peter Elliott, explained her reasons for the theme:

> First, it's one of the great themes in the Bible that was not yet celebrated in any of the [other stained glass] windows. The second reason is in British Columbia trees are very much part of our life.... Third, Jean always wanted to honour her father H.R. MacMillan and his philanthropy. MacMillan was a forester for whom the trees in British Columbia were both an opportunity for business and also a great treasure to be celebrated.[23]

The cathedral sought proposals and received three submissions, of which Susan Point's resonated the strongest with the selection committee. Her deep belief in the interconnectedness of all life, which springs from her Coast Salish roots and the environmental awareness that was an important part of her upbringing, fit well with Anglican beliefs about humans as the stewards of creation. And as Nancy Southam noted, her design impressed the committee with the "uniqueness of her approach, its beauty and elegance."[24]

It took several iterations to successfully integrate the design into the gothic window openings, and ensure the sweep and curve of the artwork matched from window to window. Susan reworked the width of the limbs and the placement of various elements over a number of months. As she worked to revise and refine her vision, her correspondence with Peter Elliott reveals her enthusiasm for the project, but also her approach to her work more broadly.

> I have done a great many public art pieces that dictate that I be sensitive to the history of the site and the community. But in this case it seems to have overwhelmed my creative juices. Thus far in my career I have strived to reach many different goals. First and foremost was the fact that there was, and still is, an art form that

OVERLEAF:

The Tree of Life, 2009

Hand-blown antique glass
5.94 × 1.03 m (centre light), 4.45 × .96 m (lights to right and left of centre; each),
3.23 × .66 m (far left and far right lights; each)

is unique to this area. And then, I have made some political and environmental statements throughout my career in some of my works. But it seems that over time it's all developed or focused on the interconnection of all life on this planet and the universe and how intricately everything depends on or is a result of that interconnection. The "tree of life" sums up what I am trying to achieve at this point in my career... spreading the word that we respect each other and all life and trying to conserve that of which we are all a part.

I've decided that because these windows are so highly elevated... being illustrative to the point of treating it like a canvas it wouldn't have as much effect as opposed to treating it like windows.... When illustrating the actual tree of life I decided to show what you would be looking at of that tree looking up (i.e. you don't see the trunk, you just see the top of the tree; the elevated tree of the branches).

Anyway, in my rough art thus far, I've tried to show that everything is connected from this vantage point so that the separation of the glass within the tree marries to the rest of the design outside of the tree (i.e. the background). In other words, the sky, the leaves and the few life forms that are depicted are all the same geometric type shapes flowing upwards, striving to give an uplifting emotion.

However, as an artist, I know that my work is always changing and if I look at it again, at any given point, I may see a totally different direction to go. This is how I work... my work continues to evolve. I challenge myself continually to do what I can't see...

I believe that the use of colour and the flow of the artwork will symbolize the connection between earth and heaven. I believe my work will emphasize the forest and landscape of British Columbia... as you say, a paramount importance in our lives. And, as you request that the design be welcoming and reflect a guiding spirit, the glass which I will use will be as light and transparent as possible.

My work strongly incorporates the leaf shape throughout the entire design, symbolizing "the healing of nations"... I hope that my work will celebrate the beauty of our lands as reflected by the Salish flavor; a legacy of the first peoples unique to this area.[25]

Susan Point was not alone in this work; she again partnered with Yves Trudeau of Studio One Glass Art, whose years of experience as a glass artisan were essential in realizing Susan's vision. From the outset she described, in considerable detail, her intention to use hand-blown glass to achieve the rich colour palette she wanted, and to ensure the glass would be translucent enough to let in as much light as possible.

The actual tree itself will transform from a darker bottom, anchoring the piece, to a lighter shade at the top, using various shades of Fraser River greens of various degrees of value. At the base of the tree, I may incorporate darker hues such as charcoal, smoke and bark colours. The background leaf shapes will incorporate leaf greens, light sky colours, clear and textured antique glass with warm highlights. Towards the lower portion of the background where the mountains and the ocean are, I will incorporate forest greens, mountain shades, mixed seasonal colours with some white highlights and also subtle sea blues and greens.[26]

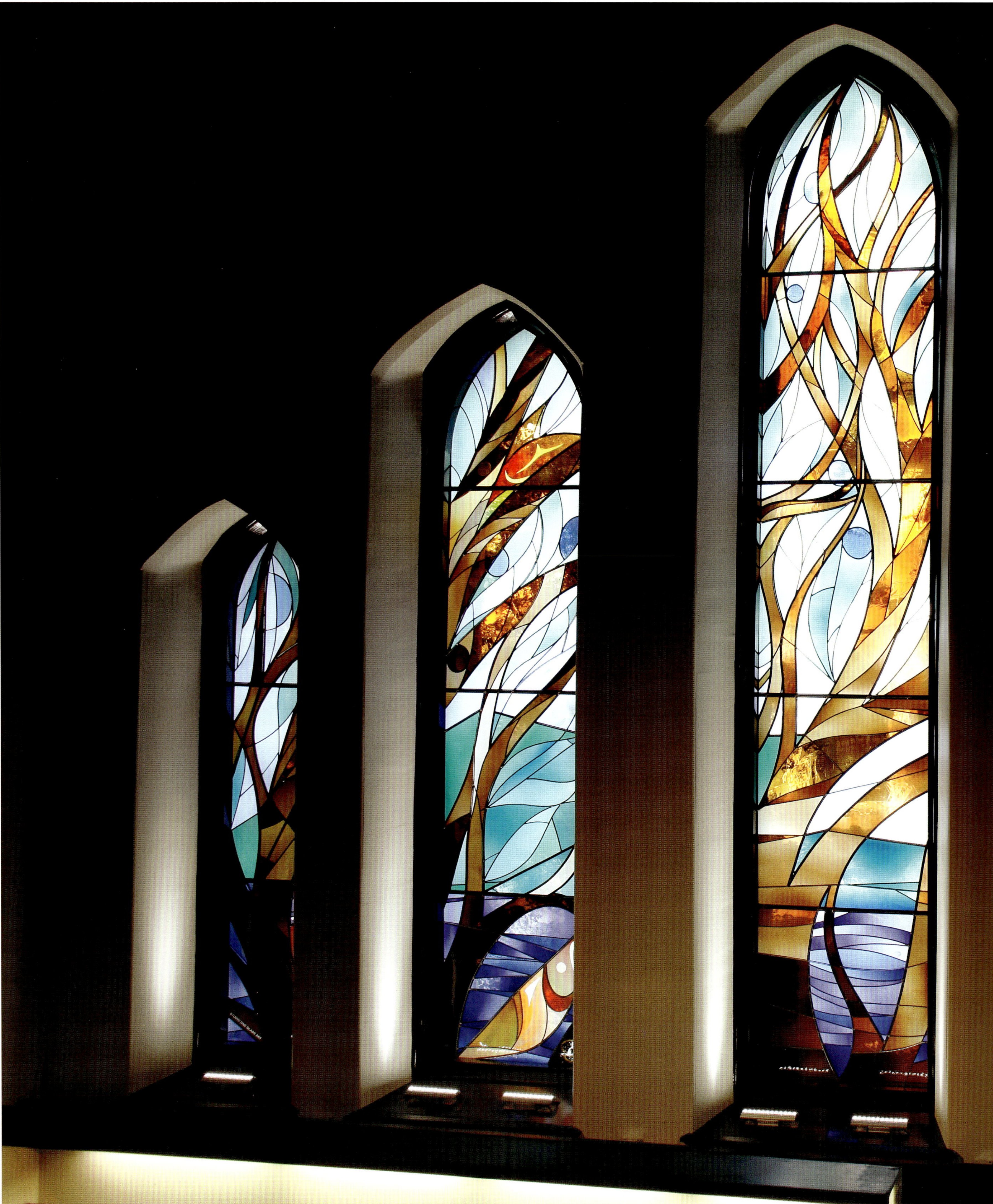

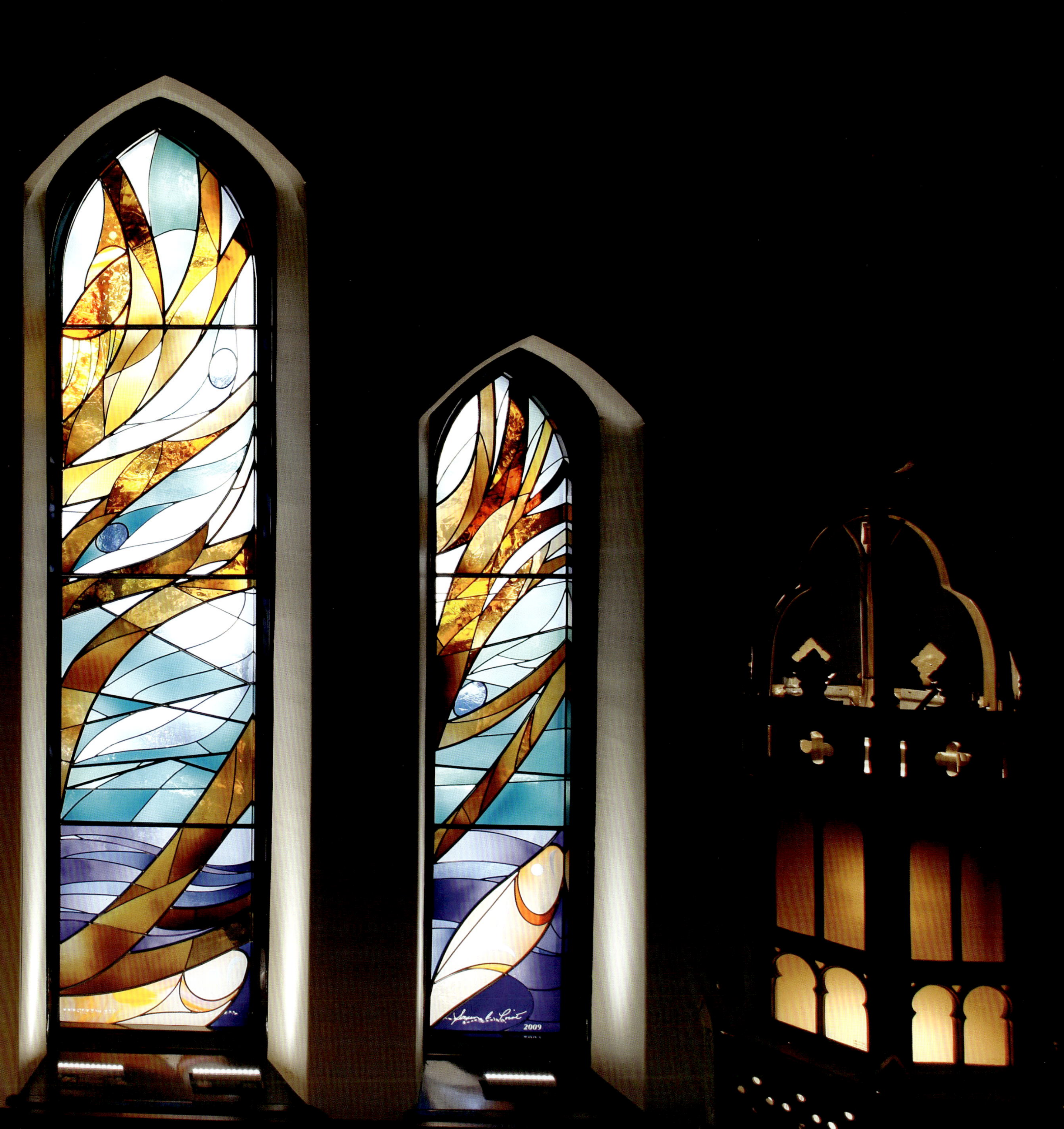
2009

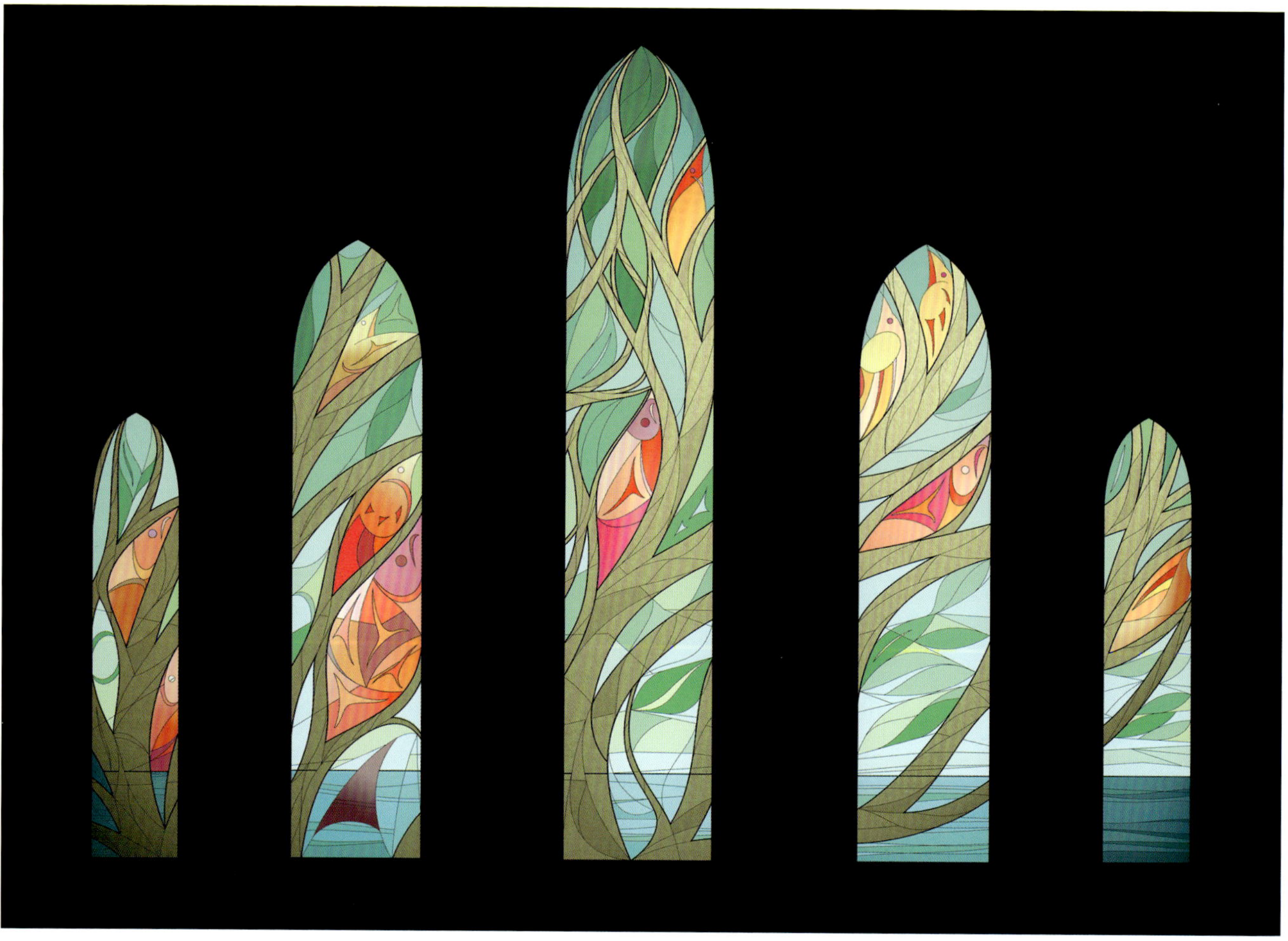

Trudeau and Susan selected Fremont Antique Glass in Seattle to produce the hand-blown glass, and supervised the production so that the rich colours Susan envisioned would be available to bring the composition to life. One of Fremont's most experienced glass blowers, Jim Flannigan, blew each sheet using a centuries-old process that resulted in beautiful sheets of vivid colour, some with gradients that Point and Trudeau requested: "The beauty of it," said Trudeau when the work was complete, "is that because each sheet is hand-blown, each sheet is different. Even in one sheet, from one end of the sheet to the other you've got beautiful shades that we requested from the glass blower, to go from a dark green to a pale green or vice-versa."[27] When the glass was shipped to Studio One in Vancouver, further adjustments to the design were made to account for the colour ranges and unique character of the glass.

When the design alterations were complete, Susan created cartoons, full-scale drawings of each "light" (or opening) of each window, to serve as guides when cutting the glass. Yves Trudeau and his colleagues, Jose Ventura and Carlos Moro, spent four months at Studio One cutting the glass to fit its designated place on the cartoons, and then assembling the pieces to make each window. This was an exciting phase for Susan and the members of the cathedral's committee, who were able to tour Studio One and watch as the windows came into being.

From 23 February to 17 March 2009, the existing windows were removed and the *Tree of Life* windows took their place. The cathedral's contractors, Scott Construction, also arranged for the installation of new interior and exterior lighting in the narthex area of the church, so that the new windows would be lit from within the church and visible from the outside.

A colour rendering that Susan made to accompany her proposal for the windows.

Less than a month later, on Palm Sunday, 5 April 2009, *The Tree of Life* was formally dedicated in the presence of Susan Point and Yves Trudeau; Musqueam Elder Larry Grant; Bishop Michael Ingham; the lieutenant-governor of British Columbia, the Honourable Steven Point, and his wife Gwen; Nancy Southam and her sister Martha Lou Henley, as well as other members of the Southam family; and hundreds of other guests.

I was privileged to be asked to speak at this celebration, and took the chance to express my belief, still firmly held today, that the generosity of Jean Southam had made possible a truly magnificent work of art, a treasure to link Christian beliefs and Salish spirituality.

> Her task was not easy as this church is a listed heritage structure in a modified Gothic style, and the other glass in Christ Church, while beautiful and historic, is very traditional in composition and subject. Characteristically, Dr. Point embraced the challenge and designed windows which are clearly contemporary in feeling and take full advantage of Coast Salish ideas and aesthetics, while being perfect complements to the glass already in place....
>
> Since the days of Chartres, Sainte-Chapelle, Canterbury, and thousands of other churches in Europe, great and small, stained glass has been used to tell stories and inspire us in our faith. I think you would all agree that Susan Point tells our story wonderfully, in glass specially blown and chosen by her in an interpretation that is alive and glistens with meaning....
>
> We can surely rejoice that Christ Church has become the home of the largest stained glass work yet created in Canada by a First Peoples artist. But these windows are about more than sheer scale. The beauty of the design and the richness of their meaning will ensure that they lift the spirit of worshippers and inspire and intrigue visitors. If this was Japan, Susan Point would be declared a national treasure and these windows would be recognized as the work of a great artist at the height of her powers.
>
> For those who have longed for the day when the wider community understands fully the importance of the cultures of the people who shared this place with us, these windows are a milestone along the way toward that understanding. Jean Southam's gift and Susan Point's art and vision are a perfect match made in heaven.[28]

I believe that it takes an artist of genius to introduce a distinctive style to a setting created in a very different style and time, and make it a perfect fit.

VANCOUVER CONVENTION CENTRE

The waterfront Vancouver Convention Centre embarked on a massive five-year expansion and renovation in advance of the 2010 Winter Olympics, adding a new West Building at the foot of Burrard Street and renovating the existing East Building in the iconic Canada Place, which occupies a site known as p̓q̓als. As the project neared completion in 2008, planners decided that the Harbour Concourse, a long corridor connecting Canada Place and the new West Building, would double as the Coast Salish Gallery.

Human Spirit

LOCATION: Vancouver Convention Centre
1055 Canada Pl, Vancouver

Of Susan's several pieces in downtown Vancouver, *Human Spirit* is one of her most intriguing compositions. It resulted from a call for "distinctive, meritorious works by exemplary Coast Salish artists," works that would "be a response to the artists' own thoughtful and creative interpretation of the vision statement and the setting." The vision was for "a celebration of the spirit of those who formed the British Columbia of today and who are dreaming of our future... as embraced by the memories of the Vancouver waterfront... and as interpreted by artists, poets and writers."[29]

Susan was understandably eager to create something different and exciting, and ensure that her ongoing exploration of the Salish roots of her art found a substantial presence in this prominent space. In her response to the call, she stated,

> This art call offers the opportunity to create artwork honouring the Salish history of the Vancouver waterfront, to re-establish the Salish footprint on the land, linking the historical past of the site with the present. It is also a chance to offer a Salish welcome to the many visitors who will be using the Vancouver Convention Centre each year—to showcase the unique culture and history of the Coast Salish people, creating a distinct sense of place while paying tribute to our Salish ancestors.
>
> I believe that Salish art has a universal appeal, celebrating the link between all peoples and the earth that we inhabit—in some way everything is connected to everything else and I strive to celebrate that connection in my artwork.[30]

She proposed a series of panels made of carved and painted cedar, each with a highly stylized human figure made of copper, arms upraised in the traditional Salish gesture of welcome. Cedar and copper are traditional Salish materials: copper was used in ceremonies and in trade; cedar, often referred to as "the tree of life," was used for houses, canoes, boxes, and domestic utensils, notably spindle whorls and mat creasers; and cedar bark was woven into mats and baskets and braided into ropes. Susan explained the significance of each element in her proposal:

> The paint and textured surface of the cedar reflects the movement and colour of the water, visually linking the artwork to the site. The carved elements (crescents and wedges) are identifiably Salish, inspired by a design on an ancient stone whorl. The overall artwork can be understood at a glance, but each panel will have enough detail and subtle variation to draw the viewer along the length of the corridor.
>
> The human figures are simply drawn and universally recognizable, water-jet cut from ¼-inch-thick copper with a subtle applied patina. They represent the Salish, along with the many

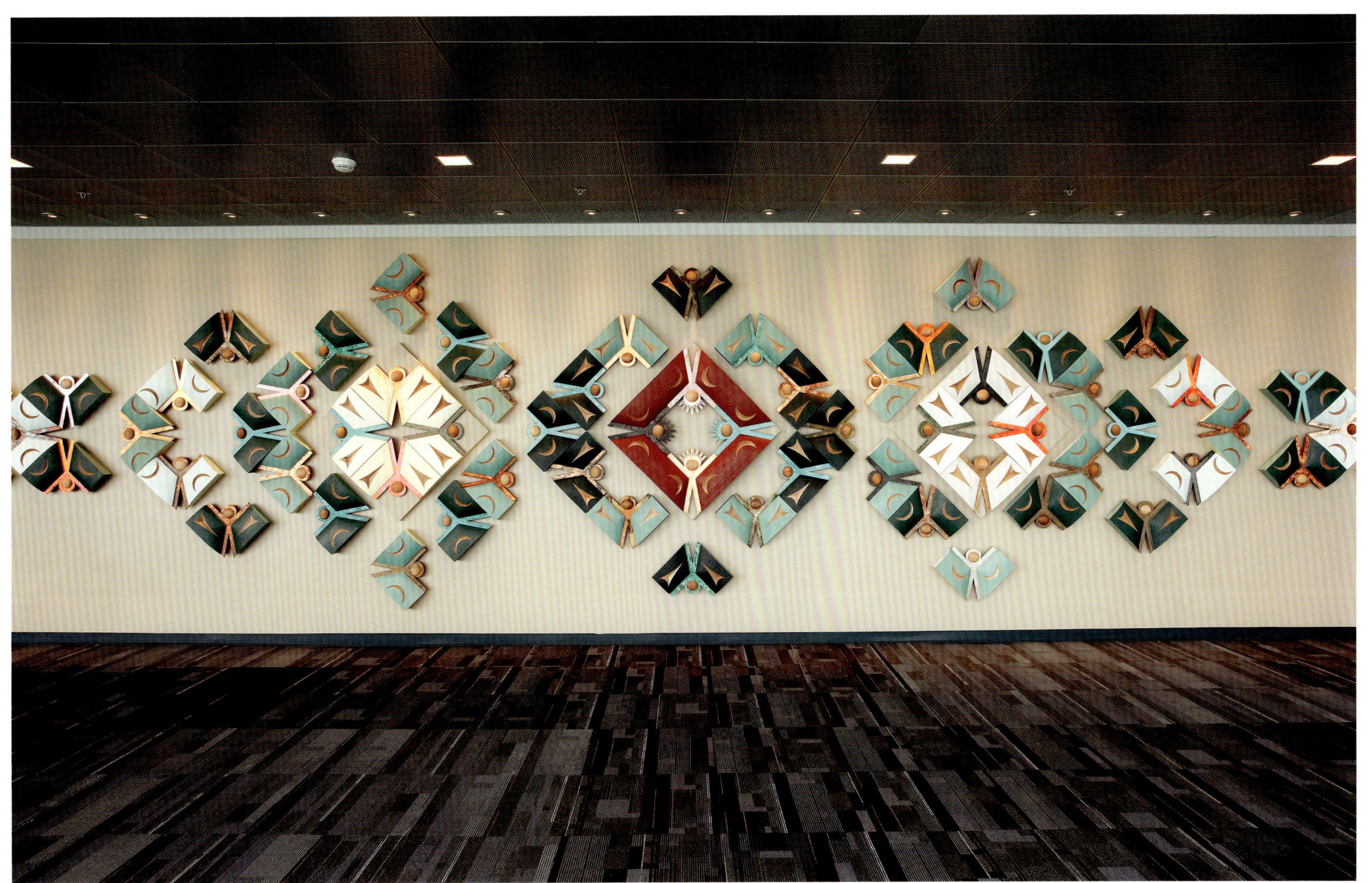

Human Spirit, 2009
Carved and painted cedar
with copper figures
2.4 × 17 m

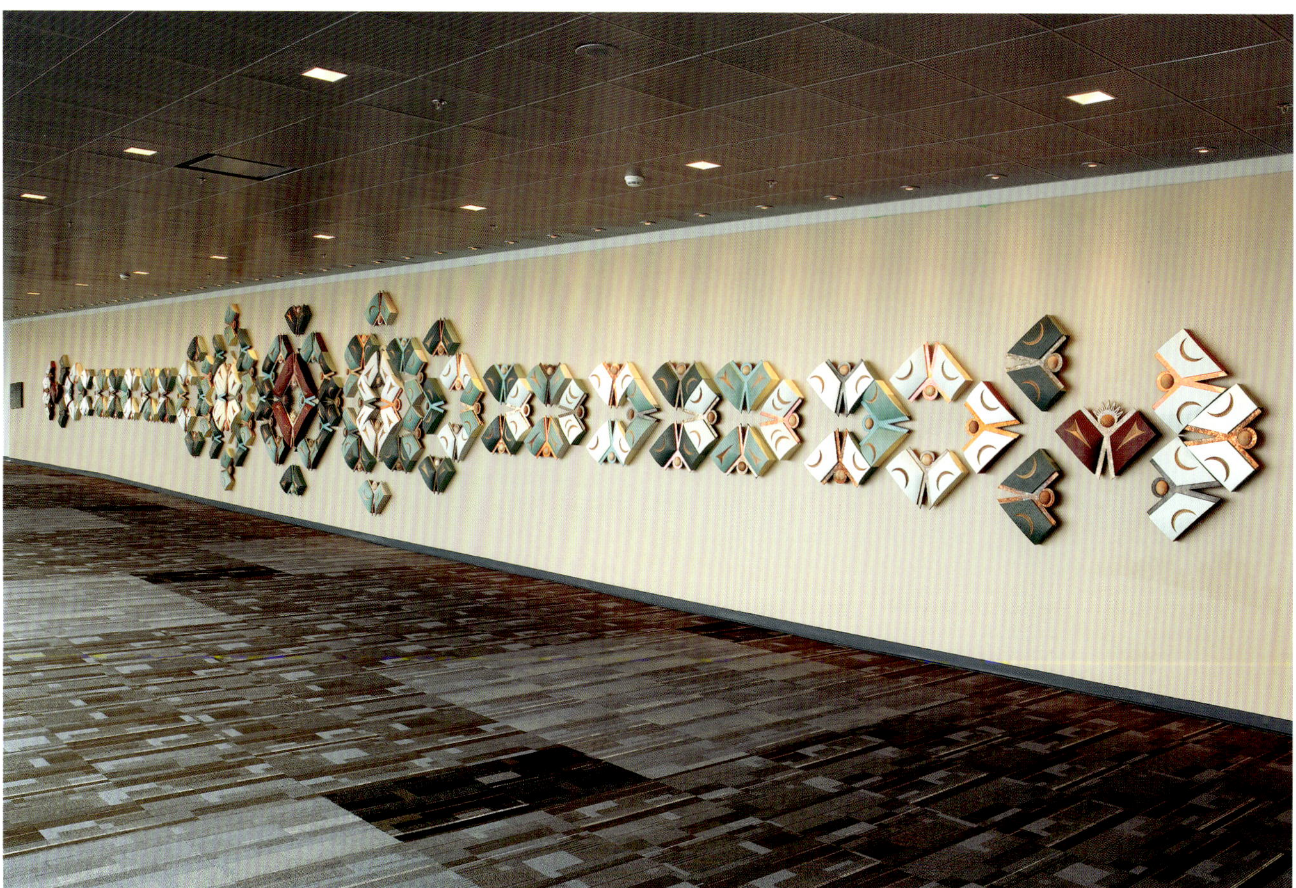

others who have chosen to make their home in British Columbia.

Six of the figures in the artwork are wearing Salish feather headdresses, and at each side of the artwork there is a welcome figure, leading the viewer along the corridor toward the central Salish "welcome" from which the artwork radiates. The three groupings (welcome figures and central area) represent the three Salish bands of the Vancouver area. The panels within this artwork are spaced throughout the corridor in a pattern inspired by Salish textile and basket weaving. Salish stories were passed on orally, and recorded through carving, textile art, and basketry motifs. Each element within a weaving or basket has symbolic value, together forming an intricate design recording the history and journey of my people...

Each panel has a multi-level, sculptural quality, curving gently toward the figure in the centre. When the panels are grouped together and seen in perspective (up close, as one walks past) this creates a sense of movement, echoing the woven form of a basket."[31]

One of the great challenges of this commission was the limited time available for completion: less than six months. Nevertheless, Susan continued to revise the design as she was working on it.

> When I actually was making the job I thought of this [holds up a pencil sketch of figures with upraised arms] and "Ah!" something related to the people. I went through months and months of revamping and redesigning the edges. The end result was I had this idea of central portions and breaking it away, stretching it right across as much wall space as I could. I wanted that broken-away effect. We're all one, although we are apart, but we can still bring it together.[32]

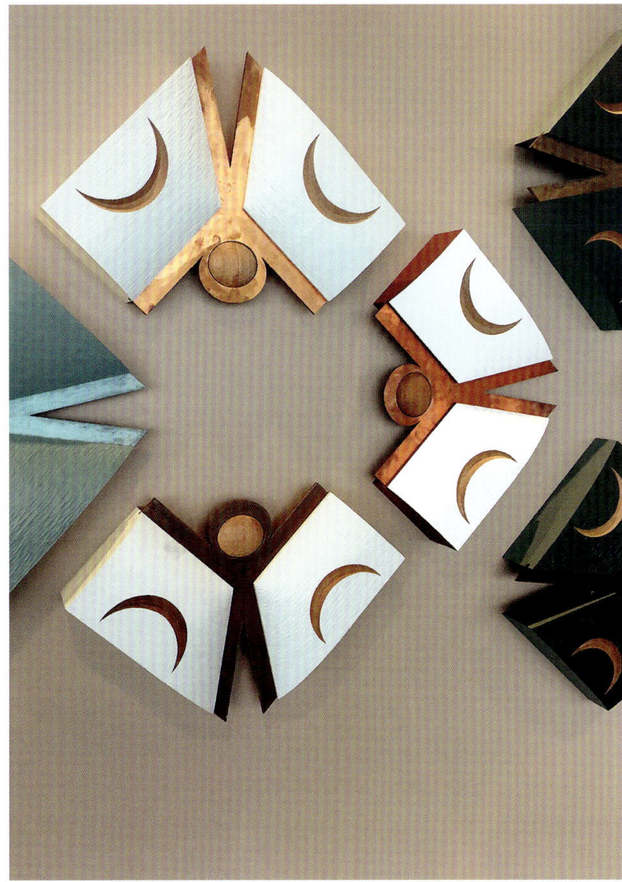

Susan and her team, which included her children and other artists, worked many long days to carve, cut, paint, and assemble the many pieces of copper and wood. The work tested Susan's experience with major public commissions, but they met the deadline.

The repetition of the welcome figures, which gesture in classic Salish style but are simplified and geometrically precise, underlines the concept of welcoming. The varied colours throughout the frieze-like work—white, turquoise, black, deep red, browns, all enfolding the burnished copper figures—are a vital part of its visual excitement, as well as a symbol of the different peoples who are being welcomed, and who are a part of the history of the city's waterfront, including Salish, European, Hawaiian, and Chinese peoples.

Once it was installed in the spring of 2009, Susan made a video commentary in which she spoke about the meaning of the work, and what she hoped visitors would carry away from seeing it.

Human Spirit, 2009

> *The Human Spirit* tells the story of the Salish, linking them to their traditional lands and welcoming those who have chosen to visit and live in British Columbia. It also represents people coming together and putting new ideas and visions together, something that is integral to the makeup of Vancouver as it is today. . . .
>
> The human figures represent all the peoples within the world. I wanted to represent everyone so I decided to use a generic figure. I took into consideration the different cultures and different values that everyone has and came up with the idea of patinating the copper men. To make them even more unique there's the green patinated men, the brown, and there's one gold-leaf figure right in the heart of the artwork. Some may look the same but no two are the same.
>
> Everything was done here [in Vancouver], the sculpting, cedar casts, the painting was all done here, all hand-done so it's not machine-made, it's all hand done. . . .
>
> People are going to wonder, you know, what is this? People are going to want to take a look, to stop and find their own story within the whole piece itself because from one end to the next, it's different. There's no beginning and no end, it can go on forever.[33]

Susan was proud of the final result and was certain that viewers would be curious about and moved by it. *The Human Spirit* bears all the hallmarks of the public art of her mature period: a thoughtful and novel approach to an opportunity, great care in design, meticulous execution, and an exciting finish. Salish elements abound, but it moves art rooted in Salish forms and ideas in bold new directions.

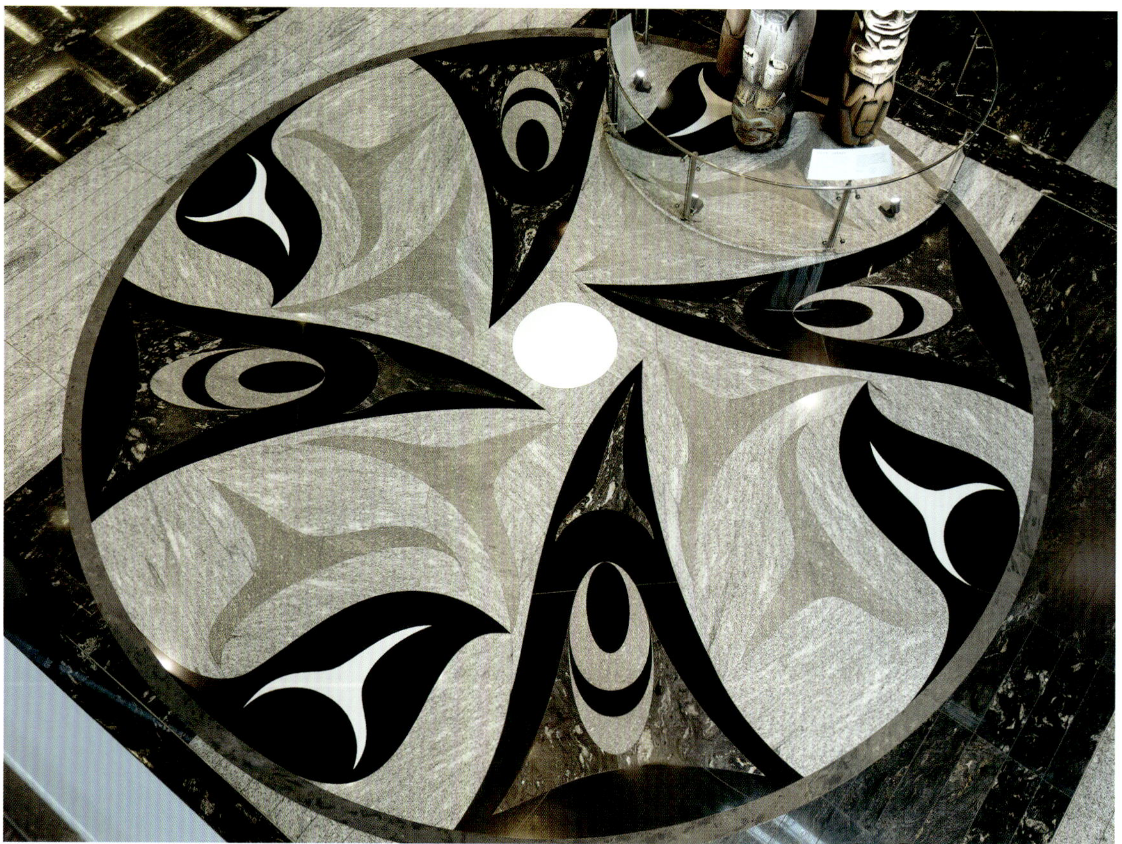

Moon Journey, 2009
Granite
10 m (diameter)

Moon Journey

LOCATION: Vancouver Convention Centre
1055 Canada Pl, Vancouver

In March 2009, shortly before the new West Building opened, Susan learned that officials at the convention centre wanted to use one of her designs to produce a mosaic in the main foyer of the renovated East Building. It would cover much of the floor in front of three historic totem poles, which were to be restored and permanently displayed.

Susan reworked a spindle whorl image that she had designed in 1997 for a print, and then revised in 2005 for a carving in paxələqʷ (yellow cedar) that she made during an artist-in-residence workshop at The Evergreen State College in Olympia, Washington. In this third variation she showed the tails and dorsal fins of four qʷənəs (whales) swimming around a full moon where the spindle shaft would have been inserted. The dorsal fins are also the shape of raven heads and beaks.

As she emphasized in her proposal, the number four has great significance for First Nations Peoples, referring to the four directions, the four seasons, and the four elements: earth, wind, fire, and water. She noted that in this work four can also represent the convention centre as a gathering place, drawing people together from the four corners of the earth.[34]

The full impact of the sweeping curves and coloured stone is best appreciated from above, on the mezzanine level. The black stone of the tails and fins really stands out, as does the white stone of the moon and the Salish-style wedges in each tail. Between the tails and the fins is the sea and the air, marked out in mottled grey stone.

The Coast Salish Gallery and the East Building were officially opened on 9 September 2009, with many dignitaries and members of the media in attendance. Susan's works have since welcomed many thousands of visitors, and introduced them to vital Salish forms and beliefs such as the central role of the cycle of the moon in Salish culture, and the importance of orcas and ravens, long a rich source of inspiration for Salish artists.

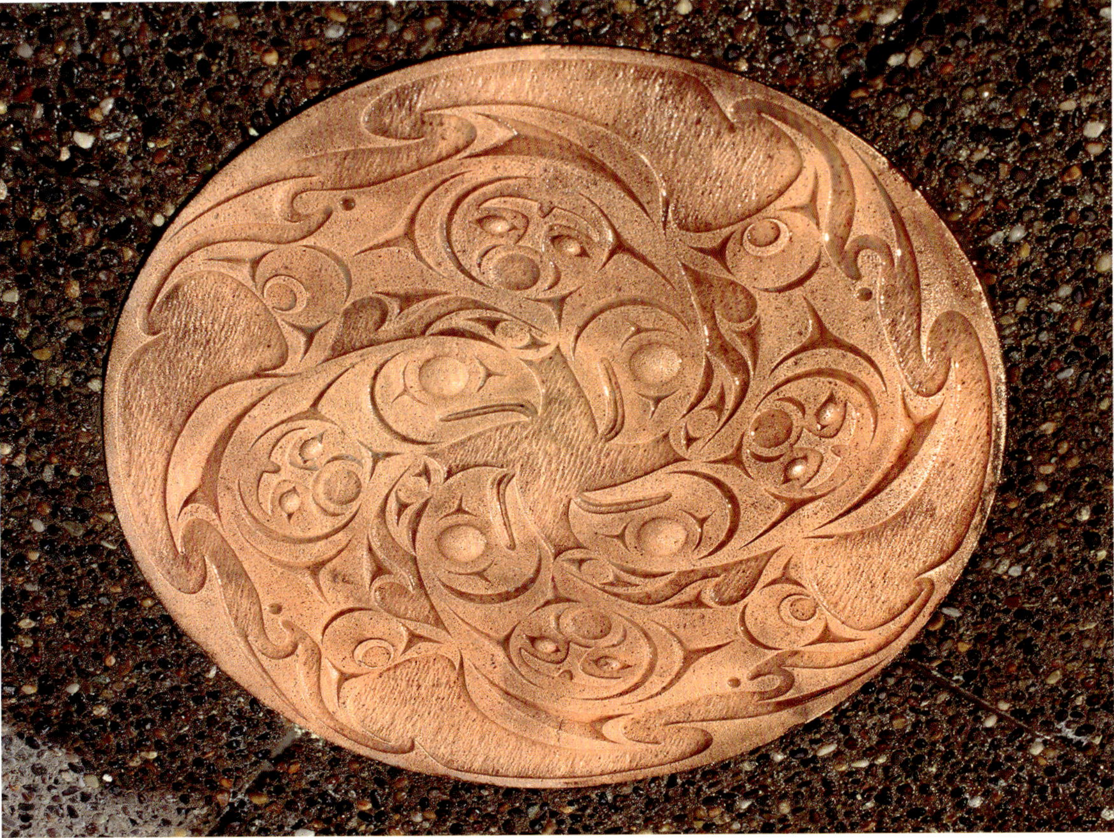

Salmon

LOCATION: Coal Harbour
600–700 blocks Jervis St, Vancouver

Salmon, 1995
Bronze
73.5 cm (diameter)

In 1995, the City of Vancouver commissioned Don Vaughan, an urban planner and landscape architect, to prepare a study of design for streets south of Coal Harbour and north of Robson Street, in a densifying neighbourhood to be known as Triangle West. Vaughan's plan called for bronze medallions, set into the sidewalks along Jervis Street, the area's main north–south thoroughfare, to become a key feature of the streetscape. The city issued a limited invitation to artists for designs, which stipulated the specifications including attributes for water dispersal and relief restrictions above the sidewalk. Susan's design was chosen, and the medallions were moulded and cast by the city in late 1995.

Using a spindle whorl shape, Susan designed a swirling arrangement of four salmon, their heads bent toward the centre. This was a new version of her frequent interpretations of the Salmon People story, with a human face forming the body of each fish. All the classic Salish elements are present: U-forms, crescents, and wedges. The wave shapes around the circumference, highlighted with wedges, are a clear reference to the proximity of the sea at Coal Harbour.

At least twelve medallions were cast and are easily found and visible today, especially on Bute and Jervis Streets north and south of Hastings Street, where they are set in the sidewalk at regular intervals of about ten metres. These beautiful works recalled Susan's first prints of 1982, and foreshadowed two similar projects: the hundreds of cast-iron manhole covers made in 2005 for the City of Vancouver from a design by Susan and her daughter Kelly (*Memory*, page 78); and, four years after that, the medallions of *The Coming Together of Two Ancient Cultures* on West Broadway (page 46).

Salmon, 1995

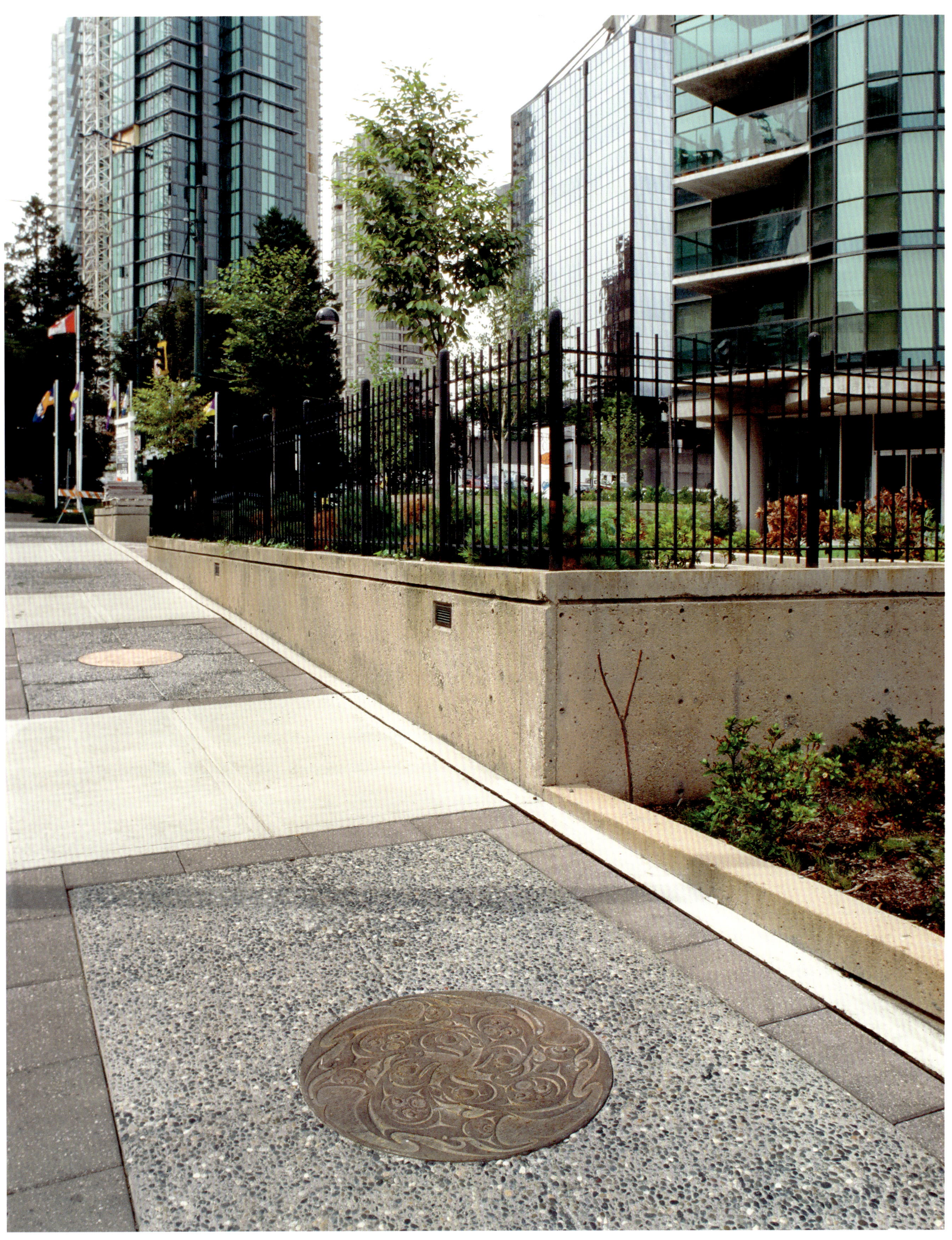

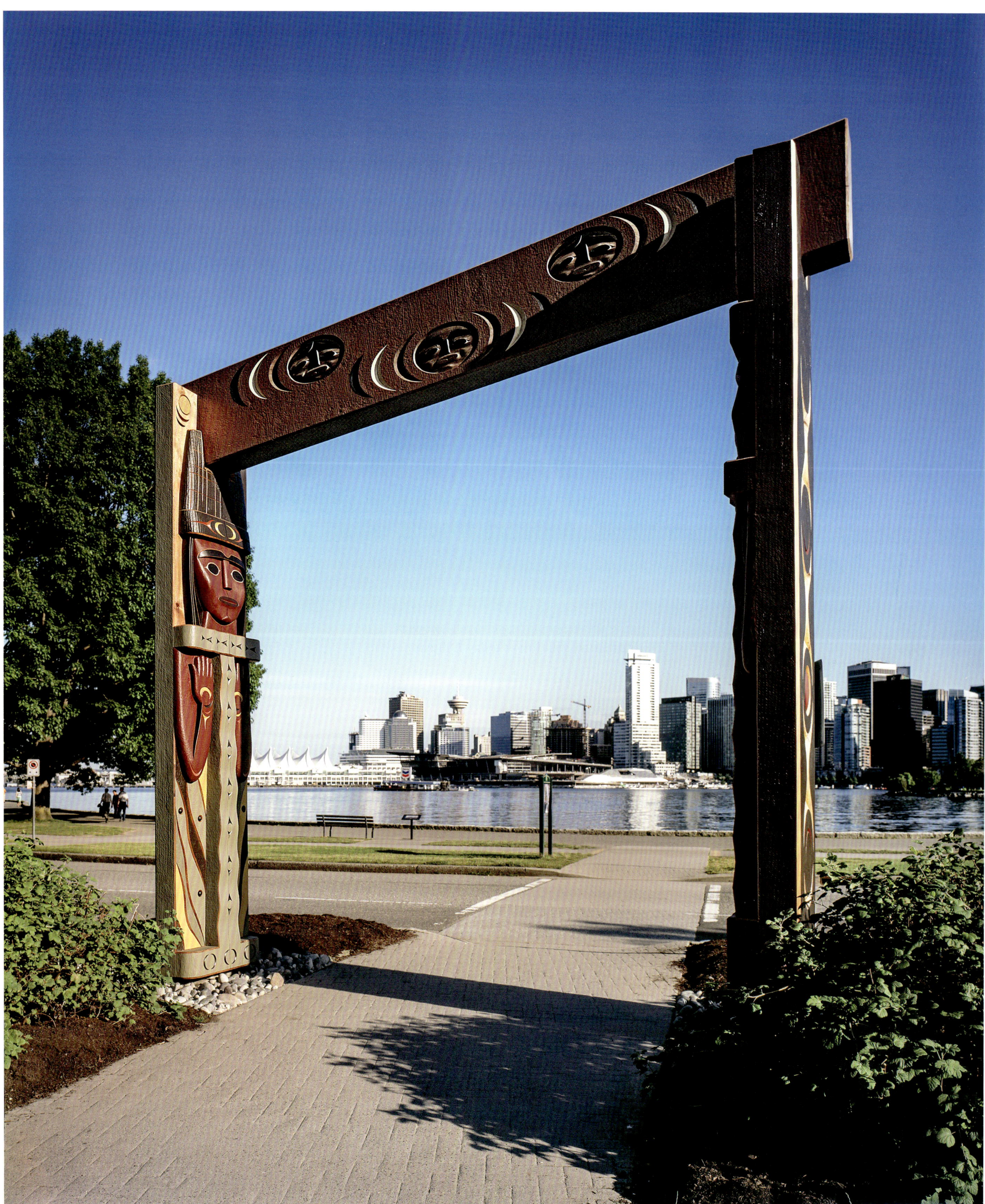

People Amongst the People, 2008
Male and Female Welcome Figures
Carved and painted western red cedar
5.2 and 4.6 m (height of uprights);
5.5 m (length of crossbeam)

People Amongst the People

LOCATION: spapəy̓əq (Brockton Point)
Stanley Park, Vancouver

The three portals of *People Amongst the People* are some of the most important works of public art commissioned in Vancouver since the city was founded in 1886. This is a masterpiece in every aspect: concept, scale, execution, meaning, and aesthetic impact. It may also be Susan's most-viewed work; the portals mark the entrance to and perimeter of the Stanley Park totem poles, the most visited tourist attraction in B.C.[35]

The genesis of the portals dates back to 2004, when the City of Vancouver Public Art Program, partnering with Vancouver Storyscapes (a city initiative to encourage Indigenous storytelling in various mediums) and the Vancouver Park Board, asked Susan first if she wanted to collaborate with another artist on a large-scale work at Brockton Point, and then if she would undertake it on her own. Susan declined both offers, and advised the city that "in respect and honour of the three Bands [and] in the tradition of my ancestors," they had best issue a request for proposals from artists from the three local First Nations Peoples, the xʷməθkwəy̓əm (Musqueam), Skwxwú7mesh (sqʷχʷaməx, Squamish), and səlil̓wətaʔɬ (Tsleil-Waututh).[36]

This was an exciting chance for artists to introduce Coast Salish art to this ancient site in the Salish homeland, to honour and represent the First Nations Peoples whose ancestors occupied this site for thousands of years before European settlement began. First Nations art in the form of totem poles from various northern First Nations have been publicly exhibited in this area of Stanley Park since the 1920s—the original plan had been to construct a "full-scale 'Indian Village' tourist attraction" and relocate nearby First Nations families to live in it, but the Squamish objected and only the poles remained[37]—but there had never been any artworks rooted in the aesthetic and cultural traditions of the Coast Salish, the First Peoples on whose territory these other artworks actually rested.

Susan decided to propose a reimagining of the traditional houseposts of her ancestors' homes, with crossbeams that not only provided structural support but also formed a gateway, a portal inviting visitors to pass through these decorated openings and be welcomed to the site. This was both an aesthetic and a political statement, as she explained:

> In the form and function of a portal, this series of sculptures is intended as a gesture of welcome by the Coast Salish people on many levels. It acts as a greeting to visitors as they explore the totem poles at Brockton Point. Many of the people may be enjoying their first experience of First Nations culture and art and this piece will provide a sense of place and occasion as they enter the site. It is also a way of welcoming visitors to the traditional lands of the Coast Salish people. The portals are also a metaphor for Burrard Inlet itself as it was once a portal for the abundance of fish and other wildlife the Salish needed to thrive and prosper.
>
> The totem poles themselves have come from other places on the Northwest Coast and are also honoured guests of the Coast Salish people. The design of these portals allows the poles within the site to be introduced to the public as friends of the Coast Salish and illustrates a cooperative meeting of cultures through art.[38]

In her proposal Susan was, characteristically, fully respectful of and inspired by the site and its deep connection to the Salish Peoples.

> In the days before the City of Vancouver grew on the land of the Salish, the narrowing of the inlet now marked by the Lions Gate Bridge was an area teeming with schools of herring and the orcas that chased them for food. As the tide left and brought the herring back out to sea the orcas and other creatures would feast on the abundance of food. The area was rich with eagles and salmon, rich with the culture and traditions of the Salish people. It was and is, a site of great energy and enormous significance to the Salish.
>
> This sculptural project is a reflection of what this area once looked like, and what it has been transformed into. Adorned with images of eagles and other creatures, the mountains and the water, as well as the weaving and basket designs of the Salish, the piece reflects both the history of the Salish people as well as the modern culture that still thrives today. It illustrates the living culture of the area as it has transformed through history.[39]

She explained that the portals would further connect to the site by using the same traditional materials as the existing art nearby, and by drawing on historic forms but with symbols, stories, and ideas highlighted in a new way.

> In developing my proposal, I felt that it was extremely important to show that Salish art is not just a historical art but that it is a living evolving traditional art form. In designing my artwork, I chose to use our unique Salish elements in a contemporary way but I wanted to use a material that has a historical significance and link to the site itself. Naturally, cedar was my first thought as a material. It complements the materials used for the totems themselves in this area; and as well, it complements its surroundings... the forests within the Stanley Park area.[40]

Susan was awarded the work in the spring of 2005. The path from that green light to the completed work was long and winding, including felling and milling the trees and transporting the posts; enlisting several other carvers, including some family members, as well as extra painters; and finally, installing the work. From the first searches for cedar hundreds of kilometres north of Vancouver to the final installation, this magnificent composition took an extra year and double the initial budget to complete, but Susan felt the work was so important that she co-produced it through Coast Salish Arts (her studio). It was, as Susan says, "a journey to produce," and the most challenging work she has yet completed.[41] Throughout the nearly three years of production, Susan remained at the centre of every stage, at times like the conductor of an orchestra, at others like a musician.

First came the search for raw material. Susan's husband Jeff Cannell and her son Thomas Cannell travelled to Port McNeill, at the north end of Vancouver Island, to source an old-growth χpeỷəɬp (red cedar tree) with the help of Susan's friend Calvin Hunt. This early stage was a highlight for Susan. "One of the most rewarding things was working with the people at Port McNeill where the wood was sourced and milled... They were super helpful!"[42] The trees were felled, trimmed, and milled, and the nine posts left to cure for six months at Calvin's home in Port Hardy before being transported to Susan's studio.

The initial roughing out took many months. In her proposal Susan had predicted that the design "would be an evolving piece of artwork; and there would always be afterthoughts and improvements once working on the project... There could be figurative work on the surfaces of the art pieces (perhaps low relief welcome figures, etc.) in a similar style to some of my previous sculptural art works"[43]—and she was right. She had to adjust many parts of the designs to accomodate the condition of the old-growth posts, and even carefully craft replacement pieces so that the colour and grain matched—one of the many hallmarks of her meticulous approach. As the work began to take shape, Susan found, as she often does when carving, that the wood also offered opportunities to enhance her ideas. She quickly found that her line drawings, often quite simple in outline and colour, became richer and more complex.

Susan was working on the runnels for the Richmond Olympic Oval at the same time as *People Amongst the People*, so she drew on the support of family and friends to complete the portals. Ron Denessen and Susan's sons Brent Sparrow and Thom Cannell helped with the carving, as did John Livingston, her original carving teacher. Others helped with the painting, including her daughters Kelly Cannell and Rhea Point, and her granddaughter Suzanne Guerin (Rhea's daughter).

The final result, which was officially unveiled on the morning of 9 June 2008, was a revelation for many. *People Amongst the People* is ambitious in all aspects: the size of the three portals; the complex, interwoven mix of symbols and colours; the visual drama of each side of the six uprights and three crossbeams; and the way in which all of these elements relate to each other and to the overall message. The naturalistic style and personal nature of the imagery is a dramatic contrast to the more stylistically structured displays of symbols and stories in the totem poles from First Peoples from north of the Salish homelands.

It is hard to avoid the conclusion that Point was the ideal artist to introduce a Salish presence into the park. Who else had spent so much time studying the surviving Salish objects in museum collections? Who else had listened to family members tell the stories that were part of the wisdom of Elders? Who else had carved in wood on a large scale when it was not felt to be an activity for a woman? Who else had embraced the artistic possibilities of new mediums, like glass, metal, and synthetic materials? Who else had demonstrated over many years a determination to explore the possibilities of using traditional Salish forms to explore themes that dealt with family structures, Salish weaving and basketry techniques, environmental concerns, and issues of intercultural relationships, personal and collective?

The portals serve a greater role than simply welcoming visitors to the totem pole display area; they also, as she wrote in her proposal,

> allow visitors to enjoy the sense that they are moving from the modern world of traffic and schedules to a unique place that is special. They become a gateway between the world of today and a timeless world removed from their everyday existence.[44]

The choice of three was deliberate, to honour the Musqueam, the Squamish, and the Tsleil-Waututh, the three Salish Peoples on whose territory the park lies, and whose traditions the artwork evokes.

All of the imagery used for the artwork draws on central Coast Salish design elements, used by Salish people pre-contact. The artwork represents and honours Salish design in its purest sense. Each of the designs incorporates a reflection of three: three portals (each made of three components—two uprights and one crossbeam) situated at the three entrances of the site.[45]

People Amongst the People, 2008
Male and Female Welcome Figures

OVERLEAF: **People Amongst the People, 2008**
Grandparents and Grandchildren
Carved and painted western red cedar
5.1 and 4.6 m (height of uprights);
approx. 8 m (length of crossbeam)

MALE AND FEMALE WELCOME FIGURES

Susan took full advantage of the six surfaces available on each portal. The main gateway to the totem pole area, on the south side, features male and female figures with hands raised to show welcome. As Susan describes the portal,

> The female figure wears a blanket incorporating traditional weaving designs, characteristic of the rich textile tradition among the Salish people. The male figure wears a blanket decorated with a salmon motif (a reference to the "Salmon People" legend). The "Male" upright is backed with a striking design using purely Salish design elements, deeply carved in large-scale to emphasize the strong graphic nature of each element. The central circle and two crescents are highlighted with red paint, representing the three Salish Peoples of the area. The other side of the "Female" upright uses a motif influenced by the border designs used for Salish berry baskets, honouring the skills of our Salish ancestors.[46]

Susan's mother and her maternal ancestors were skilled basket makers and weavers, and Susan grew up with a deep appreciation and understanding of these traditions. The main "welcome" portal was an excellent venue to reference these traditional skills, honouring both a personal and a wider community and cultural heritage.

The symbols on the north side of the crossbeam represent the three Salish settlements of the area, with the three faces symbolizing "not only the welcoming nature of the Salish people . . . but also alluding to spirit guardians or Salish warriors."[47] On the south side of the crossbeam, an elegant series of deeply carved curves in two lines, coloured alternately blue and red, is a striking reference to the waters of Burrard Inlet, just a few metres south.

GRANDPARENTS AND GRANDCHILDREN

The images of the second portal, southwest of the totem poles, are centred around Salish family structures and the transmission of traditional knowledge through the generations, a theme that encourages us to think of the world we are leaving to our descendants and the importance of environmental stewardship.

Susan explained how these themes are represented in the portal:

> An intertwined braid of hair links the three female faces of the "Grandparents," illustrating the powerful matrilineal links running through Salish ancestry as stories and teachings pass from generation to generation (grandmother, great-grandmother, and great-great-grandmother).
>
> The abstract design on the other side of the post represents the salmon that were once so plentiful in the area. Much conservation work has been done to restore the salmon streams of Vancouver, and this design is both a tribute to what was, and a symbol of hope for the future.[48]

On the inside of the south upright are six deeply carved faces representing grandchildren, a second salute to the importance of the family bond among the Salish. Curling around these faces is a brightly coloured braid that refers to χʷil̓əm (rope) weaving, a traditional skill learned by the young from their Elders. On the other side of this upright is, as Susan notes, a

> carved herring design that reflects the living culture of the area as it has been transformed through history. Hundreds of years ago, Burrard Inlet was the richest source of natural wealth in the province. Massive schools of herring,

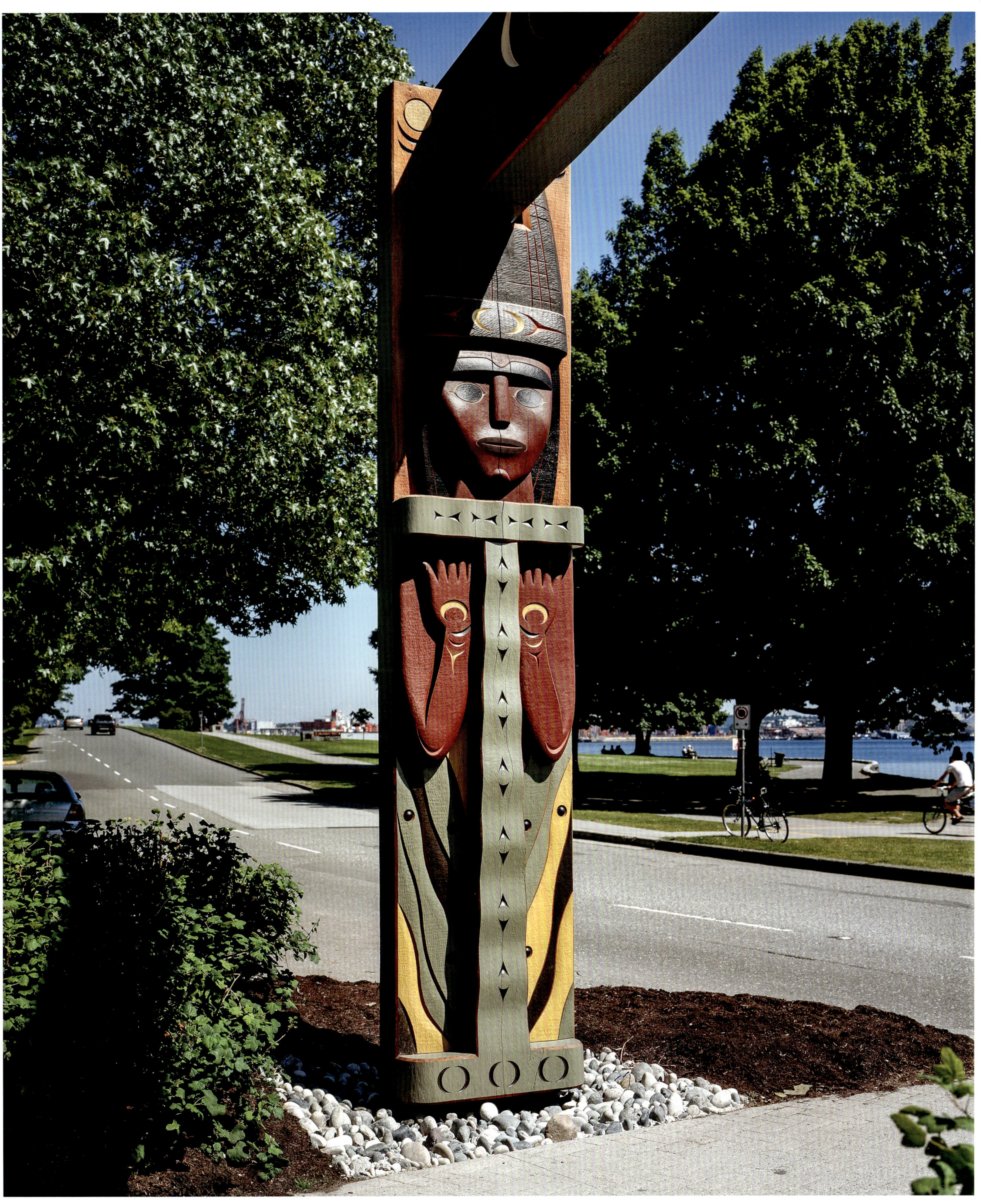

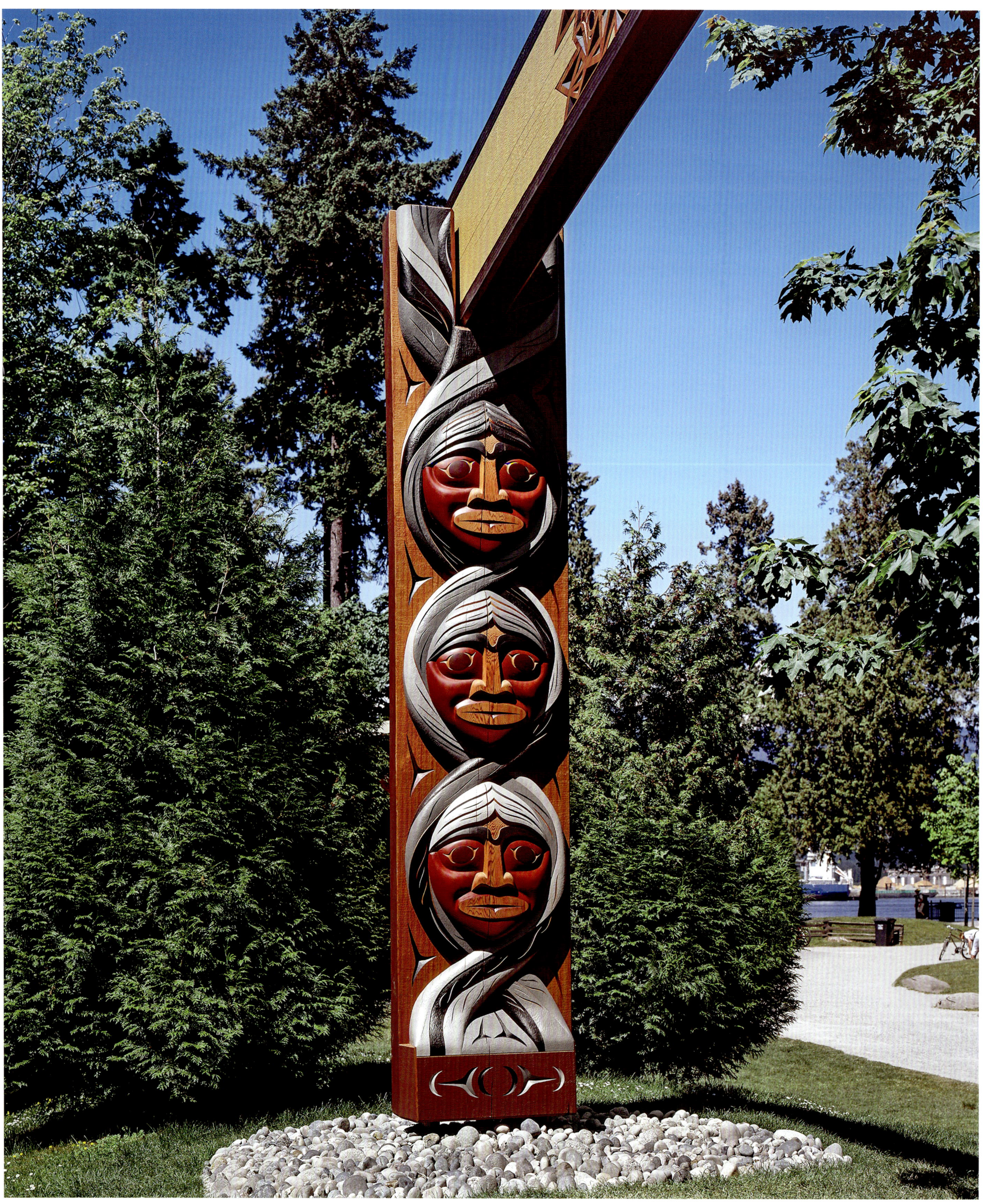

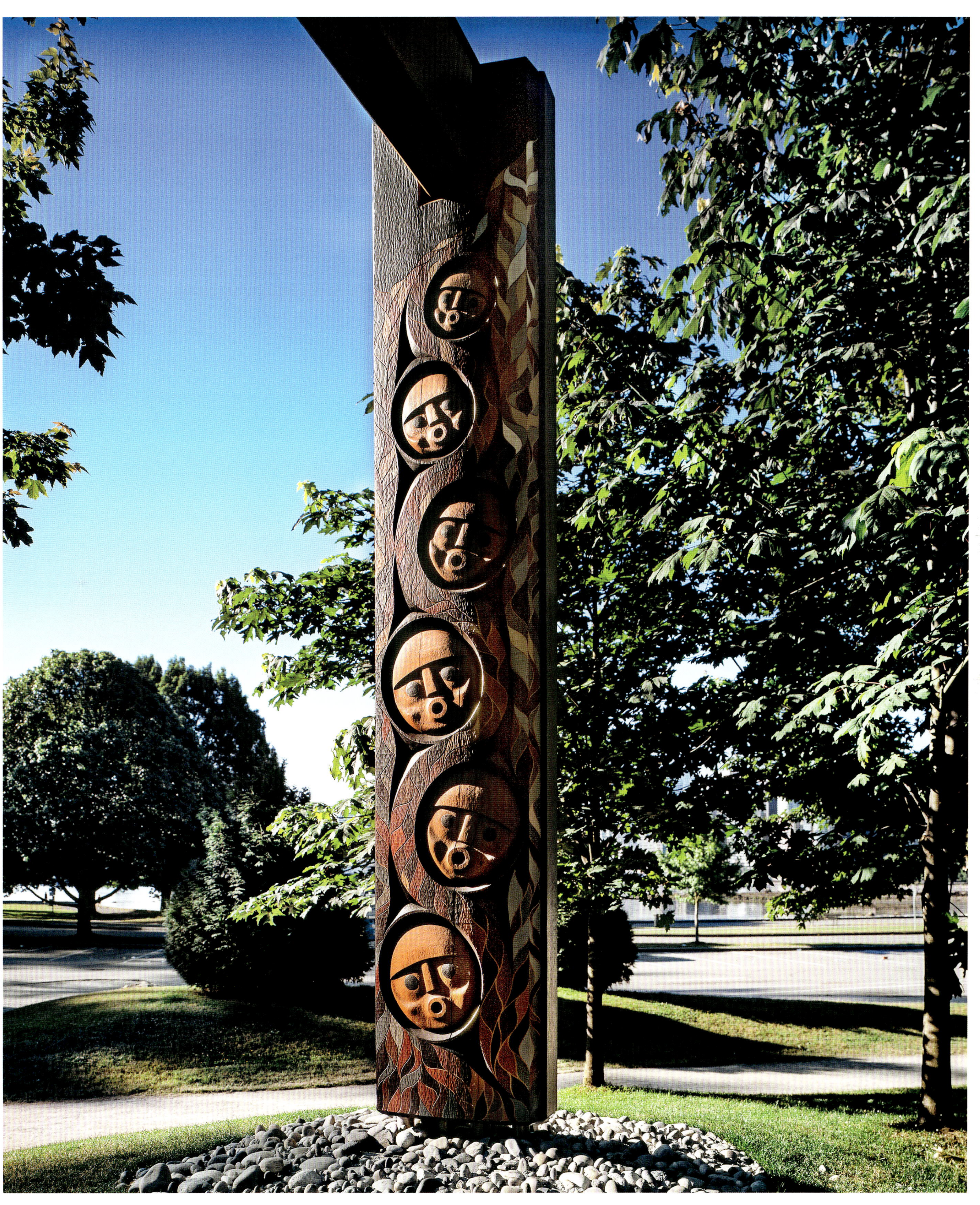

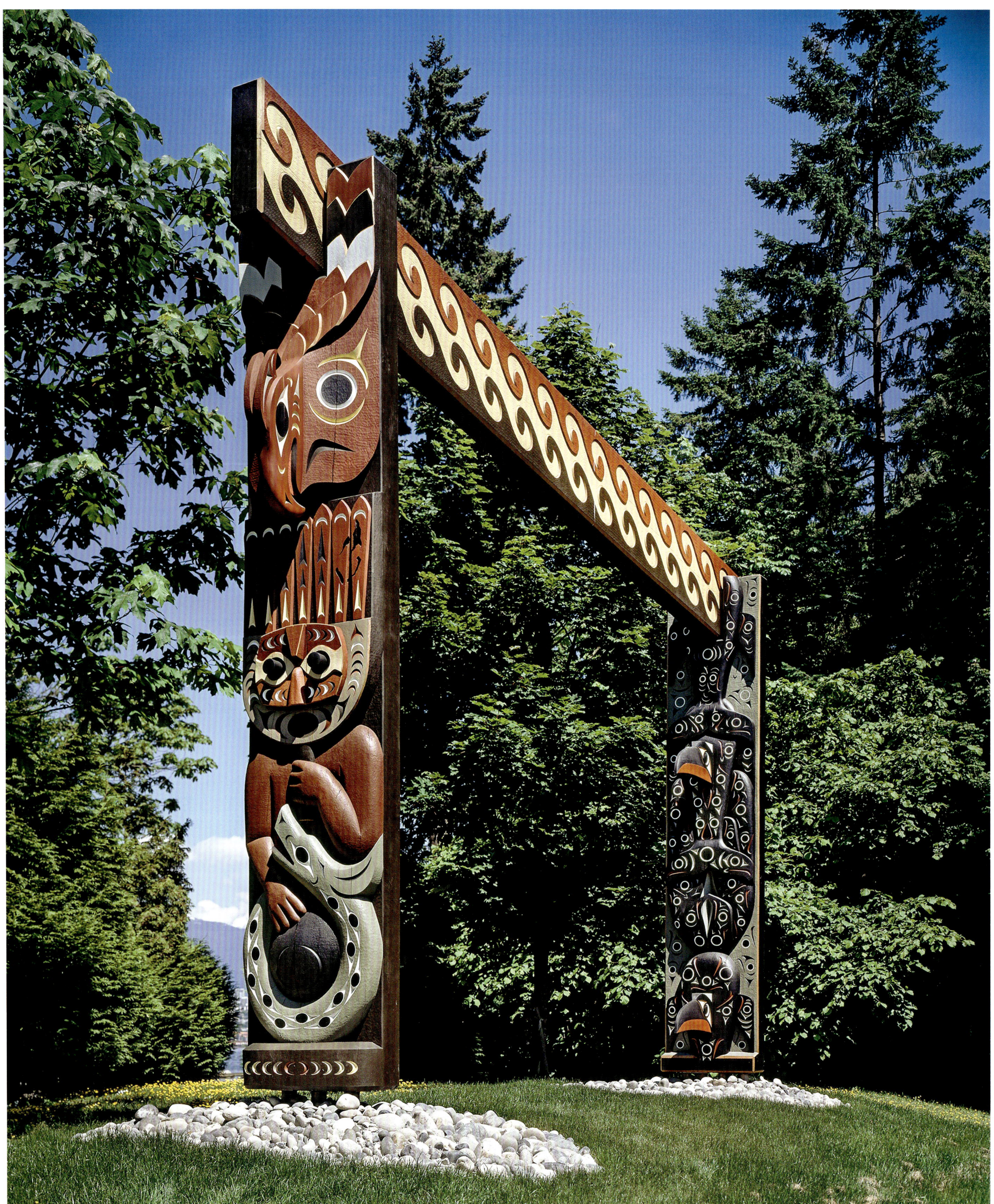

People Amongst the People, 2008
Salish Dancer and Whale
Carved and painted western red cedar
5.2 and 4.6 m (height of uprights);
7.9 m (length of crossbeam)

> followed by salmon, and then killer whales moved through the inlet in great numbers year after year. These creatures are a reflection of the abundance and natural resources that make this region so special, so in need of protection.[49]

The crossbeam features a traditional Salish wedge shape on one side, deeply carved "to emphasize both the movement and energy of the element, and the scale of the crossbeam."[50] On the opposite side Susan introduces a trio of frogs (another reference to the three local Salish Peoples), an animal with great personal significance to her that she has returned to again and again over the decades. Growing up on the Musqueam lands she often saw frogs and enjoyed their rich variety of sounds, which heralded the changing seasons. Her parents and Elders emphasized, in daily life and in the round of activities through the year, the importance of frogs to the local environment, the vital relationship between frogs and other creatures and people. Here, as in many other works in many mediums, Susan celebrates the significance of the frog even as its declining numbers in Musqueam and elsewhere reveal the pressures of continued development and growth on the natural landscape.

SALISH DANCER AND WHALE

The third portal, to the north, provides a glimpse of Salish ceremonial life and further references to Salish weaving and textile design, and continues the strong environmental message of the west portal.

Uniquely, the sculptures on the west upright do not face inward but are carved on the exterior face, dictated by the fact that visitors are not meant to walk through this portal, and the best vantage point is to the west. She explains the imagery:

> The right to "Sxwaixwe" [sχʷəyχʷəy, Masked Dance] is passed from mother to son—the female figure shown … is holding a Sxwaixwe mask and sea serpent rattle showing that she has the right to pass the mask to her sons.[51]

As one whose parents were actively involved in the winter dancing at Musqueam, and who understands the tradition and the protocols surrounding this ceremonial activity, Susan has taken every care to ensure that her representation does not trespass on the rights of any living dancer nor refer to any particular mask, but rather that it gestures to the generic *idea* of Salish mask dancing. This, then, is her idea of what a mask might look like but never did.

On the opposite side of this upright are tree roots, meant, as Susan observes, "to remind us of our natural surroundings, our connection to the land sea and sky."[52]

The eastern upright features five q̓əlƚaləməcən (killer whales) with a raven fin and salmon pectoral. Susan explains that "the Salish peoples believe that humans and orcas are closely linked, and it is thought that when great chiefs die, they become killer whales. The reverse side [of this upright] has a boldly coloured Salish design, inspired by traditional carving motifs."[53]

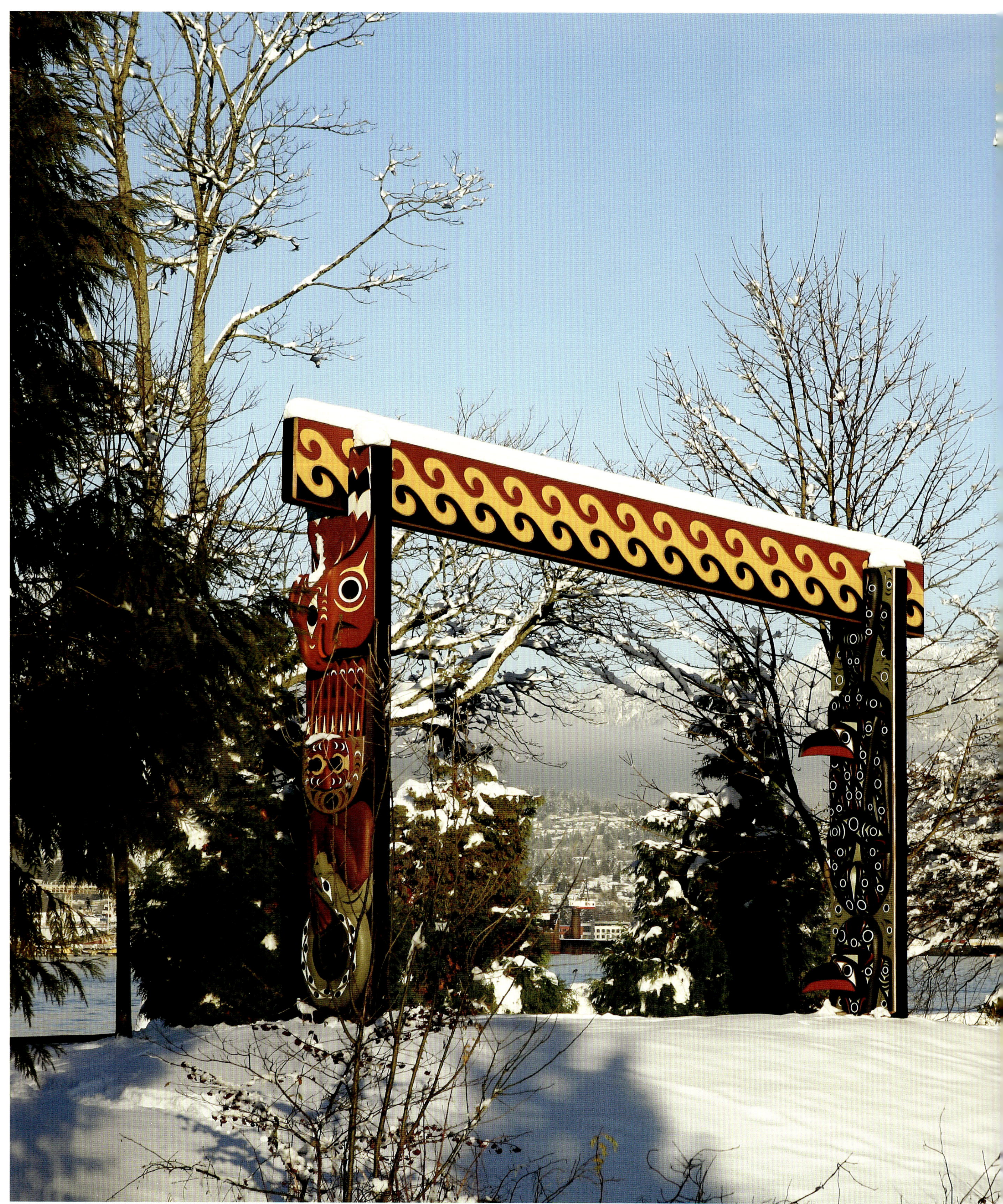

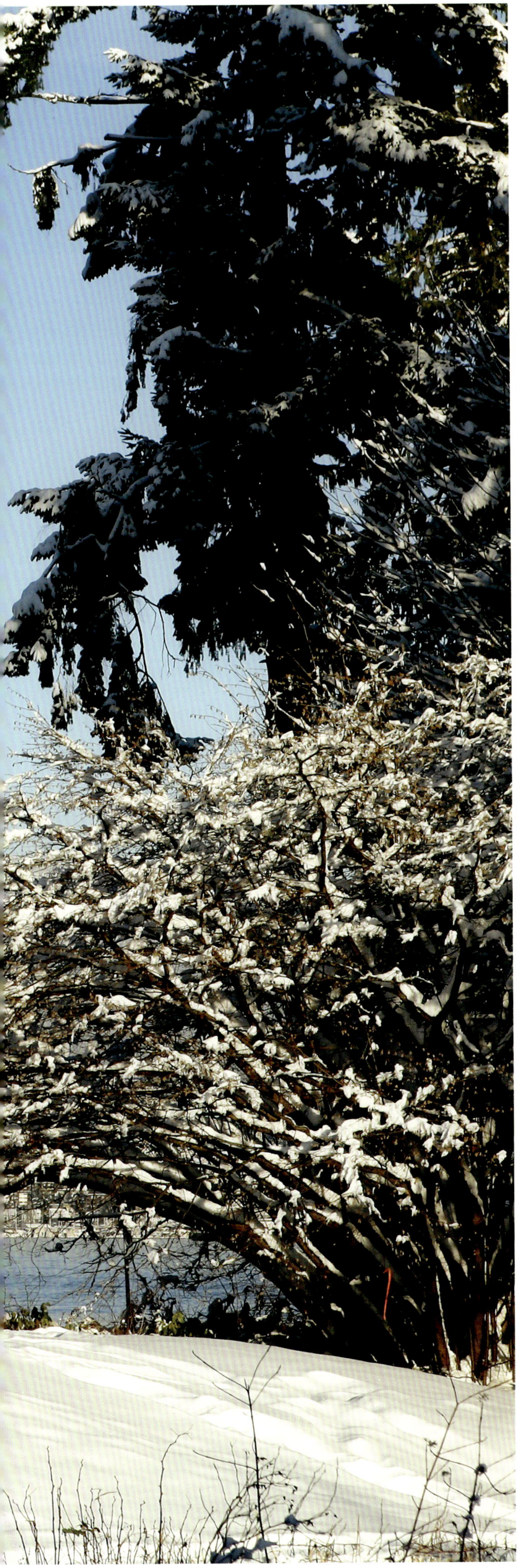

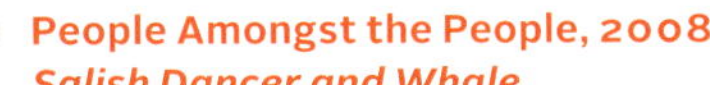

People Amongst the People, 2008
Salish Dancer and Whale

Both sides of the crossbeam are inspired by patterns found in traditional Salish weaving. The dramatic wave-like pattern on the south side, a stylization of a pattern Susan's mother used on a sweater for her when she was a young girl, is especially elegant.

PEOPLE AMONGST THE PEOPLE is a stunning and complex pageant of Salish art and culture, evoking a rich array of themes: family and knowledge transmission; traditions of weaving and basketry; and care for the shared environment and the great diversity of local marine, animal, and plant life. All of it is made possible by Susan's powerful creative spirit and her determination to be the vehicle for translating Salishness into great and timeless art. The work deserves to be more fully labelled and explained on the site, and I believe that the Park Board is working on this.

The three portals were formally inaugurated on 9 June 2008. In keeping with Musqueam practice, Susan asked her cousin Howard Grant to speak for her, and through him, she expressed the aspects of the work that she felt were most important. Hundreds of people witnessed this triumphal return of the art of the Salish to a site they had occupied for thousands of years. It was especially fitting that the vision for this return arose in the mind of the creative genius who had devoted her career to giving new life and a powerful aesthetic voice to Salish forms.

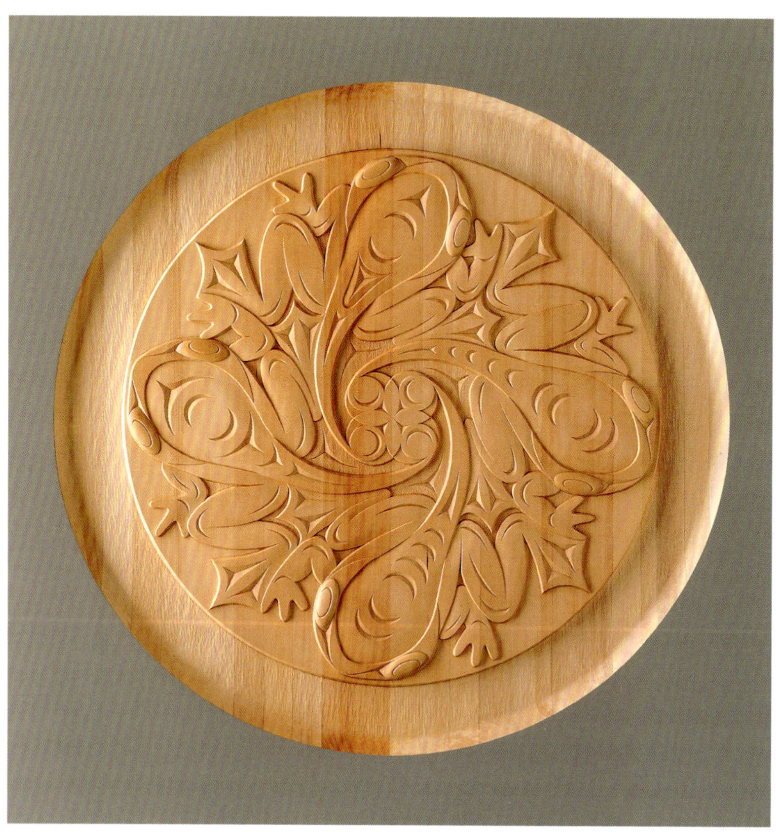

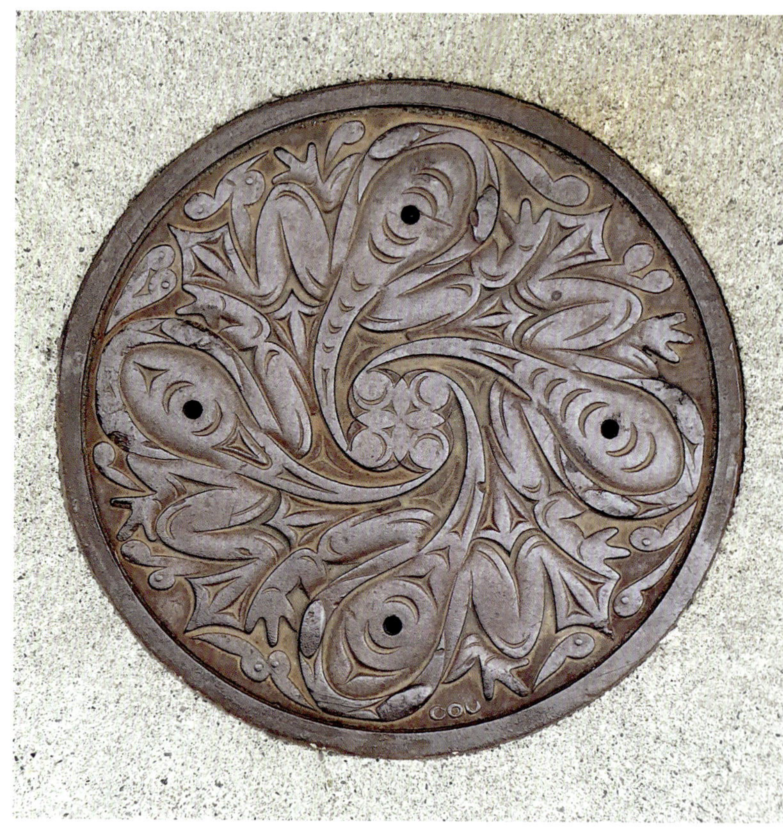

Memory

LOCATIONS: various, Vancouver

When it comes to assessing the impact of Susan's determination to re-establish a Salish footprint in the lands occupied originally by her ancestors, the manhole cover she and her daughter Kelly designed in 2004 is without a doubt her most prolific image. Carved in red cedar and then cast in iron, *Memory* is found on hundreds of Vancouver streets, from the heart of the business district to the leafy residential neighbourhoods. As Susan said recently, "We hope that these manhole covers provide moments of joy to all people when they come upon them. And, when we did this piece, we knew that everyone would see these covers."[54]

This linking of art and infrastructure originated when Councillor Jim Green suggested to his colleagues that the city invite artists to submit designs for the covers. The engineering department then teamed up with the city's public art program to organize a competition in the spring of 2004 called Art Underfoot, which combined elements of art, design, and the environment. The invitation for submissions noted that

> Vancouver's streets are lined with thousands of manhole covers, but these heavy, cast iron discs tend to disappear into the urban landscape. Manhole covers can last up to 100 years. Your design could be the one to make them an attractive, eye catching addition to the greyness of our roads for years to come.[55]

Over six hundred professional and amateur artists and designers submitted ideas. Susan and Kelly proposed two designs featuring a theme of metamorphosis, a butterfly design for the sanitary sewer covers and a frog design for the storm sewer. The winners were chosen by an expert panel of judges consisting of Daina Augaitis, chief curator

Memory, 2005
Cast iron
63 cm (diameter)

at the Vancouver Art Gallery; Douglas Coupland, writer, artist, and designer; Sonny Assu, artist; and Jim Fulton, executive director of the David Suzuki Foundation. Susan and Kelly's frog design was picked for the storm covers, and artist Jen Weih's work for the sanitary covers. Susan and Kelly described what inspired their choices.

> When we thought of our earliest memories relating to nature, two things that immediately came to mind were the metamorphosis or the life cycle of the frog and the butterfly.
>
> Imagery for the stormwater drain depicts the metamorphosis of a frog... with eggs in the center, spinning out into tadpoles then turning into frogs... In creating these designs, our goal was not to create designs that looked like they were an add-on applied to urban accessories but to create an urban accessory "using a piece of art"... thus these two low-relief sculptural designs. Water being the essence of life, these designs are intended to give the feel of "bursts of complete life," using the entire surface of the manhole covers to show that all life stems from water... Through our Coast Salish First Nations' teachings, the circular format of these designs also represents the "circle of life" and the fact that all life, in one way or another, is somehow connected. These images have also been designed in such a way that they are recognizable from any approach.[56]

This dramatic arrangement of four eggs, four tadpoles, and four frogs defined by Salish crescents, wedges, and U-forms spreads two important themes in Salish culture—the significance of fours and the symbolism of frogs, with their reminder of the imperative of environmental stewardship—to every corner of the city. Well aware of the limitations posed by material and location, the mother-and-daughter team shaped an image that was ideally suited to the low-relief specifications of the object.

The Art Underfoot initiative led to a fresh examination by the engineers of the materials to be used in the casting process. This issue was resolved in 2005, and Susan and Kelly's *Memory* cover began to be installed across the city, including several just around the corner from their home on the Musqueam lands. The covers are built to endure punishing conditions; while they haven't retained their initial shine, Susan says "we like the oxidation and wear and tear on the piece over time.... They will last a lifetime!"[57]

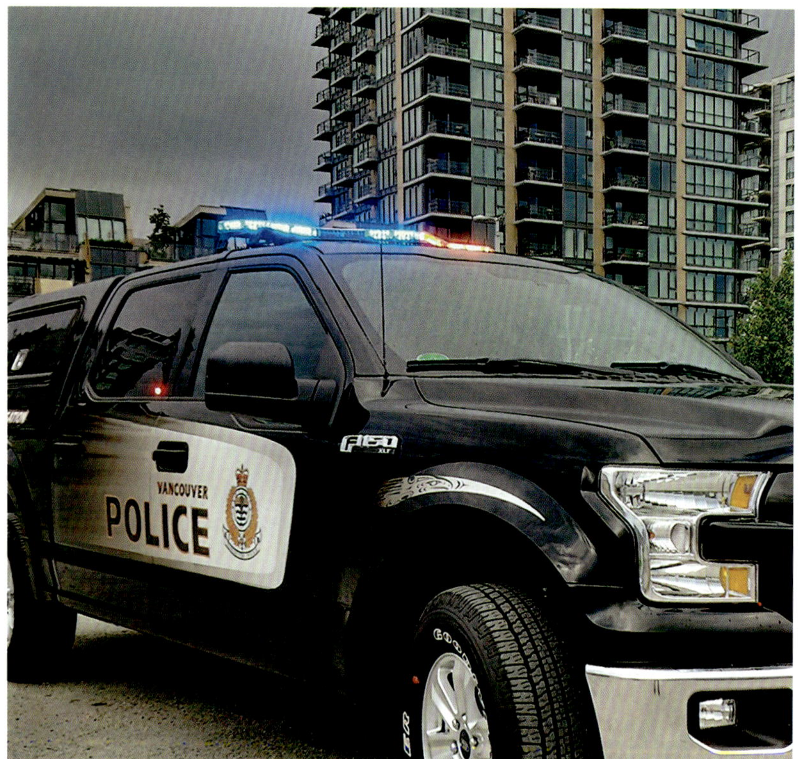

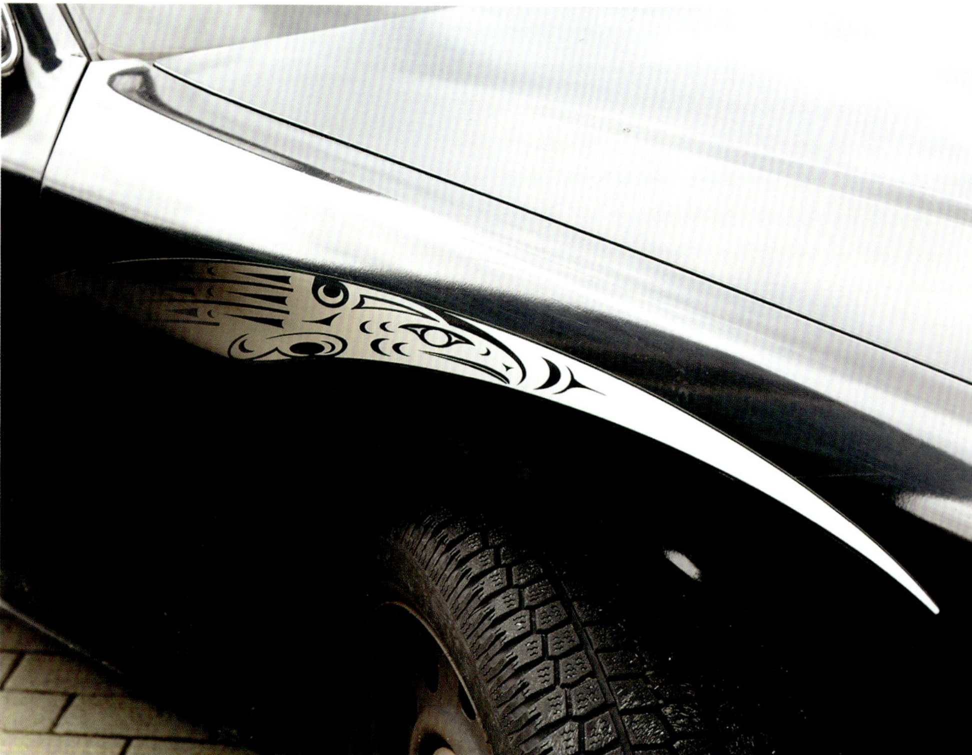

Thunderbird, 2006
White reflective paint with laminate overcoat
101.6 × 11.43 cm

Thunderbird

LOCATIONS: various, Vancouver

In 2005, Paul Patterson, then the director of public affairs and marketing for the Vancouver Police Department, invited Susan to create a design to be applied to all marked police cruisers. Her work was to sweep in an arc over the front fenders. She chose the most powerful of the spirits from the Salish world, šxʷəxʷaʔas (Thunderbird), the protector, a reference to the force's mandate to serve and protect the community.

The final design, which Susan gifted to the VPD, is centred around the thrusting head of the bird, with rapid movement indicated by three bands of feathers divided by small crescents. The department and Susan agreed the colour scheme would be blue, white, and black, to fit the colouring of the vehicles at the time and preserve the vigour of the design.

The design was formally unveiled on National Aboriginal Day (now National Indigenous Peoples Day), 21 June 2006. The chief constable at the time, Jamie Graham, acknowledged in his remarks the symoblic importance of the gesture. "We're trying to repair years and years of mediocre relationships... with many members of the aboriginal community.... We see see this as one small step that we can do to recognize the people that were here first."[58] The Thunderbird sweep was soon applied to over one hundred patrol cars.

In 2015, as part of a system-wide change of vehicles and adoption of new equipment, the VPD changed the colour scheme on vehicles from white and blue to black, white, and gold. This necessitated a redesign of the vehicle graphics, while keeping Susan's design. The new graphics and colour scheme appear on approximately 120 marked VPD vehicles, including trucks and vans, and won "Best Dressed" police vehicle in Canada. Rob Rothwell, VPD fleet manager, says of Susan's Thunderbird that "the department proudly displays it as a salute to the people who were here first, and as an icon of the Pacific Northwest."[59]

Once again, Susan's work reinforces the usefulness of Salish art and ideas in reaching out to the wider community. Other than Susan and Kelly's design for the manholes, this is undoubtedly the most widely seen work by Susan in Vancouver.

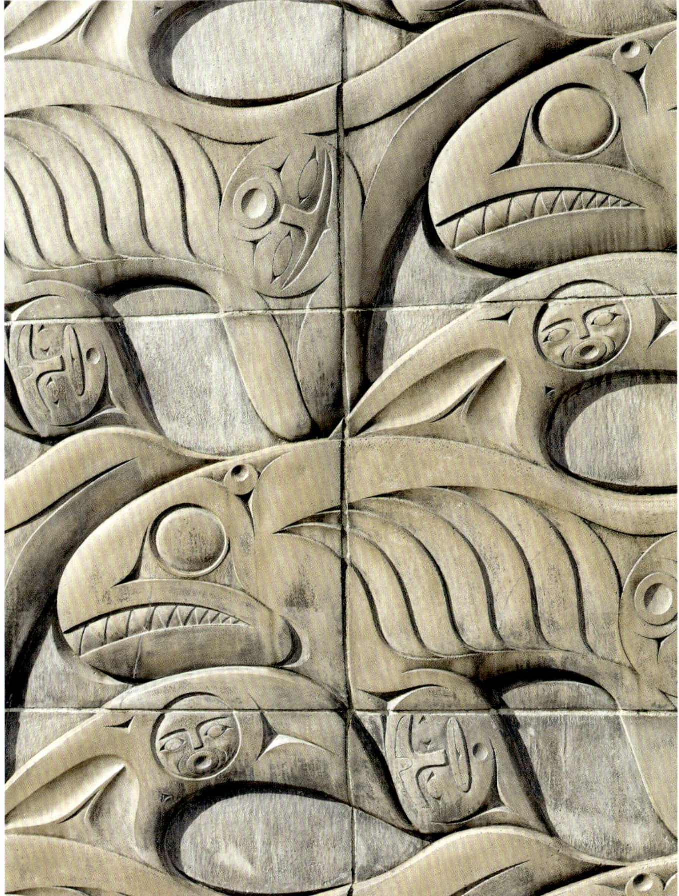

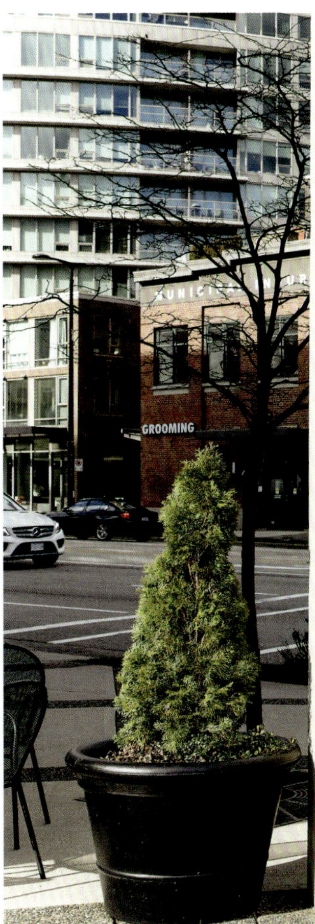

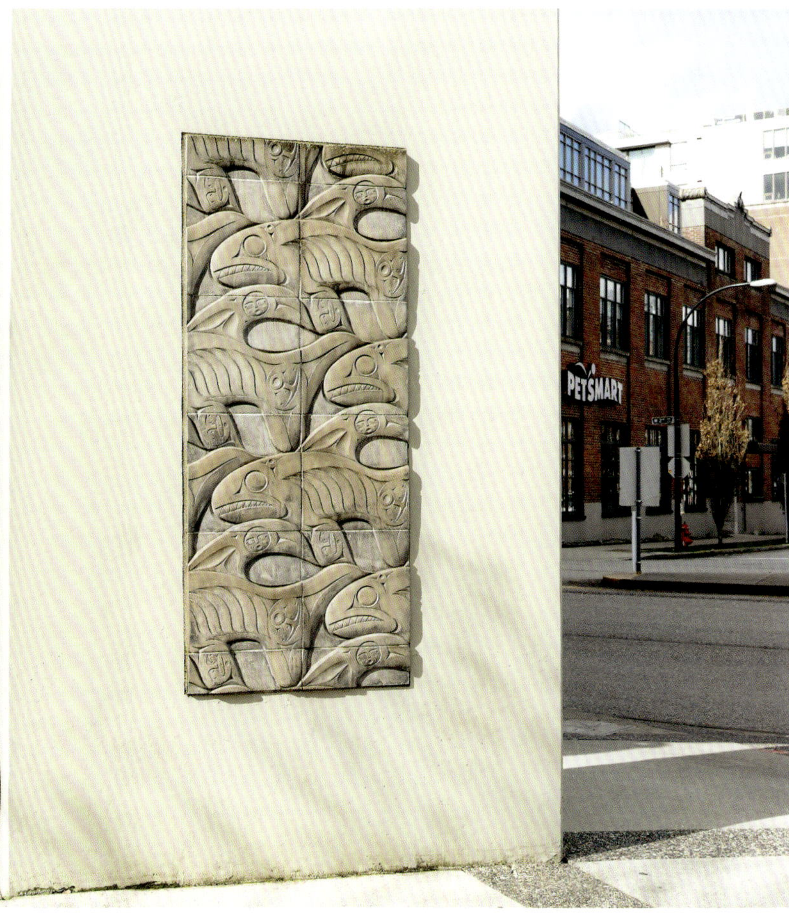

Consonance

LOCATION: Montreux Building
2055 Yukon St, Vancouver

When officials at the Bastion Development Corporation decided they wanted some public art as external ornament on a new building at the corner of Yukon Street and Second Avenue, they contacted Susan and offered her the exterior of the main pillar at the corner of the site. She chose to cast in concrete a composition from 2000 featuring humans and orcas, a symbol of long life, which she had carved in yellow cedar and cast in bronze polymer. Originally oriented horizontally, here she changed it to a vertical orientation to suit the pillar.

Susan outlines the Salish story of the Whale People that inspired *Consonance* (2000) in *Susan Point: Coast Salish Artist*. Two of a village's fastest warriors discover a group of orcas on a beach, each with its orca skin pulled back to reveal its human form. The warriors race toward them and one of them captures an orca skin, but the human form ecapes. The warrior is warned that keeping the orca skin will bring bad luck. He ignores the warning and suffers many hardships until he decides to return the orca skin. [60]

The interconnectedness of life is a regular and important theme in Susan's work, dramatized in this composition by human faces appearing on the fins of each orca. She explains that "the imagery in this piece, like many of my other pieces, is to show respect—in this case, to the whales. And to remind us of our obligation to look out and care for these magnificent creatures, who are believed to be very closely related to humankind."[61]

The mural is so accessible at street level, it's easy to admire the fluid curves defining the bodies, the human faces in a familiar Salish style, the wedges and crescents, and imagine these magnificent creatures, as Susan describes them, swimming beyond the bounds of the artwork.

Consonance, 2006
Cast concrete
213 × 89 cm

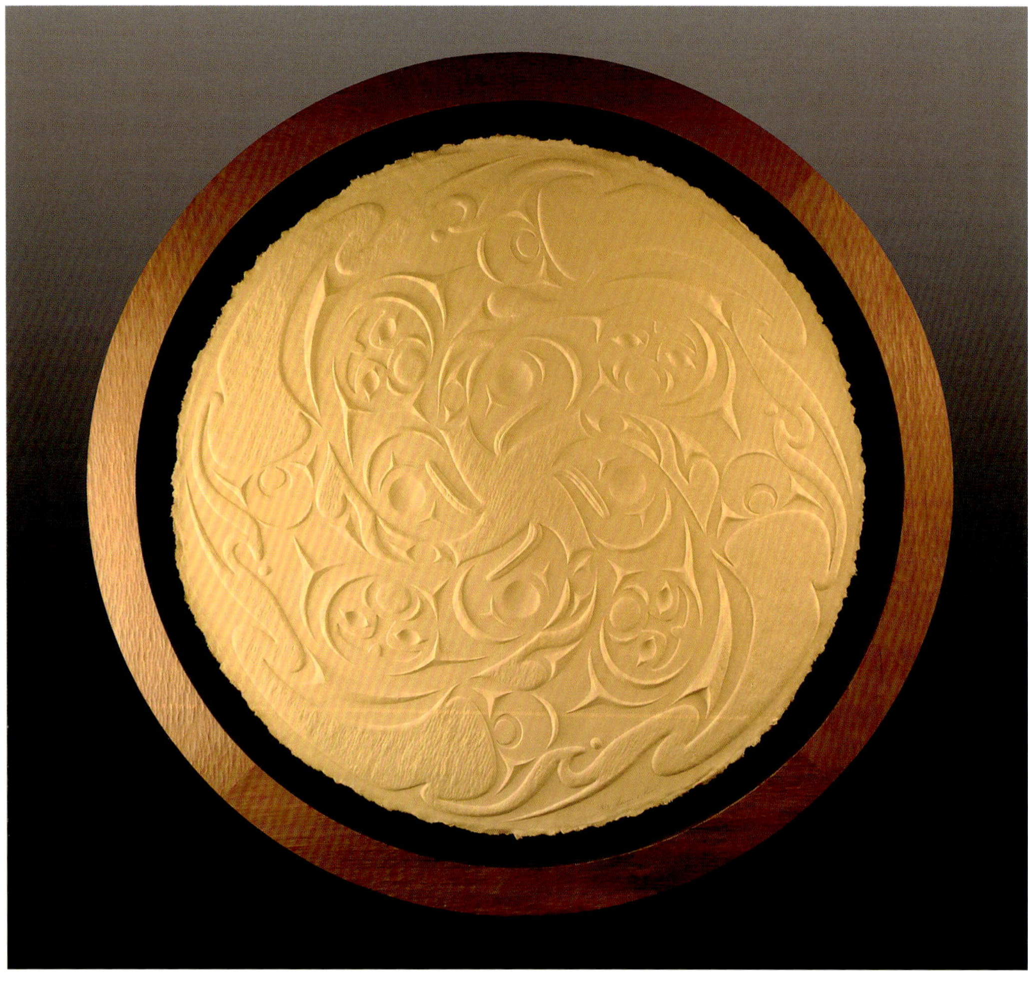

Salmon, 2003
Paper
73.5 cm (diameter)

Salmon

LOCATION: Office of the Mayor
453 W 12th Ave, Vancouver

Susan began casting in paper in 1987, following a course she took with Sharon Yuen at Kakali Papers on Granville Island. In 2000 she continued her experiments with paper casts of some of her designs. This one was made from a mould of the salmon design she did in 1995 for the bronze sidewalk medallions in Coal Harbour (see page 63). She made a pulp of cotton fibre, added pigment, and pressed the mixture into sheets using a screen. She then pressed the sheets onto the mould and allowed it to dry. The grace and fluidity of the composition appear differently than in the bronze version, but work very well as a paper cast. The result is a warm, textured image that reveals its details upon close inspection.

Salmon was installed in the mayor's office in 2003. It is a fine way to bring a Salish presence into the heart of the civic administration—salmon are known as "the giver of life" in Salish culture, and usually shown in pairs for good luck. Susan's energetic desire to experiment with new mediums allows her to render old designs in new forms, and to inspire many more people in a different context.

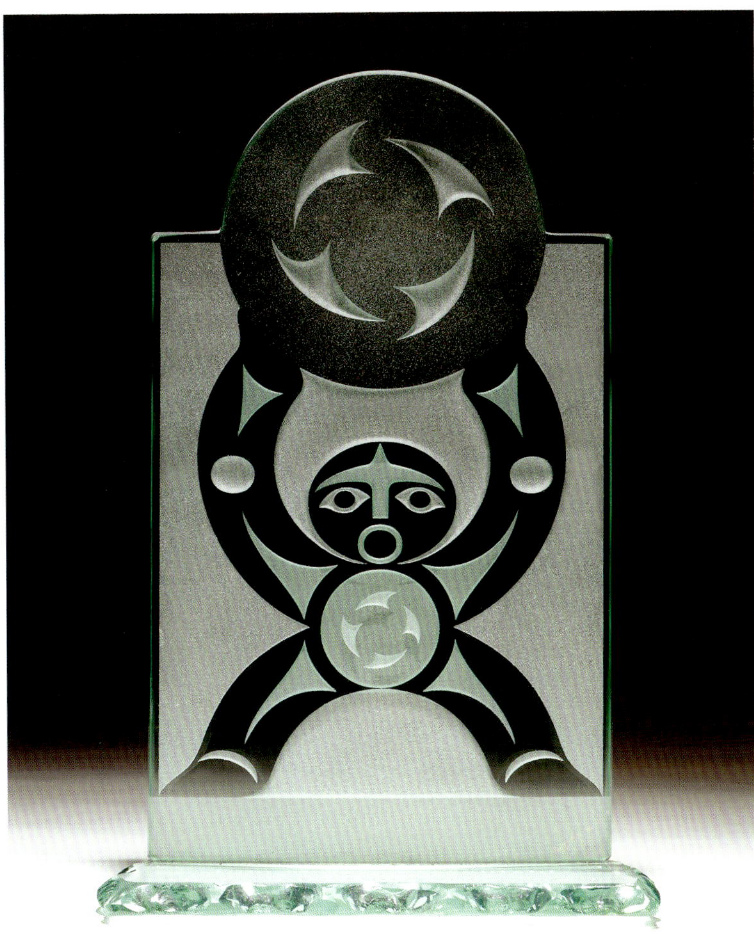

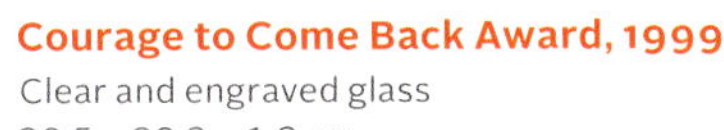

Courage to Come Back Award, 1999
Clear and engraved glass
30.5 × 20.3 × 1.3 cm

Courage to Come Back Award

LOCATION: Coast Mental Health
293 E 11th Ave, Vancouver

When Coast Mental Health founded an award for individuals who, in the words of Darrell Burnham, the non-profit's CEO, "when faced with adversity through accident, illness or social or economic circumstance, dig deep within their being to triumph over their challenges," they solicited submissions for artwork on which to base the physical award.[62] Susan submitted several images; a variation of the design she had developed two years earlier for *Generations* (see page 214) was chosen.

Yves Trudeau of Studio One Glass Art, Susan's longtime collaborator, digitally fabricated her design in glass and continues to produce the awards. As Susan wished, he uses a combination of clear and frosted glass. The spiritual and aspirational nature of the award is captured by a single human figure with raised arms holding a large circle. The curve of the legs matches that of the arms, and implies a strong and determined stance. Susan was characteristically mindful of the situations of those who might be recipients of this award, explaining that "this design is very subtle; giving the inference of human figures. As some individuals are in wheelchairs, I did not want to get anatomically correct. These figures do not display the full human body."[63] She went on to note that the Salish-style wedges in the circle highlight the importance of the number four, and the circle itself symbolizes the circle of life.

The design of the award is simple, using few lines and minimal crescents and wedges, but carries a clear message about the power of the human spirit to overcome any restrictions and uphold the promise of life. It is an excellent example of how Susan uses Salish forms to honour an important story that crosses many boundaries.

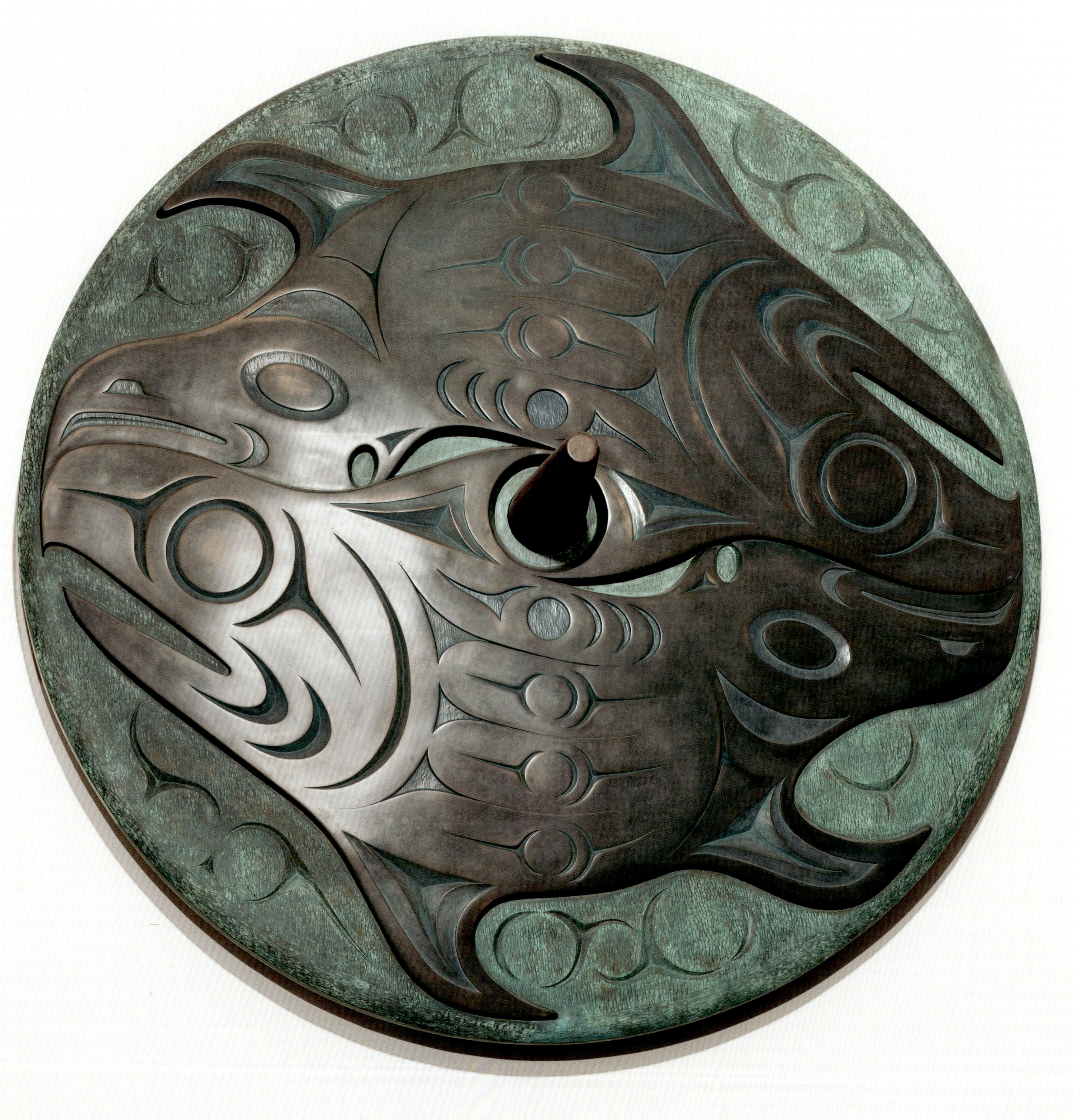

The River—Giver of Life, 1998
Patinated bronze polymer
2.13 (diameter) × .5 m

LANGARA COLLEGE

Langara College, located just a few kilometres from the Musqueam settlement, is among the closest schools to Susan's home. In 1997 the college's students' union commissioned from her a large bronze spindle whorl and a cast glass and terra cotta polymer mural, both for display in the Students' Union Building (SUB). About a decade later, the construction of a new SUB resulted in the relocation of both pieces, the spindle whorl (without its original glass backing) to the library, and the mural back to Susan's studio to await eventual rehousing on the campus.

The River—Giver of Life

LOCATION: Langara College
100 W 49th Ave, Vancouver

Susan carved this large spindle whorl—over two metres in diameter—inspired by the Fraser River, and would eventually cast it in three different materials for three different locations (see pages 138 and 139). At Langara it was placed on the south wall of the library, where it dominates the room as you enter from the east. It shows two salmon in Susan's contemporary Salish style "swimming" around the central shaft of the whorl. Susan often uses two salmon to represent a female and a male, and by extension, their four-year life cycle. Among the Salish, salmon pairs are believed to bring good fortune and wealth, and are strong symbols of the life force. The whorl also depicts two Thunderbirds facing the opposite direction. According to Susan (as recounted by Vesta Giles), "these thunderbirds, seen in the salmon tails, are transferring their power to the salmon, protecting them and overseeing their continuing cycle of renewal."[64]

The whorl invites students to reflect on the importance of the environment and their duty to care for it, and provides a dramatic visual signal of the Musqueam people's millennia-long presence in the territory on which the college now rests. Salmon are a fitting choice for the composition, given their role as a vital food source for the Musqueam and other Salish Peoples, as well as the other communities that now share the land. Susan described the whorl in a statement to the Students' Union the year of its installation:

> The imagery on this Coast Salish spindle whorl design was inspired by the Fraser River, where my two sons fish. For thousands of years my people, the Musqueam, have lived on the shores of the Fraser river; our history, rich with legends about the Fraser. This design, circular in format with water in the background, symbolizes the north arm of the Fraser, a part of the river which runs alongside our native community. This design also reflects the spirit of the Pacific Northwest Coast as well as the traditional Coast Salish style of art by use of its design elements such as crescents, U-forms and wedges or V-forms. This large scale spindle whorl sculpture . . . represents the continuing life cycle not only of Salmon but of life on our planet. As at Langara, every year students come and go, generation after generation, seeking an awakening or insight to their full potential. This whorl is a reminder of the journey we undertake.[65]

Coming Together, 1998
Cast glass, terra cotta polymer
2.13 × 6.1 m

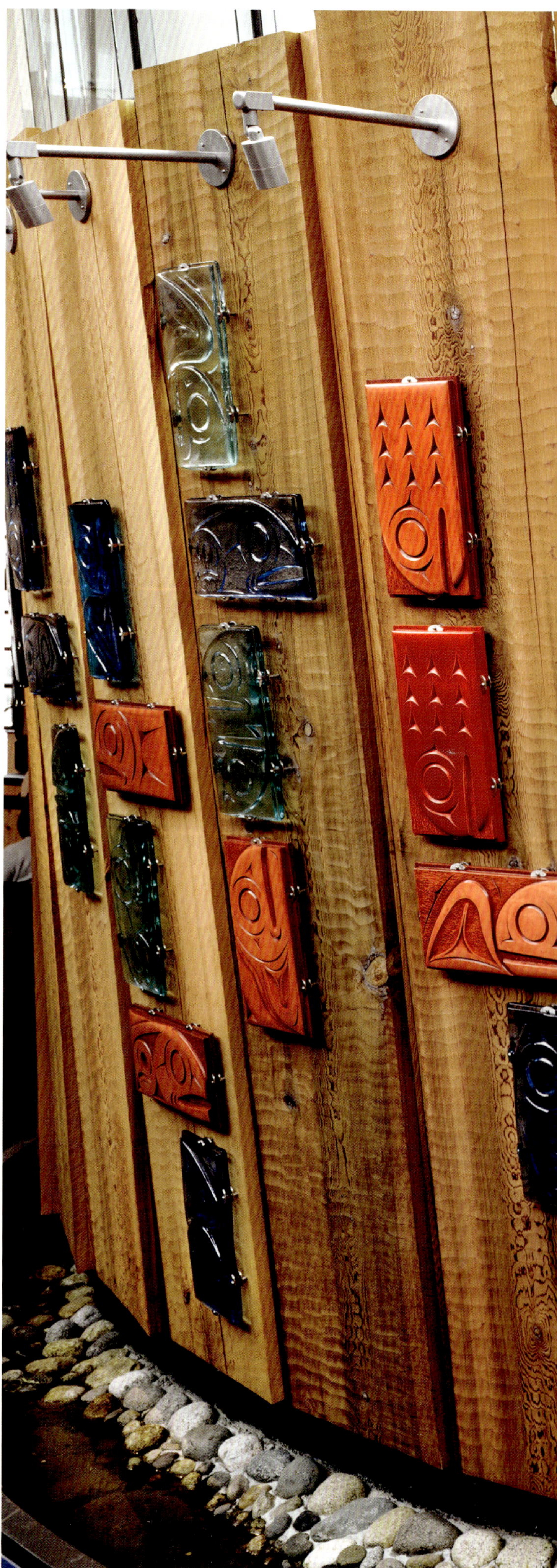

Coming Together

LOCATION: Langara College
100 W 49th Ave, Vancouver

This second part of the commission was also based on a salmon motif, with the idea that the two elements would be mounted on opposite sides of a cedar wall that would be a prominent feature of the SUB, separating the lounge from the cafeteria. As Susan explained at the time,

> Within this proposal I have developed a large-scale wall mural which could be done in cast glass or terra cotta Forton. This design was inspired by a traditional Salish panel artifact and consists of symbolic (square) salmon heads. The wall is intended to celebrate the differences of the student body and to illustrate how it exists as a community.
>
> This proposal entails carving five different original yellow cedar panels.... One of these panels would be a split panel so as to give more options for layout. Each panel represents one of the groups within the Students' Union Building. Although within each group there are diverse ethnic differences and beliefs, all co-exist and work together with common concerns for the future and goals of self-empowerment. This design also represents everyone coming together as one; fitting in with tolerance and cooperation.[66]

In the end, Susan decided to use both glass and Forton for the mural. Unfortunately, the wall and its striking artwork had to be moved when a new SUB was built in 2008–09. At the request of the Students' Union, *Coming Together* was returned to Susan's studio for temporary storage, with the union committing to eventually displaying it elsewhere at Langara. A suitable new location has not yet been found.

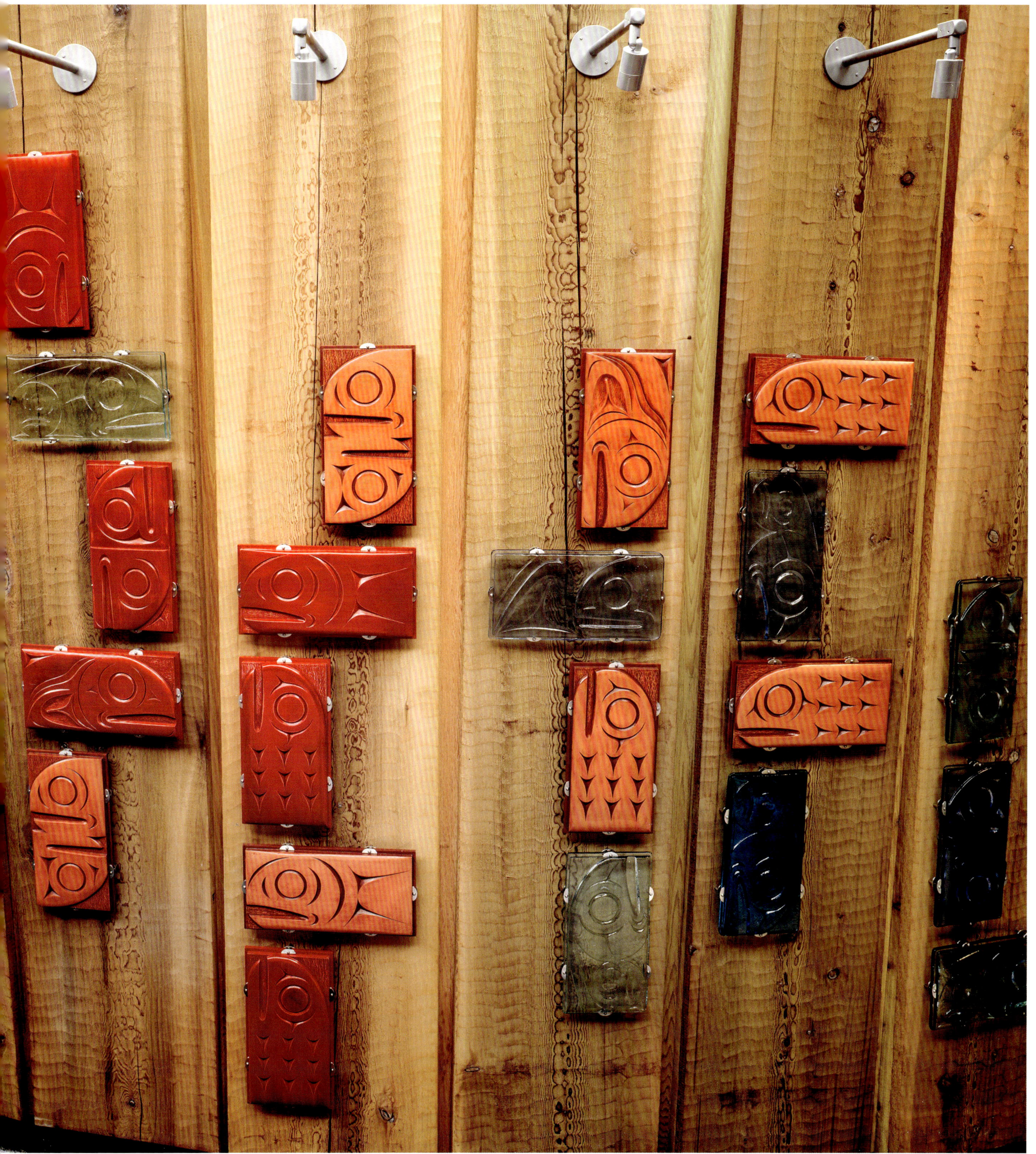

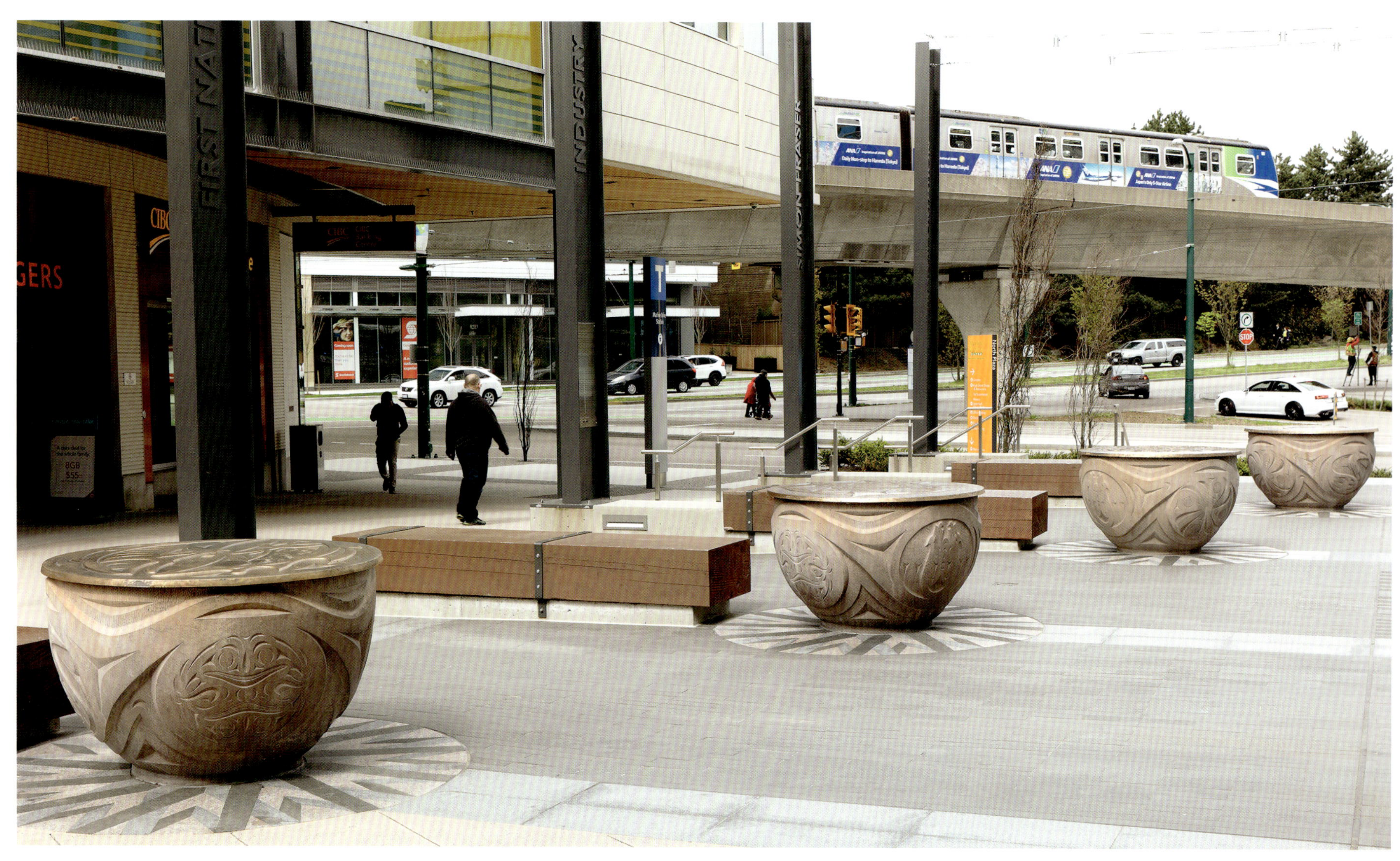
FIRST NAT
INDUSTRY
SIMON FRASER
CIBC
GERS

Salish Gifts

LOCATION: Marine Gateway
447–497 SW Marine Dr, Vancouver

Early in 2013, Susan Point learned from a long-standing acquaintance, Karen Mills of Public Art Management, about a new public art opportunity in Marine Gateway, a mixed-use development located near the Fraser River, partway between č̓əsnaʔəm (Marpole settlement) and an area upstream called skʷtexʷqən̓. The complex adjoins the Marine Drive station of the region's rapid transit system, making this striking public art commission one of the most accessible of Susan Point's creations in the last decade.

The call for proposals requested "a work created by and in honour of the Musqueam people." Susan's proposed works, four large concrete and bronze "baskets," took full advantage of the opportunity to celebrate the ancient Salish presence in the area. She explained the aesthetic, practical, and cultural aspects of the baskets in her proposal.

> My conceptual art is based on the theme of the "People of the Grass" as well as the "Salmon People" which is uniquely Musqueam. Overall, the forms/designs within my artwork represent a living thriving culture and our historical legacy; as well as this unique community today.... It is a fresh concept with limited impact on pedestrians using this area.
>
> *Salish Gifts* embraces many aspects of Musqueam culture by combining four vessels representing baskets, with lids representative of spindle whorls all sitting upon Coast Salish reed mats. The artwork is intimate, and interactive. They appear mobile but are everlasting. The view from the plaza is not affected as they are approximately three feet high, these keep the look of the plaza open with the warmth of bronze and tinted concrete. My artwork is charming as people interact with it. It is easy to comprehend. From above these four artworks are subtle and pleasing as the artwork is facing in all directions.
>
> My late mother Edna Grant-Point was one of the last Musqueam women renowned for her teaching and passing of knowledge, which included basketry. The basketry as well as woven reed cattail mats lined the inside walls of Musqueam family houses.... The designs traditionally on baskets would tell a story or depict family history. Often motifs were blended as a result of marriages between tribal families. As well, the designs on baskets depict stories of great gatherings and celebrations which they would be made especially for.
>
> Using traditional basketry as an art form, I would like to convey to the community that there is a long history of celebrated artwork native to this region. Therefore I propose hand carving a large basket pattern from windfall old growth western cedar, approximately 47″ diameter by 30″ high and casting it four times in patinated (coloured) concrete using earth tones and placing them within proposed areas of the plaza that will not impede pedestrian traffic.[67]

THE BASKETS

The art on the sides of the baskets emphasizes the historic environmental consciousness of the Musqueam people, and the interconnectedness of river, air, and land creatures. One side shows four salmon heads, a species that continues to be of vital importance to the Musqueam today. The second side carries the symbol for Heron/Crane, with "the four large Salish elements around the bird... placed in such a way as to create a circle within."[68] The

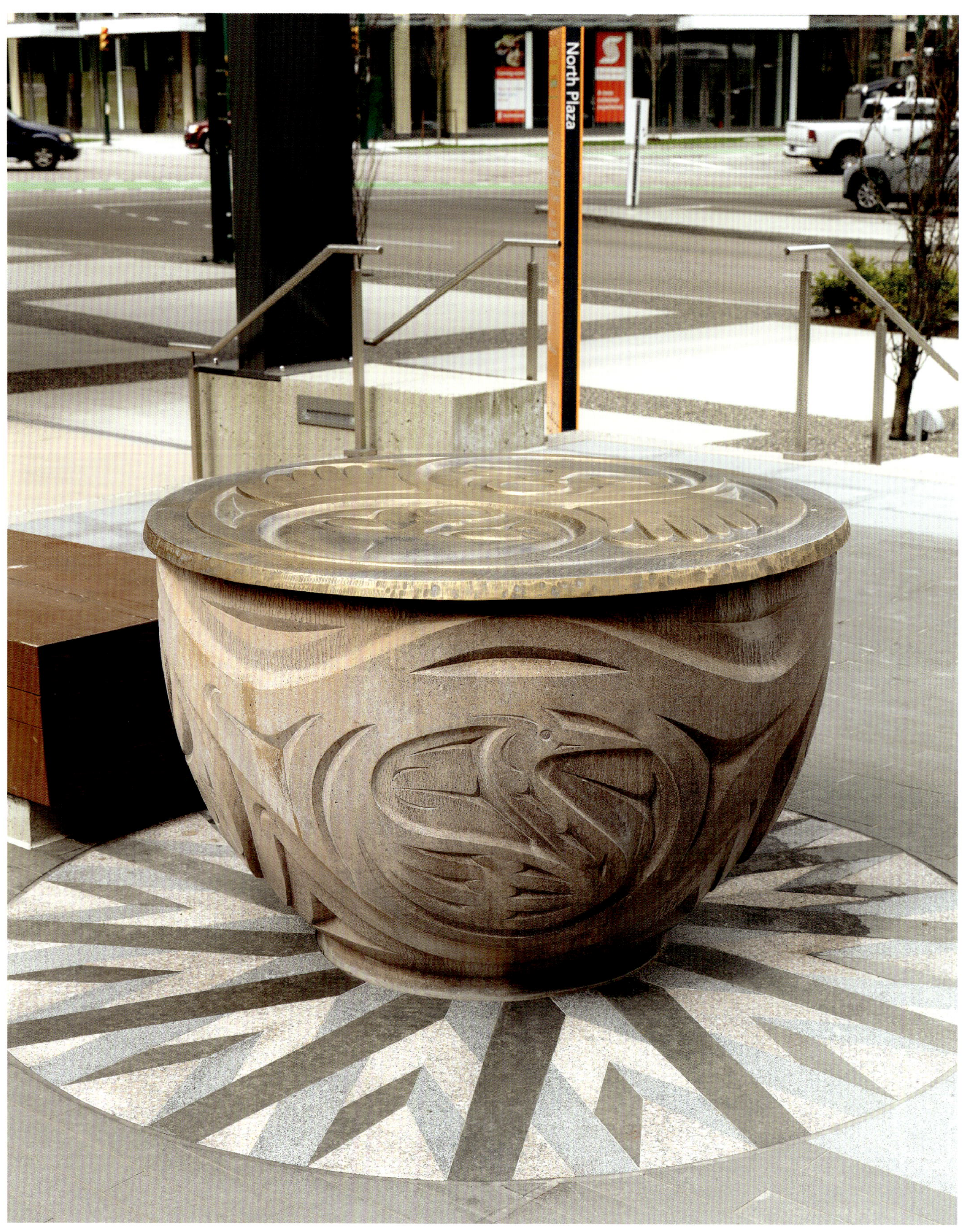
North Plaza

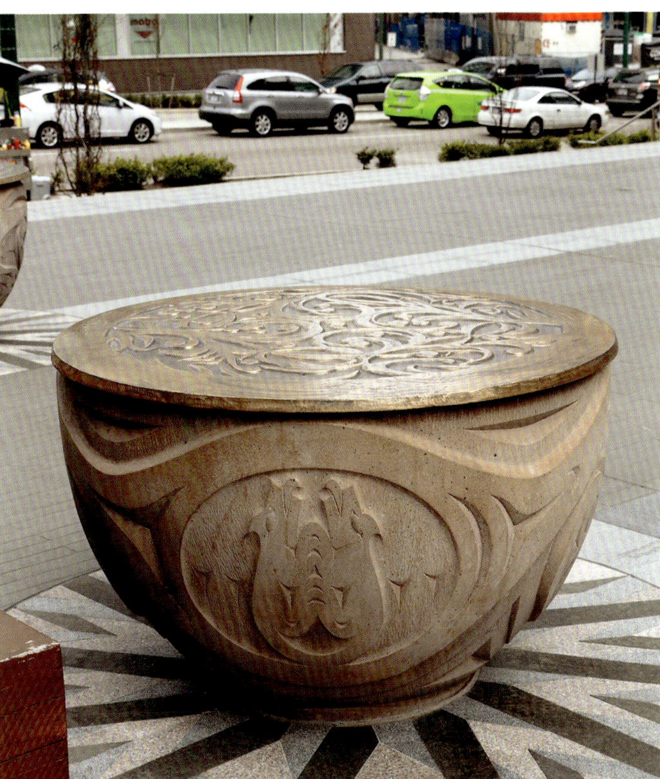

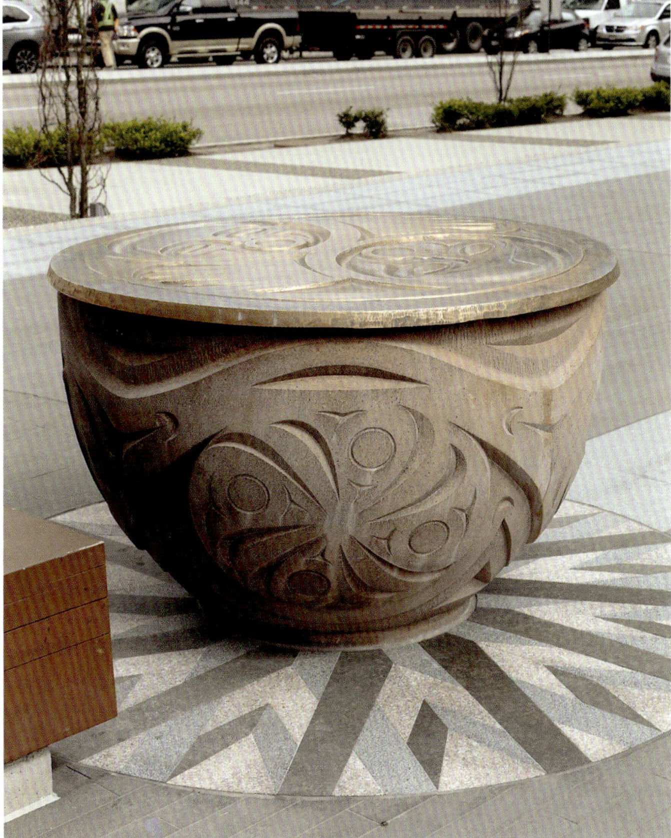

Salish Gifts, 2016
Patinated cast concrete with cast bronze lids, set on coloured stone

The Baskets
77 × 120 cm (diameter; each)

third side shows Fishers, "the most familiar iconic animal motif found in Salish imagery. At one time, the fisher was abundant along the banks of the Fraser River. It represented well-being, healing and was a sacred animal."[69] The fourth side features two frogs, a familiar motif in Susan's art that refers to the change of seasons.

THE LIDS

Recognizing that baskets would have had lids, she envisaged each of the lids as unique spindle whorls. Over the decades of her artistic career she has produced spindle whorls in a great range of mediums, including wood, metal, glass, and synthetic materials. For *Salish Gifts* she carved the whorls in wood and then cast them in bronze. In her proposal Susan touched on the origins of spindle whorls and their symbolic resurgence.

> The traditional spindle whorl, once a tool indispensable to weaving in the native household, is no longer just an artifact for museums, but a symbol that has been reborn as an icon to identify the cultural lineage of the Coast Salish people. Coast Salish women have used the spindle whorl for centuries to spin their mountain goat [p̓q̓əlqən] wool into yarn. It is a disc that acted as a flywheel on the spinning device used for making wool yarn.
>
> Traditional spindle whorls depicted outstanding "original" designs with complex integrated compositions of engraved animal and human figures as well as geometric and floral motifs . . . some depicting mythic creatures.[70]

The first whorl, "Salmon," shows a male and female fish, the latter laden with eggs, arranged to symbolize the dominant theme of much of Susan's work, the cycle of life.[71]

The original yellow cedar carvings of the lids hang in offices at the Marine Gateway complex.

Salish Gifts, 2016
The Lids
120 cm (diameter) × 3 cm (each)

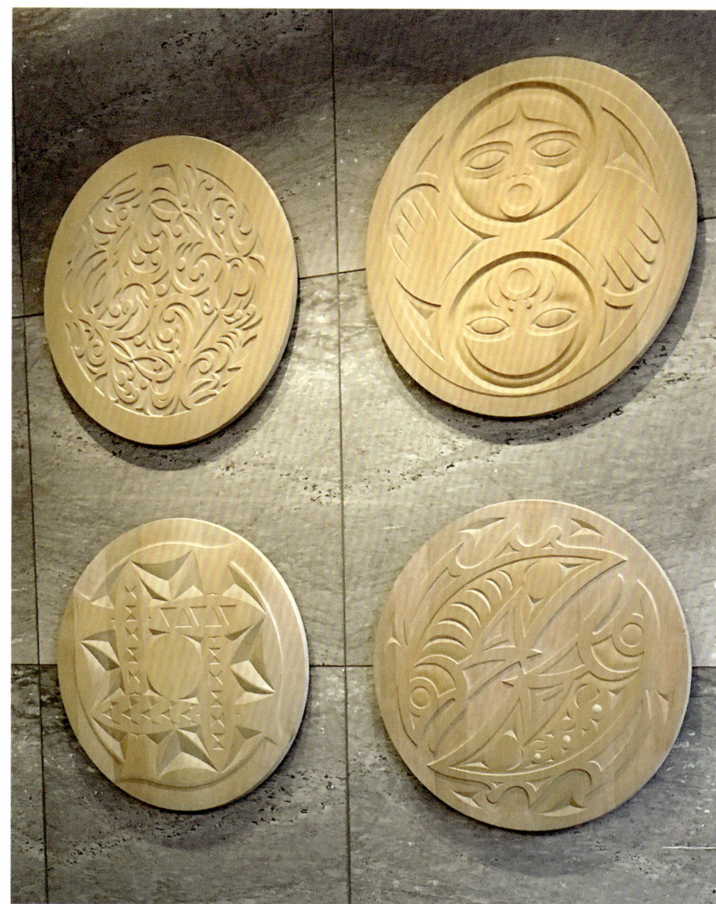

For the second whorl, "Four Paddles," Susan explained the significance of both the number and the tool.

> Paddles have been used by the Salish to navigate the Fraser River and the Salish Sea for thousands of years. Many different styles of red cedar canoes were packed with baskets full of food and trade goods including shellfish, salmon and eulachon [swiw̓ə] as well as stone tools, wool and blankets to name a few. Families climbed aboard and were whisked by the current to distant places with distant relations.
>
> ...The number four is an important number to Coast Salish peoples. This undoubtedly stems from our first breath of "the four winds," our first journey in each of "the four directions," living through "the four seasons," and understanding "the four elements."
>
> These four Paddles take us on a journey around the Salish Sea. I have used traditional basket and weaving motifs to symbolize the ancient villages... butterflies, rivers, mountains and valleys and flying geese that are all abundant here.[72]

Delightfully, Susan introduces—to this multicultural urban setting, amid towers of concrete on territory where her ancestors were once the only human presence—an image of a classic Coast Salish welcome in the third whorl, "Welcoming."

> Open raised hands are a gesture similarly used in many cultures around the world to express feelings of... friendship and welcome. Here I have two Salishan people in a welcoming gesture, almost in a full embrace.... Perhaps a journey or a spiritual quest kept old friends apart.[73]

The fourth whorl is perhaps the most intriguing, particularly for those unfamiliar with Susan Point's art or Coast Salish elements. Lines swirl seemingly randomly in every direction, but as in all her work, the design is rooted in research, stories, and ideas. For "Berries on the Shoreline," Susan explored the history and topography of the setting (as she does with all her site-specific works), and learned that a large creek once flowed beside the Marine Gateway site into the Fraser River.

> Like most West Coast streams, this one likely had small waterfalls and deep pools where fish would thrive. Huckleberries, salmonberries and thimbleberries thrived in the moist earth around

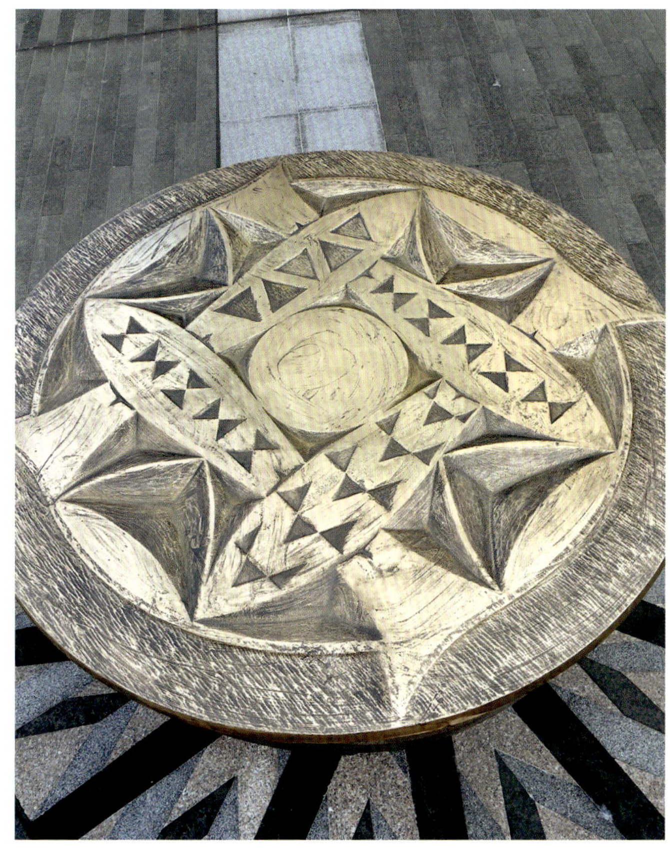

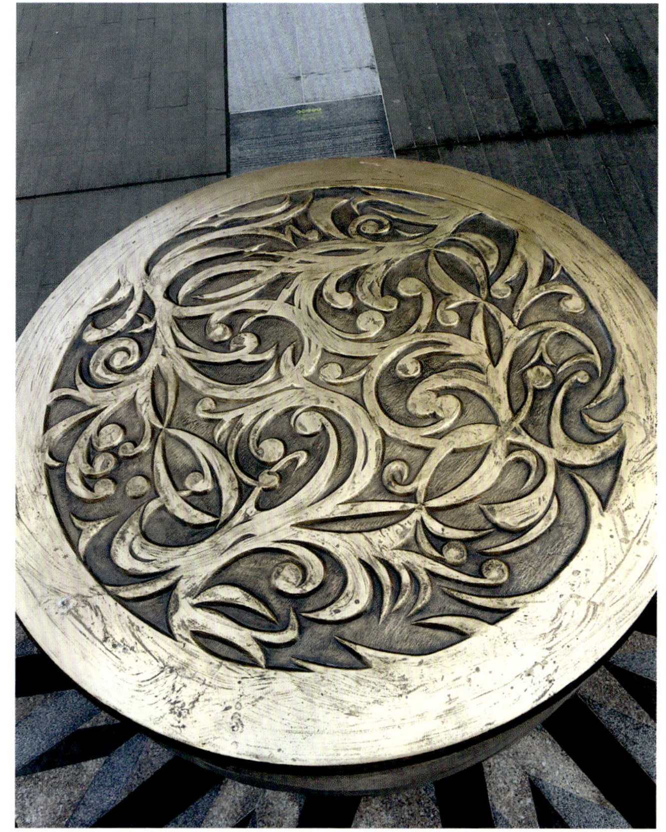

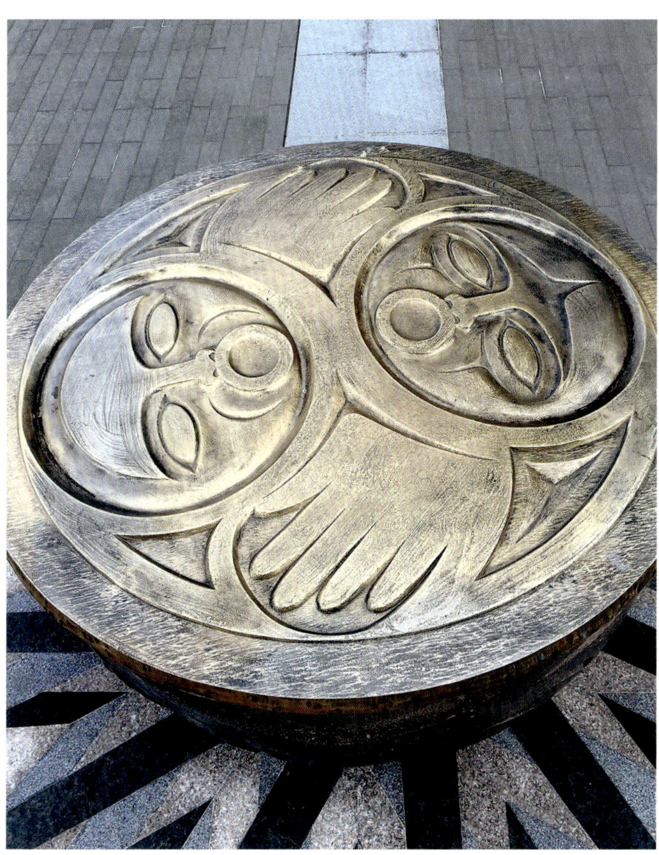

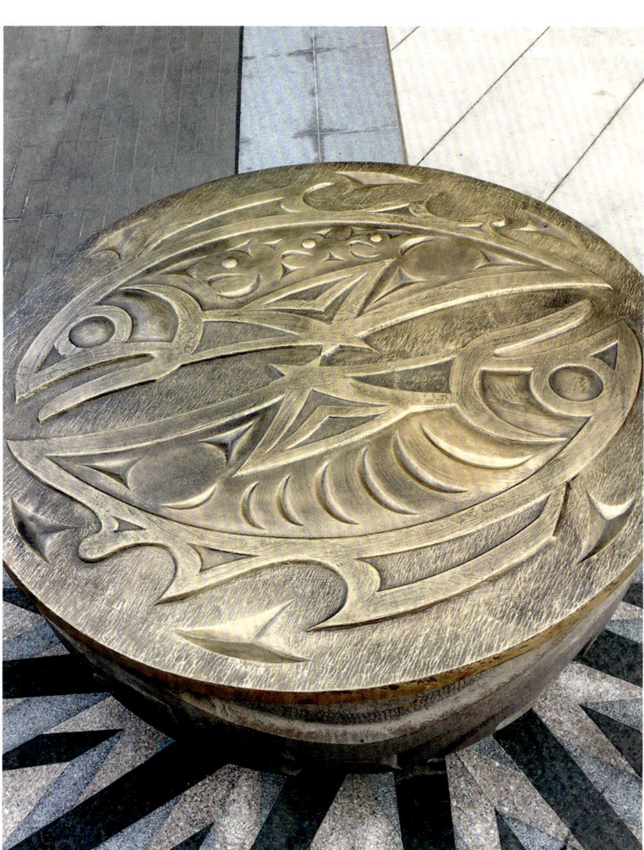

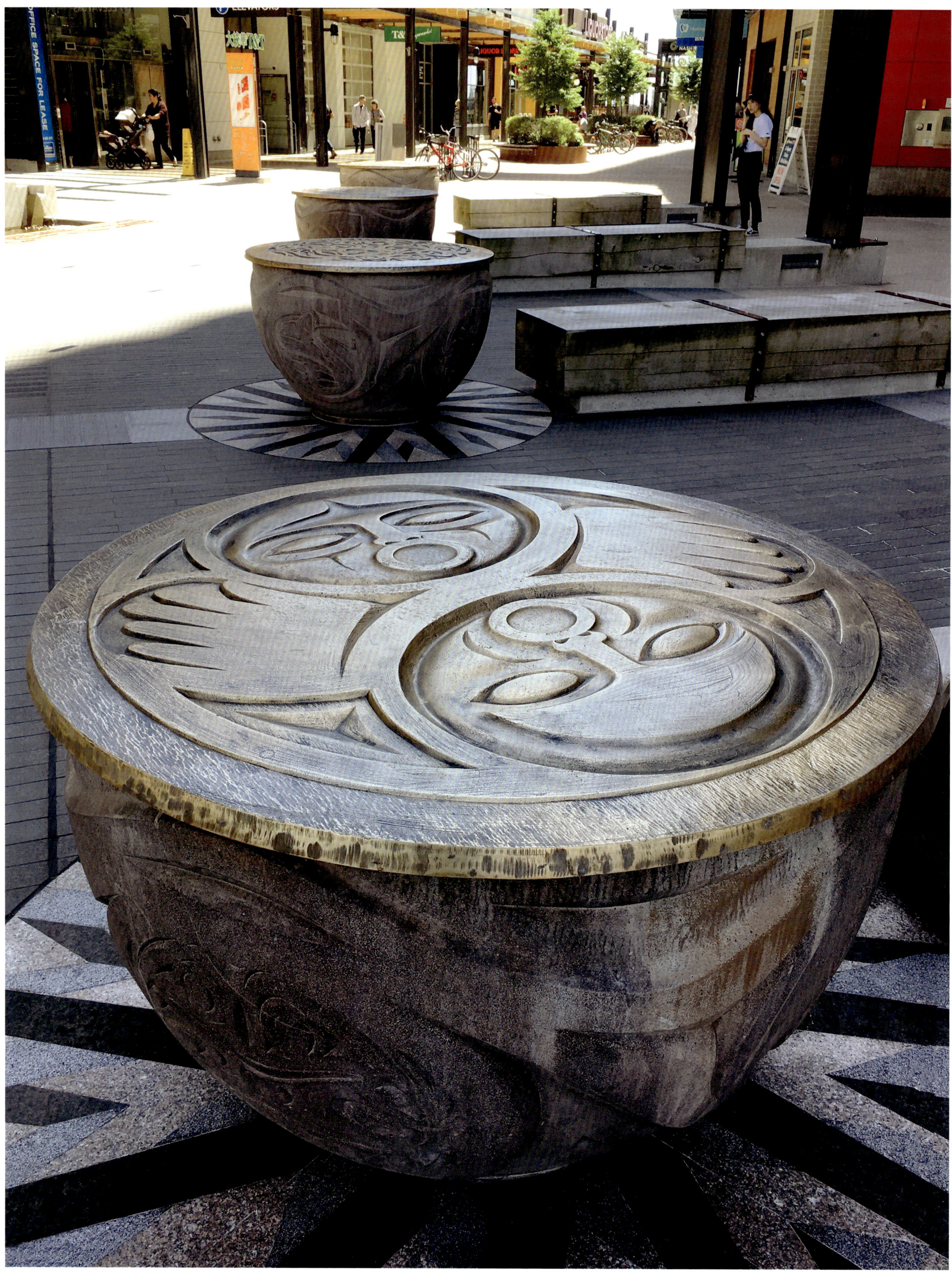
OFFICE SPACE FOR LEASE
大統華T&T

Salish Gifts, 2016
The Mats
165 cm (diameter; each)

> them. My design for this whorl embraces the wild free flowing environment that this creek existed within. The motif celebrates the nature and bounty of the Fraser River. If one looks closely around the berry branches they can see four stylized salmon heads in the branches.[74]

THE MATS

Finally, each basket was placed on coloured cut stone that was patterned to represent the mats she remembers her mother making. As she explains, Coast Salish traditional territories were very large, and so

> many days were spent away in the forest. An everyday item used [was] bulrush/cattail (reed) mats. A common practice was to bring a few reed mats along with you. These reed mats were used for a variety of things in life including quick overnight shelter and are surprisingly comfortable for sleeping. I honour these mats by laying them beneath my baskets, as they would have been at ceremonies and trade gatherings, arranging things out on the table so to speak.[75]

The series of interlaced earth-tone bands is devoid of the curves that are so prominent a feature of many of Susan's compositions. Several years later, Susan carved a version of this design in cedar and painted the various bands to produce a beautiful wall feature.

SUSAN WAS awarded the commission for *Salish Gifts* by PCI Developments, builders of the Marine Gateway complex, in late September 2013. Once she had completed the carving of the basket template in red cedar, MSE Precast in Qualicum Beach, B.C. cast the baskets in late 2015. In the meantime Susan carved the templates for the spindle whorl lids (now on display in the foyer of 450 Southwest Marine Drive). Hastings Brass Foundry in Vancouver produced the lids from these carvings, to Susan's exacting specifications—her collaborators over the years have often referred to her meticulousness at every stage of a project, and she describes herself as "fussy." The care she lavishes on a project, from design to creation and fabrication, is deeply important to the quality of her art.

The finished artwork was installed in the commercial plaza of the complex, and officially opened on 7 April 2016. As viewers walk up the short stairway off Marine Drive into the plaza, their eyes cannot help but be caught by the graceful lines of the baskets, the symbols beautifully drawn and rendered, the shining lids—all convey that here, in front of us, are important messages. Some will pause and crouch down to admire the images on the sides and perhaps run their hands across the bronze lids. *Salish Gifts* invites us all to learn more about Salish culture and to appreciate how Susan has blended her ancestral heritage with the excitement of creating shapes and images that are unquestionably appealing. This is the work of a great artist at the height of her powers.

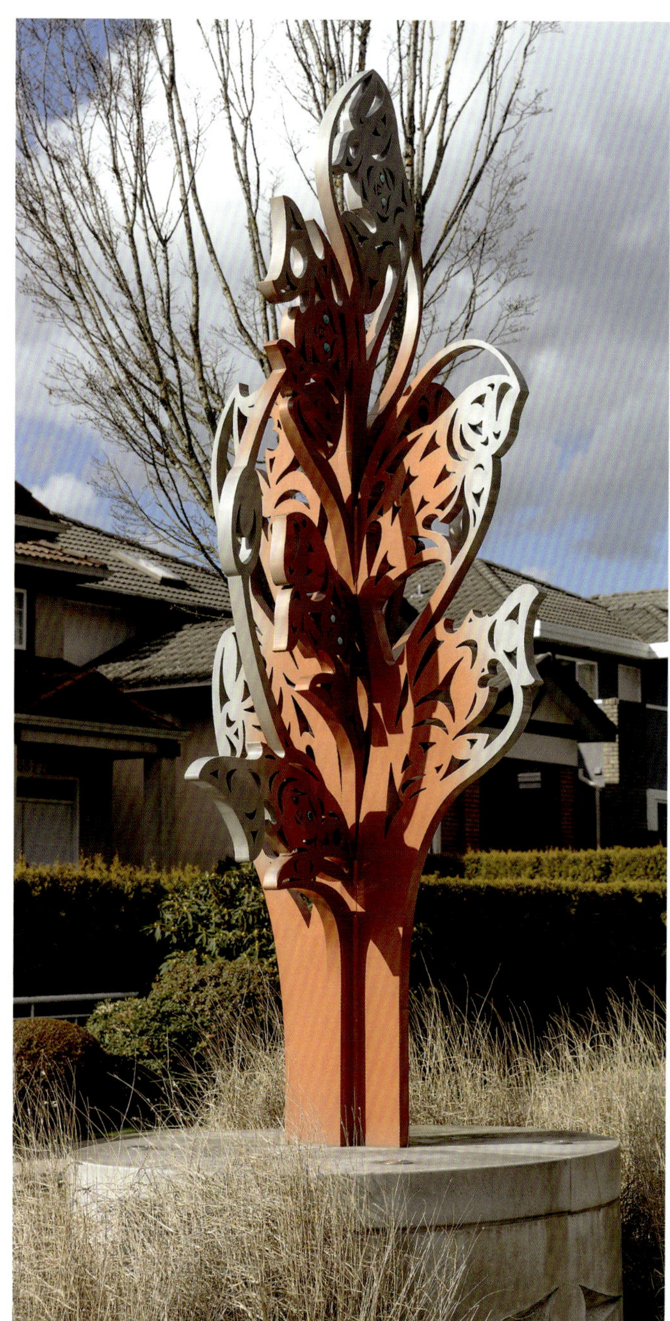

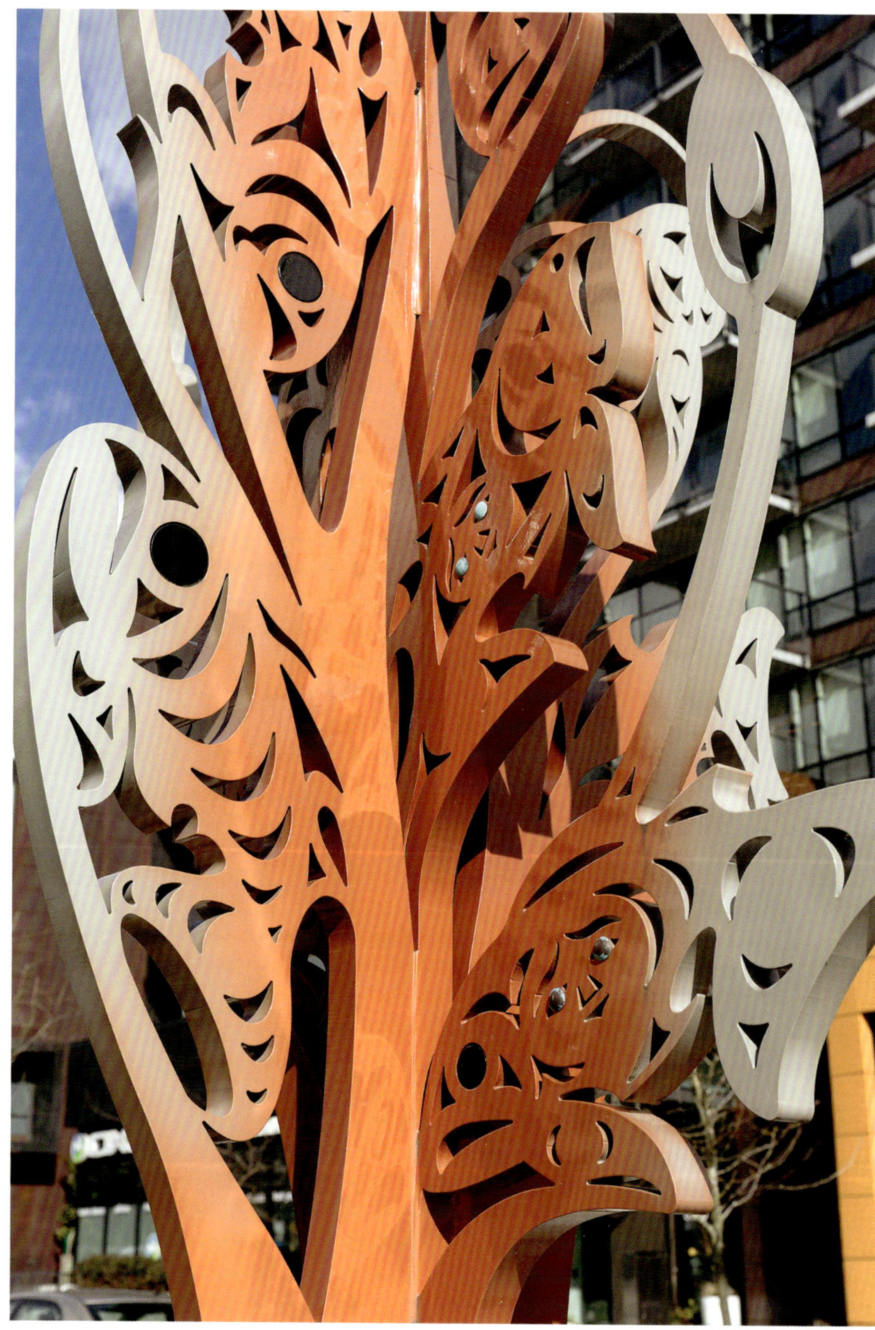

Fusion

LOCATION: Granville at 70th
W 70th Ave and Cornish St, Vancouver

The ancient Musqueam settlement of ċəsnaʔəm is just north of where the Fraser River splits around sqʷsaθən (Sea Island), roughly a third of the way from Marine Gateway to Susan's studio in the Musqueam settlement. A few blocks northwest of ċəsnaʔəm stands a traffic diverter that doubles as the venue for *Fusion*. The coloured aluminum composition, set on a base of concrete and Haddington Island stone, opens from a central axis in the four sacred directions to evoke salmon, river grass, and wi:l̓ (cattails).

In her proposal to Westbank, the developer that commissioned the piece as part of the development that backs onto Cornish Street, Susan highlighted the most important aspects of the work.

> I envisage creating a "contemporary" artwork that reflects not only the history of the area but the present as well ... an artwork that will have universal appeal to all cultures in the Marpole area.

Fusion, 2013
Copper- and silver-coloured aluminum on a concrete base
4.27 × approx. 1.1 (diameter) × .05 m (excluding base)

> *Fusion (Connecting History and Community)* is an artwork that marries mediums and cultures... as well as legends. It also, metaphorically, fuses natural imagery with modern methods.
>
> This "original" sculpture is contemporary yet unmistakably Salish. As the development project sits in traditional Musqueam territory and is close to the banks of the Fraser River, my conceptual art piece is based on the theme of "People of the Grass" as well as the "Salmon people" which is uniquely Musqueam. The human element within the salmon has universal appeal that symbolically relates to all peoples. The faces are revealed with traditional Salish elements... giving a sense of place and a landmark that respects past, present and future.[76]

Susan then describes the specifications resulting from the imperatives of the site, displaying her expertise in working with fabricators and civic engineers.

> The plinth for this sculpture is impressive. Earthen coloured concrete that has been vibrated to remove all imperfections from exposed surfaces, leaving a glass-like surface. Standing approx. 3 feet high, 6 feet wide and 4 feet deep, there will also be wedges around the outside moulded with the domed base.
>
> The domed shape is a match to the 20 domed copper eyes in the salmon. These eyes are patinated and have a chased surface, which can only be done properly by hand.
>
> The material for each of the powder coated salmon is water-jet cut three-inch aluminum. Powder coating would use a state of the art blending process whereby it will look painted, but with the extreme durability of powder coating as well as a clear topcoat.
>
> Spawning salmon on their journey up the Fraser River have passed the Musqueam people for thousands of generations. A story this big means they need to be big to be characterized fittingly. So this salmon sculpture is easily 12′–14′ high depending on final dimensions of the base and hardscape/landscape. Orientation and lines of sight will play a role in the adjustability of sizes to suit the site conditions."[77]

The sculpture epitomizes Susan's adventurous experimentation, and her determination to embrace every opportunity to work with developers (who she says are "getting better and better to work with"[78]), architects, city planners, and engineers, and to create contemporary public art that delights the viewer but also tells an important story. *Fusion* re-establishes a Salish presence in the Marpole neighbourhood near the heart of Musqueam territory, just a few hundred metres from the ancient settlement of c̓əsnaʔəm.

VANCOUVER INTERNATIONAL AIRPORT

Above the c̓əsnaʔəm site the Arthur Laing Bridge soars across the north arm of the Fraser River to sqʷsaθən (Sea Island), the island across the river from Musqueam, bounded on three sides by the river and on the fourth by the ocean. Sea Island is home to the Vancouver International Airport, which houses some of Susan's most important monumental art. The Vancouver Airport Authority and the YVR Art Foundation have commissioned six pieces from Susan to date, including *Flight*, the largest spindle whorl in the world. Over twenty million passengers travel through YVR each year, allowing Susan's work to impress upon visitors from around the world the beauty and richness of her art, and the continued vitality of the Musqueam people in their home territory.

Land, Sea and Sky

LOCATION: Vancouver International Airport
3211 Grant McConachie Way, sqʷsaθən (Sea Island), Richmond, BC

Susan's long and fruitful relationship with the airport began in 1993, with a request to create several pieces of art exploring the theme "Land, Sea and Sky," to be located near Gates 9 and 10 in the main terminal (now the domestic terminal). She created a triptych in cedar (now on display in the pass control office in the domestic terminal), and a series of images produced once in etched copper and again in glass, based on an original series of aquatints (all three series are now in the waiting area for Gates 90–96 in the international terminal). The glass series is an early example of her adventurousness in working with non-traditional materials.

Susan had only been carving in wood for three years when she made *Wolf, Killer Whale, Eagle and Salmon*, the cedar triptych. She carved the design, sandblasted the negative spaces, then painted the raised parts with acrylics. Stylized mountains across the base unite the three images, which Susan chose to represent land, sea, and sky.

On the left are two black wolves, tails in each other's mouths, curling around a circular space that represents the shaft of a spindle whorl. Wedges and crescents help define the shape of the animals and underscore the sense of circular movement. The killer whale, in the centre, anchors the composition. It makes a powerful visual impression with its red crescents that give a sense of three dimensions, helping the viewer to imagine the orca is leaping out of the sea. On the right is an eagle, wings outstretched, grasping a female salmon in its talons. Red and white wedges and red crescents in the eagle's wings imply swift movement, and the human face in the centre of the eagle's back represents the link between humans and the natural world. Six small red circles with eyes and mouths on the salmon's belly represent eggs, and new life. The use of turquoise elements in all three images reveals Susan's openness to non-traditional colours. Even for viewers unfamiliar with Salish-style art, these three compositions are clear, distinctive, and accessible.

In the glass and copper works, Susan represented "land" with two wolves around a sun, flanked by

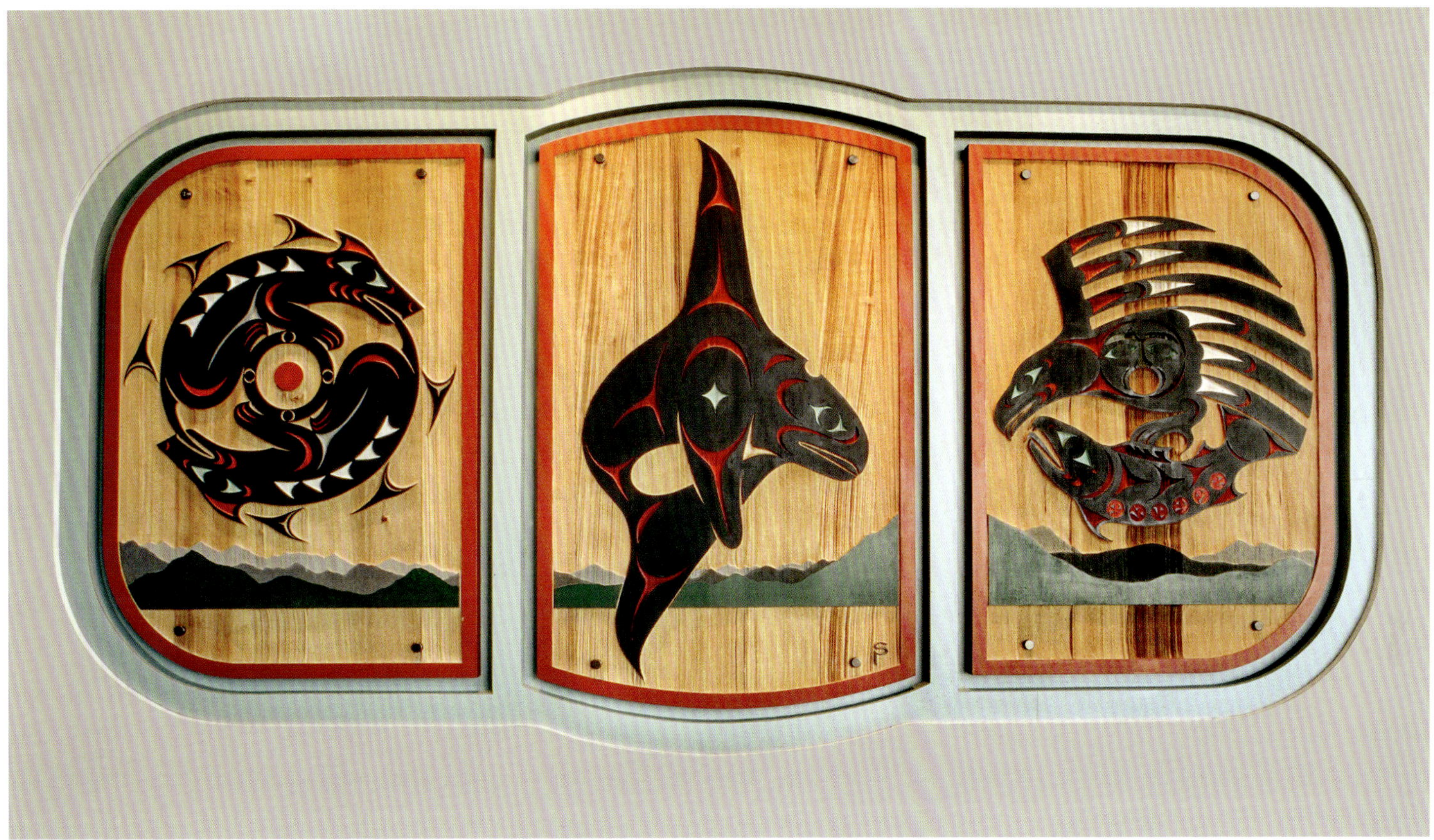

mountains and stylized trees; "sea" with two salmon heads and two eggs, along with a moon and stylized kelp; and "sky" with two eagles, again with a sun and mountains and trees. She chose a rectangular format instead of a whorl, though the symmetry of the designs makes it appear as if the eagles, the wolves, and the salmon are curving around a central circle.

In 1993 Susan had been working in glass for only a few years, but the glass versions are impressive, able to fit the contemporary architecture around them without any sacrifice of their Salish roots. Susan's decision to also etch the designs in copper, a symbol of wealth for the Musqueam and many other Indigenous Peoples of the Northwest Coast, is noteworthy.

After little more than a decade of production in various mediums, Susan's skillful use of traditional Salish elements in a modern context is very apparent. As she noted in her description of these works, "Although these images are very contemporary in their appearance they are entirely created with traditional Coast Salish elements; crescent and wedge shapes."[79] She has translated the elements she saw in various museum collections with confidence. No wedge, crescent, or U-form seems out of place or extraneous.

Land, Sea and Sky, 1993
Wolf, Killer Whale, Eagle and Salmon
Carved and painted cedar
152.4 × 289.5 cm

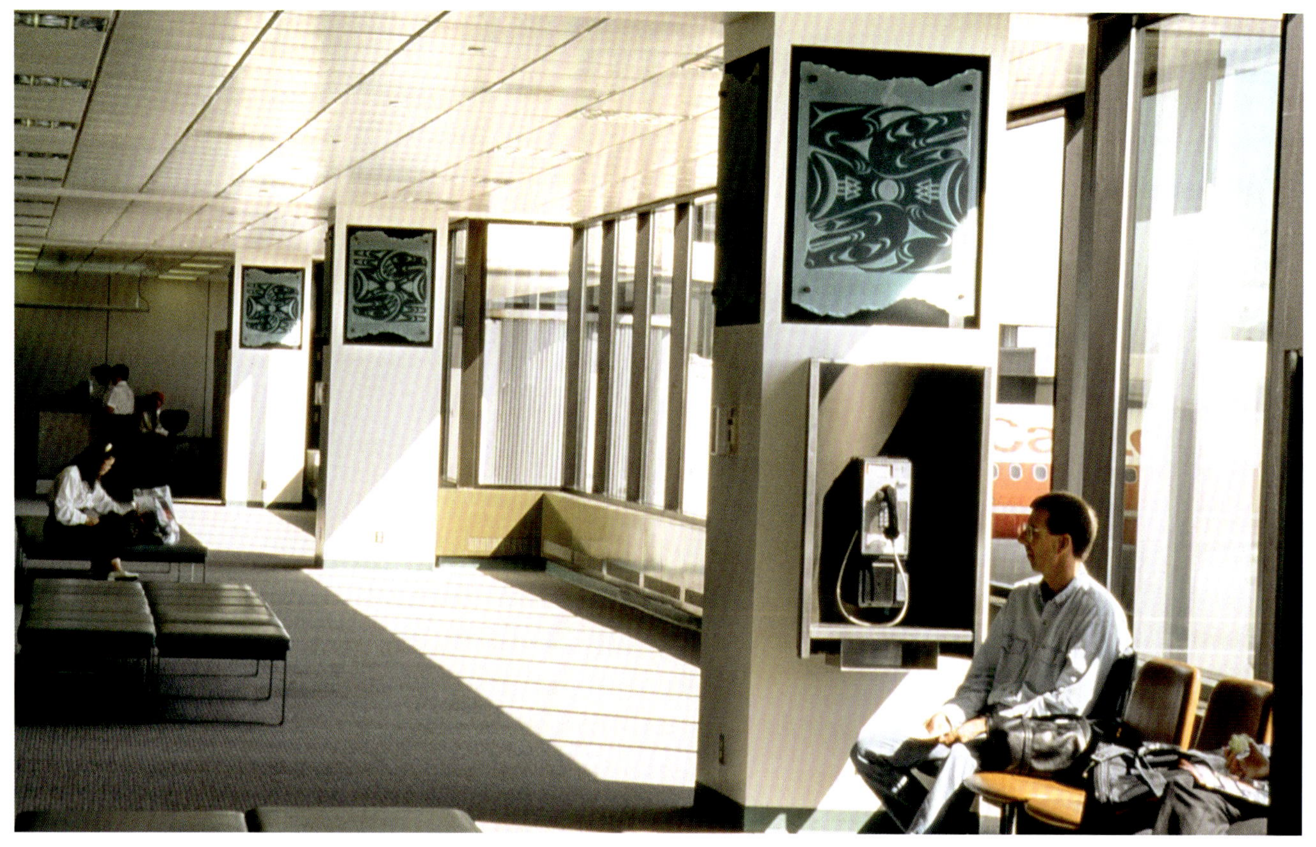

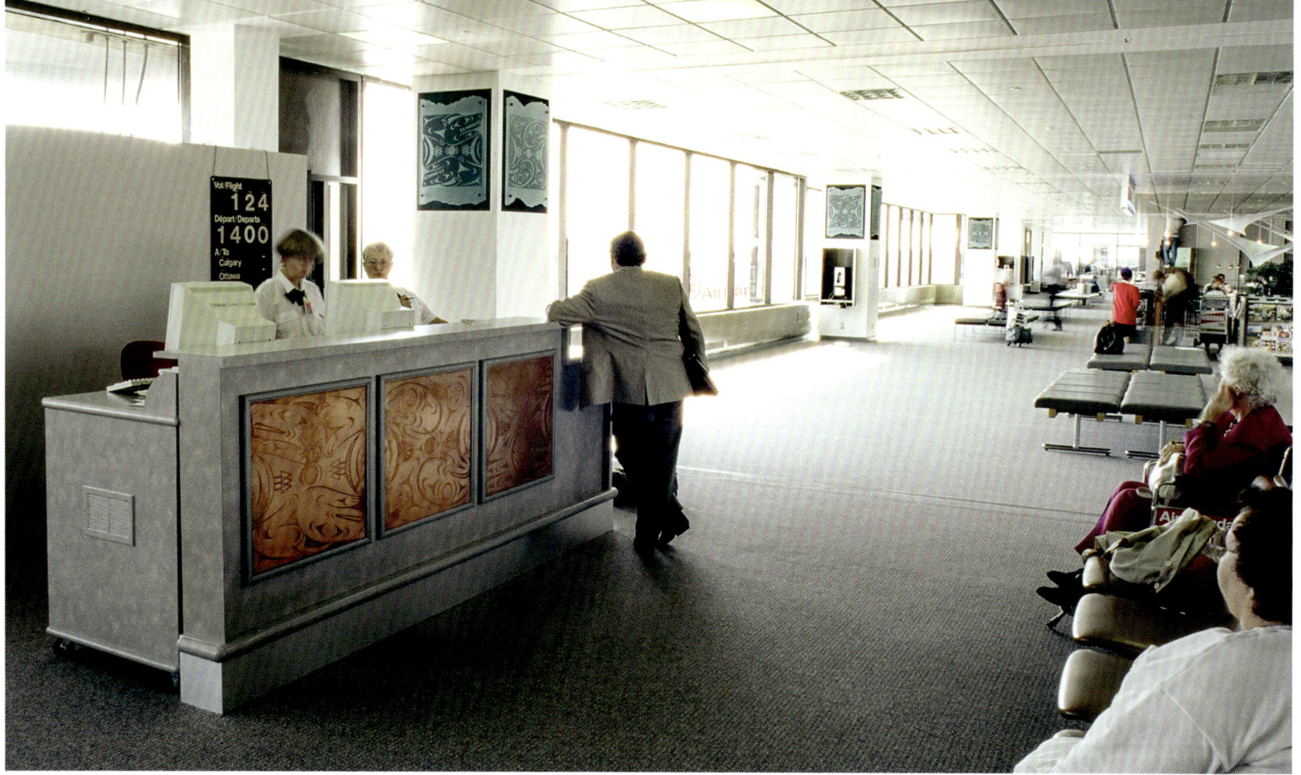
Vol/Flight
124
Départ/Departs
1400
A/To
Calgary
Ottawa

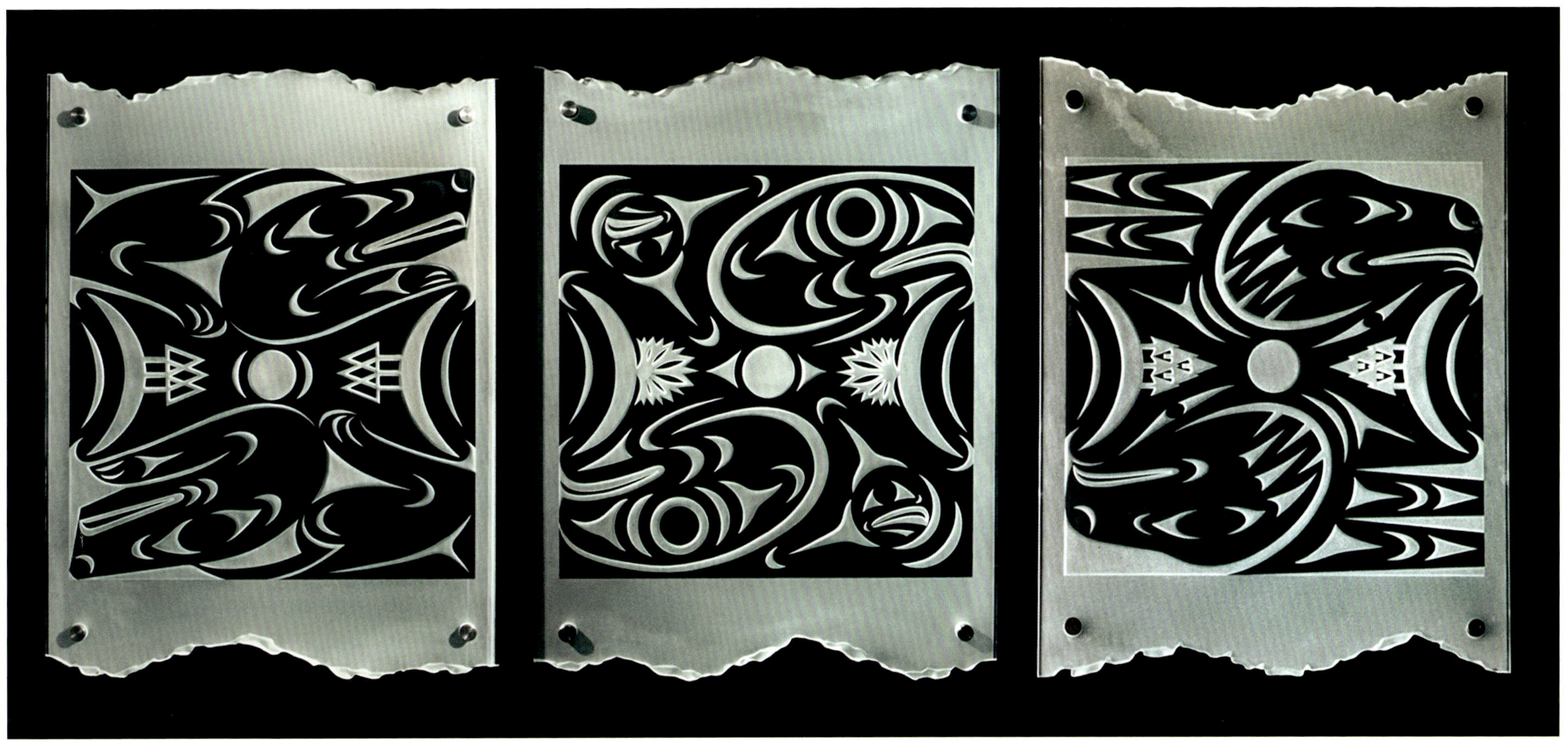

Land, Sea and Sky, 1993
Abrasive carved glass (above and top facing); copper (bottom facing)
114.3 × 68.6 cm (each panel)

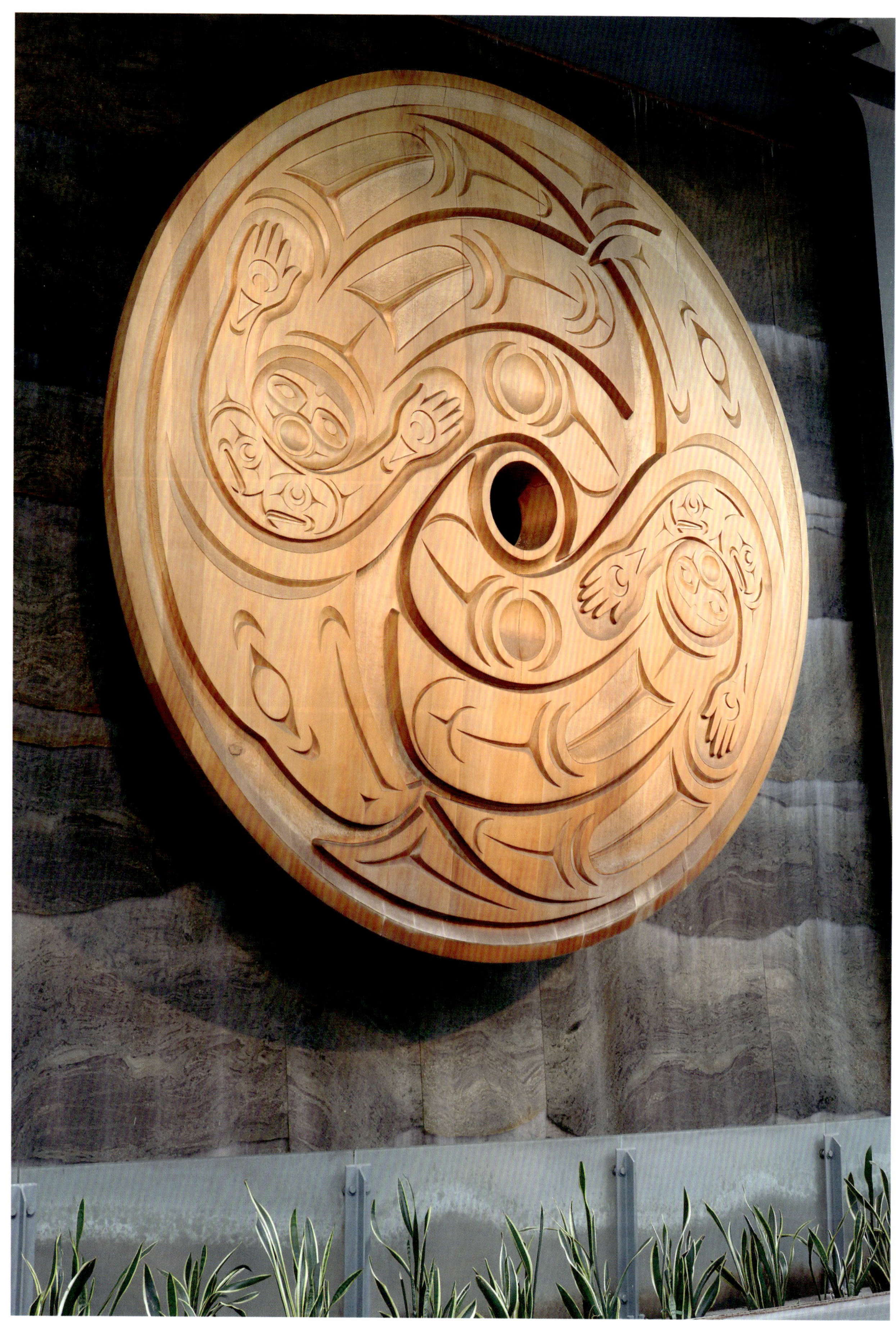

Flight, 1995
Carved and oiled western red cedar
4.8 m (diameter)

Flight

LOCATION: Vancouver International Airport
3211 Grant McConachie Way, sqʷsaθən (Sea Island), Richmond, BC

The Musqueam Welcome area in the international terminal is part of the airport's efforts to share a sense of the special character of this area of the world by showcasing the finest art from the various Indigenous Peoples of the Northwest Coast.

As international arrivals near Canada Customs they encounter the magnificent *Flight*, the largest spindle whorl in the world. The setting of *Flight*, framed by trees and in front of a waterfall representing the great Fraser River, adds to its striking impact. Many people stop to take a photo. They may not understand the traditions and meaning embedded in this art, but the beautiful wood, the superb carving, and the swirling, curving design are no less captivating. As Susan says, "I definitely set my Salish footprint!"[80]

Spindle whorls are among the most distinctive objects from traditional Coast Salish culture. Whorls in museum collections provide some of the best examples of Salish art forms, showing carved and engraved humans, fish, animals, birds, and on occasion abstract patterns, where the inspiration of the artist remains a mystery. As whorls were used by women, they are a perfect symbol of the special place of women in Salish culture, and of the weaving that is justly celebrated. Whorls have been at the centre of Susan's studies of historic Salish ʔeləw̓k̓ʷ (belongings), and at the heart of many of her compositions, in various mediums, her entire career.

The western red cedar that would become *Flight* was found in the Nimpkish Valley on Vancouver Island. After it was cut and kiln-dried in Duncan, the two halves that would form the whorl were laminated in Nanaimo and shipped to Susan's studio in Musqueam. The carving itself took just over a month, thanks to a collaborative effort in which Susan was assisted by her carving mentor John Livingston and her husband Jeff Cannell. It was physically demanding and creatively challenging to fill this grand circle of wood with meaning and exciting forms.

In her artist's statement, Susan said she felt it important

> that this design represent not only the flight theme relating to the airport, but... the human element as well....
>
> ...The contemporary style of representation in this spindle whorl image depicts two eagles, two human forms and salmon. The eagle, which is considered a symbol of power, is designed around the image of a man whose arms are raised welcoming visitors and also gesturing flight. Also, the upper torsos of the men represent the peoples of this area, namely the Coast Salish. On the chests of the men are salmon motifs, which represent the fact that the Coast Salish peoples, still today, live and fish along the shores of the Fraser River; salmon being a substance of life and a symbol of wealth.[81]

It had long been Susan's goal to create a large-scale spindle whorl, and with *Flight*, her vision was marvellously realized. She personally dedicated the artwork to her friend and one of her earliest champions, Potlatch Arts owner Bud Mintz.

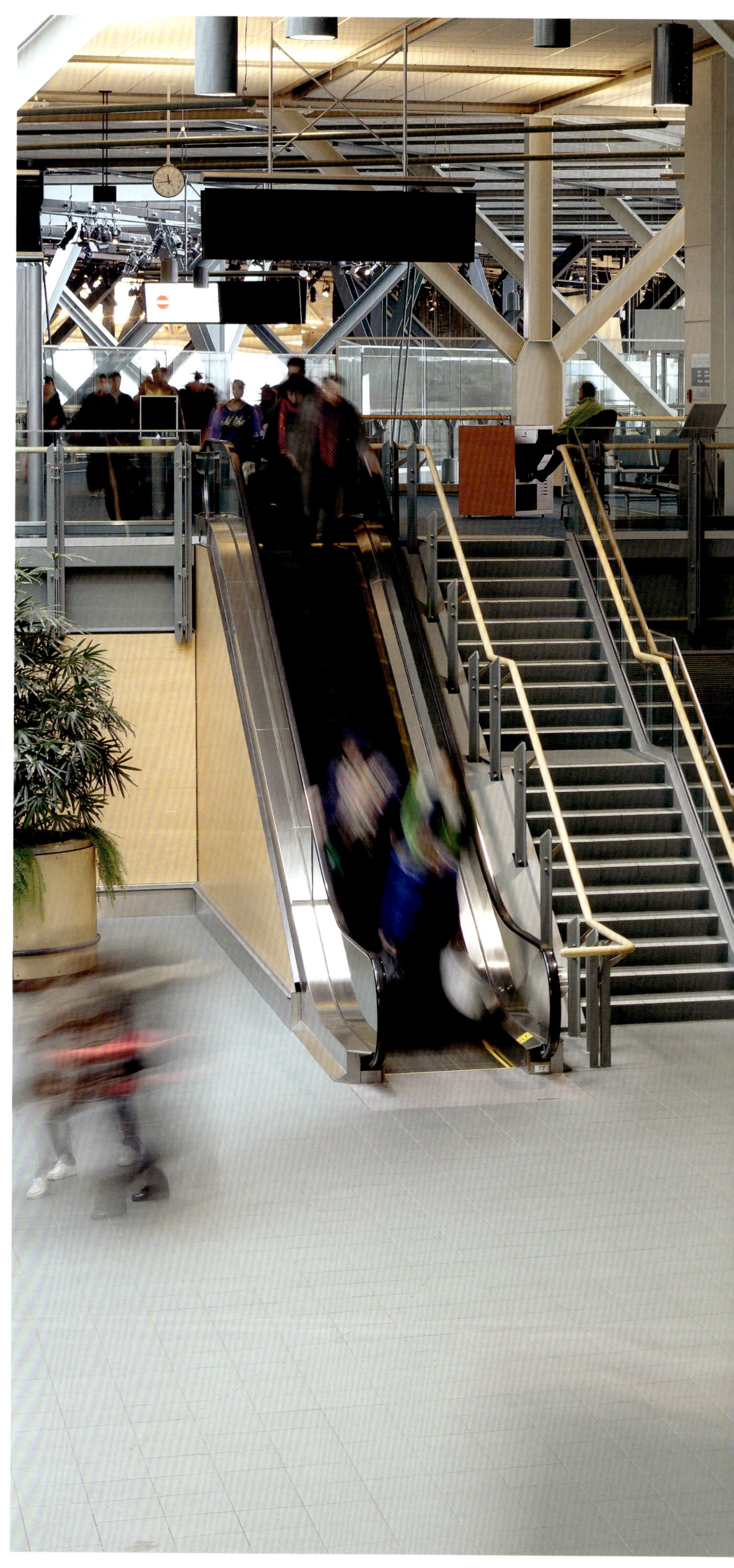

Flight, 1995

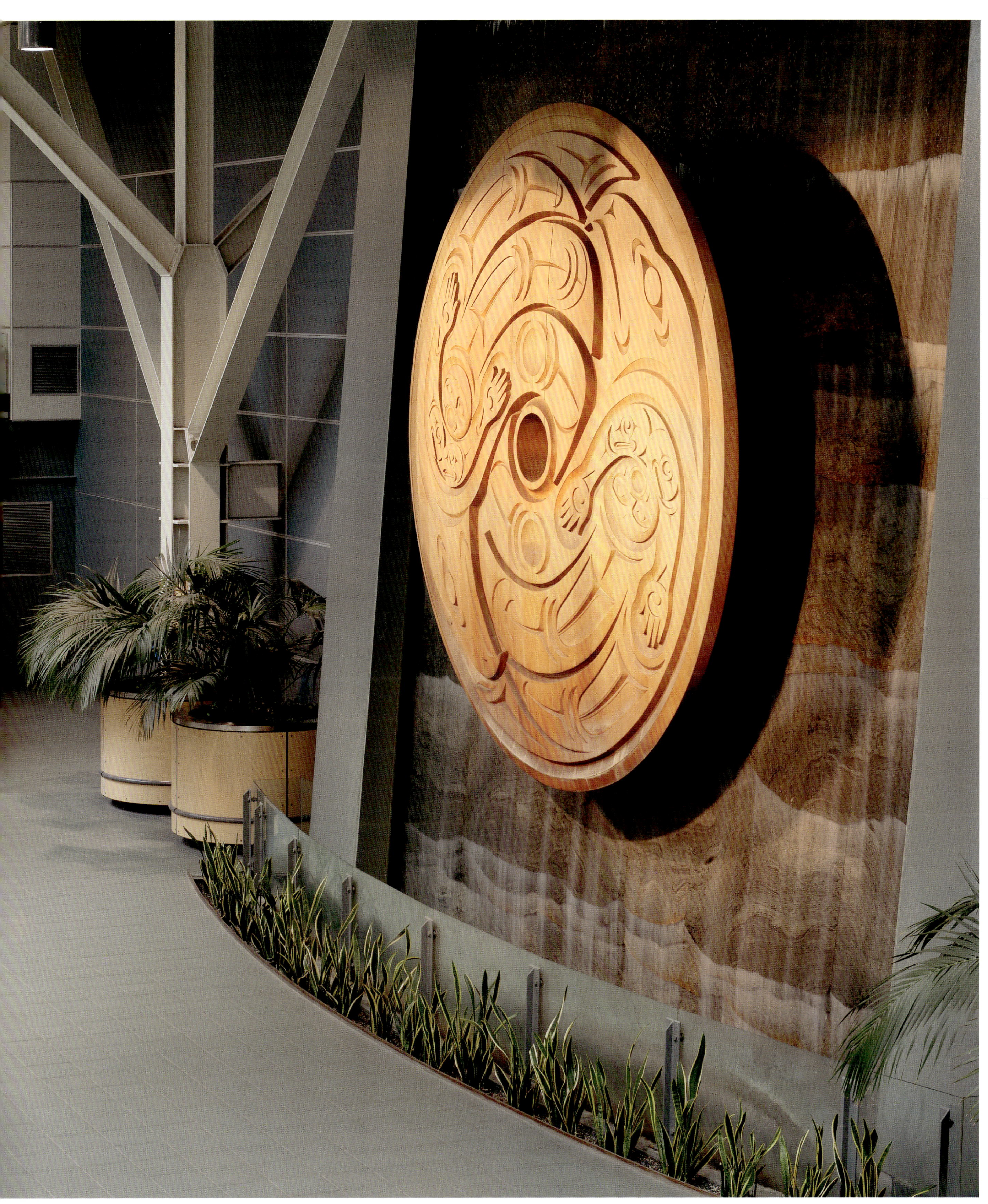

Musqueam Welcome Figures, 1996
Carved and oiled western red cedar, glass
5.2 × 1.3 × .2 m (each)

Musqueam Welcome Figures

LOCATION: Vancouver International Airport
3211 Grant McConachie Way, sqʷsaθən (Sea Island), Richmond, BC

Across from *Flight* are escalators and stairs that descend into the main level of the customs hall, where travellers are welcomed by *Musqueam Welcome Figures*, two traditional Coast Salish–style houseposts. On the left is a female figure and on the right a male, both deeply carved from one red cedar log. The high-status Salish woman wears a traditional blanket-style front with carved buttons down the middle and across her shoulders. The blanket is decorated with four fishers, an important figure with cleansing powers in traditional Coast Salish culture, often seen on historic carvings in museum collections. The woman wears a traditional hat and a dignified and formal facial expression.

Beside her, the male bears a similar expression. Susan describes the male figure in a letter to an airport official in 1997:

> This male housepost was inspired by the traditional Coast Salish style houseposts; many of which are housed in the Royal B.C. Museum. It is 17′ × 48″ and carved out of red cedar. It is the "mate" to the female housepost and is also the "other half" of the log from which she was carved. . . .This housepost represents a high status Coast Salish male depicted with a traditional blanket style front; buttons running down the front and across his shoulders which are represented by the use of Salish crescents. Two contemporary style eagles similar to that on the 16 foot spindle whorl and also representing "flight" decorate the front of his blanket; the eagle being a symbol of power. A circular motif depicting a legendary two headed serpent also decorates the front of the blanket. The large circular motif on his hat represents the sun and is enhanced with Salish elements on either side.[82]

In Salish longhouses, houseposts were not carved in the round, as they would have been set against a wall. These two are freestanding, so Susan decorated the back panels as well.

> Each of these panels has been carved with sand to make them look ancient creating a sharp contrast between the slick contemporary polished look of the new International Terminal Building. On both panels, the human figures from the spindle whorl have been used, one depicting a male the other a female. These figures with their arms raised in a welcome fashion, represent the native peoples of this area, namely the Coast Salish. On the chests of these figures are salmon motifs which represent the fact that the Coast Salish peoples, still today, live and fish along the shores of the Fraser River . . . on the bottoms of the panels, the flying geese pattern from the weavings has been incorporated; these motifs representing the flight theme.
>
> On the top of the left panel the circular motifs symbolize the stars, the moon and the sun, and on the right panel, the figures symbolize the sun carrying two valises of valuables—both these images are from traditional Coast Salish houseposts in the region.
>
> 7 feet from the floor, on each panel, is a 42″ diameter carved glass eagle head; these eagles again representing the flight theme. When one stands back from these panels, the carved glass eagle heads flanking the spindle whorl on the back wall again emulates the traditional Coast Salish motif found on the top left panel; the stars, the moon and the sun.[83]

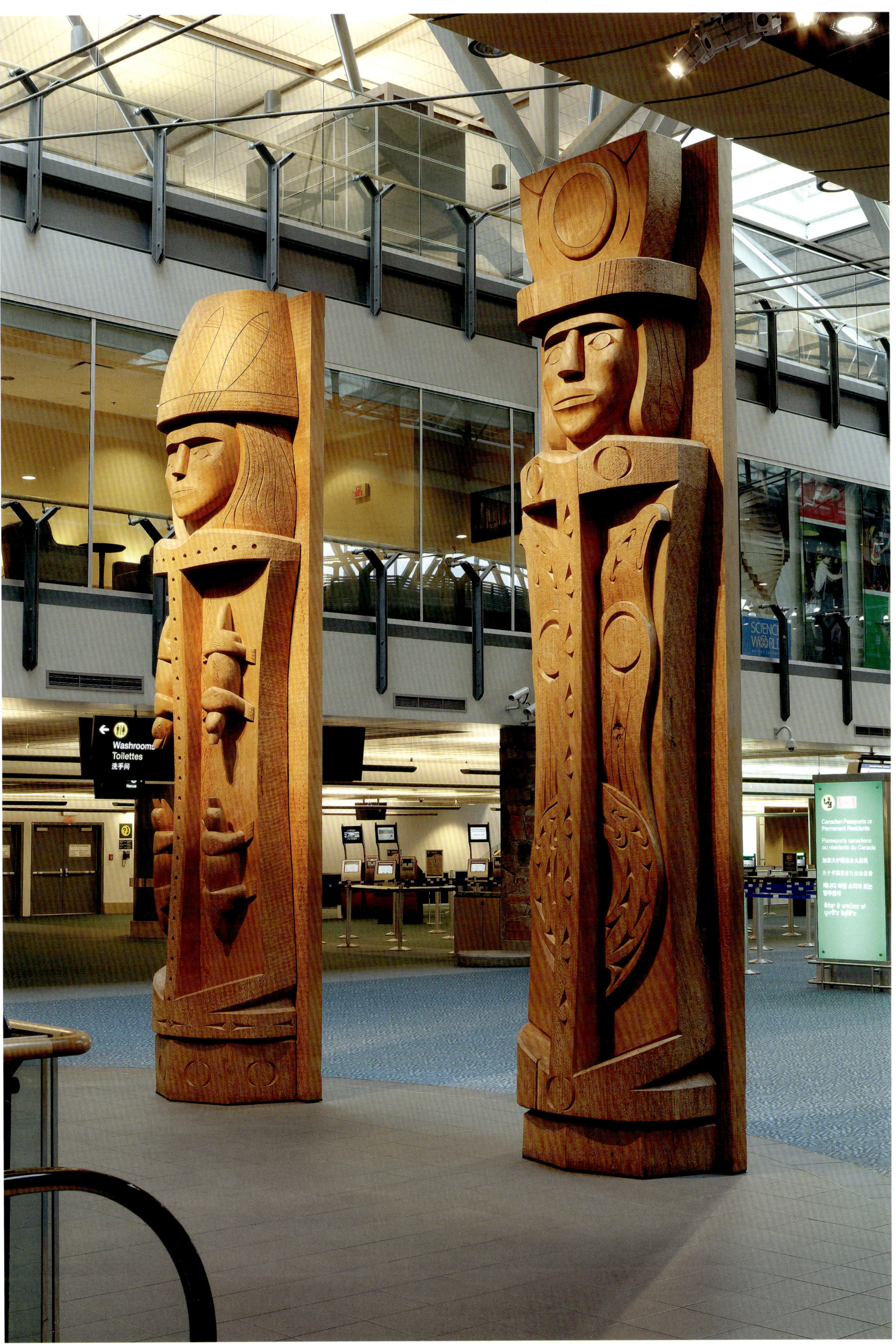
Washrooms
Toilettes
Canadian Passports or
Permanent Residents
Passeports canadiens
ou résidents du Canada

A detail from the female *Musqueam Welcome Figure*.

Facing: From the Musqueam Welcome Area, the carved glass eagle heads on the back of the *Welcome Figures* frame a view of *Flight* (1995), visible at the top of the stairs.

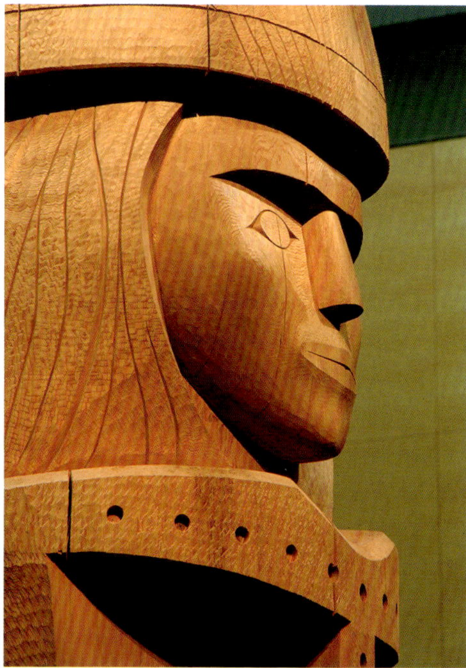

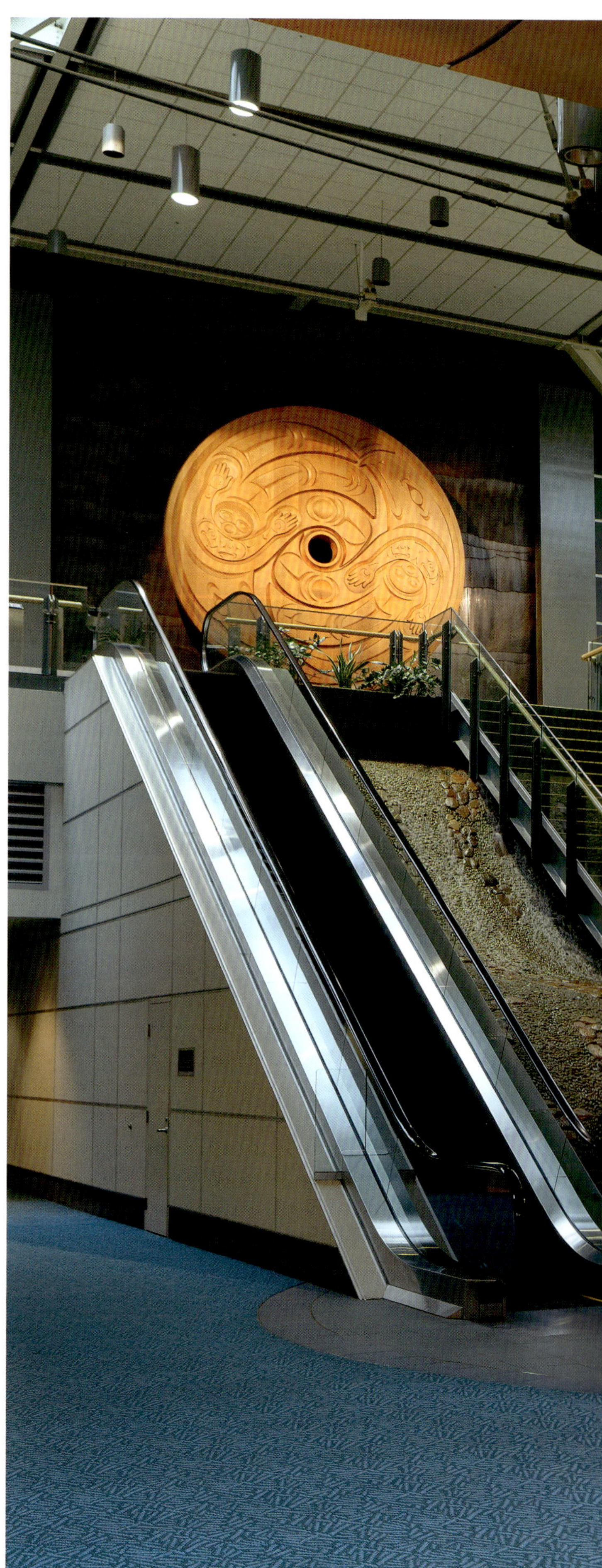

From the whorl and the welcome figures it became clear to many that Susan was able to breathe new life into Salish forms and interpret them on a scale and in a manner that is truly memorable. In her hands and from her mind, the traditional art of her people has been reborn.

At the official opening of the Musqueam Welcome Area on 20 April 1996, Susan recognized that the art of her people was being given a new prominence.

> It is always nice to see art of any kind incorporated into public places and YVR should be commended for their commitment in making this airport unique with its Northwest Coast atmosphere. Most particularly, I am pleased that YVR has shown respect to the aboriginal Coast Salish peoples of this area by having Salish art incorporated into their project; and I am honoured that I was able to contribute on behalf of my people.
>
> Although Salish Art was almost a lost art form after European Contact, today it is becoming better known. Much of the native art you see around Vancouver today is from Northern B.C. It was because of this that I, over the past 16/17 years, devoted my time, as a Coast Salish artist, to its Renaissance.[84]

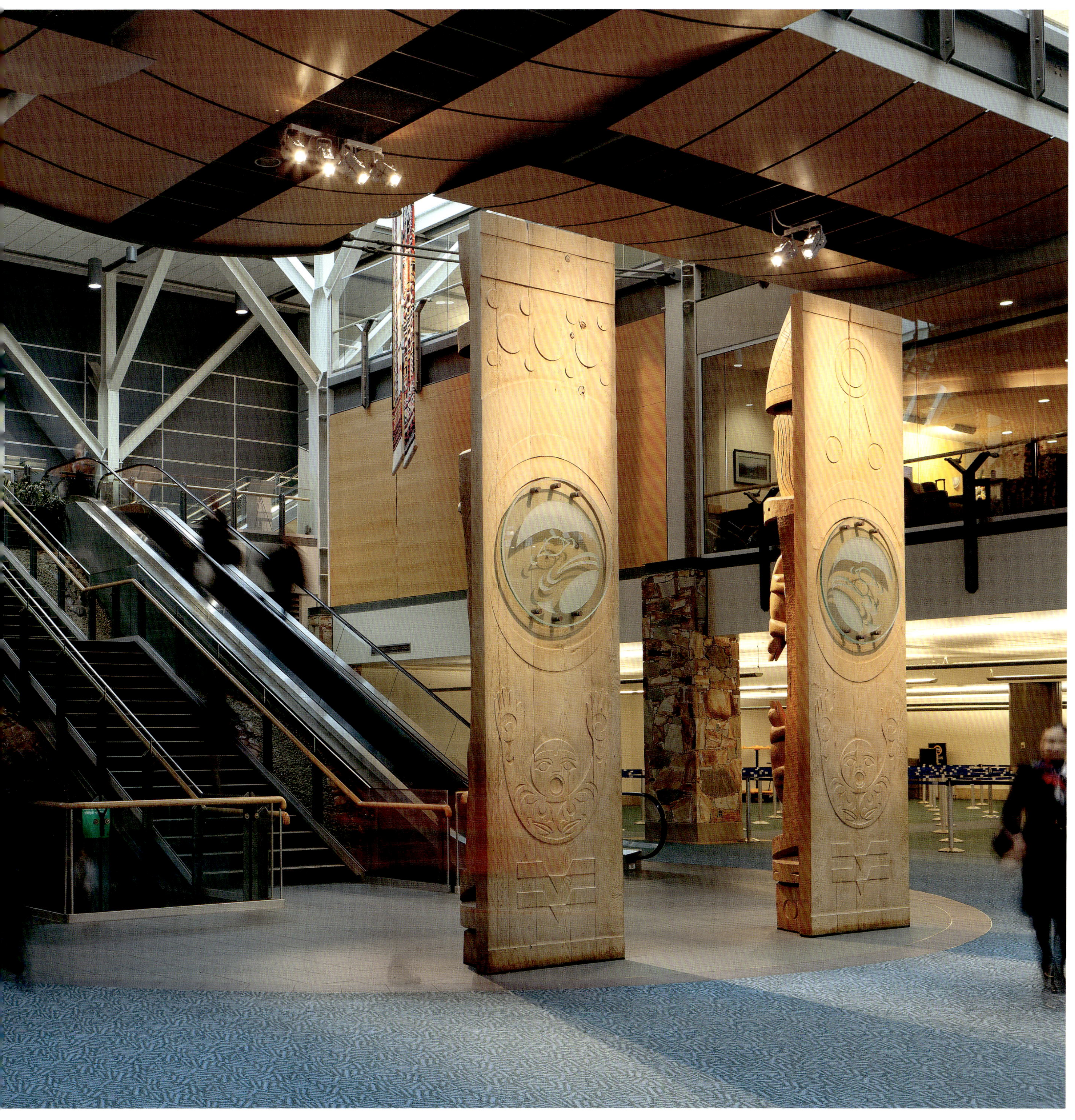

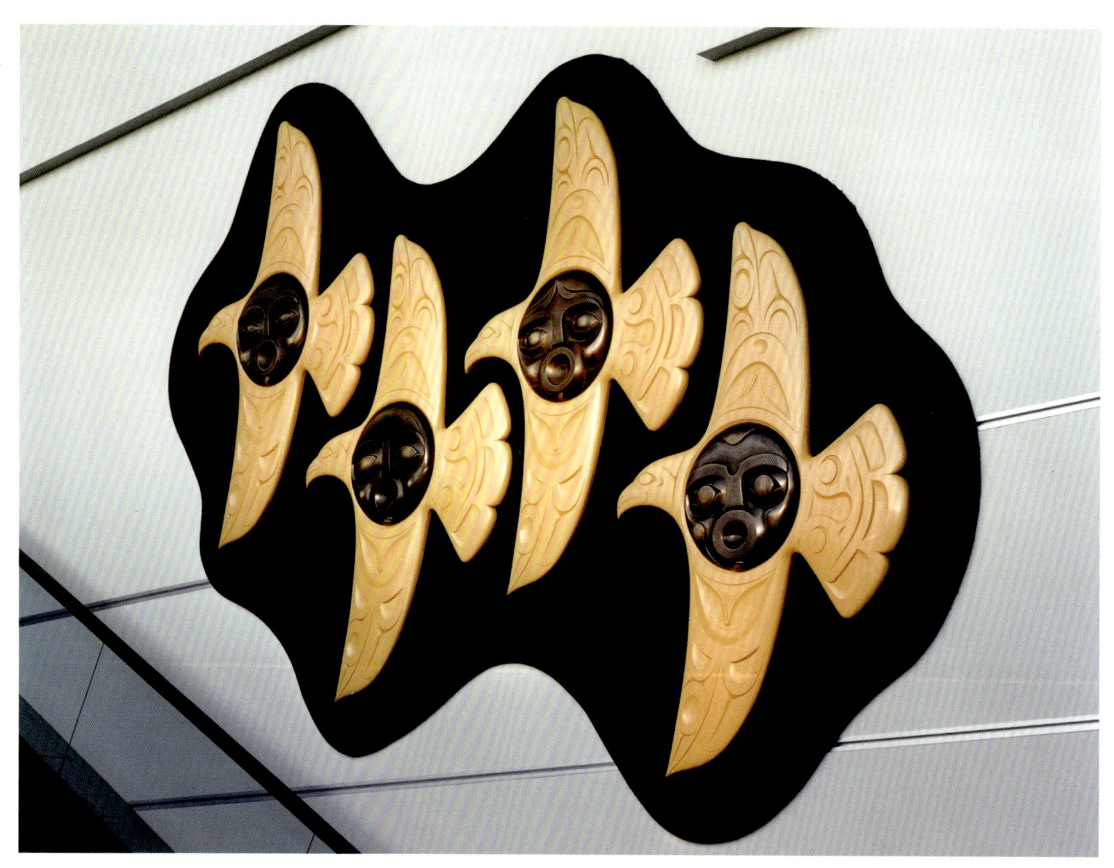

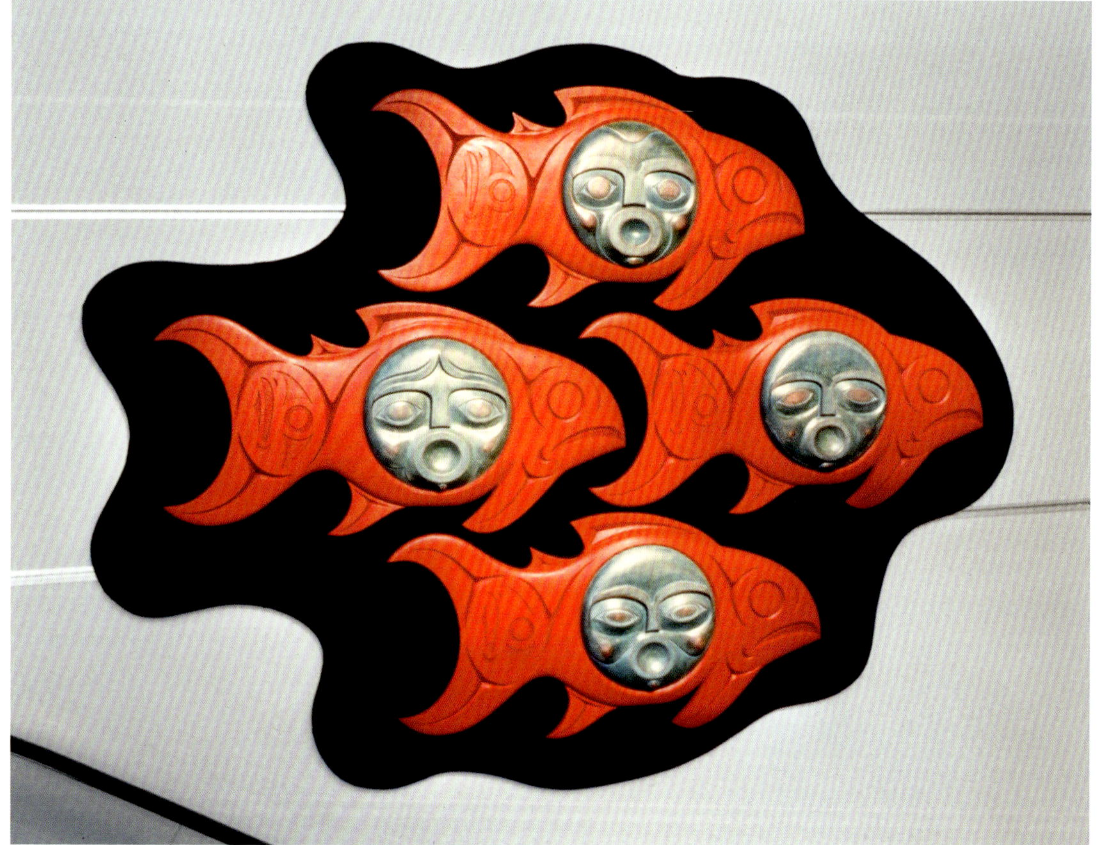

Arrival, 1998
Forton
3.1 × 4.3 m

Salmon People, 1998
Forton
2.9 × 2.3 m

Arrival *and* Salmon People

LOCATION: Vancouver International Airport
3211 Grant McConachie Way, sqʷsaθən (Sea Island), Richmond, BC

In an August 1997 proposal for two new artworks for the arrivals area of the international terminal, Susan remarked that "I feel either of these proposals will enhance this area and add to the excitement of the traveller's journey. I have tried using my traditional Salish design elements to integrate my style with the global culture of the 21st century."[85] She chose familiar themes for these works: flight and salmon.

She carved both works in laminated red cedar. She then had them rubber moulded, cast in plaster to eliminate distortion of the design, then produced in Forton. Susan came to favour this polymer when she wished to have multiples of one original carving, or when she wanted to vary the treatment for colour and surface finish. In the years that followed, Susan worked with a number of other artists on the production of the casts of her work, notably Rosa Quintana and her husband Michael Edwards, whose studio is in Agassiz in the upper Fraser Valley.

Salmon People depicts four identically shaped salmon bodies, but two of the fish contain a male human face, and two a female. Their mouths are open wide, a sign of the importance of Oral Traditions for sharing knowledge between the generations. The human faces symbolize the human spirit living within the fish, as explained by the legend of the salmon people, which is outlined in the plaque accompanying the work: salmon people live in undersea villages and every spring they change into salmon form and set out on a journey across the ocean to the rivers of their birth. An eagle head appears in the tail of each fish. The deep orange of the salmon and the green of the faces are examples of Susan's ongoing experiments with strong colours.

The four eagles of *Arrival* appear to be "flying" alongside people riding up the escalator. As with the salmon, the body of each bird is made from a human face, two women and two men, mouths open, again evoking the idea of the human spirit in these creatures and the interconnectedness of life forms. Crescents and wedges fill every space on the bird's body. As with the salmon, the contrast of the bright bodies to the grey faces highlights the separate spirits of the animals and humans without losing the central idea—that these beings are connected in a larger world.

Salmon People and *Arrival* are a colourful introduction to Salish aesthetics and culture. They certainly achieve an important objective shared by Susan and the airport authorities—they offer a distinctly Salish welcome to travellers.

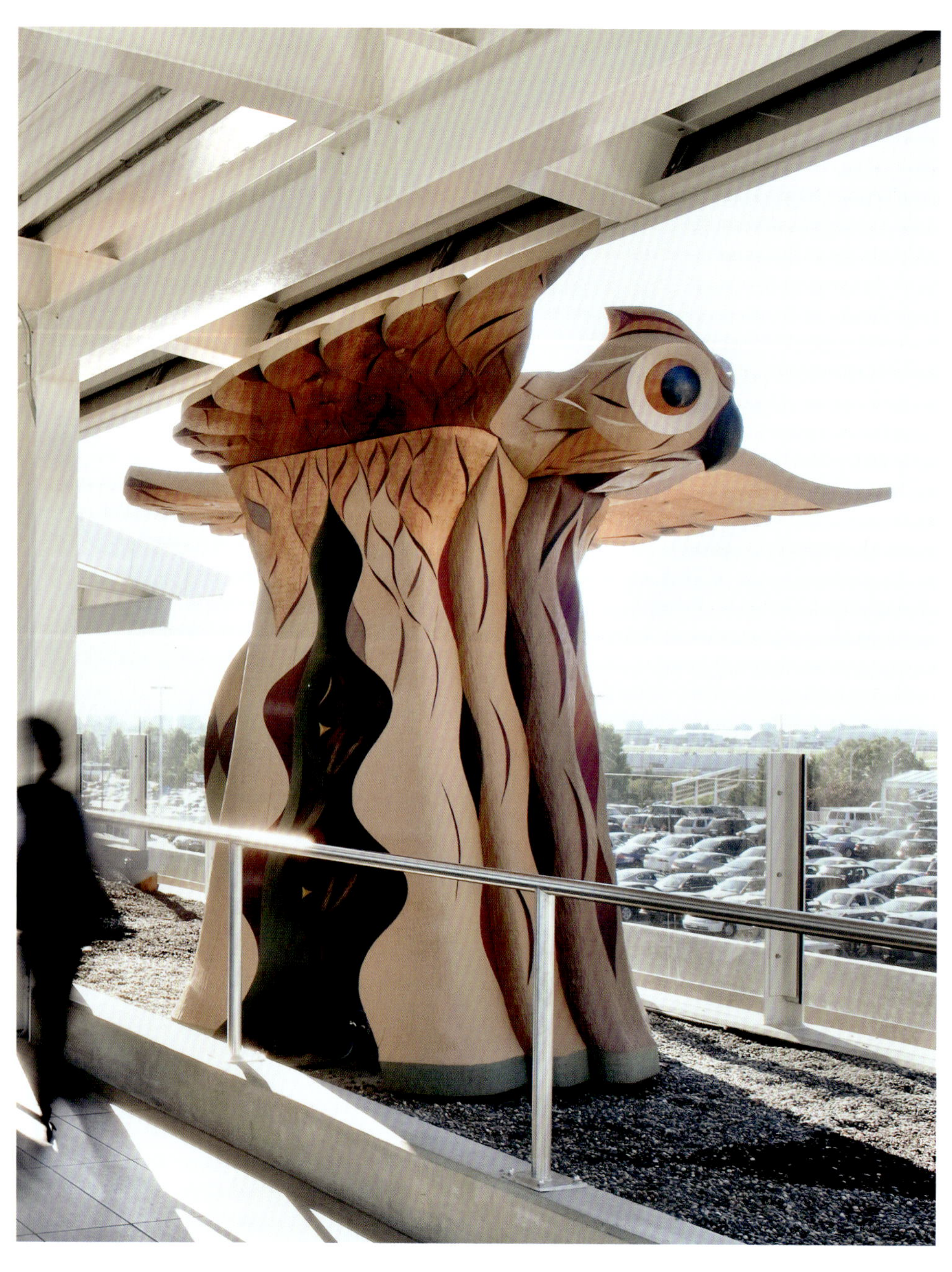

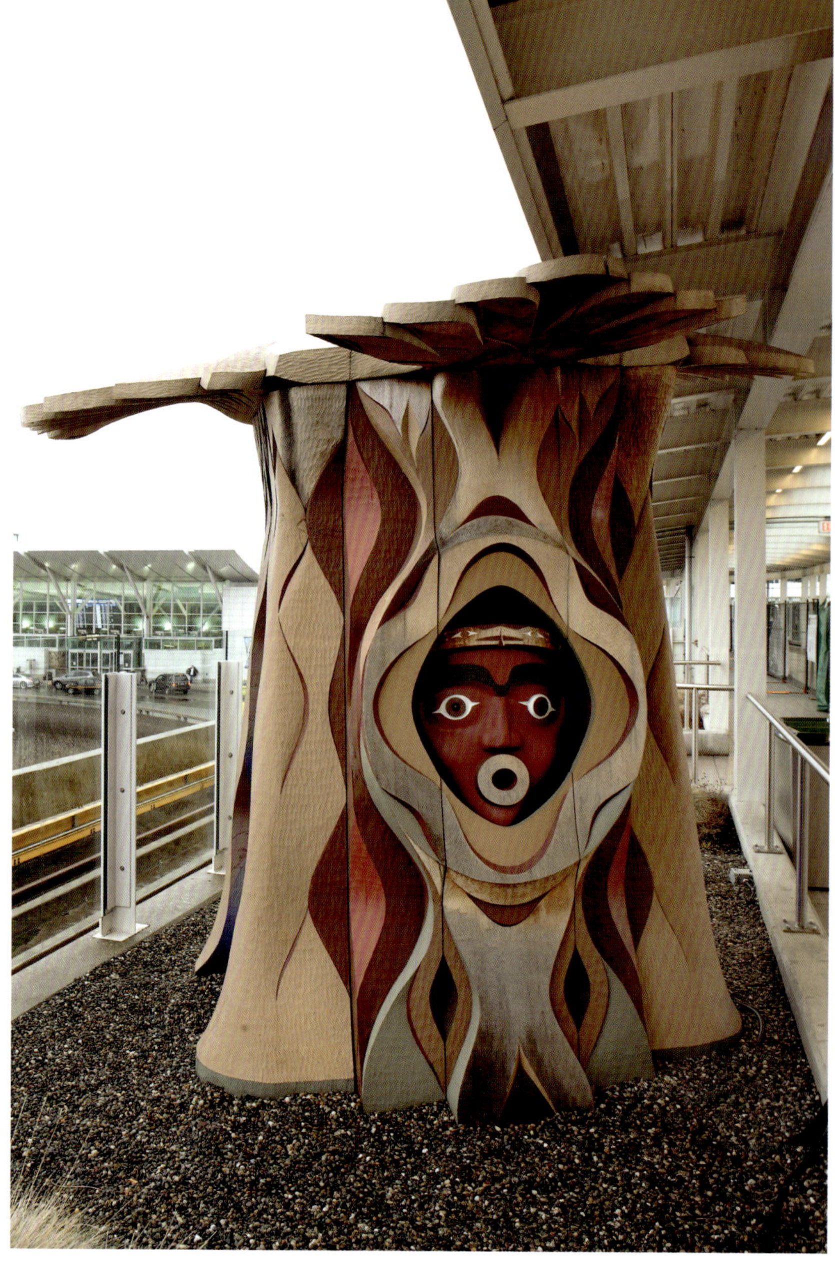

Cedar Connection, 2009
Carved and painted western red cedar
3.35 × 3.04 × 3.04 m

Cedar Connection

LOCATION: Vancouver International Airport
3211 Grant McConachie Way, sqʷsaθən (Sea Island),
Richmond, BC

The most recent and accessible of Susan's works at the airport is located alongside the walkway that connects the terminus station of the Canada Line to the domestic arrivals building. *Cedar Connection*, the result of a competition held in 2008, is a fresh exploration of the theme of flight, and the only Susan Point work at YVR that is not behind a security checkpoint. Even if you are not taking a flight it is worth a train ride to take a good look at this complex carving.

Susan and her helpers carved the sculpture from fourteen pieces of western red cedar laminated into a large block. It includes a powerful rendering of an owl in flight and a human face with an open mouth, peering out from the trunk of an old-growth cedar, the "tree of life." It is a gesture of welcome, but also represents the way the land looked before modern settlement. Shaping the artwork around the image of a stump evokes the cycle of life; cedars grow to great heights before falling to the earth and decaying, providing nutrients for the next generation of trees.

Each main part of the composition carries a particular theme. The human face refers to the Oral Traditions of the Musqueam and other Salish people, the central method for transmission of knowledge and understanding. It is also intended to honour Susan's late uncle, Dominic Point, a master storyteller and Elder from whom she learned so much about Salish life and legends, especially early in her art career. Susan opened up the piece through the centre and designed a series of wave shapes that move through the whole composition, representing the waters of the Fraser and nearby streams. The owl, which soars away from the upper portion of the stump, is a keeper of wisdom in traditional Salish beliefs. It can also be seen here as a delightful symbol of the modern activity of the buildings toward which the sculpture is a guidepost.

In correspondence with airport officials, Susan summarized the intentions behind her work.

> My people are children of this Land. The land has shaped our beliefs and our history. The cycles of our rain forest, river, sea and ancestors complete the circle. We are people of Strong tradition... a Tradition of respecting our homeland and our visitors. We are people of Oral tradition. Our stories go back before the Great Flood. Under the watchful eye and protection of the Thunderbird, our people thrive today. We continue our unique Salish legacy with song, dance and story. We will always continue to shape our future; we are Musqueam.[86]

As jets take off and land just south of Musqueam, Susan's art links past, present, and future. *Cedar Connection* is a stunning creation in which she takes full advantage of her understanding of Salish aesthetics and stories, which she has developed over many years, to send a complex message about stewardship of the land, cycles of life, respect for šxʷtəhim̓ (traditional teachings and customs), and moving forward, like the owl in flight.

Part Two

From shíshálh to Semiahmoo

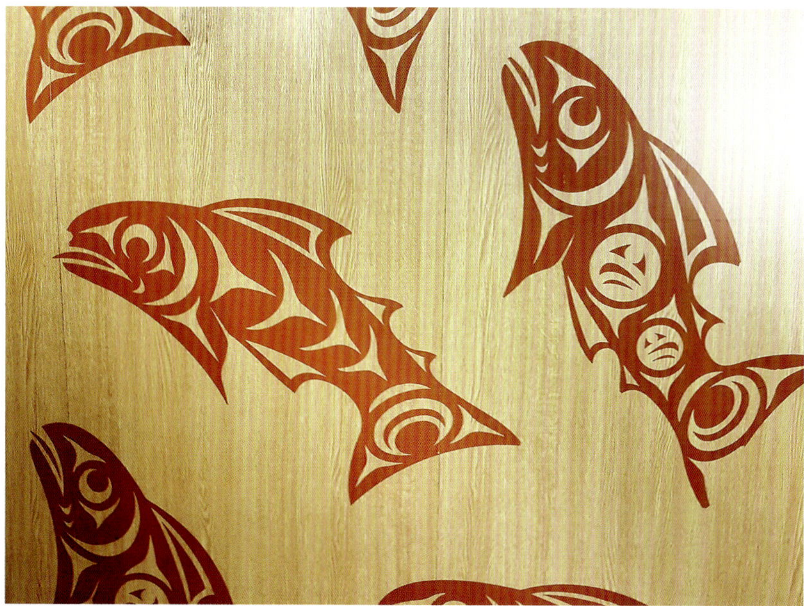

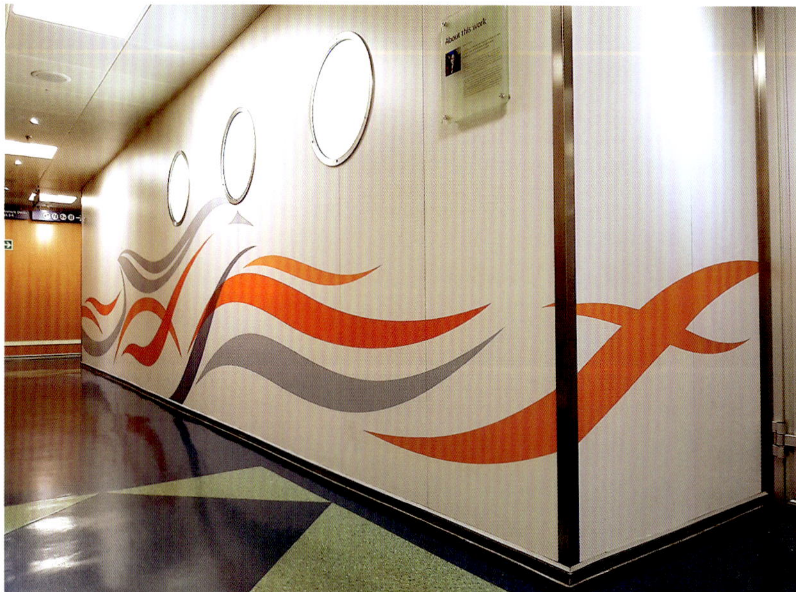

Salmon Life Cycle, 2003
Adhesive plastic and engraved glass
64 × 76 cm (salmon, each); various (wave motif)

Salmon Life Cycle

LOCATION: BC Ferries vessels
Salish Sea, BC

Every day, thousands of residents and visitors who cross the Salish Sea on BC Ferries routes between the mainland and Vancouver Island have a chance to enjoy art by Susan Point. Depending on which vessel you are travelling on (her works are on *Coastal Celebration*, *Coastal Inspiration*, *Coastal Renaissance*, *Spirit of British Columbia*, *Spirit of Vancouver Island*, and *Queen of New Westminster*), her lively stencilled sce:łtən (salmon), drawn using classic Salish motifs, can be found at the Pacific Buffet or the Seawest Lounge. Her art also includes sweeping and brightly coloured curves that recall the sea over which the ship carries you.

A placard identifies the work and includes a statement by Susan about the importance of salmon to Coast Salish Peoples, and the goals of her art.

> Over the years I have spent a great deal of my time, as a Coast Salish artist, trying to revive traditional Coast Salish art in an attempt to educate the public, to the fact that there was, and still is another art form indigenous to the central Pacific Northwest Coast. In creating my art, I feel a need to continually express my cultural background and beliefs, yet at the same time my work continues to evolve with changes within and outside my community.

Every day these ships sail waters that are home to the salmon who remain, for both First Nations and other inhabitants of this territory, an important source of food and wealth. As with all her art, Susan interprets the salmon life cycle in Salish terms, and once more establishes a legacy of Salishness—this time, on powerful vessels that now ply the routes once traversed by the canoes of her ancestors.

SHÍSHÁLH (SECHELT) FIRST NATION

A short ferry ride west from West Vancouver is the Sunshine Coast and the town of Sechelt, known as shíshálh in the local Coast Salish dialect of she shashishalhem, and sxəxeʔɬ in həndəminəm. The Sechelt First Nation's government, education, and cultural centre is home to four of Susan's earliest public artworks, including the facade of the House of héwhíwus (House of Chiefs), her first experiment with a large-scale exterior, and three works for the Raven's Cry Theatre. Completed near the end of the first decade of her career, the four works illustrate her developing ability to work across mediums using a variety of techniques.

Spawning Salmon

LOCATION: shíshálh First Nation, House of héwhíwus, 5555 Sunshine Coast Highway, shíshálh (sxəxeʔɬ; Sechelt), BC

The Dominion Company commissioned Susan on behalf of the Sechelt First Nation to create a design to cover approximately ten thousand square feet on several sides of the facade of the newly built complex, resulting in one of her most widely admired and successful works. As Susan describes it,

> the challenge in this project, due to a limited budget, was to create an entire wall mural using only two grids (65 × 65"). This was accomplished by using the theme "Salmon Run" where the inter-connecting squares of salmon designs bled off each grid but leaving parts showing on the adjacent grid (i.e. fins, tail and nose) thus creating a large flowing image of a male and female salmon swimming upstream to spawn. The original patterns were fabricated from wood and then rubber moulds were taken from each and castings were made from reinforced concrete. The walls were then formed on the castings and then tilted up to incorporate the design as part of the overall wall structure itself. This entailed working very closely with the Dominion Company's design consultants.[1]

The collaboration produced a lively, rhythmic mural that dramatically highlights the Salish-style spawning salmon motif. Although the concrete casts are painted a uniform white, Susan designed the original grids deep enough to add dimensional interest to the moving fish. The repeating grid design works equally well across the vast planes and at the corners, so that the impact is felt from every vantage.

The composition celebrates a deeply important story from the traditional life of the Sechelt First Nation. It was fortuitous that, as Susan entered the second decade of her life as an artist, she was able to experiment on this scale for a Salish First Nation, and prove on her first attempt the success of grid compositions cast from wood carvings.

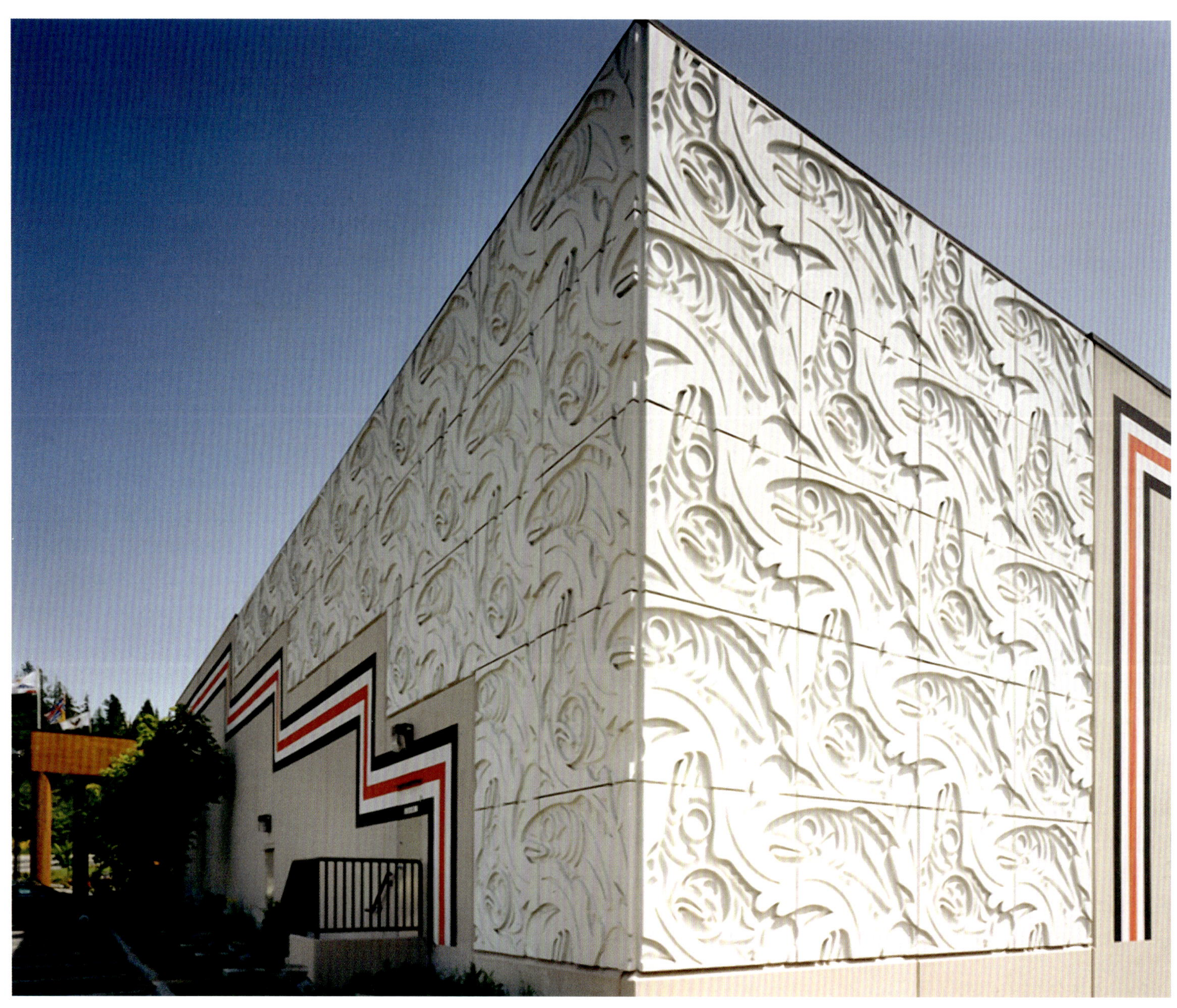

Spawning Salmon, 1991
Cast concrete
929 sq. m

Two Headed Eagle, 1991
Cast concrete
1.6 × 3.35 m (each)

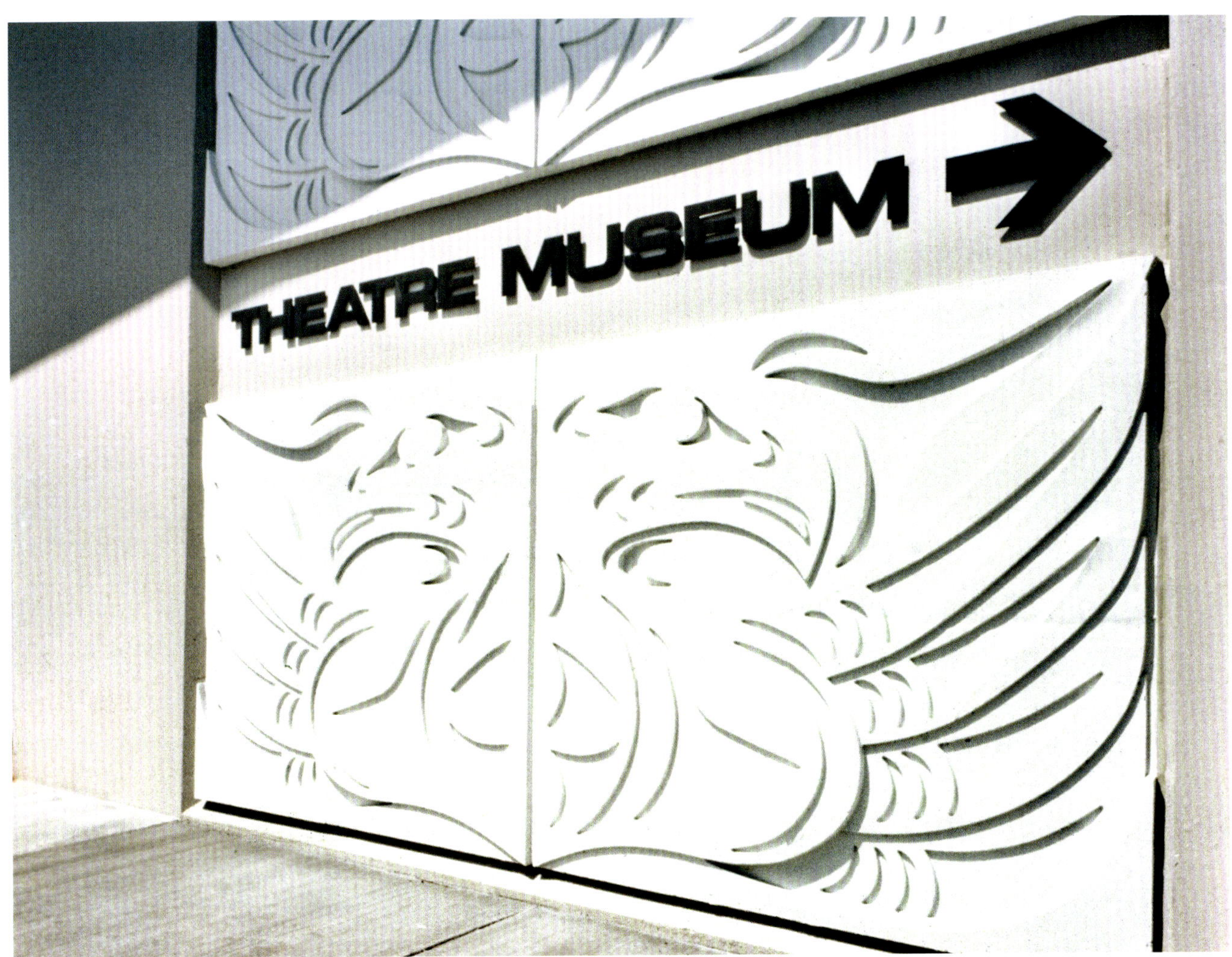

Two Headed Eagle

LOCATION: shíshálh (Sechelt) First Nation, Raven's Cry Theatre
5555 Sunshine Coast Highway, Sechelt, BC

One of the most important components of the House of héwhíwus is the Raven's Cry Theatre, which shows movies, live performances, and concerts. The Sechelt First Nation commissioned three pieces from Susan for the lobby. *Two Headed Eagle*, the painting seen in the lower right of the right-hand photo on page 121, is based on the low-relief casts pictured here, which are mounted near the entrances to the theatre and the tems swiya Museum.

The styling of the bird has very traditional roots. Susan would have seen many examples of bird heads treated in this simple, powerful way—but this is very much her own interpretation. The eagle is composed of the smallest number of parts needed to define its spirit and purpose, including wedges and crescents that highlight the body. The upward position of each wing implies flight or soaring. This double-headed eagle is a powerful guardian spirit, and looks as though it could call out to you at any moment.

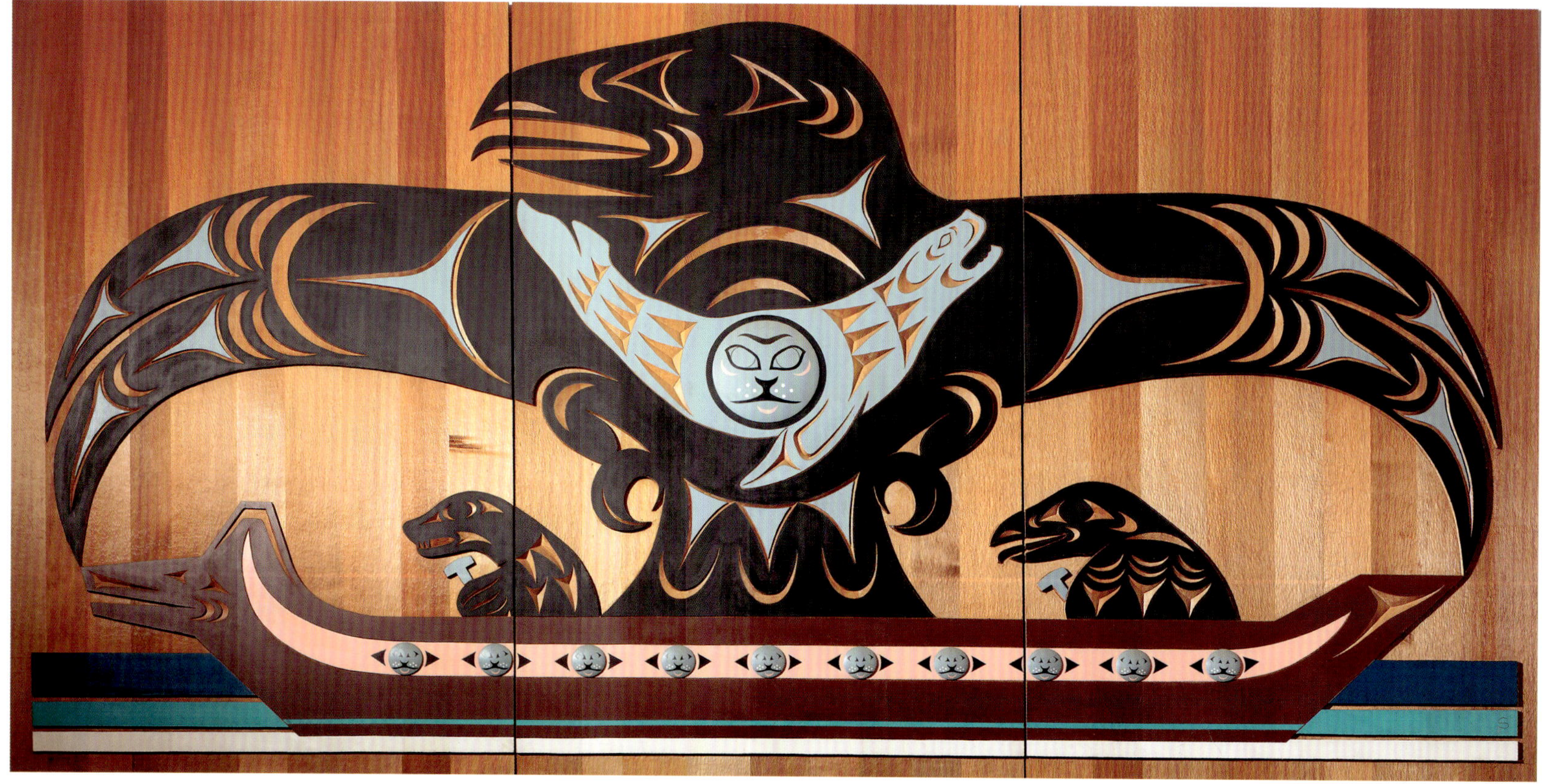

The Seal and the Raven, 1991
Carved and painted western red cedar
2.29 × 4.27 m

The Seal and the Raven

LOCATION: shíshálh (Sechelt) First Nation, Raven's Cry Theatre
5555 Sunshine Coast Highway, Sechelt, BC

For her largest and most complex design at the theatre, Susan was asked to illustrate a local Coast Salish syəθ (Traditional Story) about an interaction between ravens and a ʔešxʷ (seal). She prepared a large panel of laminated red cedar and carved the figures in low relief.

The central figure is a raven rising from a canoe paddled by a seal (on the left) and another raven. On the large raven's chest is a swimming seal, and on the seal's chest is another seal, facing the viewer. Susan's continual exploration with colour is evident in the light blue that is used for the seal and other elements, the pink band across the canoe (which is decorated with baby seal faces), and the white, turquoise, and dark-blue stripes of the sea. The Salish elements of wedges, crescents, and U-forms—which Susan had been researching, studying, and adapting for ten years by this time—are a vital part of the central raven and seal, serving to define wings, muscles, and other parts of the creatures' bodies and emphasize the Salish roots of both the story and the design. Susan had been carving in wood for only a year, but her growing enthusiasm and talent for the medium are already clear in the strong outlines and carefully rendered detail of the work.

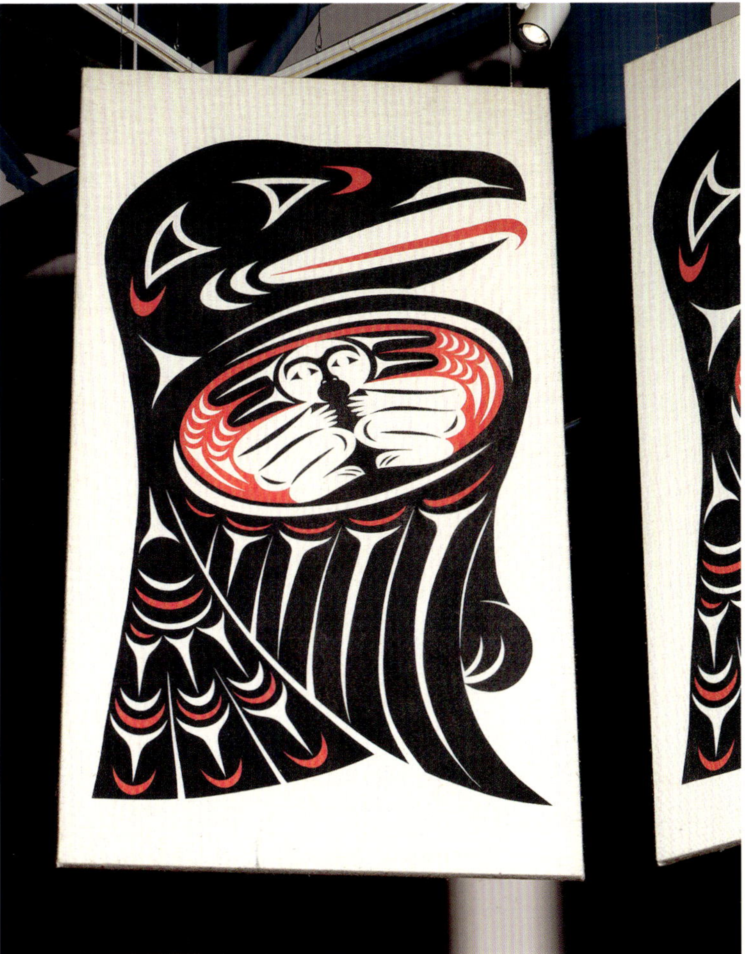

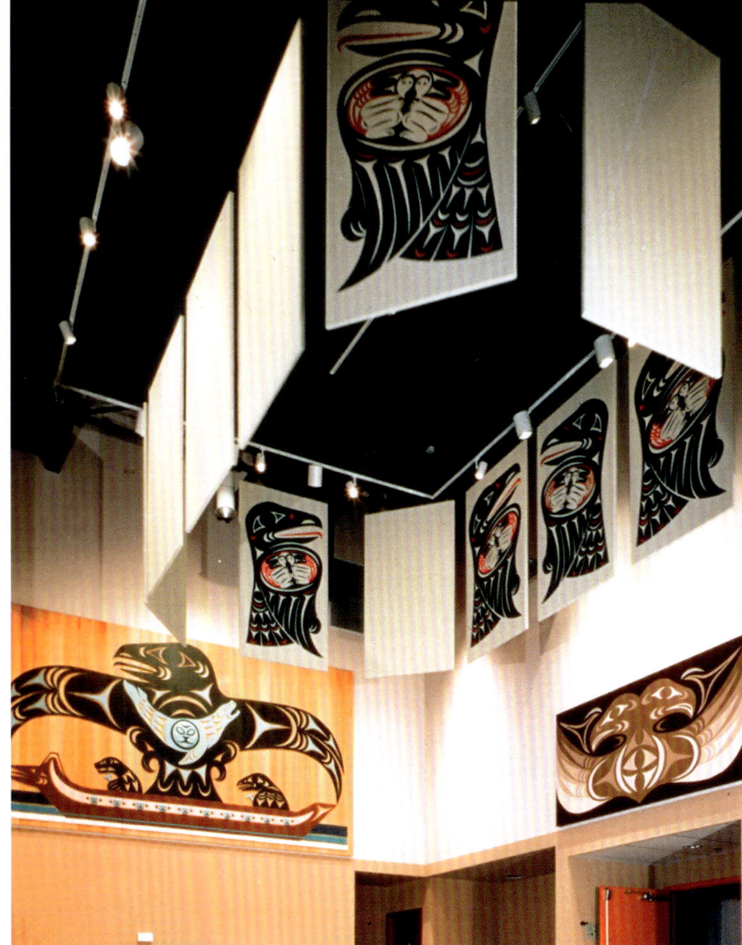

Cry of the Raven

LOCATION: shíshálh (Sechelt) First Nation, Raven's Cry Theatre
5555 Sunshine Coast Highway, Sechelt, BC

Susan's final contribution to the theatre is this set of twelve acoustic panels, which reduce noise levels in the lobby. She transferred her growing skill in printmaking to the production of a large-scale design for textile. She designed, cut, and printed the image, which is based on an original logo design she developed for the theatre's exterior signage.[2]

Cry of the Raven speaks again to the interrelatedness of all creatures: in the centre oval of the body of the spa:l̓ (raven) is a human figure, face forward and mouth open. Crescents and wedges of various sizes define the wing and tail feathers of the raven, in traditional colours of black, red, and white. This is a superb flock of Salish-style ravens to welcome visitors to the Raven's Cry Theatre.

Cry of the Raven, 1991
Cloth
Approx. 152 × 92 cm

A Timeless Circle, 2016
Cast bronze on painted iron frames
24.8–48.3 (diameter) × 5.1 cm (faces; each);
approx. 43.2–61 × 99.1–125.7 × 10.2 cm
(frames; each)

A Timeless Circle

LOCATION: Maury Young Arts Centre
4335 Blackcomb Way, Whistler, BC

In recent years the mountain resort town of Whistler, about one hundred kilometres northeast of Sechelt, has gained important new cultural institutions, notably the Squamish Lil'wat Cultural Centre in 2007 and the Audain Art Museum in 2016. Eleven days before the Audain Museum opened to the public, *A Timeless Circle*, Susan's most recent large-scale public artwork, opened in a small plaza just steps away. The work was unveiled in a special ceremony attended by, among many others, the Líl̓wat Nation's Taya (Cultural) Chief, Leonard Andrew; Musqueam Elder Larry Grant; the mayor of Whistler, Nancy Wilhelm-Morden; Whistler councillor Andrée Janyk; members of the Public Arts Committee; and Susan and her son, the artist Thomas Cannell.

Susan was inspired to create this composition by her time demonstrating carving during the 2010 Winter Olympics. The Vancouver Art Gallery had set up a tent on their grounds for Susan, several of her family members, and other artists from her studio to practice their art for the benefit of tourists and passersby. Meeting so many people from around the world, who welcomed the opportunity to speak with her and learn something of her traditional culture and the art of the Coast Salish people, was a powerful experience that stayed with her for many years.[3]

A Timeless Circle is a legacy of those interactions, and of the enormous public interest in Vancouver and Whistler that the Olympics generated. Susan originally conceived of a sculpture with forty-three different faces, representing all the visitors, hosts, athletes, and volunteers, both from local communities and around the world. As her design developed she decided to double the number of faces so that they could be viewed from either side, meaning she had to design and carve an additional forty-three faces. This required fresh consideration of the relationships among the sizes of the pieces and the various faces. In the end, the project took five years to complete.

The careful refinement of each line is captured in the gleaming bronze. While all the faces are circular in typical Salish fashion, the features of each are unique. First, Susan carved each one from cedar with help from other members of her team; next, Jacob Burton, of Burton Bronze Foundry, made the wax master moulds and cast each face in bronze. Burton then welded them together into the five sections that Susan had designed to symbolize the gathering of all the people who had created the spectacle of the Winter Olympics. Each section includes faces of varying sizes, some facing the viewer, others looking up or down, and is held in a painted iron frame that echoes the curves and composition of the faces. The work is arranged in a small plaza so that viewers can study the faces from both sides and linger to appreciate the fine details. *A Timeless Circle* is an unforgettable, Salish-style telling of a story that deserves to be told and retold across the generations.

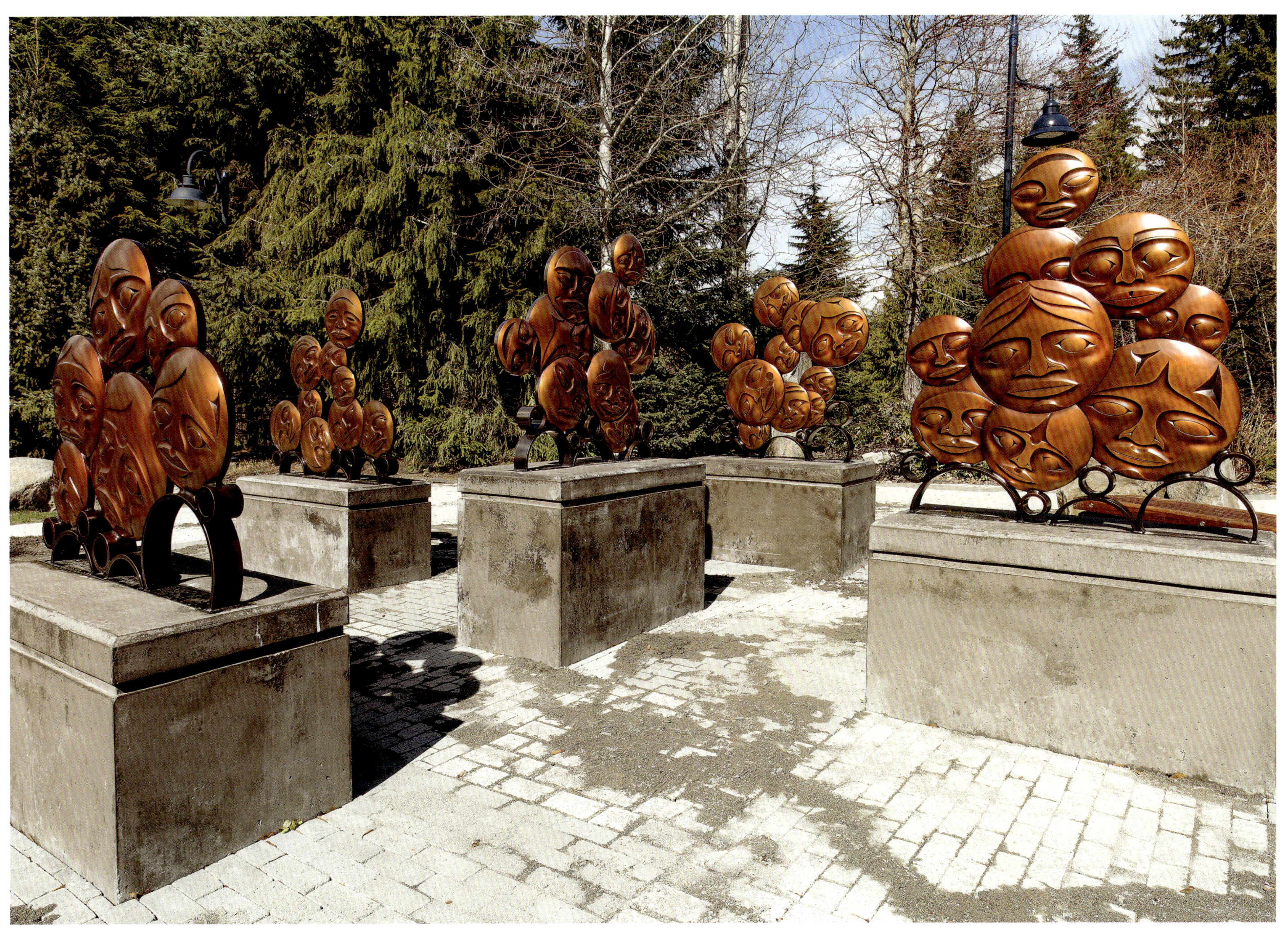

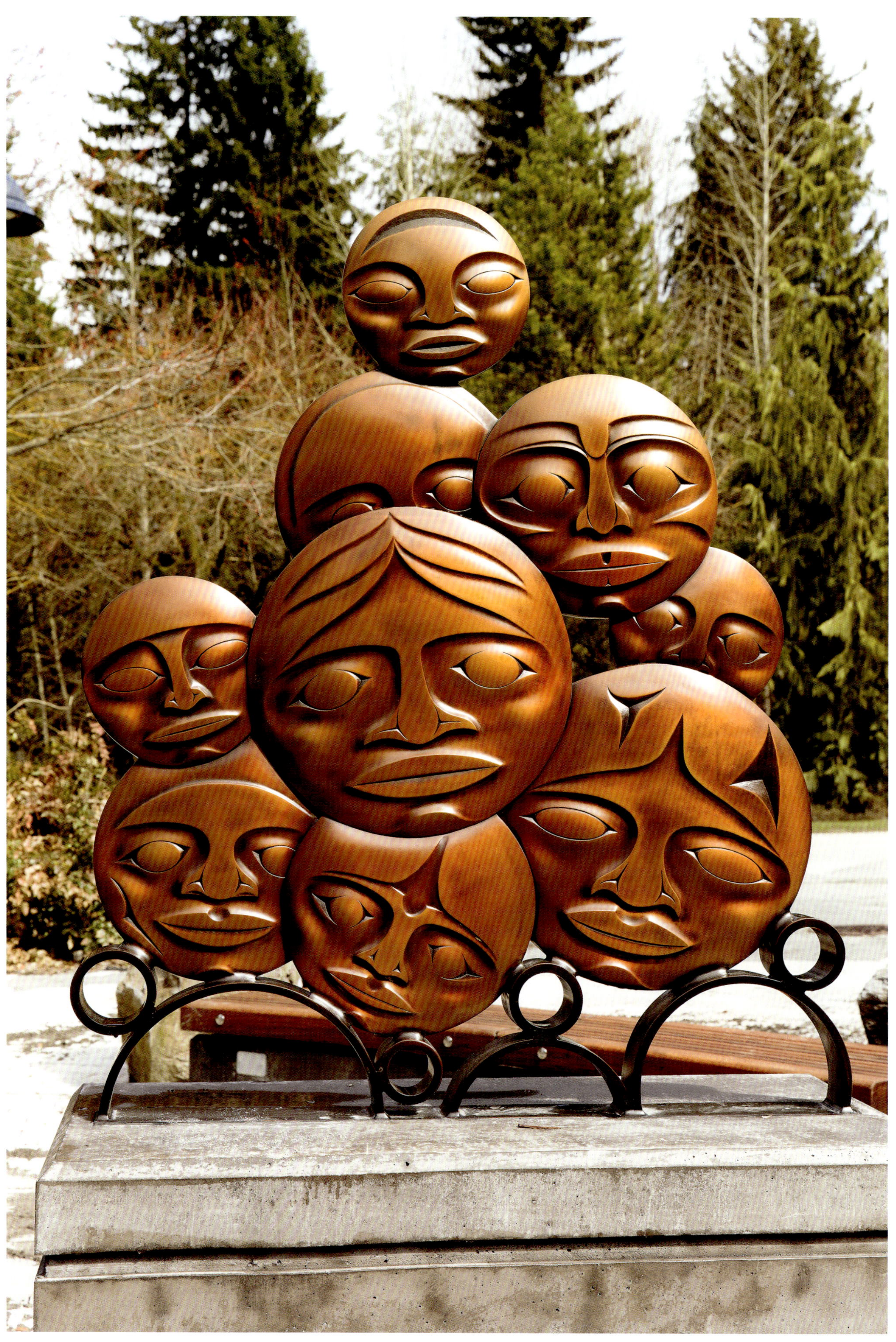

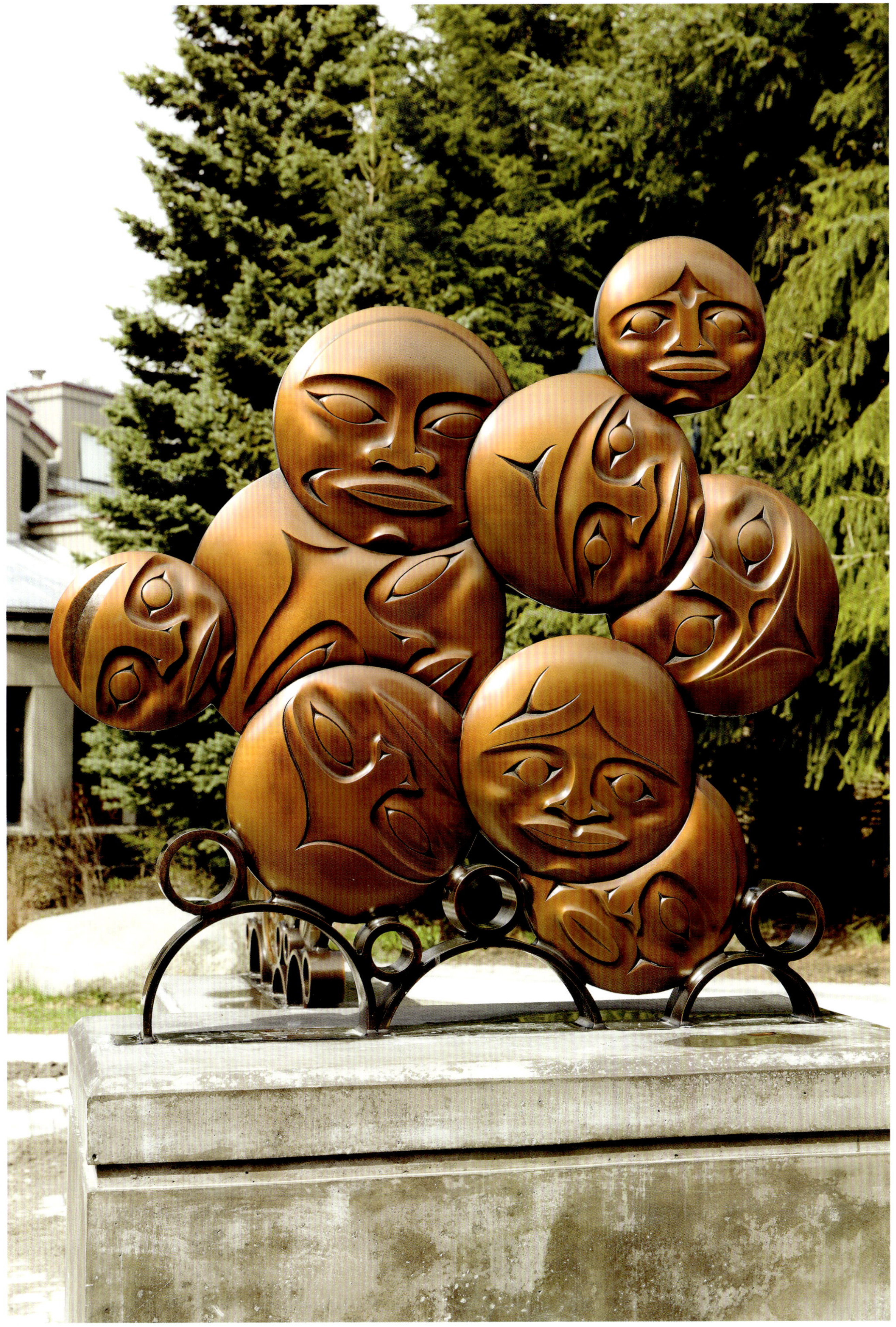

Salish symbols, 1982
Paint
Approx. 25 × 110 cm (each)

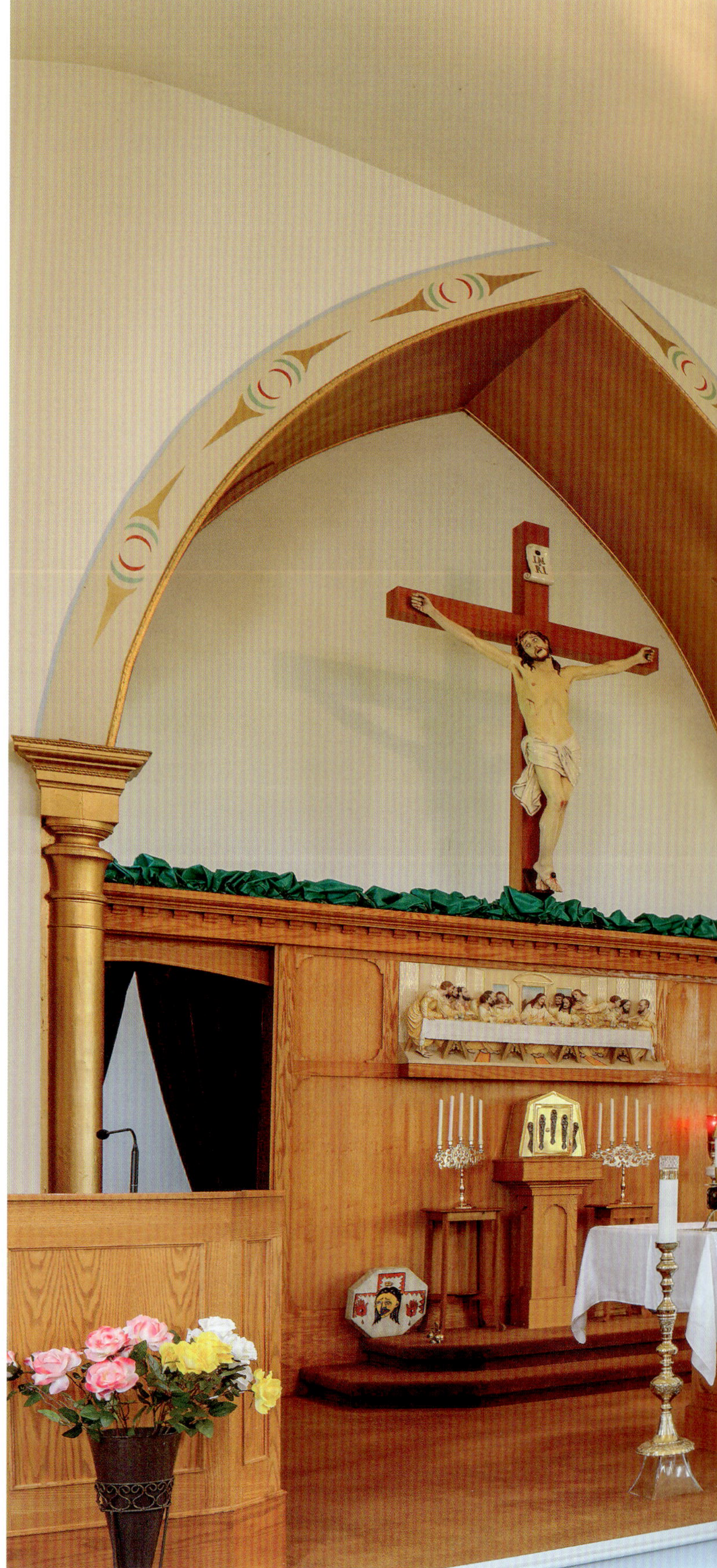

Salish symbols

LOCATION: St. Paul's Church
424 Esplanade W, Eslhá7an
(Ustlawn/Mission Indian Reserve No. 1)

Passengers crossing Vancouver Harbour on the SeaBus are afforded a fine view of one of region's oldest buildings, the twin-spired Gothic Revival-style church of St. Paul's Church. Inside is the earliest public art designed by Susan Point.

St. Paul's Indian Church, as it was originally known, is located in the Squamish Nation community of Eslhá7an (Ustlawn), also known as Mission Indian Reserve No. 1, on the shores of North Vancouver. A church was first built on the site in 1868, then replaced in 1884 and remodelled in 1909/10. In 1980 it was designated a national historic site in Canada. Concerned about the long-term viability of the structure, Squamish Elders and elected leaders—including some who were active in the St. Paul's parish—then embarked on a comprehensive restoration effort. To reach out to the wider community for support they formed the Save St. Paul's Indian Church Society.

In *Mission on the Inlet*, a history of the church published in 1984, the society's chair, Yvonne Schmidt, describes the impetus of seeking a First Nations artist.

> Within the church interior... historic values (there were several layers of history there) had to be blended with the contemporary requirements of the living institution... The introduction of a Coast Salish Indian Motif around the arches rather than the fleur de lis which had decorated the arches in the period before 1910, serves as an example of the fusion of historic values, here with the emphasis on the Indian origins of the parish rather than the French origin of the missionaries.[4]

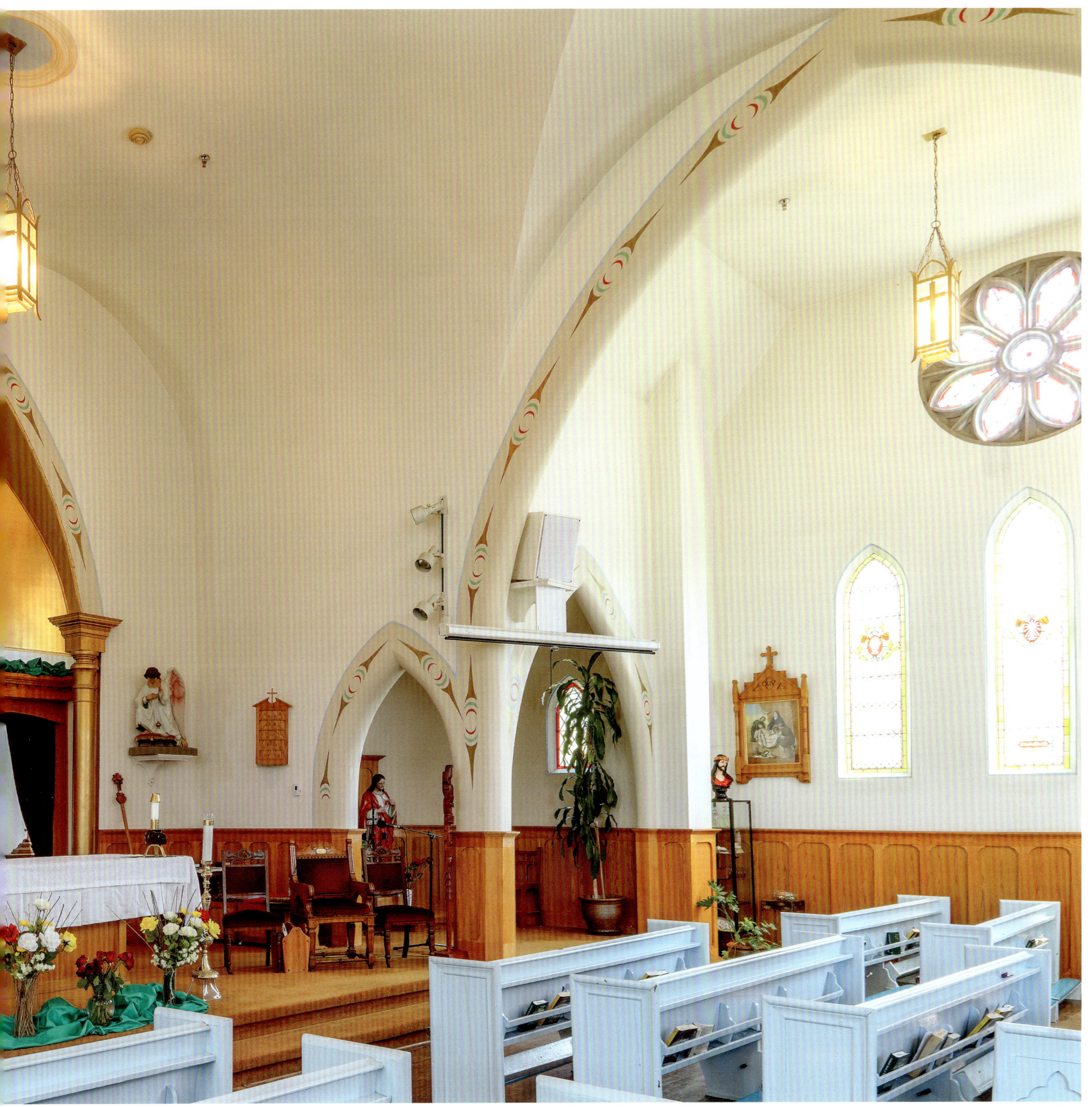

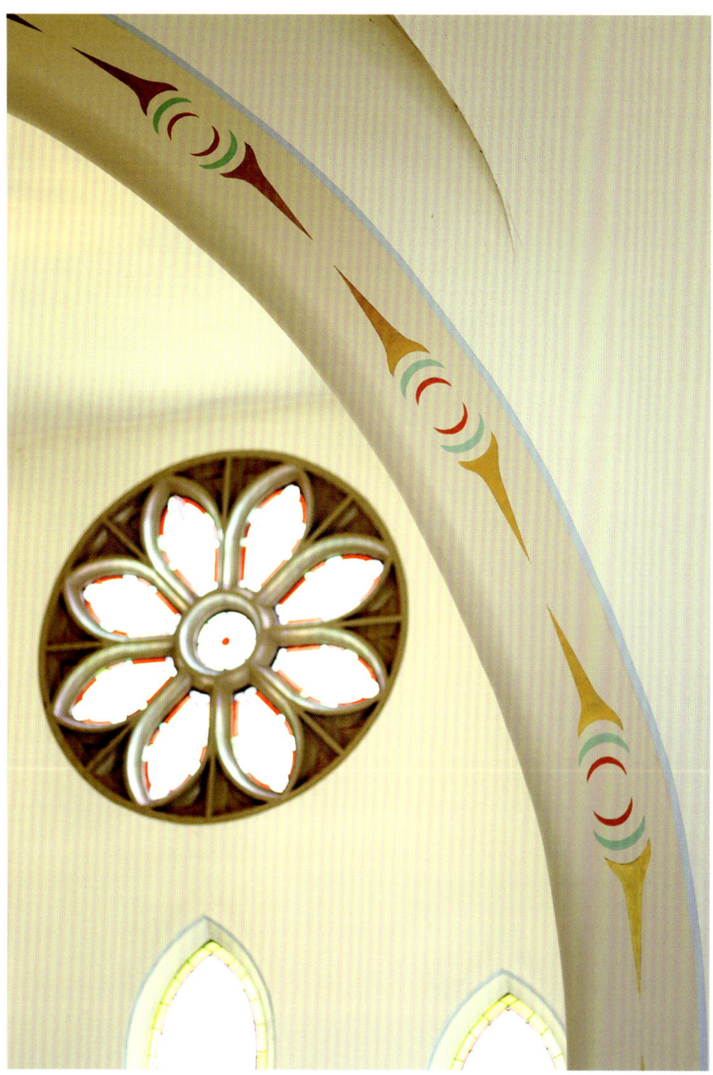

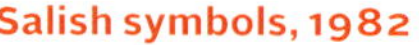

Salish symbols, 1982

This renovation began in 1982, when Susan was in the second year of making prints and, with the guidance and support of her uncle Dr. Michael Kew and other family members and Musqueam Elders, studying historical Salish art. These were the years when few scholars and even fewer artists understood the special nature of Salish art, and it was only just beginning to be introduced to Salish communities, scholars, and collectors. Percy Paull, a Squamish Elder and parishioner of the church, explains how Susan came to be involved.

> The Committee decided to explore the possibility of introducing some Indian Art into the Church. The architect was consulted and he approved the concept, subject to the choice not being in conflict with the general unity of the Interior design.
>
> With the anticipated volume of visitors that will be coming to St. Paul's, we saw this as an opportunity to bring into a place of high visibility our own traditional Coast Salish art. This is considered some of the most beautiful of all native art and is just recently experiencing a revival. We are learning more and more about it. We also knew that whatever we did would be subject to the scrutiny of experts.
>
> Accordingly, we contacted the renowned authority on Salish Art—Dr. Michael Kew at UBC. He arranged a display of slides and artifacts which reflected the very highest quality of traditions of Coast Salish work—mostly more than 100 years old. It was a thrilling and inspiring evening.
>
> Subsequently, the design for the arches was chosen—this incorporated some of the frequently used non-representational traditional symbols—crescents, wedges and circles. The design was produced by Susan Point (formerly Sparrow), a Musqueam artist, and the pattern painted on by myself, Walter Joseph and Willis Baker.[5]

While Percy Paull does not state so directly in his report, it seems evident that Michael Kew recommended his niece for the commission.

Susan chose to repeat simple Salish elements—an eye, two crescents, and two wedges—in rich, non-traditional colours: darker red for the inner crescent, light blue for the outer, and gold for the elongated tapered wedges. The motif fits well within the architecture and the prevailing colour scheme, echoing the blue paint of the pews. The work is a quiet statement, set within a non-Salish architectural and spiritual space, that speaks to a culture much older than the Gothic shapes it adorns.

Story of Life

LOCATION: Low Level Road
600 block Low Level Rd, North Vancouver, BC

To improve rail operations and vehicle and cyclist traffic, Port Metro Vancouver and the the City of North Vancouver completed a dramatic realignment and elevation of nearly three kilometres of Low Level Road in North Vancouver. The work resulted in a long, high retaining wall that faces grain elevators on the harbour shore and sits immediately below the Spirit Trail, which links this site, the beginning of European exploitation of the great coastal forests, with the ancestral lands of the Squamish to the west: a perfect location for public art.

An invitation to artists was posted on the Musqueam Band website on 22 January 2013. The scale of the space to be filled was enormous, and as the road would not have space for pedestrians, only for cars and for cyclists, the design would have to be appreciated by viewers travelling by at speed. The challenging site was a perfect match for Susan, as she explained in her proposal.

> In 1990 I produced my first bas relief commission that was integrated into the Sechelt Indian band Government Complex on the Sunshine Coast ... a totally new approach. This I achieved by designing and fabricating two 5′ × 5′ grids, made of wood, which when cast, repeated and covered approximately 10,000 square feet of wall space ... Based on my need for pushing my limit in the art world and my love of experimentation, since 1990, I have used this grid system process in many of my artworks: paper, glass, concrete, polymer, cast iron, wood etc. This is a normal part of my daily artwork creations ... so I am very familiar and have the experience with public art projects of this scale and scope.[6]

Susan's proposal also offered important background on her personal story, noting that her ancestry made her a particularly fitting choice as an artist, and then describing the considerations and thematic content of the story she proposed to tell on the huge wall.

> This is an exciting project that gives me the opportunity to design a "contemporary" public art theme in my Coast Salish art style based on the history of the site. I feel a close connection personally, as I am the great, great, great granddaughter of Chief Capilano. My family's crest is that of the Thunderbird, passed on to my children from my great, great, great, grandfather.[7]

She then explained the various site-specific considerations that went into her design, including the surrounding landscape (past, present, and future), the need for longevity, and the particular parameters of the site. To achieve her desired effect she chose to use "traditional Coast Salish iconography in a story book form" to create

> an illustrative mural depicting a changing landscape. There is a center focal point and a beginning lead-in at each end. The three panels do not repeat monotonously over and over. The interaction between the three panels changes from one end to the other in an attempt to reduce repetition. This is done by casting one of the three panels six times, and the other two panels nine times each. Even though there is repetition to the imagery, it gives a different appeal from both directions.
>
> Because of the scale that the artwork must fit within on this retaining wall, I decided to go with one level in this relief embossed process ...

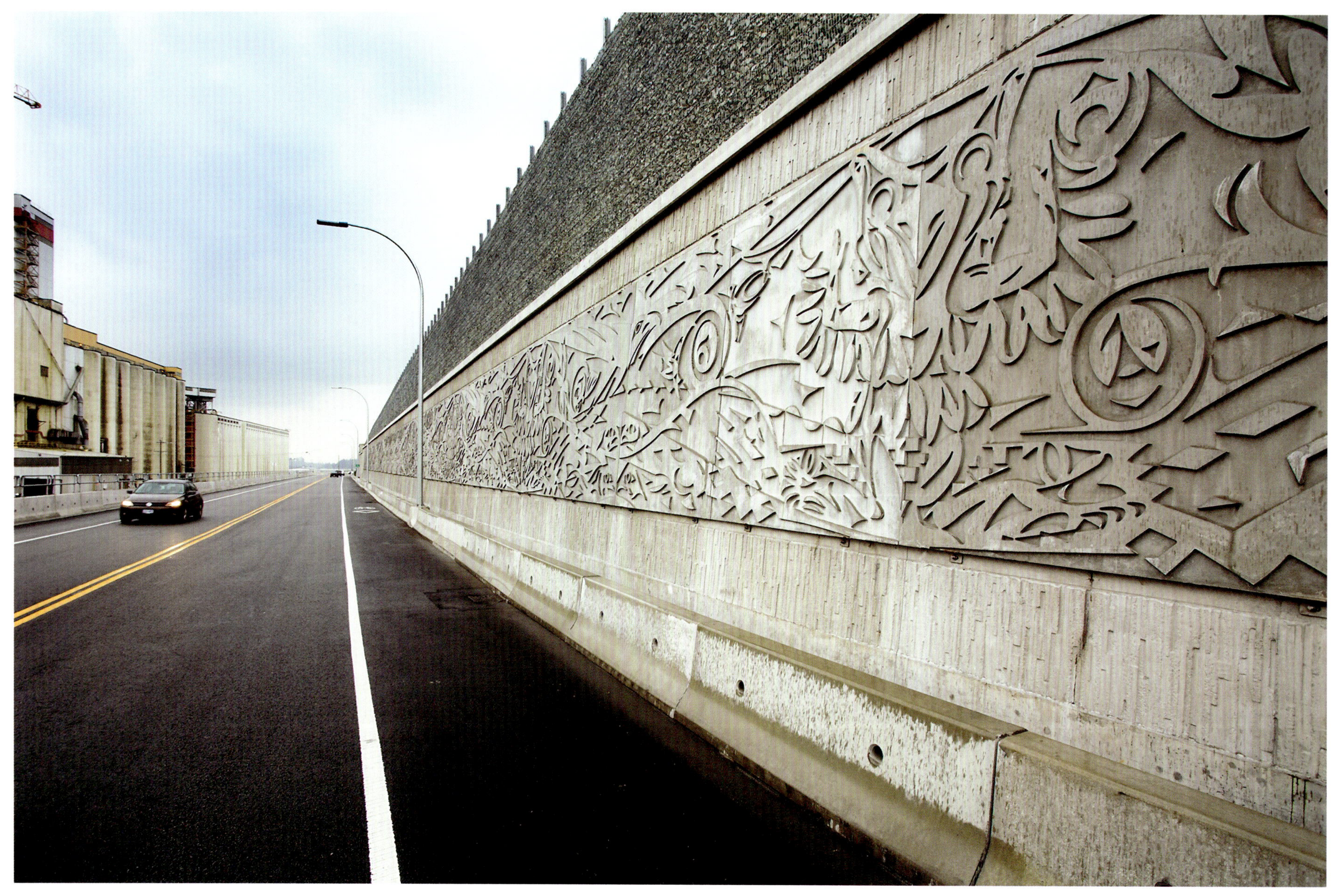

the lowest level allowed and the highest level allowed... giving the mural design depth.

The overall imagery in my design reflects on the history of the site, the change of the site and the natural site itself. I have incorporated male and female figures that are welcoming all peoples to this land. As well to beautify the site with a gentle rhythm of the land, butterflies, frogs, hummingbirds, salmon, eagles and plant life have been incorporated into the overall design. However, the imagery within the design can suggest many other images by the simple Salish forms that are used. The imagery also shows habitat, just briefly, in the beginning... concentrating on the center, which shows a thriving community. The subtle flora and fauna motifs represent the future generation; the knots represent the ties within all cultures.

The imagery in the design has been designed so that the shadows emphasize the flow and rhythm of the overall art piece.

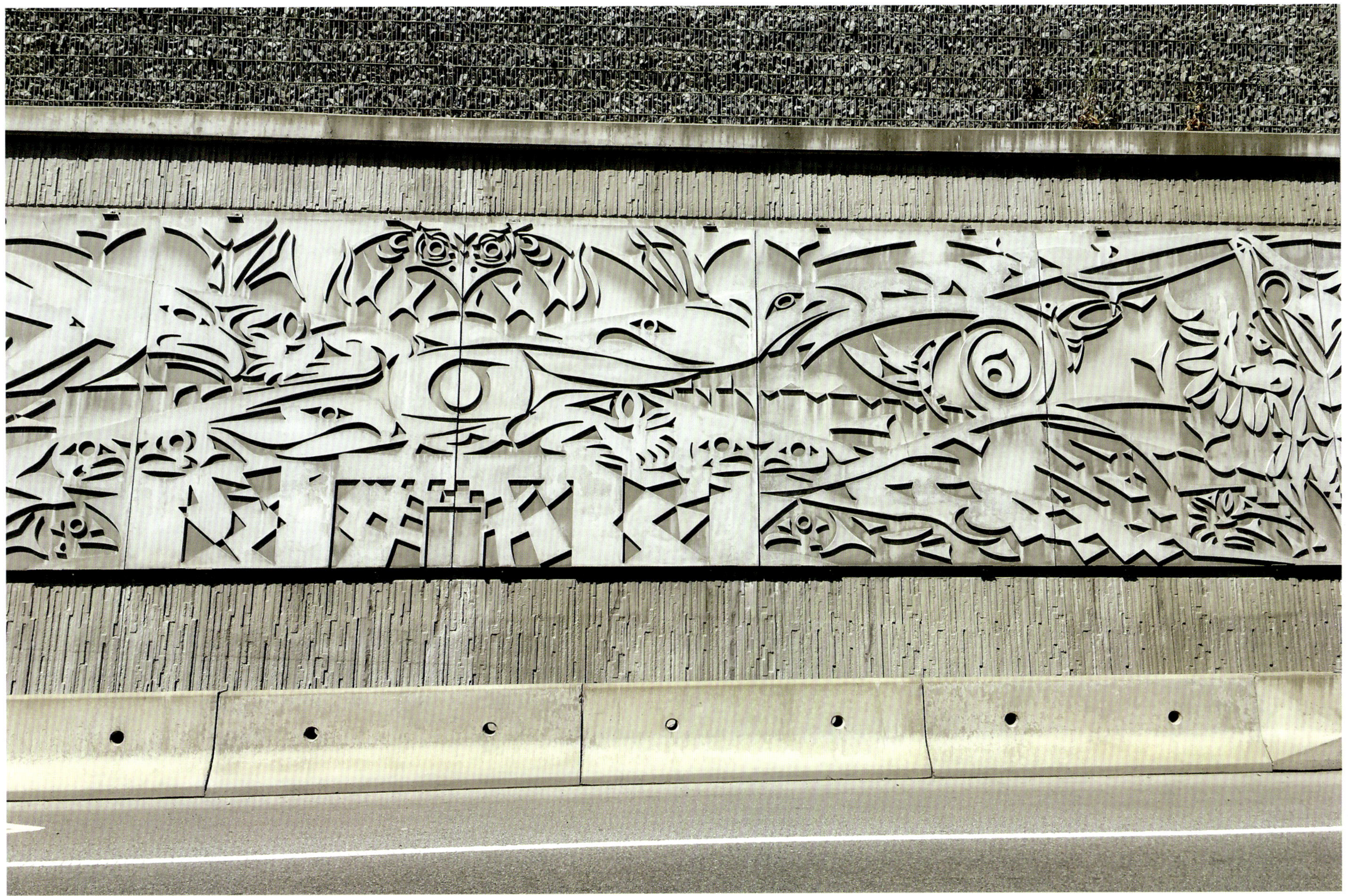

The completed mural is a great pageant of life in Salish style, but from a passing car you have only a limited opportunity to appreciate the elegance, complexity, and rich symbolism of Susan's work. A fuller and more comprehensive understanding of the composition is available to cyclists. The forty-six large panels include nine full welcome figures and half a figure at either end of the mural; grand sweeps of lines composed of birds; flowing qaʔ (water) with salmon; and six stylizations of houseposts, each with a small door incised in low relief, symbolizing community. Susan's work reaffirms the importance of this land that has changed so much in the last two hundred years, and offers a Salish-style welcome to those who come from so many parts of the world to find work here beside the sea and in the shadow of the mountains. ■

Story of Life, 2013
Cast concrete
Approx. 1.8 × 240 m

Salish Wolf, 2002
Bronze
60 × 60 × 3.5 cm
Iron circle: 1.58 m (diameter)

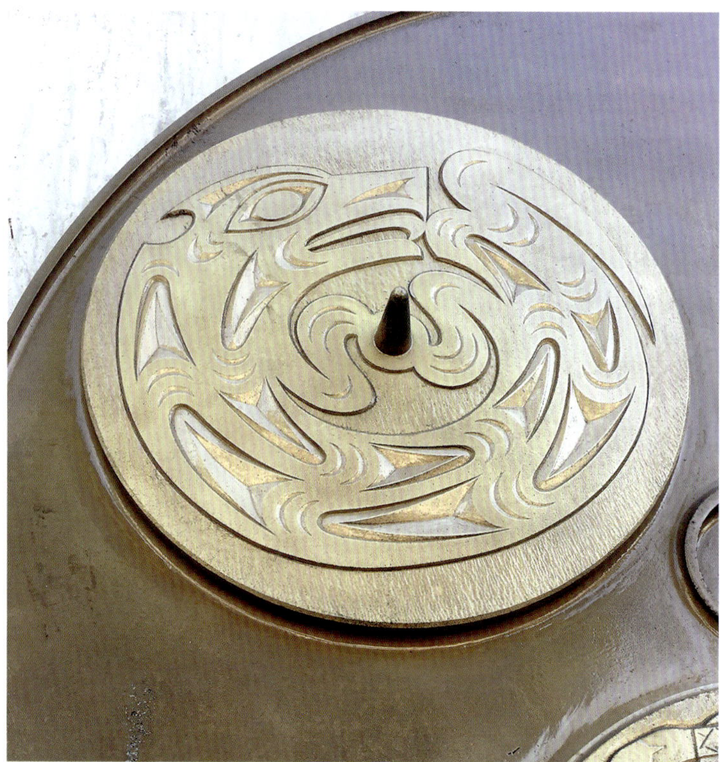

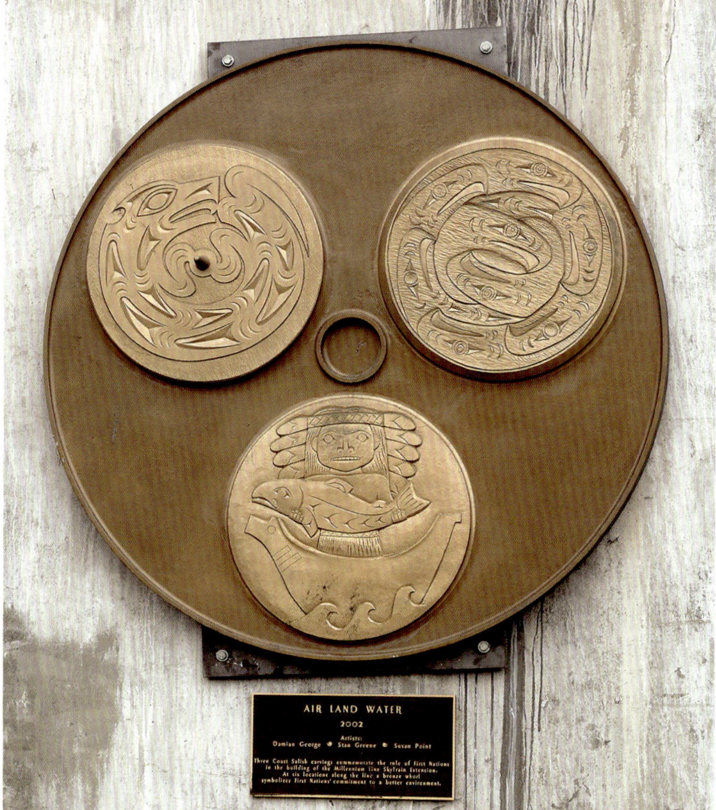

Salish Wolf

LOCATION: Gilmore Station
Gilmore Ave at Dawon St, Burnaby, BC

To honour First Nations contributions to the new Millennium Line extension of Metro Vancouver's SkyTrain system, officials chose three Coast Salish artists to create works for several new stations. Susan was chosen, along with Stan Greene (Stó:lō) and Damian George (Tsleil-Waututh). The theme was "Air Land and Water," a celebration of the environment.

Each artist produced spindle whorl designs, which were carved in cedar, cast in bronze, then mounted on a large iron circle and bolted to several of the concrete supports for the elevated track, near station entrances.

Susan's whorl shows a stqəyeʔ (wolf), defined by strong wedges with crescent accents in a classic Salish style. Susan explained to officials of the Millennium Line that

> the design in this image is taken from a traditional Coast Salish spindle whorl. In this particular sculptural placement, the wolf here represents "land." It is believed that the wolf is a great hunter that is often associated with the special spirit power a man had to acquire to become a good hunter. The wolf also represents the family and togetherness.[9]

Originally, there may have been as many as six of these iron circles, but unfortunately most have disappeared since their installation—probably victims of theft—and the art has not been recovered. It is always distressing when important public art goes missing. Perhaps the work's inclusion here will inspire the corporation to recast the three whorls, including Susan's *Salish Wolf*, to renew this reminder of the interconnections between us and the creatures of the air, land, and water.

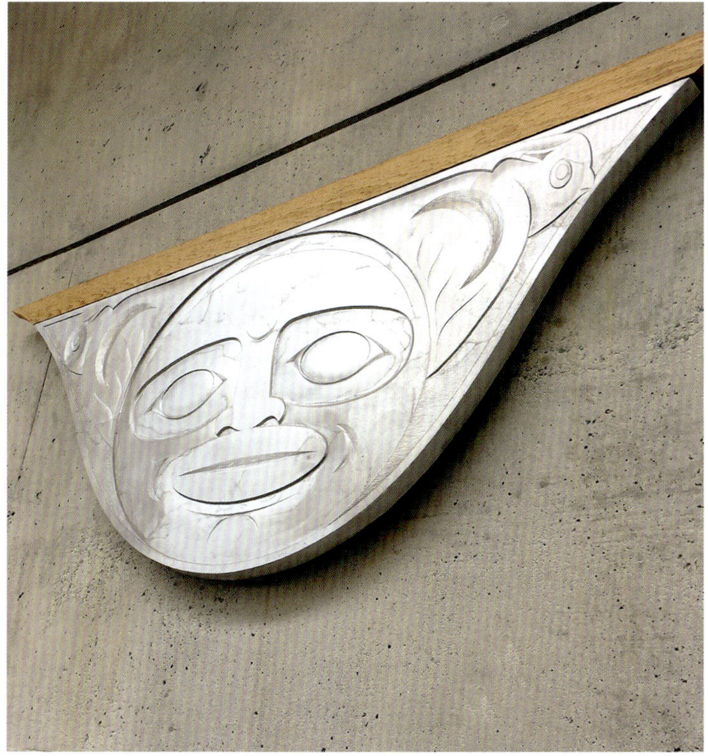

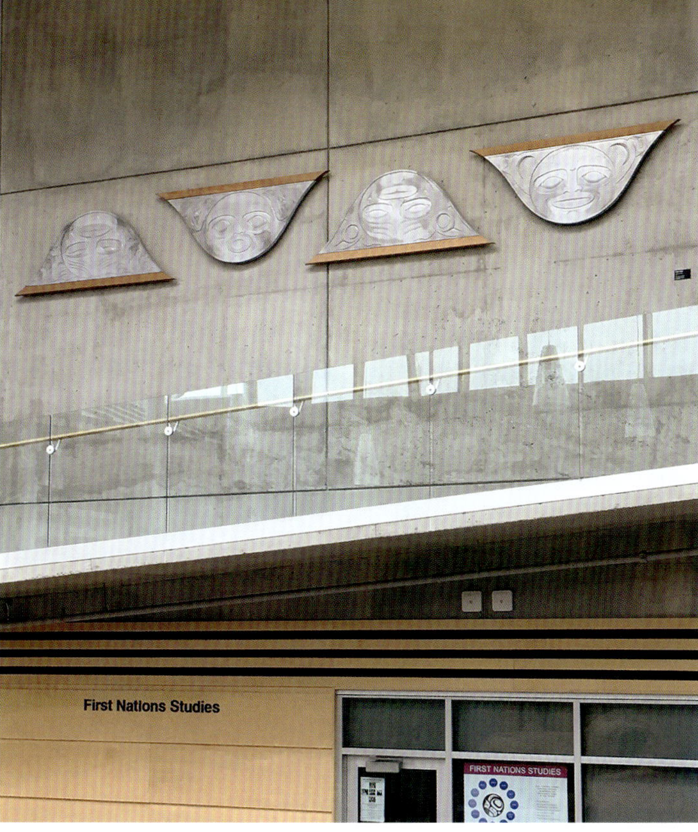

SIMON FRASER UNIVERSITY

In 2010, George and Christiane Smyth donated to SFU several works from their Salish Weave Collection. They began the collection a decade earlier after moving from Ottawa to Victoria, B.C., and deciding to collect Coast Salish art within a one-hundred-mile radius. The collection is named after Susan Point's *Salish Weave* (2003; see page 223) and has become the largest and most important collection of its kind in Canada. George and Christiane's encouragement of Salish artists, and the outreach they have achieved through bringing the collection into schools and siting pieces such as these, have been pivotal to increasing knowledge of Salish artists and art in B.C. and elsewhere in Canada. In 2018, Canadian Heritage granted "certification of cultural property" to both *Written Into the Earth* and *Blue Herons*. Students and visitors to SFU can view and learn about these and many other Indigenous artworks with the imesh mobile app (imesh means "to walk" in Sk̲wxwú7mesh snichim [Squamish Language]). The app was developed by the Bill Reid Centre for Northwest Coast Studies at SFU as "a step, however small, toward decolonizing the university and the surrounding landscape."[10]

Written Into the Earth

LOCATION: Simon Fraser University
8888 University Dr, Burnaby, BC

Susan originally created these four faces for an arc of bronze casts set in pavement at the north end of the stadium in Seattle, described more fully in the *Written Into the Earth* entry on page 182. The carvings translated well into a contemporary medium, and are on a scale that suits the architecture of their setting, the atrium of Saywell Hall. George and Christiane Smyth acquired the casts in March 2008,[11] and donated them to SFU in service of the university's ongoing commitment to promote respect for, and understanding of, the First Nations Peoples on whose lands the university is located.

Written Into the Earth, 2002
Aluminum
64 × 147 cm (each)

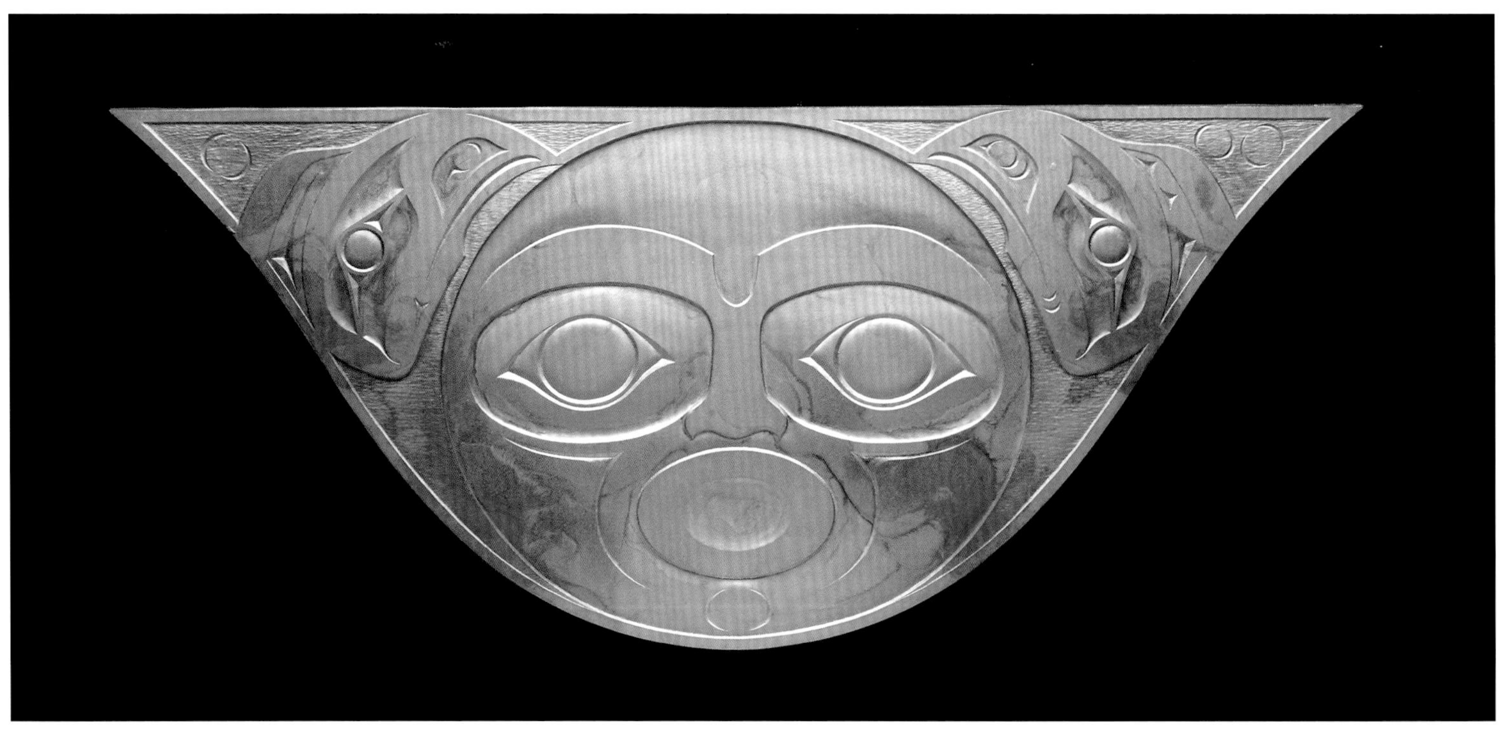

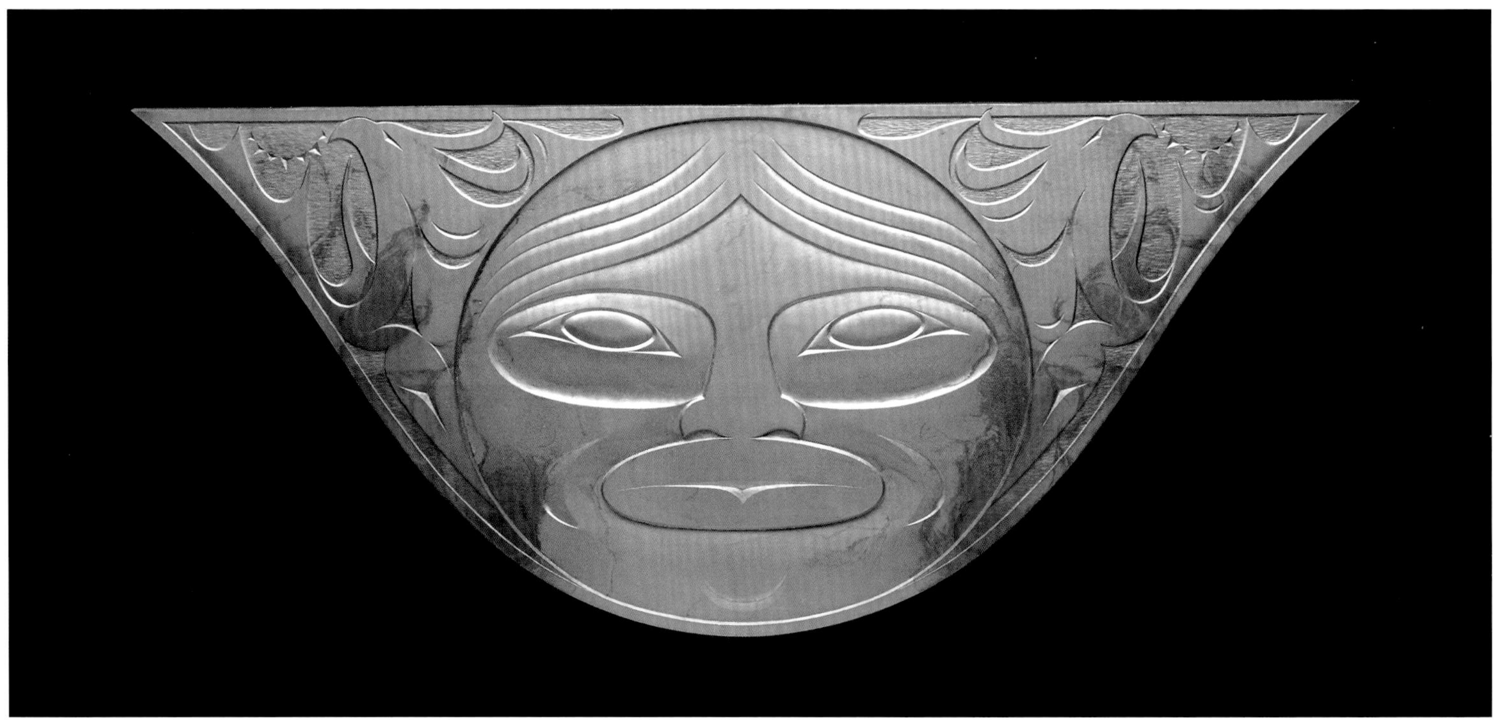

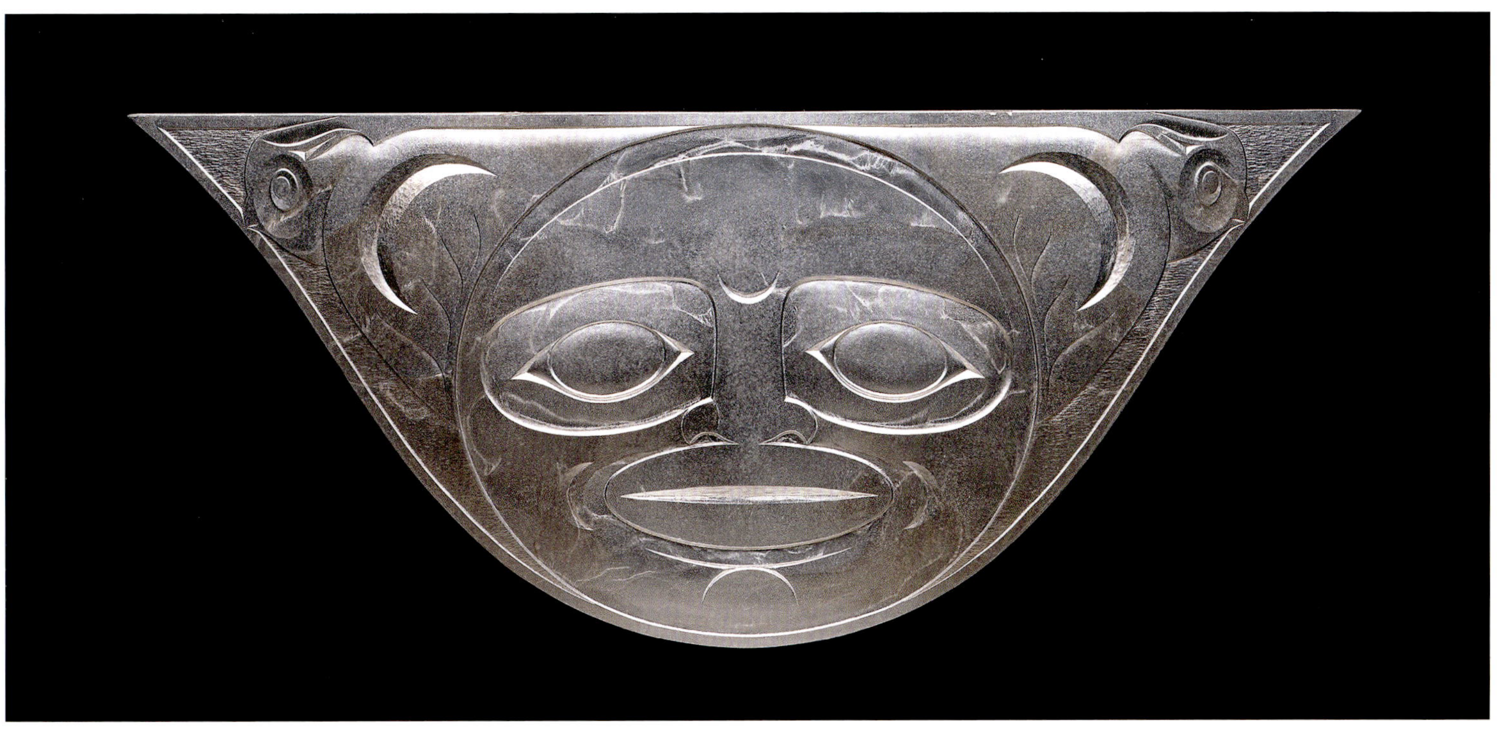

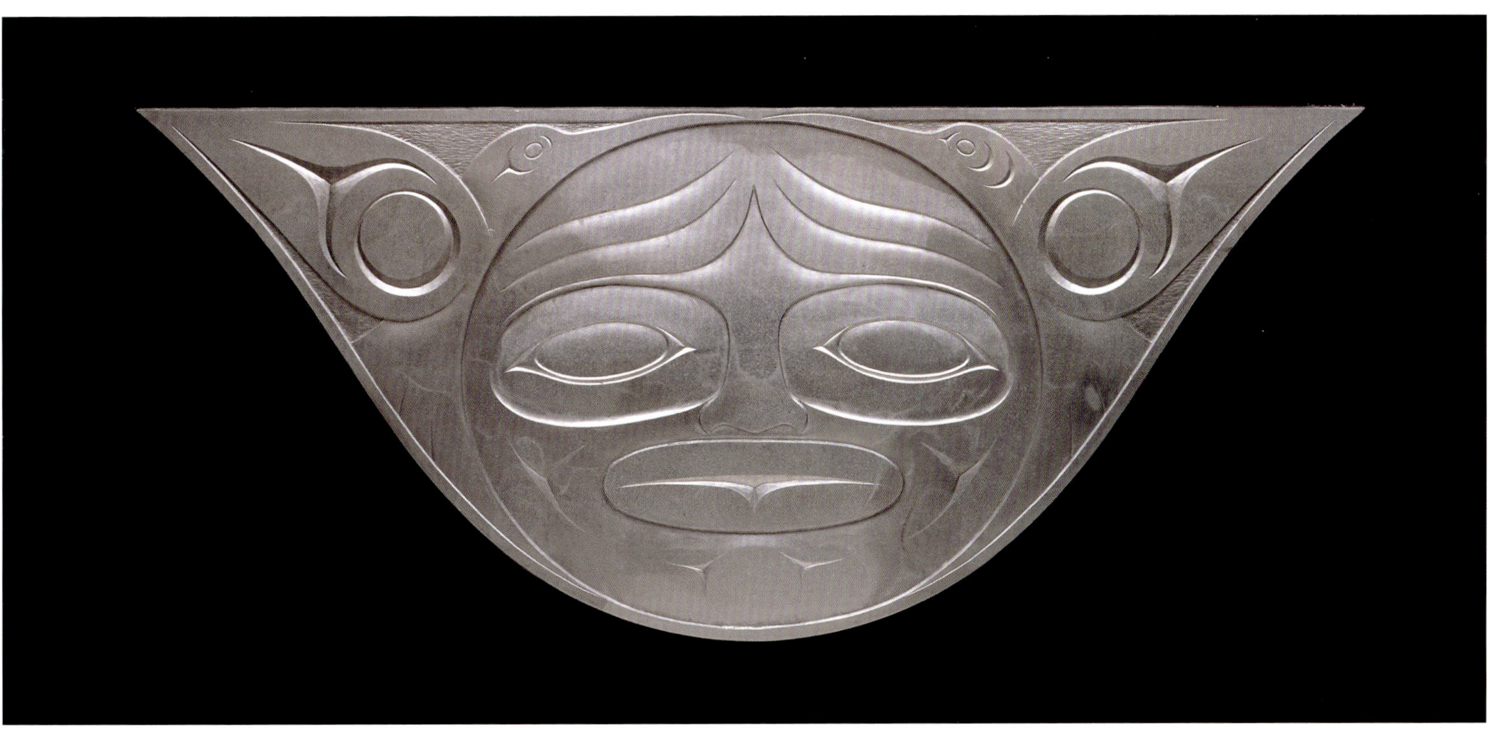

Written Into the Earth, 2002

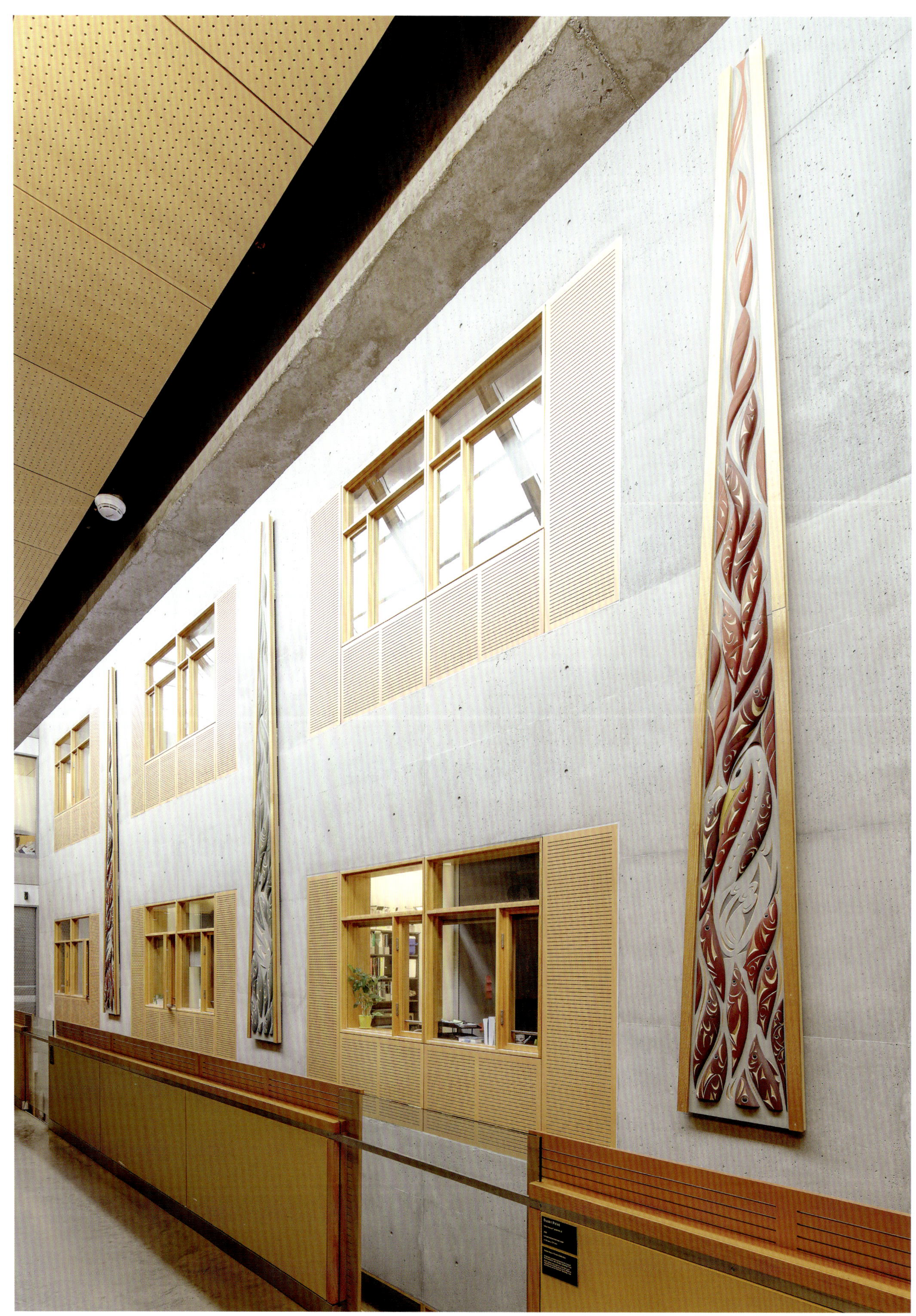

Blue Herons, 2008
Carved and painted western red cedar
6.73 × .79 m (each)

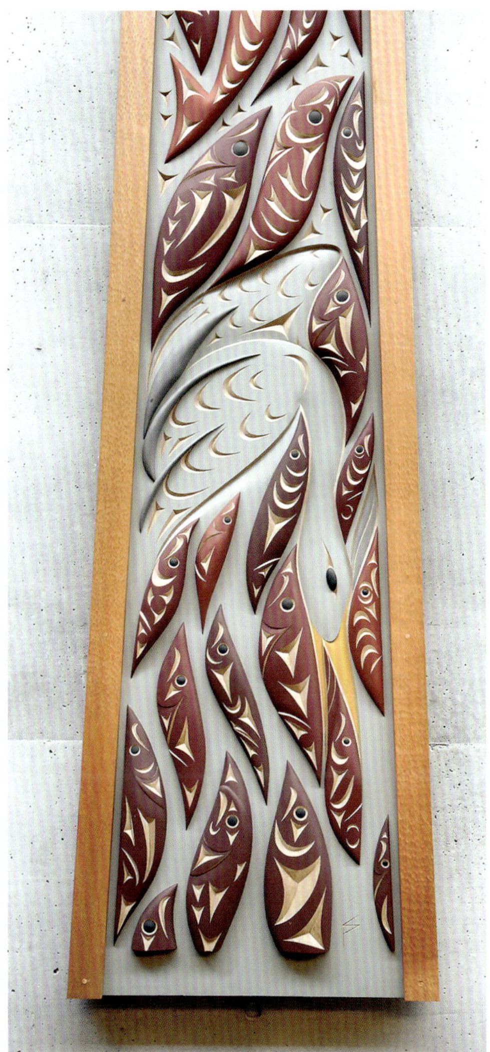

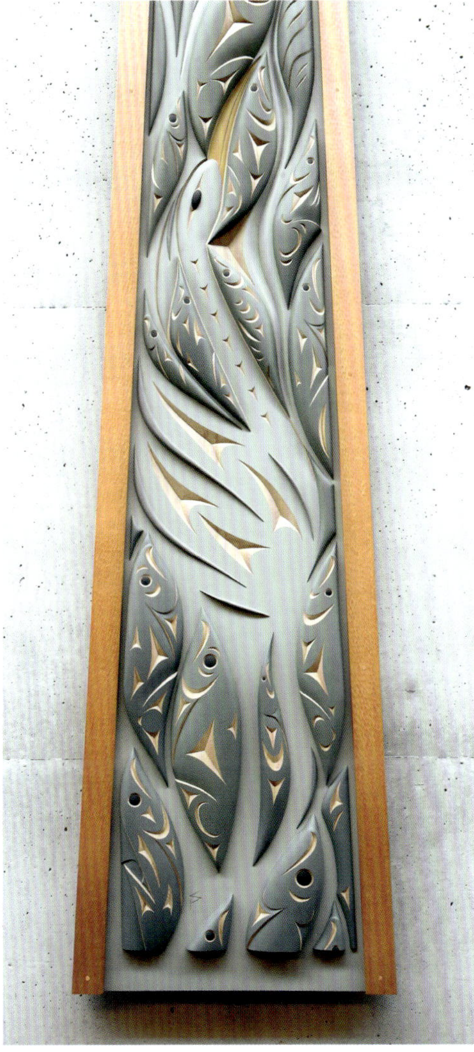

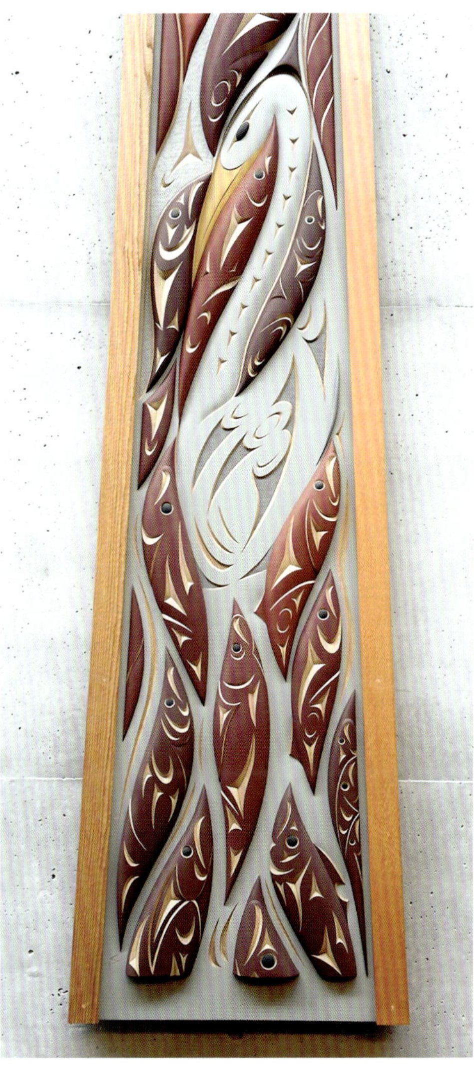

Blue Herons

LOCATION: Simon Fraser University
8888 University Dr, Burnaby, BC

These impressive sculptures were carved in cedar to create moulds for the concrete runnels of the Richmond Olympic Oval—see page 151 for more on their design, meaning, and creation. The original carvings were beautifully painted by Susan, predominantly in reds and blues, and are now on permanent display and accessible to the public in the atrium of the Technology and Applied Science Building 1 on Burnaby Mountain.

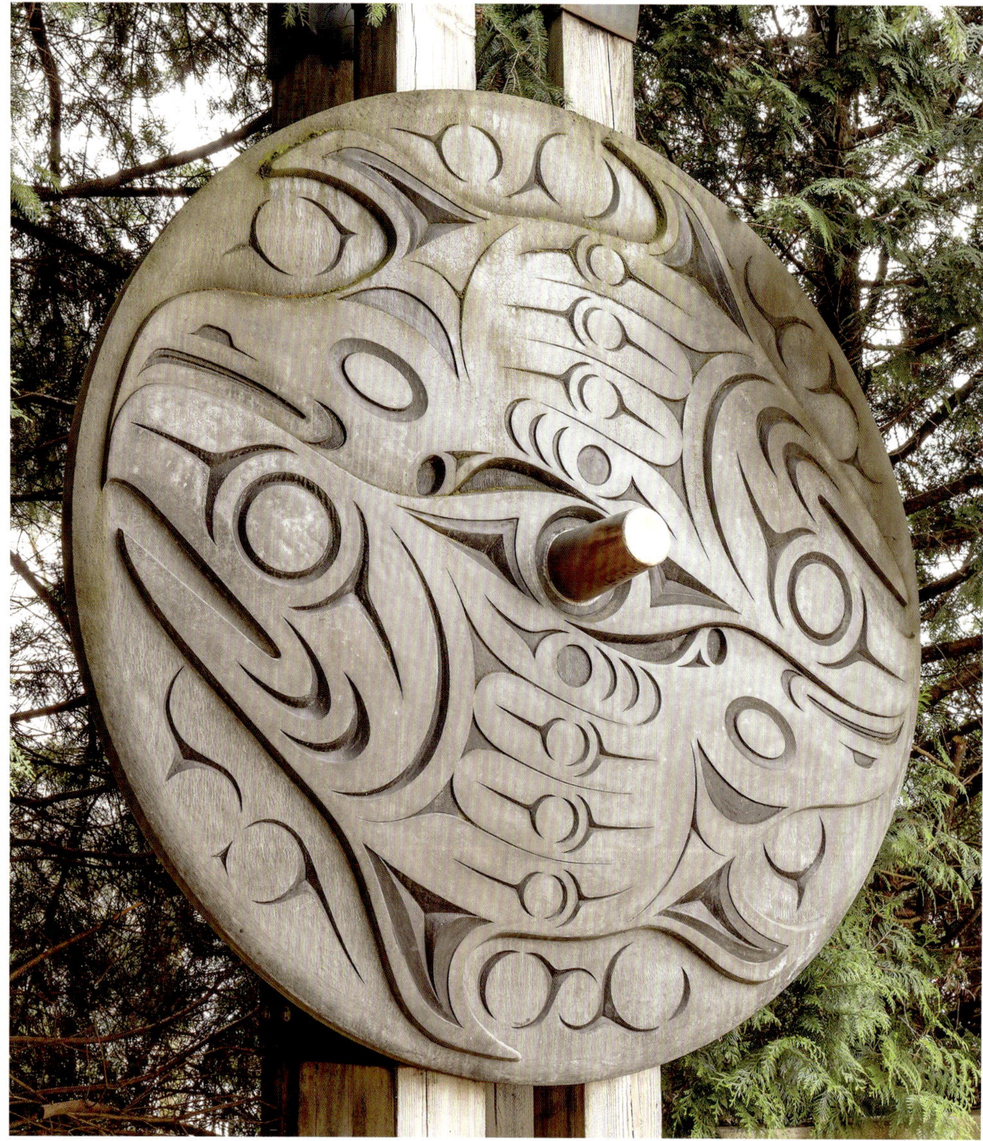

The River—Giver of Life

LOCATION: Klahanie
Klahanie Dr, Port Moody, BC

First designed and carved in 1998, this is the second of three iterations of this splendid composition (see pages 85 and 139). It is located at the entrance to Klahanie ("the outdoors" in chinuk wawa, or Chinook Jargon), a housing development built by Polygon Homes. Polygon's chairman, Michael Audain, has a long-standing interest in the art and culture of First Nations Peoples, and under his direction Polygon decided to make Susan's whorl the centrepiece of the entry to the development.

Some months before the whorl was installed in August 2004, Hugh Ker, the director of development for Klahanie, told Susan, "I am very excited and think it's a great fit for the community of Klahanie and Port Moody. Your piece will be viewed by thousands of weary commuters a day who I know will be uplifted by it."[12]

The whorl is many times the size of those used by Susan's ancestors to spin yarn for swəq̓ʷaʔɬ (woven blankets). The large scale better allows viewers to admire the two salmon, whose tails are formed by Thunderbird heads, that swim around the central pivot, symbolizing the cycle of life. When Susan carved the original, she described how the design was inspired by staľəẁ (the Fraser River), a source of salmon and therefore sustenance and wealth for hundreds of generations.

The scale, the material, and the dramatic shape of the circle are all very contemporary, but the images tell a universal story, in Salish style, about the life cycle of salmon and of all life, and the deep connections between people and the river, the land, and the air. It is a timeless introduction to a contemporary subdivision whose residents are given a glimpse of the culture of the region's original inhabitants, and of the art of a woman who was at the forefront of the renaissance of Coast Salish art forms.

The River—Giver of Life, 2004
Concrete
2.13 (diameter) × .5 m

The River—Giver of Life, 2006
Ruby sand, polymer, steel, copper
2.13 (diameter) × .5 m

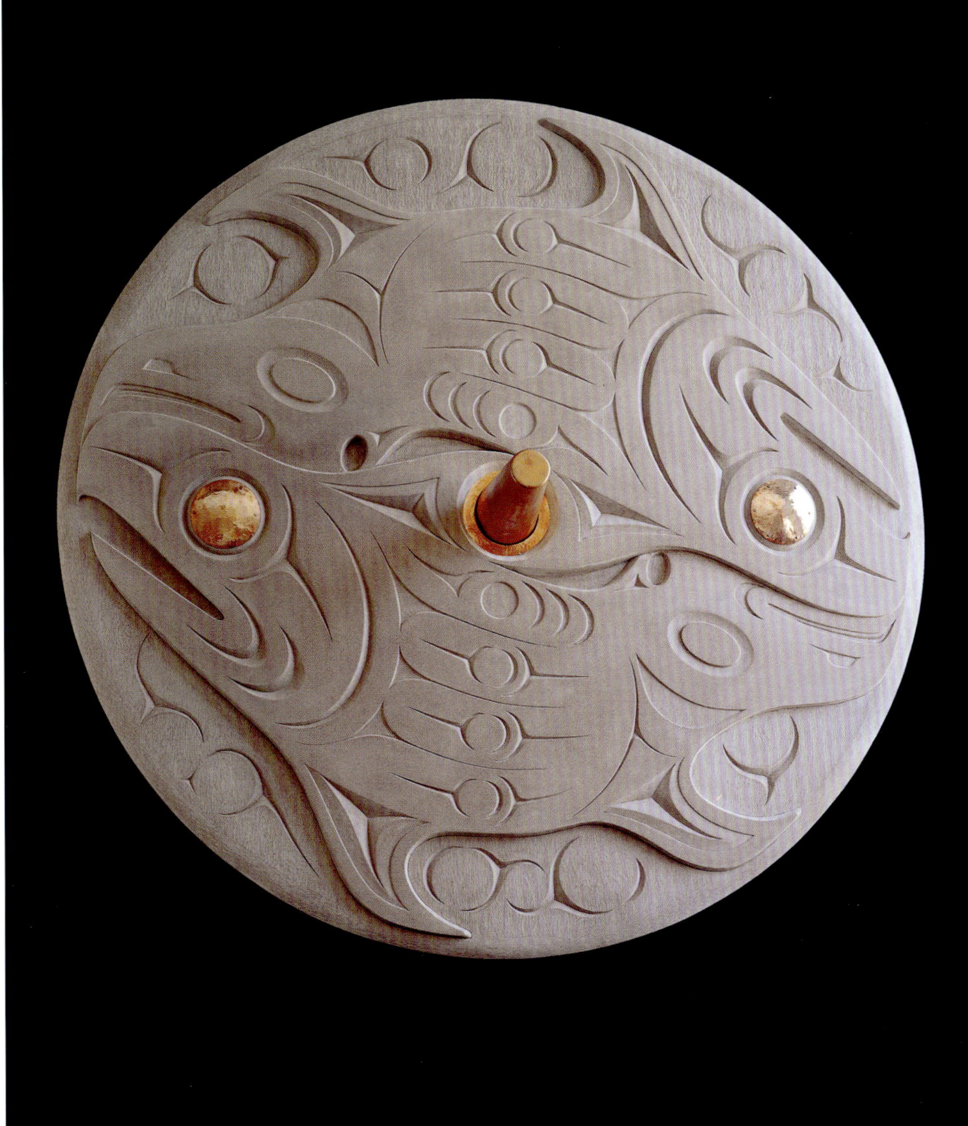

The River—Giver of Life

LOCATION: Weatherhaven
2120 Hartley Ave, Coquitlam, BC

The third variation of Susan's powerful spindle whorl (see page 85 for the polymer version and page 138 for the concrete) caught the eye of Brian Johnson, president of Weatherhaven, a manufacturing company specializing in shelter systems. Johnson acquired the work in connection with a donation to a bursary for First Nations students at Shawnigan Lake School on Vancouver Island; he felt the work would provide a dramatic conversation piece in the reception area of Weatherhaven's corporate offices, and be an excellent link with the bursary project.

Weatherhaven issued an illustrated leaflet that explains the central role of the Fraser River in Musqueam life, and describes the meaning of the whorl.

> With water flowing in the background, *The River—Giver of Life* depicts two salmon swimming in a circle. One swims inland to spawn and the other out to sea, completing their life cycle. . . . Moving in opposite directions to the salmon are two magnificent thunderbirds. According to First Nations mythology, the thunderbird, living high in the mountains, is the most powerful of all spirits. . . . In *The River—Giver of Life*, these thunderbirds, seen in the salmon tails, are transferring their power to the salmon, protecting them and overseeing their continuing cycle of renewal.[13]

In the same leaflet Susan describes the manufacturing process and further emphasizes the importance of the river.

> The spindle of the whorl is leafed in copper and the eyes are copper domes, but structurally, this piece has been created entirely as a sand cast. This technique involves pouring a mixture of sand and polymer resin into a mould. The use of sand further demonstrates the commanding presence every aspect of the Fraser River has in the lives of the Musqueam people. The sand moves through the twists and turns of the river as it flows out to sea, not unlike how members of the community must navigate their own journey through life.[14]

Happily, although Weatherhaven's office has since moved from a Burnaby location upriver to Coquitlam, the whorl remains in their reception area, affirming the story of the salmon and Thunderbirds, the eternal cycle of life, and the story of one of the Salish Peoples who paddled past this location over many generations.

ts'u-hey-us, 2011
Carved and painted western red cedar
with copper features
Approx. 3.5 × 1.3 × 1.1 m

ts'u-hey-us

LOCATION: Douglas College
700 Royal Ave, sχʷeyəməɬ (New Westminster, BC)

Recognizing that significant numbers of First Nations students attend Douglas College, the school opened an Aboriginal Gathering Place in April 2011. As you enter this large room on the fourth floor of the main campus building, Susan Point's stunning, larger-than-life sculpture dominates the east part of the room, beyond which lies the Fraser River. The work's label reads, "Our pole faces both the river and the sunrise to welcome both visitors from the river and the dawn of a new day."

Susan, with her daughter Kelly and son Thomas, carved the welcome figure from windfall old-growth western red cedar. She named it *ts'u-hey-us*, the hən̓q̓əmin̓əm̓ word used mainly by women to mean a gesture of respect, acknowledgment, and welcome. It is a striking sculpture, fully in the round. A regal woman, her gaze dramatized with inset ovals of patinated copper, stands with her forearms out, palms upward in the classic Salish welcome gesture. She wears a blanket ornamented front and back with motifs that represent traditional Salish weaving patterns, and a bracelet, possibly representing a Salish horn bracelet, that repeats motifs from the blanket. Her long hair falls in beautiful masses of flowing lines to the centre of her back. Susan has recently described this figure as "one of my favourite pieces," explaining that she finds it particularly successful as a sculptural piece because of the styling of the hair.

In this contemporary space of glass, steel, and twenty-first-century furnishings, the welcome figure seems like a messenger from another time, reminding visitors of older ideas rising from a natural environment of forest and water. When you follow the gaze of the figure eastward it is easy to imagine the scene two hundred years ago: great cedars and firs covering the steep slope down to the Fraser, some of Susan's ancestors paddling upriver to trade and visit relations among the Stó:lō as the sun rises over the swift, muddy waters. We can also let our imaginations stretch forward into the future. Will the students who are welcomed by this Salish woman be careful stewards of the creation that gave birth to the tree from which she has been carved?

In recent reflections on this artwork, Susan has recalled childhood memories of her mother telling her of trips she made as a girl, in the 1920s, to visit relatives near the present-day site of the college. Edna Grant-Point travelled by horse and buggy along Marine Drive (then a dirt road), which still links the Musqueam settlement to sχʷeyəməɬ (New Westminster).[15] Susan's grandmother owned one of two houses that were inhabited by Musqueam families, located near the river on a small reserve that is no longer there. The memory adds a special layer of meaning to the welcome figure—Susan's contemporary art gives fresh expression to the welcomes given to visitors by her maternal ancestors on this very shore.

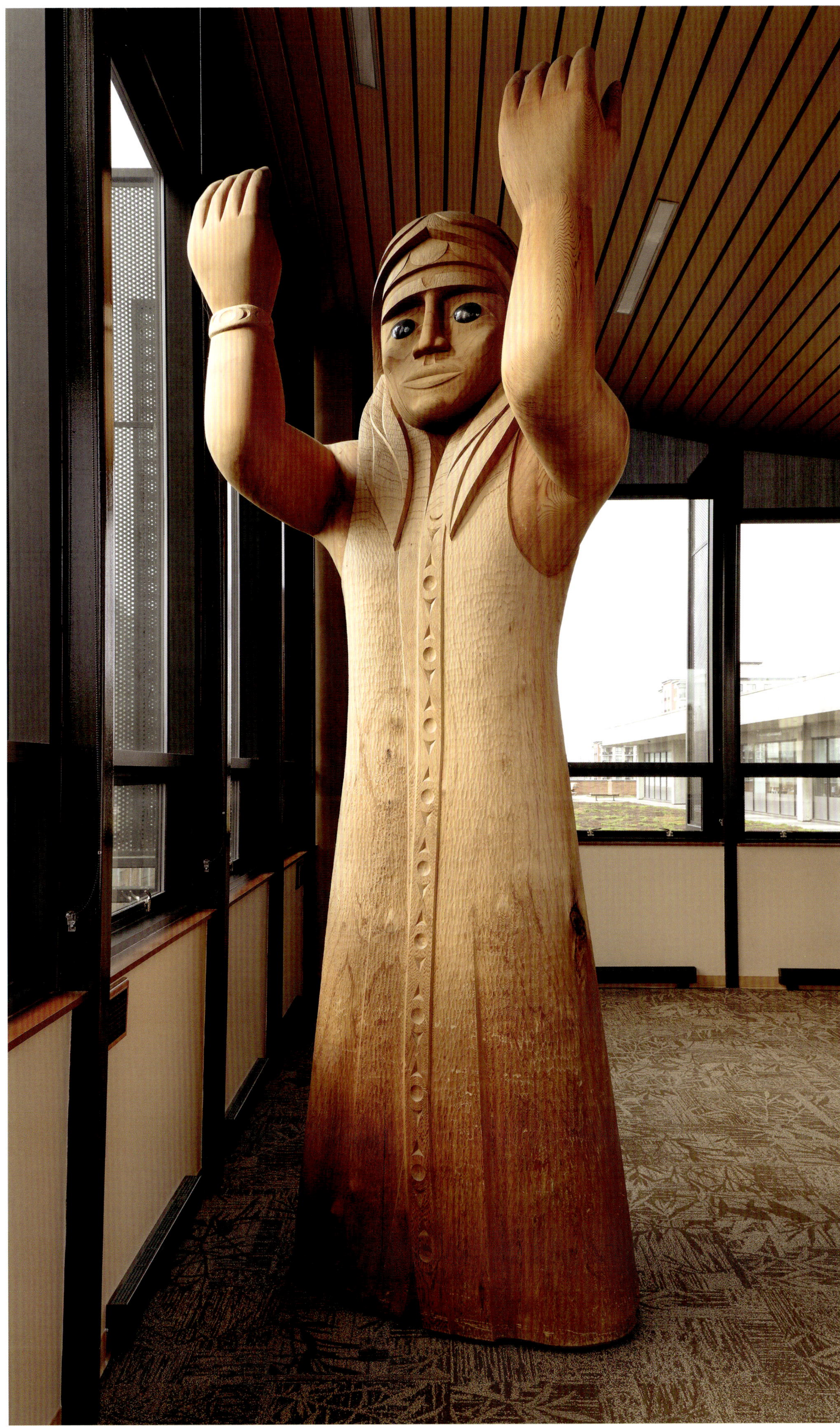

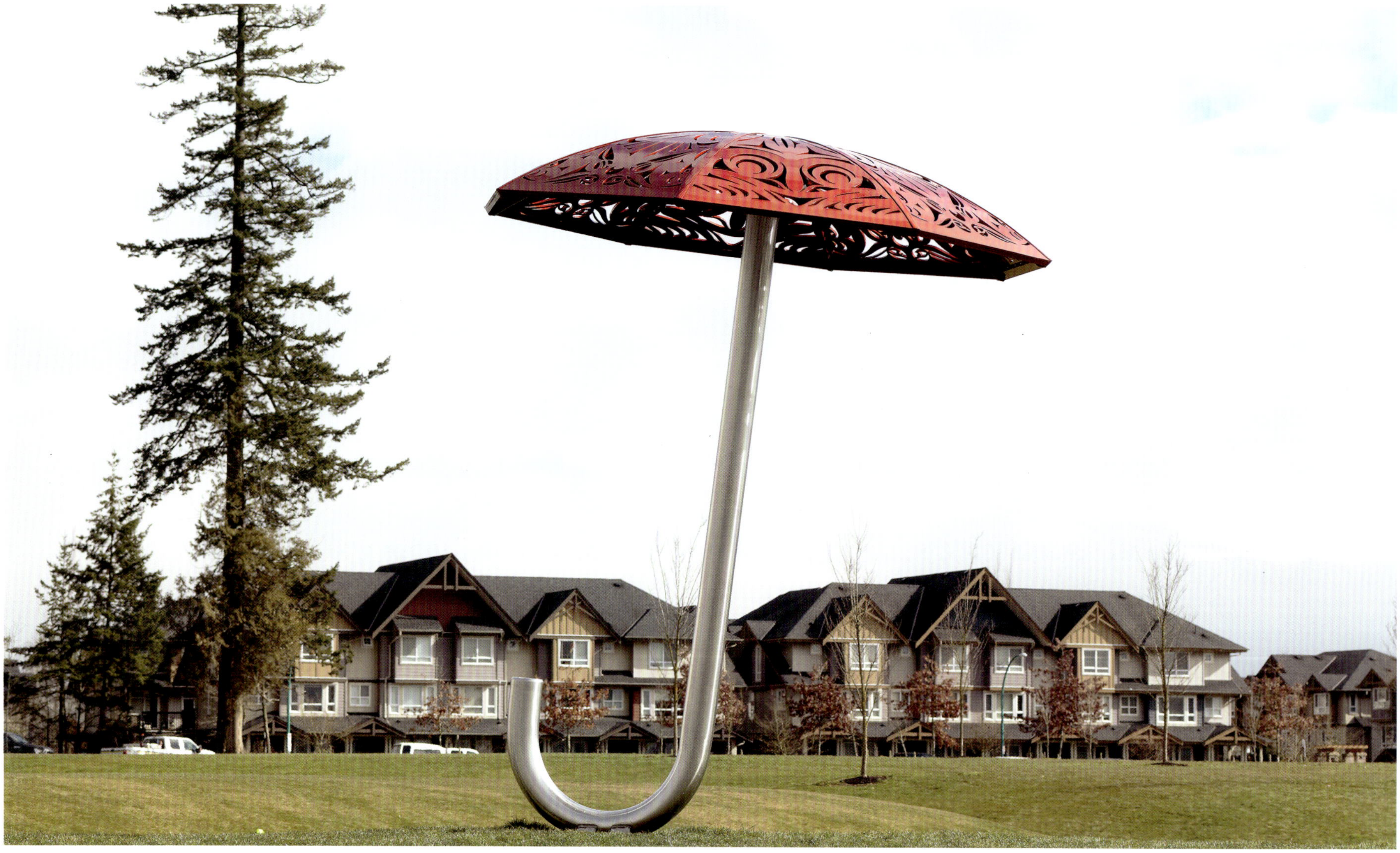

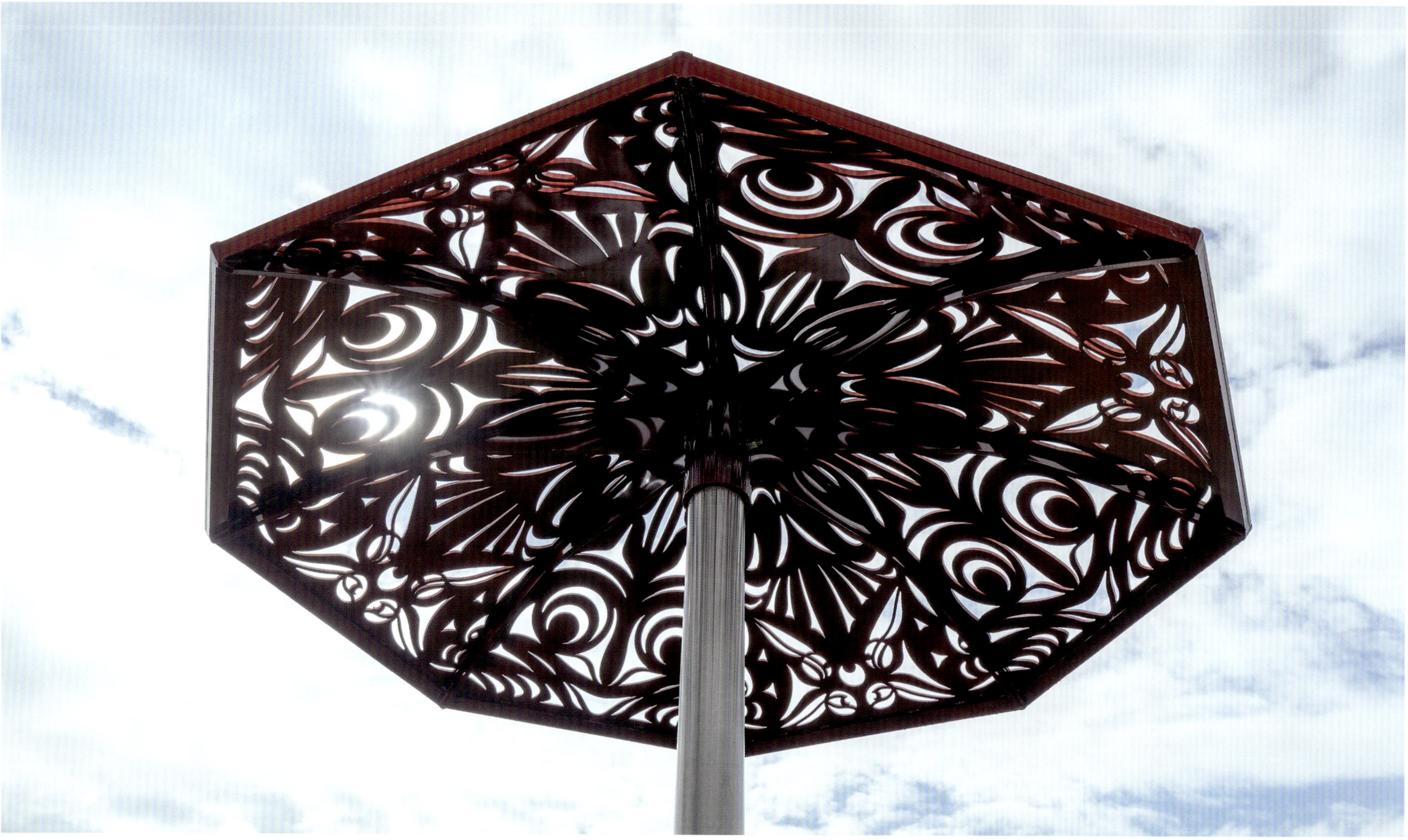

Water Guardians, 2016
Powder-coated aluminum and stainless steel
3.66 × 3.5 × 3.5 m

Water Guardians

LOCATION: Hazelgrove Park
7080 190 St, Surrey, BC

When Susan was a child, frogs were the watches and calendars of her people. She enjoyed the sound of frogs as they marked the coming of spring and, as they fell silent, the coming of winter. She feels fortunate to have experienced their song, as development of all kinds has altered the ancient habitats of many beings with whom humans share space, and from whom we get sustenance and stories. Of these creatures, frogs were among Susan's favourites. Over the years she has used them as the basis for designs on paper and in wood, metal, and glass.

In the summer of 2015, Susan won a commission from the City of Surrey to create art for a new park in an area known as East Clayton. In keeping with the ecology of the area, and the family-oriented demography of the park's main users, Susan proposed a large red umbrella made of waterjet-cut, powder-coated aluminum set on a stainless-steel handle. The motifs for the open-work design were a combination of frogs and tadpoles in Susan's contemporary Coast Salish style, as she outlined in her proposal for the work:

> I feel water has always been a primary requisite of my life.... If I am not fishing, or beachcombing, or watching frogs from the shoreline of a pond, I am imagining the world through the eyes of the creatures that have survived here since time immemorial....
>
> My artworks throughout my career are thoughtful examples of my passion for aquatic relationships and dependencies... I feel I am capturing the whimsical feelings of a young person within my proposal for this waterpark sculpture.
>
> My water theme design, "Frog Umbrella" [later changed to *Water Guardians*] is an original design created specifically for Hazelgrove Park that interacts with the intended young family-oriented audience.... All design elements are created from Coast Salish iconography in a form that represents the past, present, and future....
>
> The umbrella offers no shelter from rain, but does provide shade on hot summer days... I want the rain to fall through the umbrella... the frogs welcoming the rain to ensure their survival....
>
> I have incorporated smiling frog and tadpole motifs representing the continuance of life, and small transformative beginnings. I also chose frogs to symbolize the rhythm of the land (as songs sung by frogs have always been the indicators of changing seasons to First Nations people of the Pacific Northwest).
>
> What I really like about this design is that while viewing from the outside, you can likely see one frog... but while standing underneath, the viewer sees the whole design, which creates a kaleidoscope effect.
>
> The imagery within this design can suggest many other images by the Salish forms that I use including bird and butterfly inferences.[16]

Young children and adults both are drawn to the outsize scale of this brightly coloured umbrella (a deeply familiar object to all who live in this part of the world) that stands in for a water lily. Underneath the umbrella they can admire the Salish patterns when they look up, or, on a sunny day, when they look down—Susan ensured the sculpture is tilted so that the umbrella casts frog-shaped shadows on the earth beneath.

Frogs, 2005
Forton
274.3 × 137.2 × 5 cm

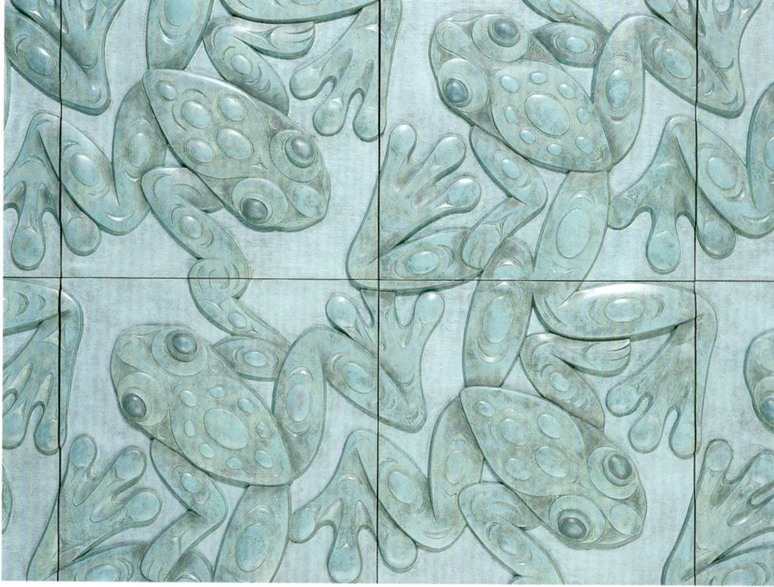

Frogs

LOCATION: South Surrey Recreation & Arts Centre
14601 20 Ave, Surrey, BC

One of Susan's favourite creatures appears again in this vivid green composition located in South Surrey, a neighbourhood that was once a forested area filled with streams and ponds where pipá:m̓ (frogs) would have flourished. Many Coast Salish Peoples believe, as she says in the label, that "the frog is the voice of the people. It symbolizes innocence, stability and communication. The voice of the frog heralds the coming of spring and its silence is the first sign that the environment is suffering." The work is a tribute to the original First Nations inhabitants of the area, including the Semiahmoo and the sc̓əwaθn məsteyəxʷ (Tsawwassen people), while at the same time inviting reflection on the impact of unrestrained human settlement on the environment, with the frog symbolizing the riches of the natural world.

Once again Susan used the grid approach that she first mastered with *Spawning Salmon* (1991; see page 117). She cast original wood carvings in polymer to create eighteen panels that fit together to form a much larger artwork. The mural was initially placed in a vertical orientation in a stairwell near the entrance to the building, and later moved and set horizontally behind the main reception desk.

The frogs achieve considerable three dimensionality, with Salish-style wedges and crescents providing additional emphasis. The liveliness of the work reveals another objective of Susan's, which she explained in a statement to Surrey officials: "The frog is also a playful image, which I believe has an appeal for all age groups.... By using this kind of universal image, I hope to create a focal point for the community, something which will draw people to the facility and enhance the sense of pride which they feel in their community."[17]

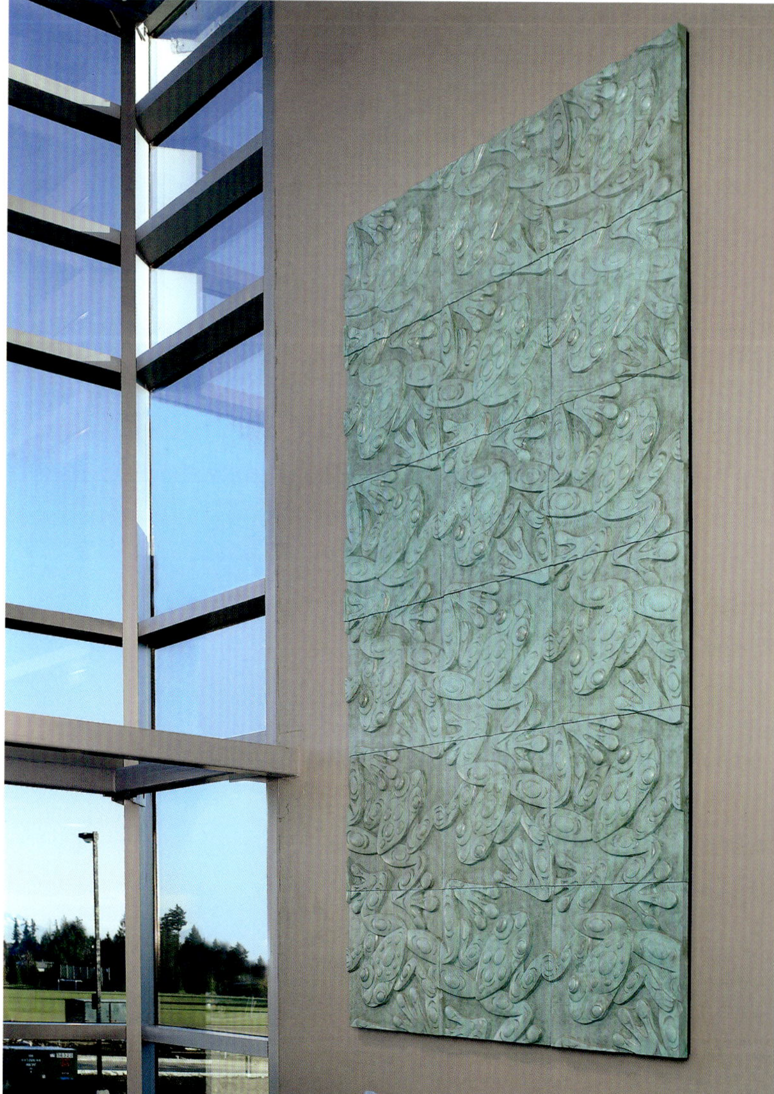

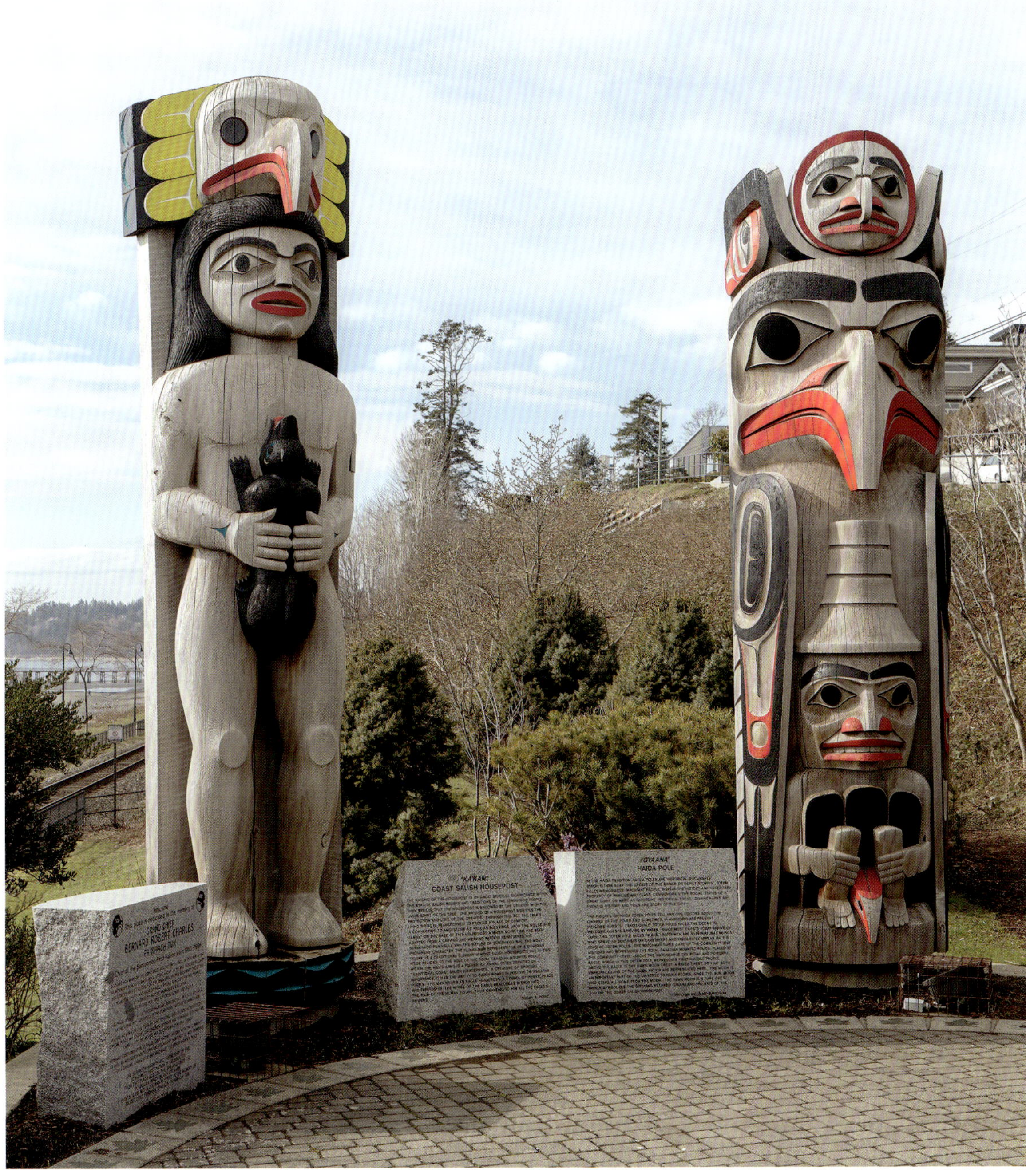

Ka'kan (left; designed by Susan Point) and Gyaana (designed by Robert Davidson), 1999
Carved and painted western red cedar
Approx. 4 × 1 × .68 m (Ka'kan)

Ka'kan

LOCATION: Totem Plaza
15000 block Marine Dr, White Rock, BC

In a small circular plaza above a huge arc of beach, overlooking the sea at Semiahmoo Bay, stand two First Nations wood sculptures. The Haida pole and Coast Salish housepost were formally raised in a traditional ceremony on 25 April 1999.

In 1997, a year before the 125th anniversary of the establishment of the Royal Canadian Mounted Police, the White Rock RCMP invited the renowned Haida carver Robert Davidson to create two totem poles to be installed in the city in permanent commemoration of this milestone anniversary. Davidson's studio at the time was on the traditional lands of the Semiahmoo First Nation, just southeast of White Rock. Titled *The Gift*, the two works were meant to signify a relationship between the RCMP and the First Nations, and to be an important site for the whole community to gain a deeper appreciation of First Nations art.

Davidson was mindful of the importance of ensuring that the project respected the distinctive traditions and art of the (Coast Salish) Semiahmoo First Nation, which vary in important ways from those of the Haida. So he reached out to Susan Point, who designed a housepost in traditional Coast Salish style but did not carve the housepost, instead accepting Davidson's proposal that he supervise the carving with the help of Leonard Wells and Leslie Wells, young Semiahmoo men whom he would train to carve. Susan sent Davidson notes on the details and meaning of her design.

> This Coast Salish housepost is scaled at 2″=1′. I was told that the log was about 4′ in diameter. I have designed this housepost at 3.5′ to be safe. The arms can take advantage of the 4′ if it is necessary or the elbows can be brought in if necessary. Originally, houseposts used to hold up cross beams for the roof of a longhouse. They in turn supported long interlocking planks of red cedar, the roof of the longhouse.
>
> This housepost is representative of a guardian figure. Above his head is an eagle, the eagle being a symbol of power; its down is a symbol of peace and friendship. The wings of the eagle is also the hair of the man. Within his arms is a fisher—an animal that is quite often seen on traditional houseposts and which has the ability to carry power in positive or negative form. On the base is a water motif which has been adapted from a weaving pattern.[18]

Susan expanded on these ideas for an inscription that now accompanies her housepost under the title "Ka'kan Coast Salish housepost" ("Ka'kan" is an Anglicization of qeqən, the hən̓q̓əmin̓əm̓ word for "housepost").

> The raising of the housepost is of great spiritual significance within the Straits Salish beliefs and traditions of the Semiahmoo People. They believe that the housepost is endowed by the Creator with the living spirit of the tree. The raising of the housepost signifies the protection and love of the Creator. Through this act the tree's living spirit is transformed to provide a place of comfort, a connection to ancestors as well as blessings upon the house and family. On the base of this housepost a water motif that has been adapted from a carving and weaving pattern represents the waters of Semiahmoo Bay. The most prominent character, the human man, representative of a guardian spirit is a traditional element in most Salish houseposts and in this piece relates to the role of the Royal Canadian Mounted Police.

These two sculptures provide a rare opportunity in the Greater Vancouver area to appreciate in one location the differences between Haida and Salish art. The proportions of the Salish figures are much closer to those in nature, while the Haida style is more structured and formal, with the figures sometimes less immediately recognizable to the viewer. Both these artworks speak powerfully to their own traditions and stand as unique expressions of X̱aayda (Haida) and Salish cultures.

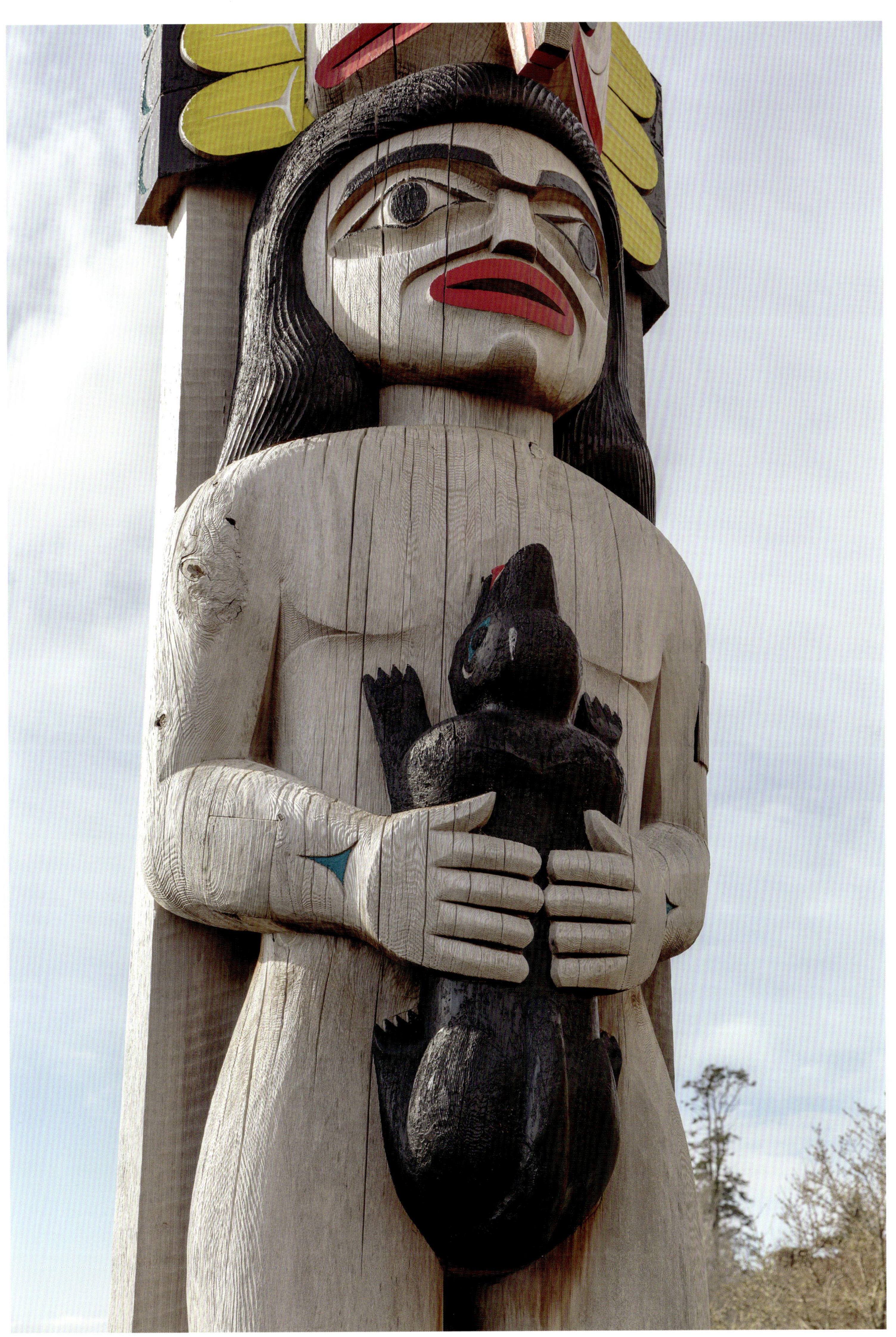

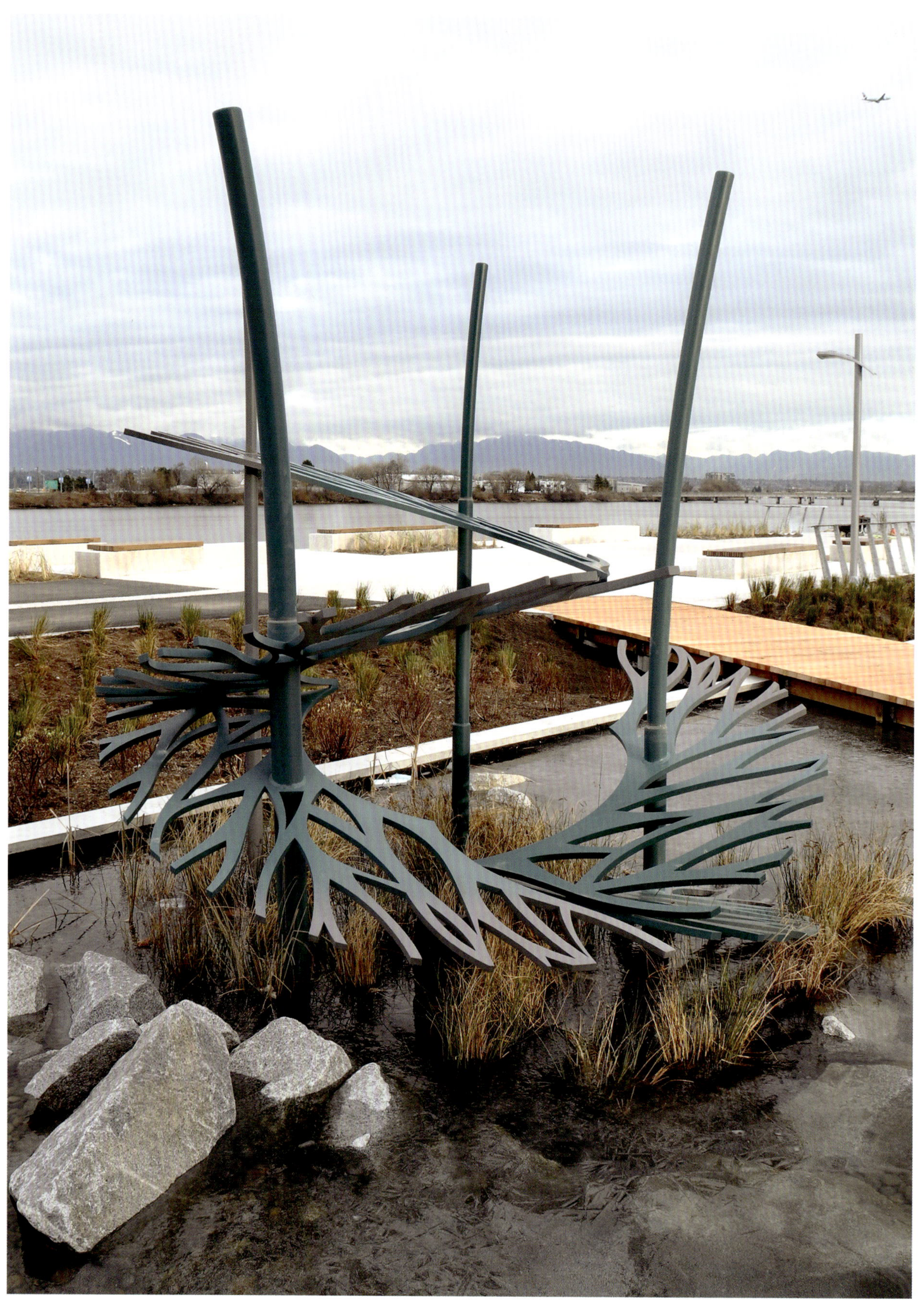

Fish Trap Way, 2014
Powder-coated aluminum (fish trap)
2.13 × 2.74 × 2.74 m

Fish Trap Way

LOCATION: River Green
5111 Brighouse Way, Richmond, BC

Three important works of Susan's are located within a short distance of each other, all a short paddle upriver from sp̓ələk̓ʷəqs, the site of a former Musqueam settlement at the mouth of the Middle Arm of the Fraser River. The first is a tribute to salmon made in collaboration with her son, Thomas Cannell, and installed in a new riverfront development called River Green. Susan and Thomas named the work *Fish Trap Way* after the path that runs atop a dyke, connecting the development to the Richmond Olympic Oval.

In their call for expressions of interest from Coast Salish artists, the developers requested "a public art interpretation of the 'fish trap' and/or similar Fraser River use ... suggested by an imaginative interpretation which would be a source of education and play."[19] Susan and Thomas's chosen proposal drew on family tradition to convey the longstanding and vital importance of salmon to the Musqueam people.

> For thousands of years, salmon have been integral to the maturity of our Musqueam people and culture. Salmon face grave dangers all of their lives; only one out of every one hundred salmon return to their spawning grounds today making them a very precious gift.
>
> This site on the middle arm was, and continues to be used by Musqueam people for harvesting salmon. Traditionally members from each of the big-house families would set two large poles in the water at low tide. These poles were set so well they would last for years unlike the intricately woven cedar traps tied between them. Family members would camp at these spots to ensure that their traps would catch enough fish to get their families through the winter months and have enough for commerce.[20]

Susan and Thomas also recalled a story passed to them by the late Dominic Point, Susan's uncle, telling of recent dramatic changes in the salmon story on the Fraser River. He told of a particular name given to the site: Black Waters. "Black because so many salmon gathered in this area waiting to come up the river to spawn. The salmon would wait for just the right high tide, a full moon, and then they would begin up the river."[21] The proposal then goes on to describe each element of the four-part work in detail.

> Two (Basalt) Salish markers are each representing the journeys that salmon must make in order to continue the cycle of life and maintain their survival. From granite juvenile fish splashing around their tributaries, to the determined adults swimming against the current, splashing over waterfalls, breaching the surface to reach their homeland, it's a reminder of our own playful beginnings and our trepidations later in life. The adult salmon represented on our Salish Markers even include copper domed eyes, a form of currency used by first nations of the Northwest ... showing the trade value of the salmon between communities.
>
> While pondering the legacy of the salmon, two Salish stools each with a design reflecting the importance of the cycle of life and the connections in nature vital to a balanced ecosystem are offered.
>
> Off the side of Fish Trap Way, a bright Coast Salish Medallion inlay represents Salmon waiting for the full moon. They have already

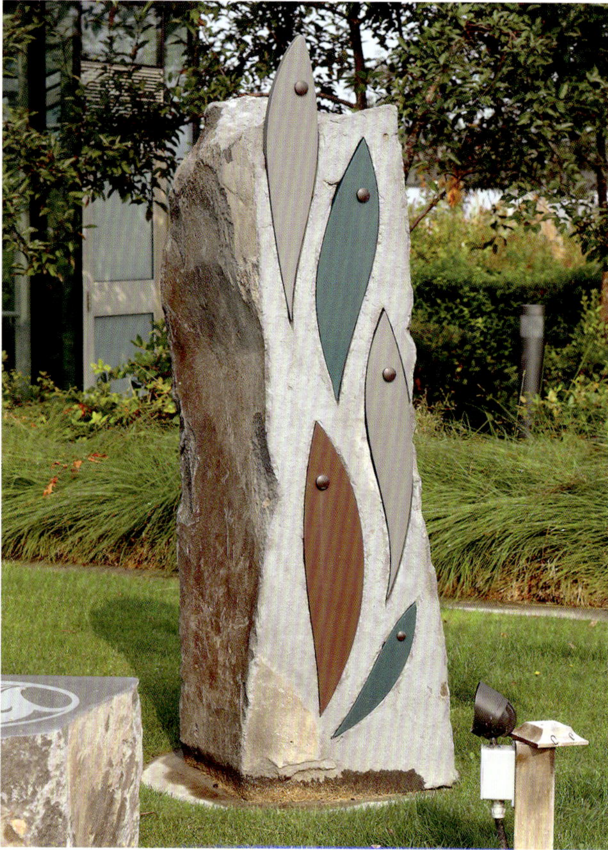

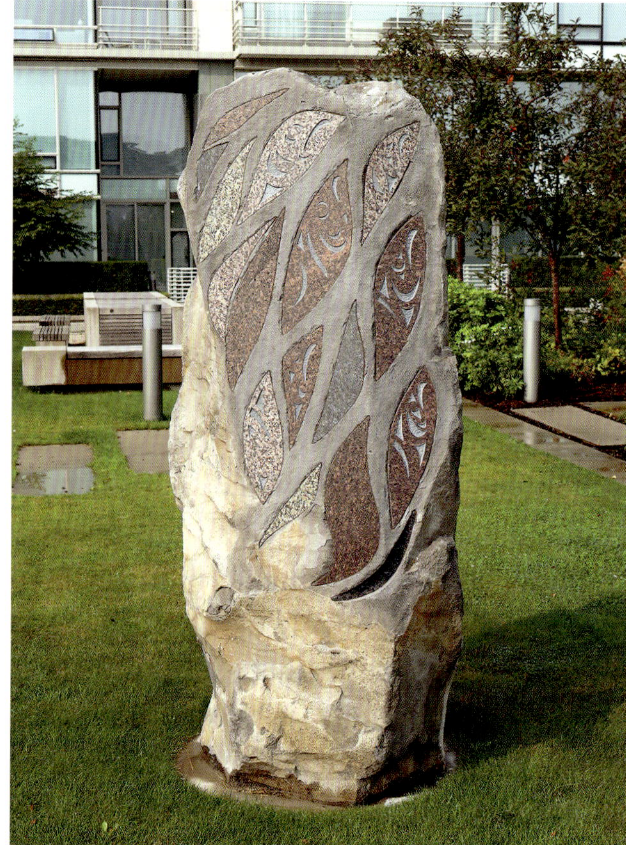

Fish Trap Way, 2014
Basalt with coloured granite inlays and copper features (markers, pictured at top); sandblasted basalt (stools, not pictured); coloured granite (inlay, pictured at bottom) 182.9 × 76.2 × 76.2 cm (markers; each); 76.2 × 63.4 × 60.9 cm (stools; each); 121.9 × 121.9 × 2.5 cm (inlay)

started changing colour and millions gather in this tide. It used to be told that you could walk across the backs of the millions of fish in the water; therefore we have chosen to place this motif in the path so that their backs can be walked across, a tribute to the history and once abundant numbers of these marvelous fish.

[In] the piece that harmonizes the salmon theme, a contemporary colour-blended aluminum Fish Trap, fish silhouettes are pieced out from the one-inch aluminum and gently rounded so as not to leave any sharp edges. The negative fish elements make a positive design element . . . roots, from the great western red cedar. It also resembles the cedar boughs hanging loosely in the wind. Motifs of plants and even a suggested heron's wing are symbolic of the local wetlands while the entire design symbolizes fish caught in a trap.

The design was also influenced by an aerial view of the tidal waters around Richmond; at low water the drainage ditches around the shoreline resemble roots, the lifelines of our culture.

Clean lines make for an elegant sculpture with subtle design elements incorporated within the piece. That is the art style of our Coast Salish peoples.

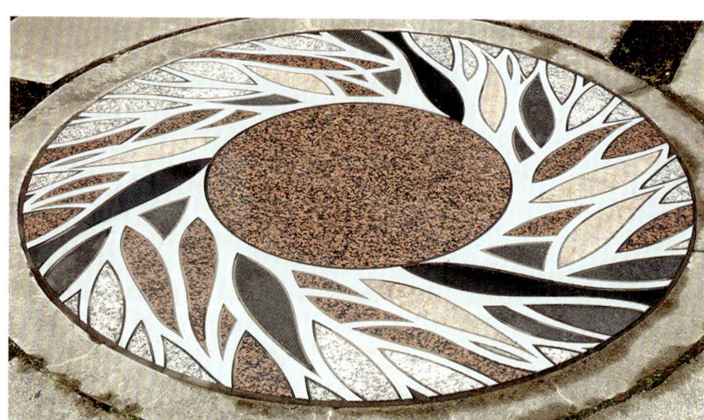

This design incorporates the land, the water, the plant life of both, and the rich history of the site well defined by the fish trap with bountiful fish. The sculpture to us means keeping a Musqueam footmark on the traditional land of our past, present, and future.[22]

This dramatic and complex work is best appreciated in a walk around the various components, which vary in medium from traditional basalt to modern powder-coated aluminum. The trap itself is elegant and ingenious, the four vertical aluminum poles forming a support for the upward curve of roots and branches formed from the outlines of salmon and other elements.

Blue Herons

LOCATION: Richmond Olympic Oval
6111 River Rd, Richmond, BC

One of the most architecturally dramatic of the facilities built for the 2010 Winter Olympic Games is the Richmond Olympic Oval. Set on the south bank of the Middle Arm of the Fraser River (immediately east of River Green), the building faces a large festival plaza with superb views across the river and the delta lands, toward the traditional settlement of the Musqueam people.

A prominent feature on the north, river-facing side of the oval is a series of fifteen concrete buttresses. These include runnels to carry stormwater from the roof, and were designed to be wide enough to feature high-relief decoration. Jane Fernyhough, then manager of Heritage and Cultural Services for Richmond, set out the plan in a report to city council.

> These buttresses are massive structural elements, and establishing human-scaled and intimate detailing at the pedestrian level will create a more welcoming facility.... Because of their form and function, the concrete buttresses can be viewed as a contemporary interpretation of housepost forms, an important element in Coast Salish Culture. Building on this connection, using Musqueam motifs in the runnels would add meaning that is authentic to the site.[23]

The request for proposals from "artists with demonstrable skills in the expression of Musqueam heritage and contemporary art practice" stressed the need for experience casting relief sculpture in concrete and creating large-scale public artworks, and also emphasized the significance of the location to the Musqueam First Nation, noting that "Musqueam historians and storytellers have told us that this location is one where they fished and gathered, and is not far from an historic village site." The plan for the runnels was that "deep articulated relief patterns will activate the water as it flows downward, and will make the runnels more dramatic when no water is flowing. The Musqueam designs will also bring a human-scale and authentic meaning to Oval visitors."[24] The timelines were very tight for this project; less than a week elapsed between the three proposals being received and the project awarded.

Based on her experience, her knowledge of Salish imagery, and her knowledge of the site, the project fitted Susan's creative approach especially well. In her submission she remarked:

> This artwork is a dedication to the Fraser river, on whose shores my people have lived and prospered for countless generations. It is also a tribute to all rivers that shape the destiny of those who live by their cycle and spiritual encounters. The river alters its shape and course over time, yet remains at the heart of the changing communities around it.
>
> The artwork incorporates a series of positive and negative elements, which (when rendered in three dimensional form) allow water to flow down the face of the runnel—the artwork, like the river itself, will change with the seasons. Each design includes the heron/crane as a central image—a symbol used by the City of Richmond. The subtle inclusion of the heron/crane as a negative image allows rainwater to flow over and through the body of the bird. The heron/crane is also a prominent bird featuring in many legends told by my elders and often seen on traditional Salish implements.

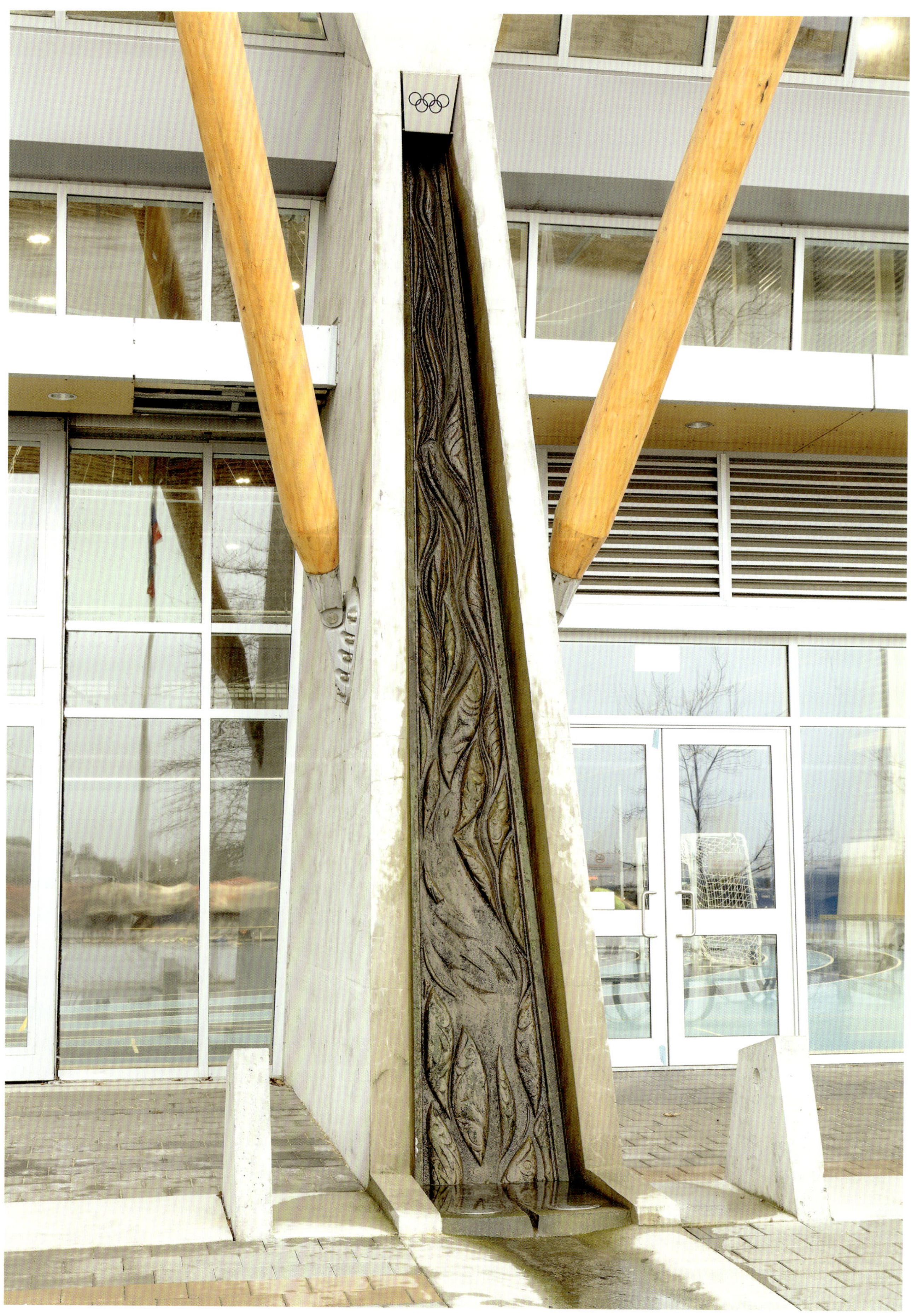

Blue Herons, 2008
Concrete
5.5 × .76 m

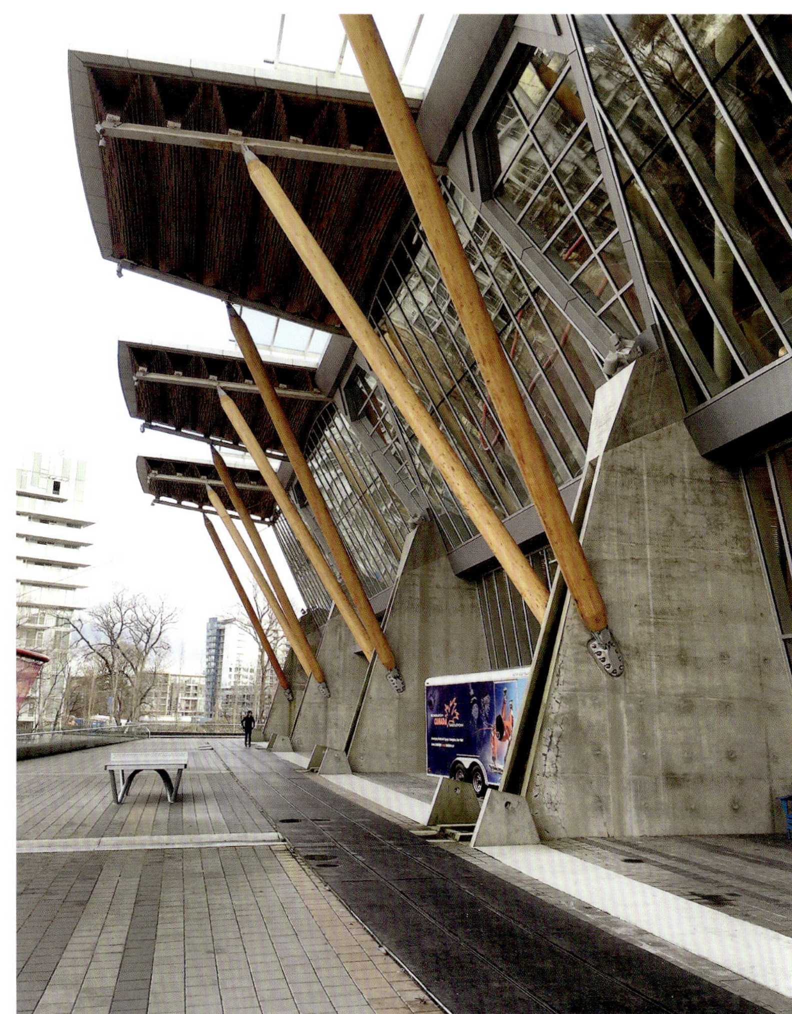

> The third element in my design depicts contemporary salmon, and symbolically represents the delta. The salmon populating the river were a form of wealth, sustenance for our peoples, and used in trade with other tribes. . . .
>
> The imagery reflects the land, sea and sky—and the connections between all forms of life and the earth, which we inhabit. Recent scientific research reveals the central role of the salmon in the ecology of the Pacific Northwest. Nitrogen 15 (a traceable essential element originating in the deep ocean) is found in Salmon, bears, songbirds, and even the trees of the forest. The bears drag their catch of salmon under the trees, which absorb the traces of Nitrogen 15 through their roots—these chemical links illustrate the connections between all living things as this element is transferred through the web of life.[25]

Richmond City Council approved Susan's pencil drawings of three different designs in July 2006. Each of the three designs was reproduced five times and fitted alternately into the central spaces of the buttresses. Susan was on-site to supervise the installation, an important and increasingly necessary aspect of her work.

> I love supervising my art installations to ensure that nothing ever goes wrong. Also, I often oversee site conditions and develop a plan for execution. I, as well as my sons, Thomas and Brent, have learned a thing or two with respect to engineering, consulting with architects and contractors, and fabricating for equipment required.
>
> Nowadays, it's not just being an artist(s) creating a work of art . . . you have to know everything there is to know about structural engineering, site preparation for your art piece, the ins and outs of fabricating your art piece, the proper and safe way of installation of your artwork among many other technical issues . . . these requirements I and my boys have learned hands-on and abided by with all my public art projects.[26]

Since the oval's opening in 2010, the flowing water has stained the relief forms to varying degrees, in places obscuring the imagery. Time spent with the original carvings at SFU (see *Blue Herons*, 2008, page 137) is well repaid by giving the clearest idea of the vision that Susan had for her work. The imagery of the runnels is now softer than the precise shapes and lines of the carved and coloured red cedar at SFU, but both ensure that contemporary Salish art produces a long-lasting statement in a modern building, using imagery central to the traditional economy and beliefs of the Musqueam.

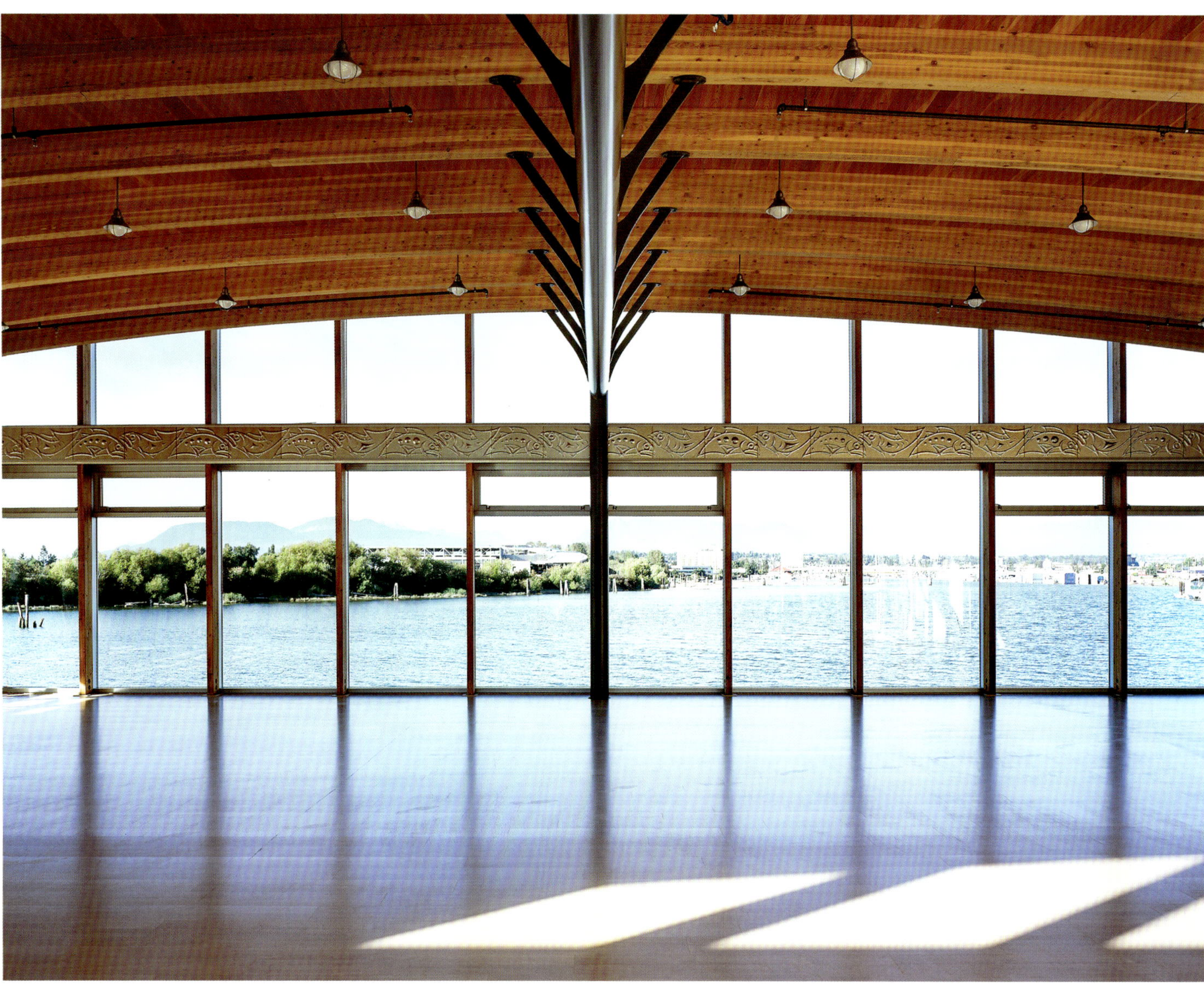

Golden Salmon

LOCATION: John M.S. Lecky UBC Boathouse
7277 River Rd, Richmond, BC

As a symbol of cultural traditions and economic livelihood, salmon appear in many of Susan's artworks and are among the most important references in her iconographic palette. In 2006, she employed them as the central motif in a beautiful glass mural created for the newly built home of the famed UBC Rowing Club.

Because the boathouse is on the Middle Arm of the Fraser River, traditionally fished and occupied by the Musqueam people, the committee responsible for the project recognized that discussion with the Musqueam was as important as the choice of an artist to provide the main aesthetic embellishment for the hall. The committee strongly felt that Susan Point was the logical and best choice of an artist.

Susan met with the committee on 6 March 2006 and presented her proposal for a frieze consisting of two panels of two salmon, each sixty centimetres wide, in classic Salish style, repeated to form a graceful arc over fifteen metres across the entire north wall of the hall. The principal architect

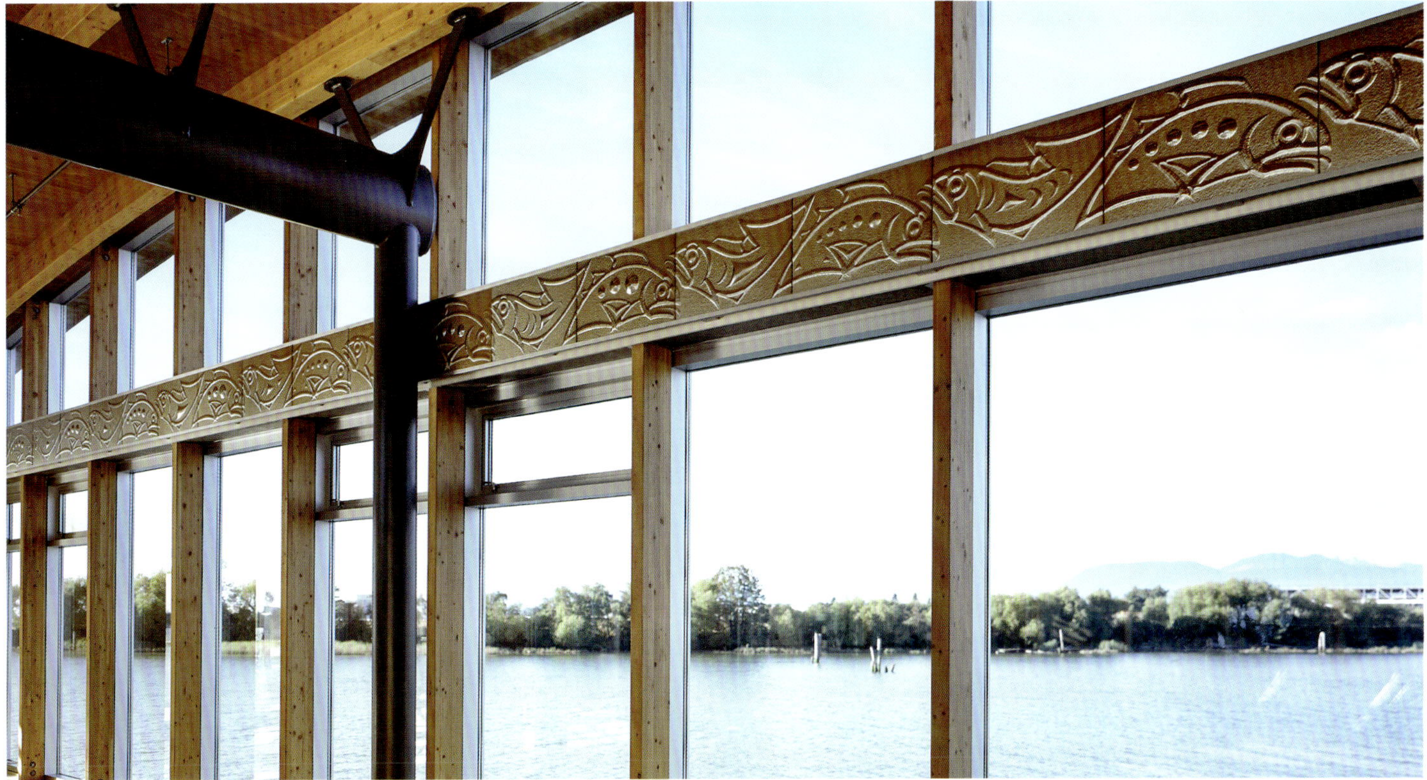

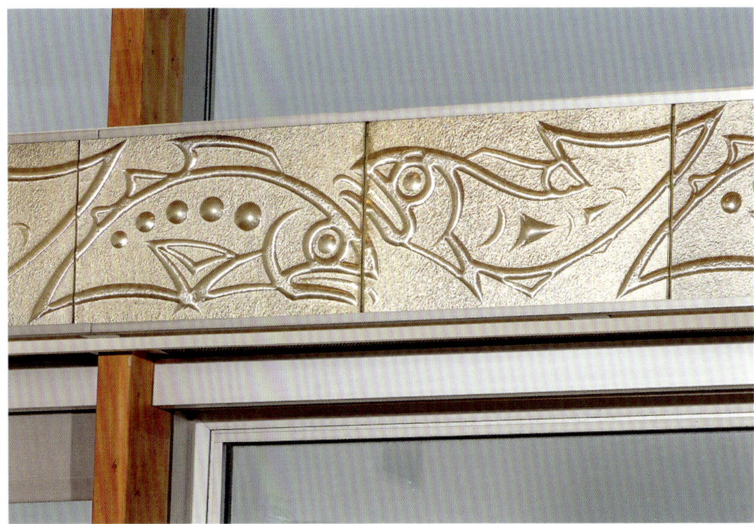

suggested the work be cast in silver-coloured glass, but fortunately Susan's desire for gold glass prevailed.

Adele Weder described the boathouse and Susan's work in glowing terms in *Canadian Architect*: "With its clean simplicity and floor-to-ceiling glazing, the event hall opens up a panoramic river view. The ceiling is a splendid expanse of Douglas fir. Below the curved clerestory, an otherwise neutral space is enriched by a frieze with a fish-motif bas-relief sculpture created by Musqueam artist Susan Point."[27]

"Enriched" is a perfect description of the contribution of Susan's salmon frieze, which tells a story that honours the Musqueam people, the salmon, and the rowers, all highly skilled navigators of the Fraser's waters. The gold of the glass can represent the economic value of salmon, so central to the historic and present-day life of the Musqueam, but also the medals won by rowers who have come to the banks of this ancient river to test themselves and their bodies against the power of the water.

Golden Salmon, 2006
Kiln-cast gold glass
.6 × 15 m

Part Three

Salish Lands

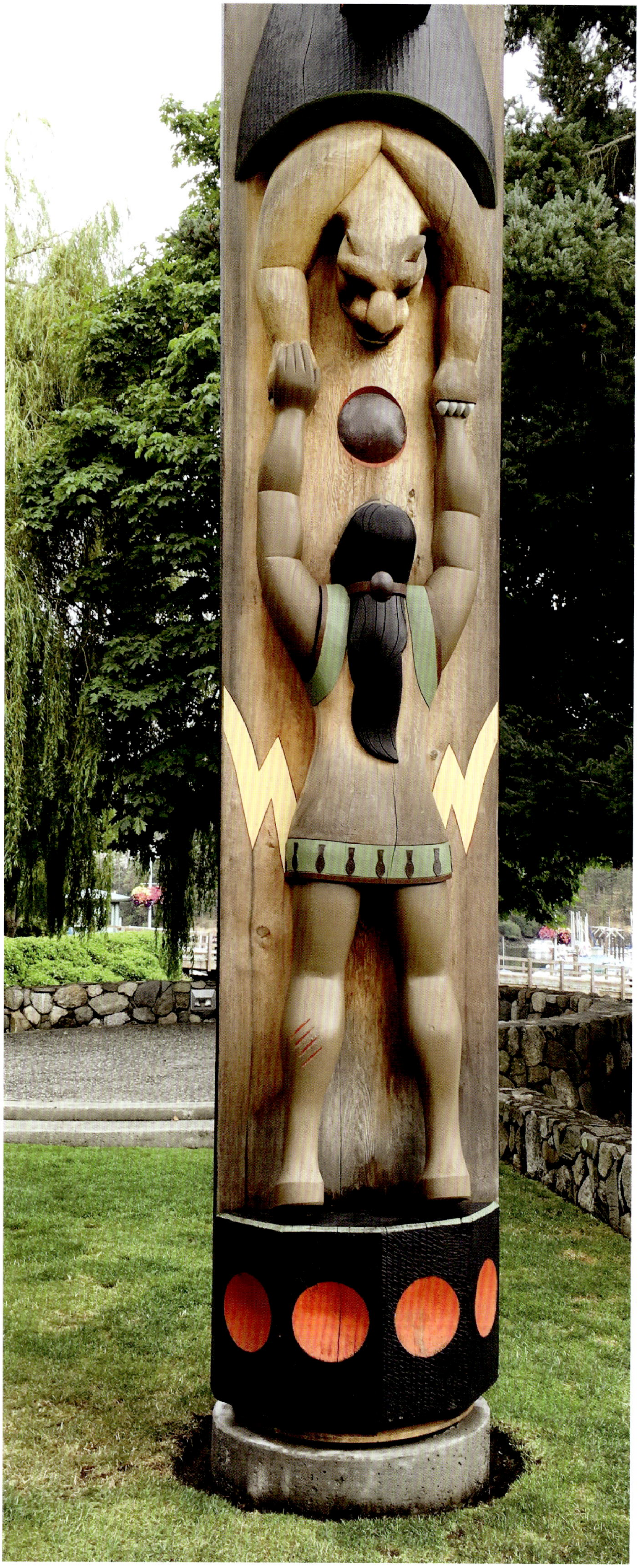

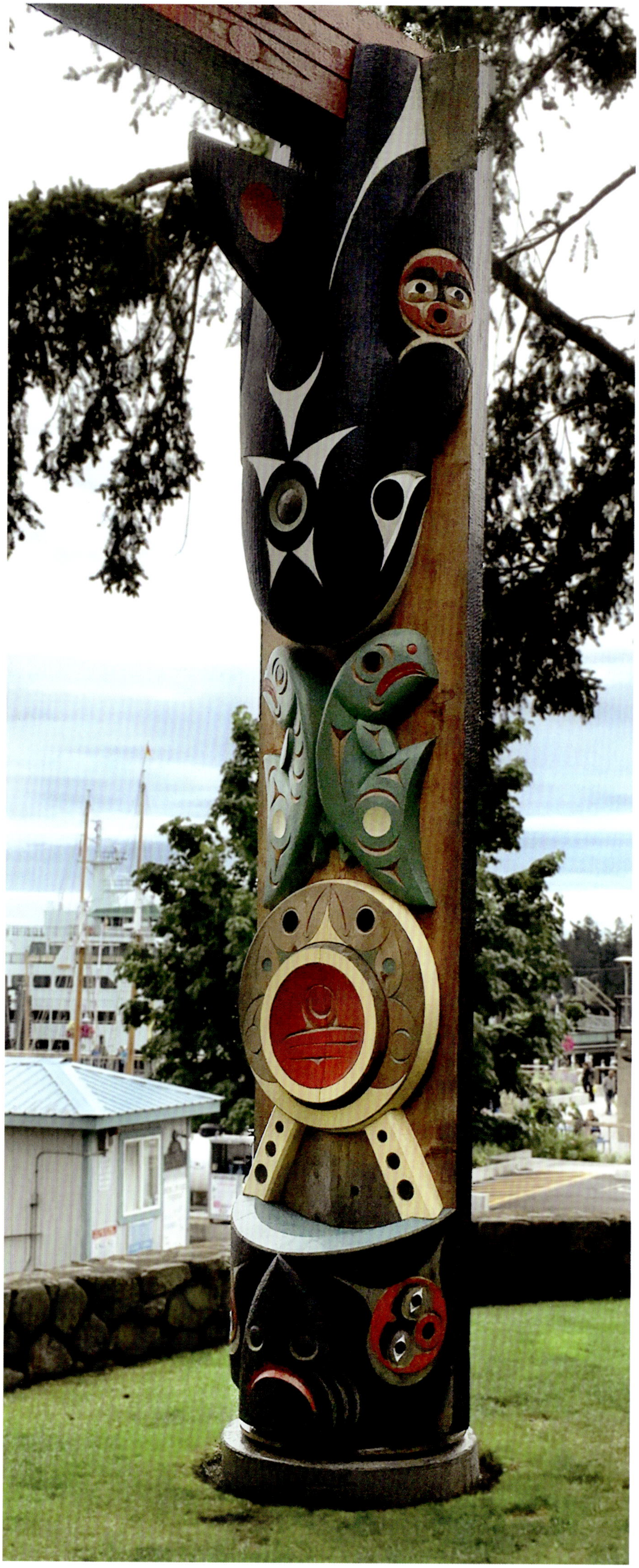

Interaction, 2004
Carved and painted western red cedar with copper features
4.98 × 4.47 × approx. .8 m

Interaction

LOCATION: Fairweather Park
204 Front St, Friday Harbor, San Juan Island, WA

Susan completed carving these old-growth posts in 2000, and her children Thomas and Kelly Cannell helped her paint them. They were displayed at the Spirit Wrestler Gallery in Vancouver, then returned to her studio at Musqueam where they remained until 2004. Their destiny, which unfolded in the intervening years, was to be moved south across the international boundary that artificially separates many of the Salishan-speaking Peoples from relatives and ancestral lands.

On one post, a full-length figure of a woman stretches up to place a hand on the paw of a cougar emerging from a cave, who in turn is holding a paw on her hand. A copper dome between them represents their shared environment. This imagery is inspired to a degree by a 120-year-old housepost originally from the Musqueam settlement and now on display at MOA. The overall impression is of mutual respect between humans and animals in a world of shared resources.

The emphasis in the second post is on the sea and its resources. At the top of the post is a killer whale, its mouth facing down toward two salmon above a circle representing the sun. Bill McLennan, former curator and technician at MOA, continues the description of the post: "The sun is life, and the salmon egg within the sun, new life. Two sɬewəƭ (herring) are carved on the outer ring of the sun; two containers of valuables carried by the sun are indicated by copper disks. The whale's head at the base, carved with a shark's head motif, is designed as a seat. It is the artist's intention that the individual who sits there completes the sculpture by connecting to the life cycle."[1]

Susan linked the two posts with a lintel (or crossbeam). McLennan describes how she chose symbols appropriate to the lintel's position in the structure: "As this is the highest point in a house, celestial images are an appropriate embellishment. On one side of the beam is Xels, a being from the past, who could fly and transform itself into any creature or object it wished. The other side of the beam features two eagles with a silver dome representing the full moon. Stars and a new moon adorn the top and bottom of the beam respectively."[2]

Two determined individuals, Barbara Marrett and Lee Brooks, residents of Friday Harbor and owner-operators of the Arctic Raven Gallery there, visited Susan's workshop—accompanied by two friends from San Juan Island, art collectors Karen Westrell and her husband Bill Rosser— and were captivated by the houseposts and lintel. They conceived a bold plan to fundraise in their community, purchase the posts, and install the town's first public art on the waterfront in Friday Harbour. They formed the volunteer-run "Portals of Welcome Committee" to raise awareness about what they saw as a unique opportunity, and succeeded in getting a significant donation from the town council of Friday Harbor. As Brooks expressed it in March of 2004, when the committee was nearing completion of its fundraising activity:

> There is a set of Coast Salish house posts that yearns for a new life along their traditional shores. . . . Their message of respect for our ecosystem empowers all the people that now share this land. . . . These portals provide a window to the richness of the past, create a critical framework to view the present and are a catalyst for a promising future. . . .
>
> [The proposed location of the houseposts] reflects our mission to promote an invigorated environmental stewardship and re-emphasize sustainability. The extended purpose of our

committee is to acknowledge the Coast Salish presence in the San Juans.[3]

Susan and her family were willing participants in the plan. The objectives of the committee fit well with the consistent themes of Susan's art, and she worked regularly with the group toward their shared goal of educating the public about the nature of Salish art forms and lifeways, in a place where the Salish had had no visible artistic presence for many decades. She approached this opportunity with her characteristic sensitivity.

The Musqueam people, in the time before European settlers entered the area that became known as the San Juan Islands, did not have settlements as far south as San Juan Island, but they undoubtedly travelled and visited the original inhabitants of the islands, their Coast Salish cultural cousins the xʷɬəməy̓ (Lummi), sabš (Samish), and sxʷdabš (Swinomish) Peoples. The Lummi had a longhouse in Garrison Bay on San Juan Island in 1858, and shell middens attest to First Nations occupancy long before the nineteenth century. [4] Most notably in relation to the portals project is the ongoing struggle of the Mitchell Bay Band, whose territory lies closest to Friday Harbor, to be recognized by the U.S. government. In the meantime, as Susan noted, one of the goals of the project is to "re-instate the footprint of the Salish peoples on these lands."[5]

Susan ensured that the various First Nations in the area be invited to view the portals and give their blessing to these posts by a Musqueam artist coming into their lands. A series of consultations and engagements were held with representatives of the Lummi, Samish, and Swinomish Peoples, all of whom saw the posts and expressed enthusiasm that Coast Salish art would once again be on public display in their traditional lands. On 20 March 2004, the unofficial leader of the Mitchell Bay Band, Billy Chevalier, gave a blessing for Point and the portals and offered thanks for their imminent arrival in Friday Harbor.

Susan and her family joined hundreds of local residents on 22 May 2004 to watch as a tarp was pulled away to reveal the houseposts in their new permanent home. It had taken more than two years for Marrett and Brooks to fulfill their vision. The program for the ceremony stated, "*Interaction* is dedicated to welcoming all who work together in the stewardship of our precious marine ecosystem. Working together we can help restore it for future generations. These Coast Salish houseposts also serve as an acknowledgement of the thousands of years of Native presence in the San Juan islands and the Salish Sea." Once again, Susan's art had been at the centre of a major educational and artistic effort that would pay dividends for years to come. As Billy Chevalier said when he introduced Susan at the dedication ceremony, "She took these logs and brought them to life."[6]

Kneeling Stool, 1993
Carved and painted western red cedar
67 × 71 × 35.5 cm

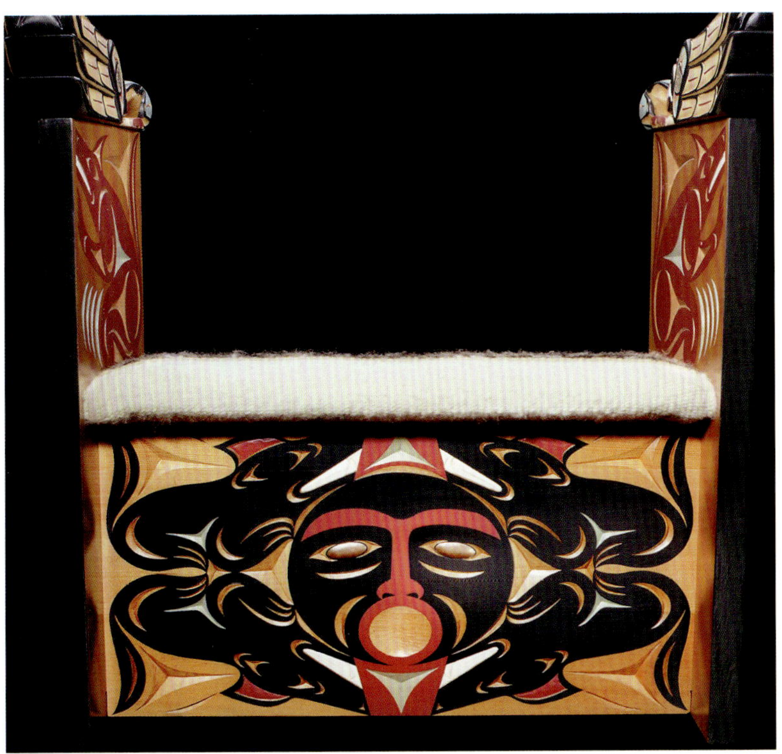

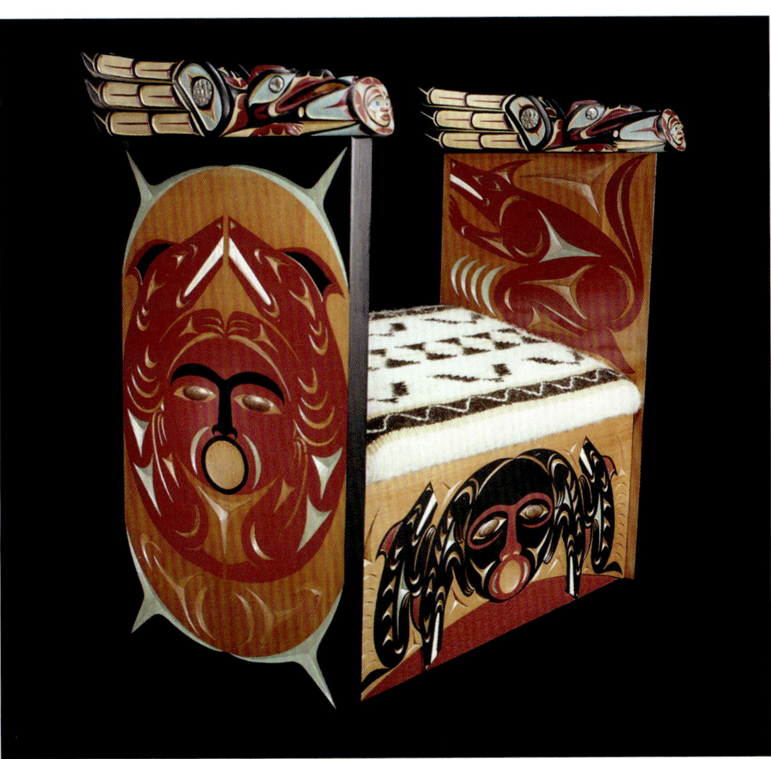

UNIVERSITY OF VICTORIA

Michael C. Williams, a prominent Victoria property owner, philanthropist, and benefactor of the University of Victoria, was also a great admirer and supporter of Susan Point and other Indigenous artists of the Northwest Coast. He collected nearly nine hundred sculptures and paintings and commissioned many works, including a collection of ceremonial furniture by Susan and several other artists.[7] Before his death in 2000 he willed virtually his entire estate to the university, including one of Susan's largest spindle whorls.

Kneeling Stool

LOCATION: University of Victoria
3800 Finnerty Rd, Victoria, BC

In 1993, Michael Williams arranged for some of the finest Indigenous artists working on the coast to produce a chancellor's chair, lectern, kneeling stool, speaker's staff, and mace stand for convocations at the university, which is on the traditional unceded territory of the Lkwungen (Songhees), Xwsepsum (sχʷəymeɬəɬ, Esquimalt), and W̱SÁNEĆ (xʷse:nəc, Saanich) Peoples. John Livingston (adopted Kwakwa̱ka̱'wakw) coordinated the effort, carved the lectern and part of the chair, and helped select the other artists: Art Thompson (Ditidaht), Calvin, Richard, and Tom Hunt (Kwagu'ł), Glen Tallio (Nuxalk), Don Yeomans (Haida), Norman Tait (Nisga'a), Ann Smith (Tutchone–Tlingit), Cheryl Samuel (adopted Tlingit), as well as Susan and her cousin, Roberta Louis, a weaver.

Susan generally avoids collaborations with non-family members, but makes exceptions "if it feels right," as in this instance.[8] She carved the entire kneeling stool with spindle whorl patterns and traditional Salish elements, except the upper handrails, which Glen Tallio carved in a Nuxalk style. Roberta Louis weaved the Salish-style covering. Susan used the faces of the stool to explore different aspects of a

Musqueam story about the Wolf People, which she tells as follows.

> Once there was a man who wanted to become an Indian doctor. As part of the ritual, he spent a great deal of time in the forest bathing in the creeks and lakes to cleanse his body and soul.
>
> One day while he was walking in the forests he was confronted by a pack of wolves. Because there were too many wolves, he was unable to defend himself, so he decided to play dead.
>
> Thinking that the man was dead, the wolves decided to carry him to their encampment.
>
> While the wolf was trotting along with the man on his back, he realized the man was still alive because the man groaned each time he was jolted.
>
> Reaching their encampment, the wolves laid the man down beside the fire. The man then saw the wolves taking off their hides to reveal their human form. One of the elders who was also lying beside the fire noticed the man open his eyes and announced to the other Wolf People that the man was still alive.
>
> After realizing that the man was still alive, the Wolf People offered him anything that he desired if he were not to reveal their secret about their disguise. Because the man told them he wanted nothing more in life than to be a good hunter, the Wolf People bestowed on him good luck and from that time forward the man always enjoyed the best of luck in hunting and became known as a good hunter.[9]

Each of the artists was invited to speak at a ceremony commemorating the gift of the furniture on 27 October 1993, the university's thirtieth anniversary year. Susan said:

> It was an honour to be selected as "The Coast Salish artist" to design and carve the kneeling stool. . . . It has just been in the past three years that I have been able to add wood carving to the list of media that I work in. This is due mainly to the teaching and direction I received from John Livingston.
>
> . . . Because the spindle whorl has been a key element that I have been working with for years—in my quest to revive Coast Salish Art—in creating the design I have incorporated circular forces within the design along the lines of the spindle whorl format. While working on this project, I very much enjoyed the challenge of working on all six sides of the kneeling stool.[10]

Good Luck

LOCATION: University of Victoria
3800 Finnerty Rd, Victoria, BC

Toward the end of Susan's first decade as a wood carver (a few years after the ceremonial furniture), Williams commissioned *Good Luck*, one of the largest spindle whorls Susan has yet carved. The work was displayed in his oceanside home near UVic until shortly after his death, when it was bequeathed to the university. It is now prominently featured in the Diana M. Priestly Law Library at UVic.

Good Luck is carved on both sides, unusual for a spindle whorl. The "front," carved in high relief, features two sce:ɬtən (salmon) whose tails terminate in a Thunderbird head. The styling of the salmon foreshadowed the design of *The River—Giver of Life*, which Susan would later carve and cast in three different materials (see pages 85, 138, and 139). Wedges and crescents mark the sṫθaṁ (bone) and muscles, conveying the strength of the fish. Salmon dominate the design until a closer look at the tail reveals the Thunderbird. The reverse side is not as dramatic, in part because it is almost monochromatic, mostly painted in a deep red. On the reverse is a shallower carving of four salmon moving counter-clockwise around a centre ring decorated with eight yellow circles.

Good Luck is another of Susan's rich tributes to Salish domestic arts and to the economy and Oral Traditions of her Musqueam people and their Salish relatives. The title refers to the widespread First Nations belief that showing two salmon in a design brings good fortune. The combination of the salmon and Thunderbirds symbolizes the interrelatedness of all creatures and the richness of the natural world.

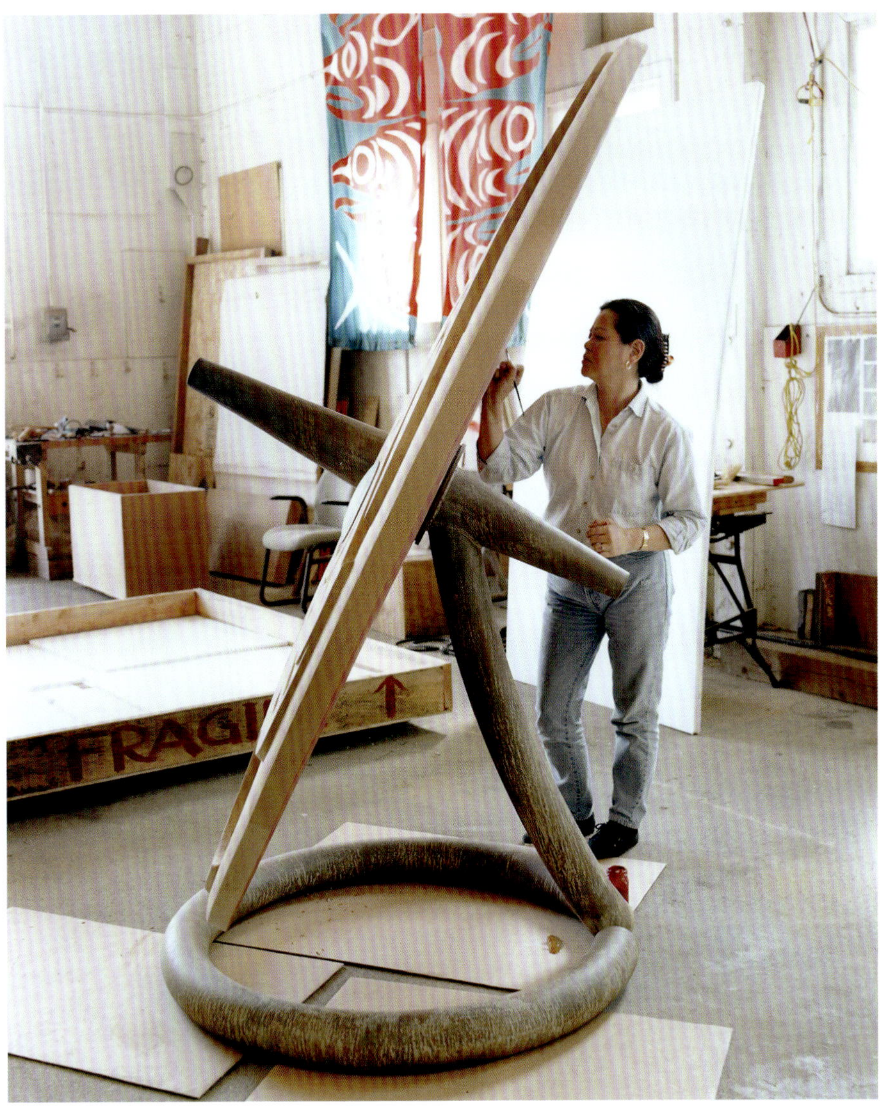

Susan puts the finishing touches on *Good Luck* at her Celtic Shipyards studio, c. 1998.

The four salmon on the reverse speak to the importance of four among the First Nations, referencing the elements, the seasons, and the life cycle of the salmon. The whorl must have delighted Michael Williams, who would have recognized the skill of the artist and the deep cultural references that are embedded in this contemporary masterwork.

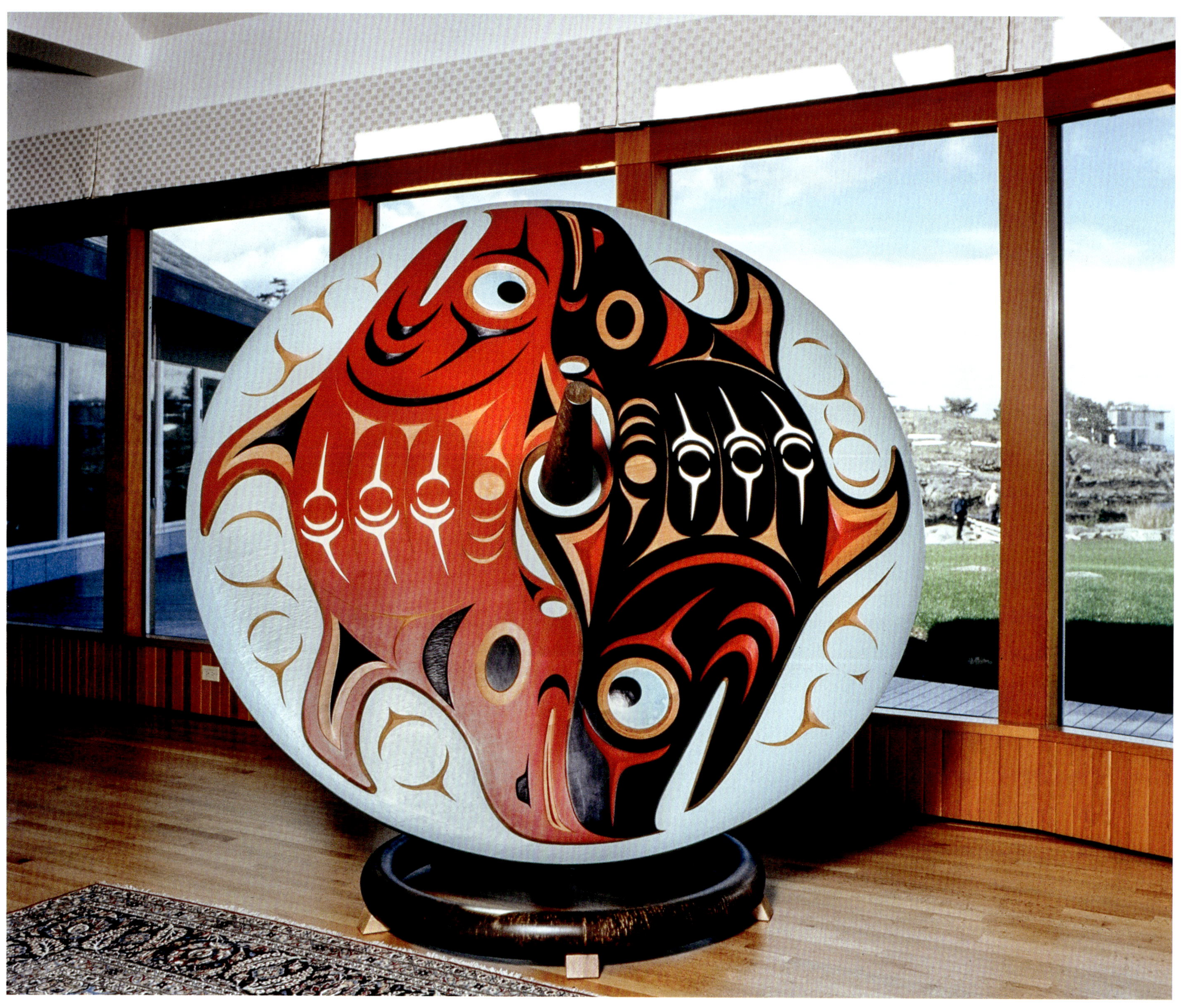

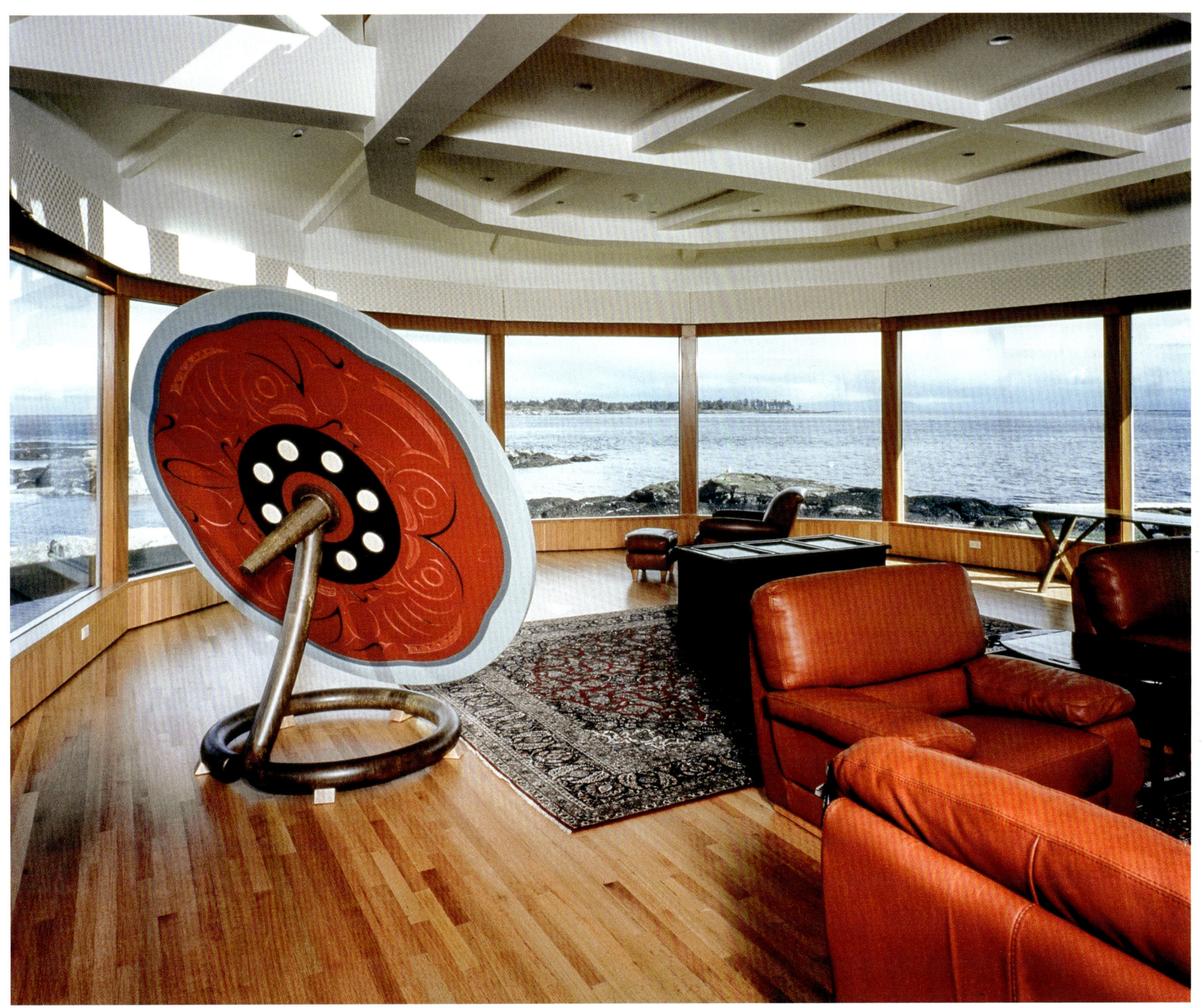

Good Luck, 1998
Carved and painted western red cedar
with copper and steel features
205 × 205 × 5 cm

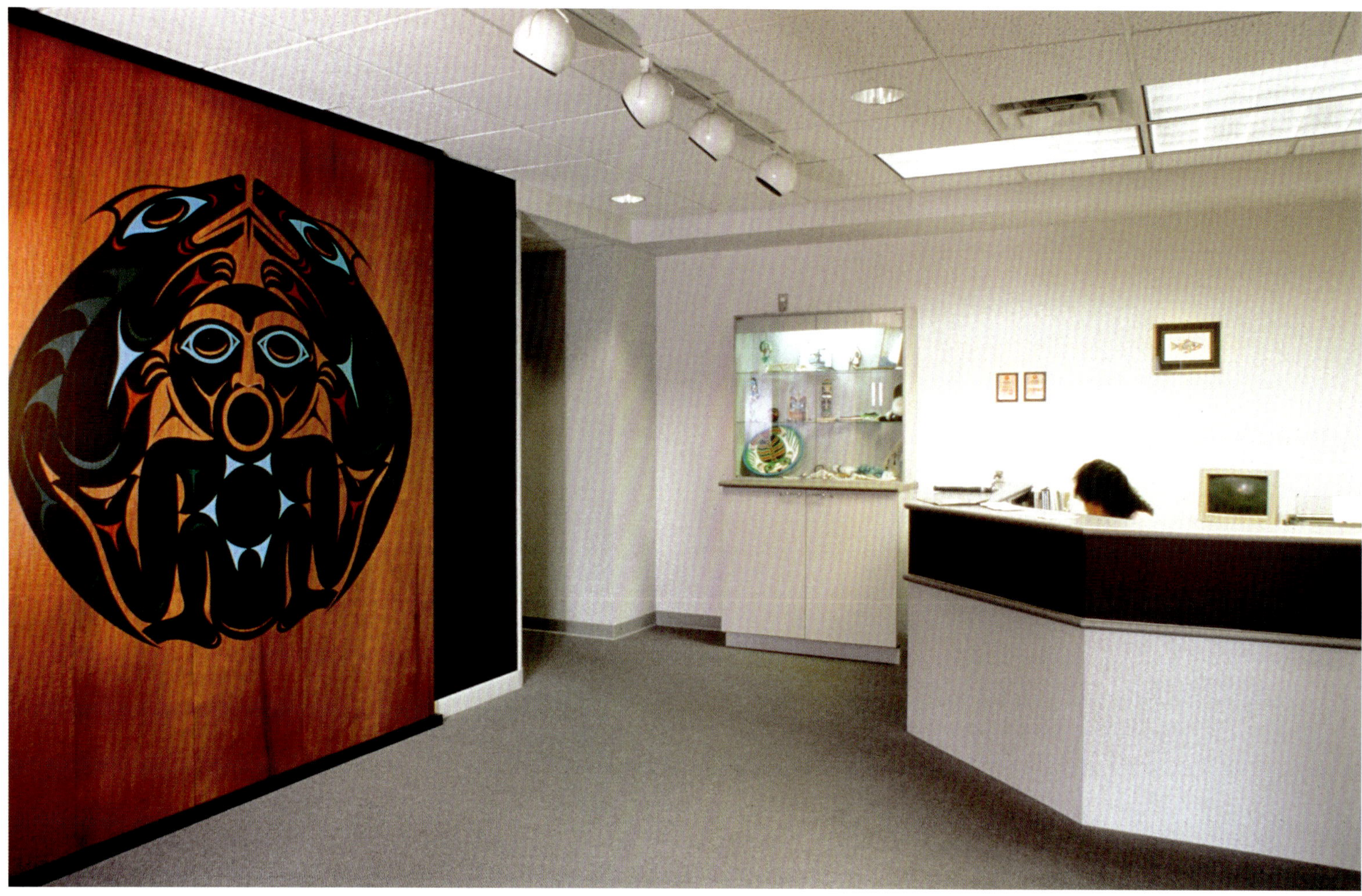

The Man and the Sea Otters, 1993
Painted western red cedar
2.74 × 1.98 m

The Man and the Sea Otters

LOCATION: B.C. Ministry of Indigenous Relations and Reconciliation
612 View St, Victoria, BC

By the time the provincial Ministry of Aboriginal Affairs (as it was then known) commissioned this work to mark the United Nations–declared International Year of the World's Indigenous People, Susan had been continually exploring designs based on the traditional spindle whorl for over a decade. *The Man and the Otters* honours the riverside lifestyle of her Musqueam ancestors and their belief in the deep interconnectedness of all life, and remains a powerful example of her ability to represent one of the most important objects from the Musqueam lifeways.

The design of Susan's first monumental public art in sṫ$^{\theta}$aməs (Victoria) recalls those of historic whorls she had seen in museum collections: a human figure in the centre surrounded by one or more creatures, their bodies following the circumference of the whorl. The mouth here is a perfect circle in the centre, where the spindle shaft would pierce the whorl, and is open to signify the Salish Oral Traditions. The human's hands are open, palms raised to support the hind quarters of the otter. Almost every feature—cheeks, limbs, hands, feet—is accented with Salish crescents and wedges. The turquoise elements are a non-traditional and rich choice.

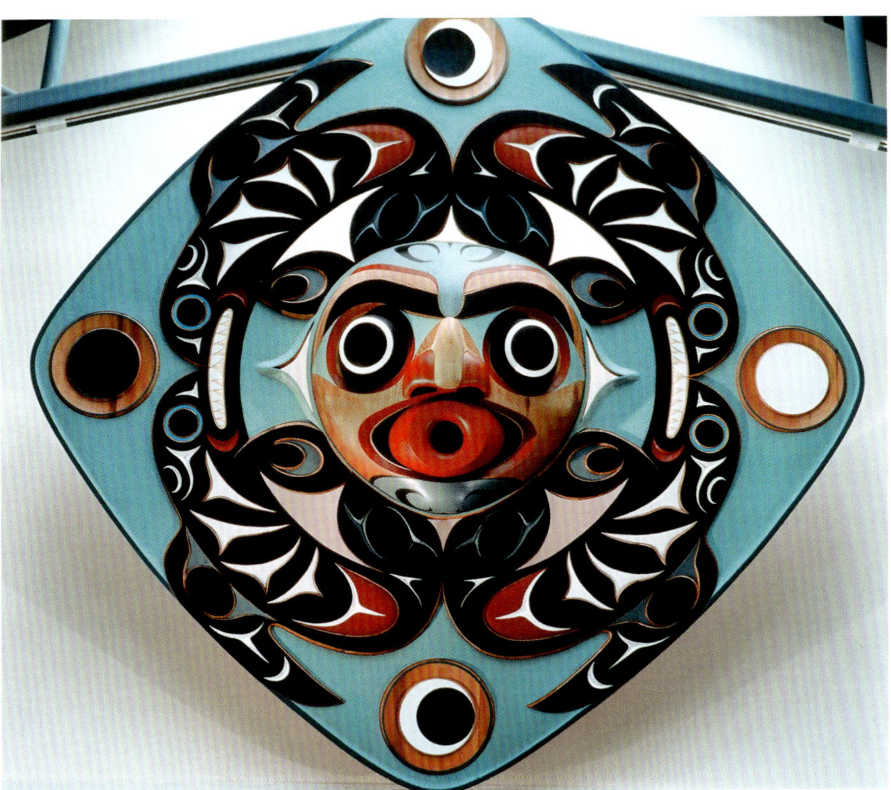

The Whale People, 1998
Carved and painted western red cedar
Approx. 3.2 × 3.2 m

The Whale People

LOCATION: Victoria Convention Centre
720 Douglas St, Victoria, BC

Susan was commissioned to create this large-scale spindle whorl to commemorate the convention centre's tenth anniversary. It was the first piece by a Salish artist to join the centre's collection, which included poles by Kwakwa̱ka̱'wakw, X̱aayda (Haida), and Nuu-chah-nulth artists.

In light of the steady popularity of whale-watching cruises, several of which depart from docks mere steps away from the convention centre, Susan's choice of theme was very fitting. As she explained to David Titterton, the centre's manager, she was inspired by "old Salish stories and legends about the 'Whale People'; these stories being handed down from our ancestors—their legacy tells of respect for everything around us. The imagery in this whorl is to show respect to the whale people and to remind us of our obligation to look out and care for these magnificent creatures who are believed to be very closely related to humankind."[11]

The carving is not only large, but complex in its composition and construction. In her letter to Titterton, Susan noted that historically, whorls were not always round; some were oval and others were a soft-cornered square shape. She felt the latter format best suited the whorl's setting on the mezzanine level of the centre. The base of the whorl was carved from five-centimetre-thick kiln-dried red cedar, with the central human face deeply carved from a separate log thirty to thirty-five centimetres deep so that it rises dramatically from the plane. The face represents the human obligation to respect the killer whales, which encircle the face oriented in different directions to symbolize their migratory paths. In the four corners of the whorl are representations of the four phases of the moon. As with so much of her art, Susan's use of colour is both personal and adventurous, dominated by a distinctive green hue.

By the Salish Sea that is home to several resident pods of orcas, Susan uses Salish forms to celebrate the magic of their presence in the world, and honour the traditional Salish belief of the links between humans and whales.

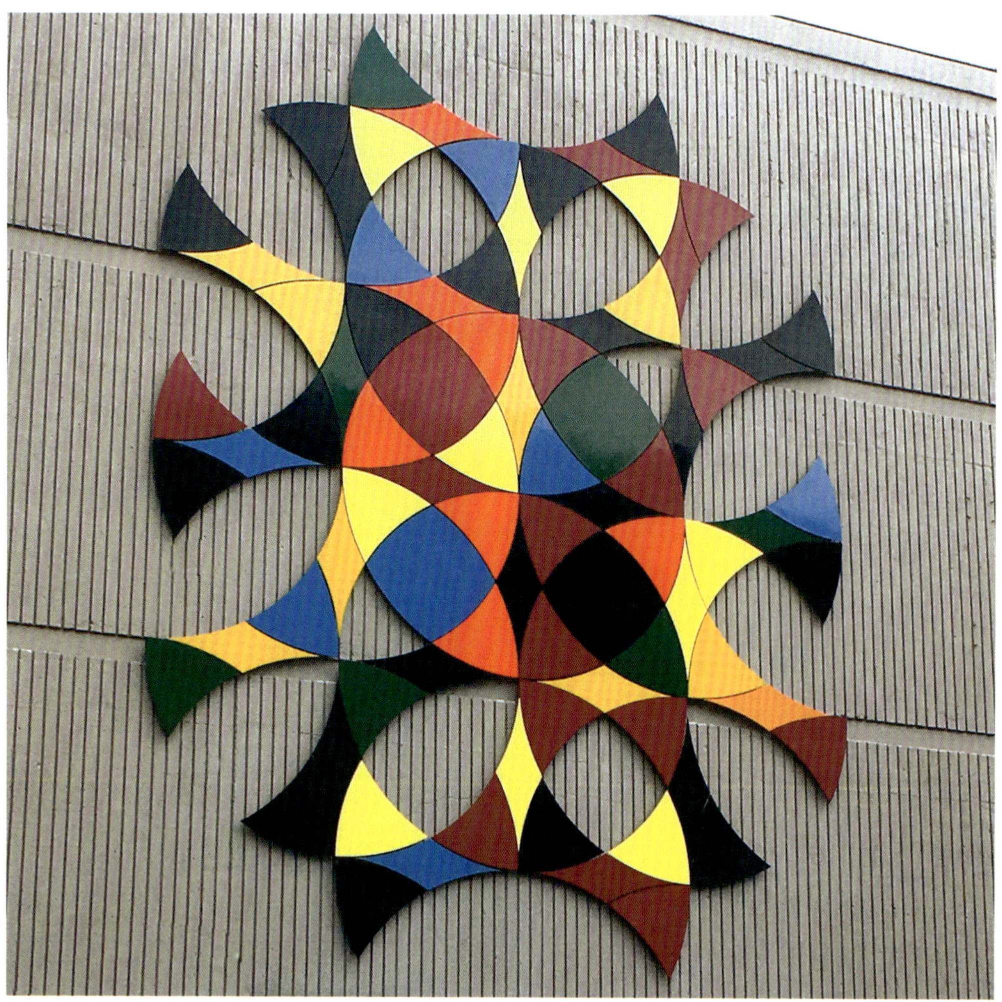

Woven Together

LOCATION: Johnson Street Parkade
750 Johnson St, Victoria BC

This piece is dramatic evidence of how far Susan has travelled as an artist, and of her willingness to experiment with expressing traditional Salish forms in an unquestionably contemporary, almost abstract composition. The geometry, the outlines, the intersections of circles and blending of colours are a fascinating evolution from her earlier work.

Susan shaped this creation with her son Thom Cannell in response to a national juried competition held by the City of Victoria to "beautify and enhance" the parkade,[12] a prosaic four-storey concrete structure in the heart of downtown Victoria. How far removed, in so many ways, from a winter house in the Musqueam settlement! But Susan and Thom recognized an opportunity to explore how their art might add visual excitement to a familiar utilitarian urban structure.

Salish forms, in their hands, were about to be reshaped in new ways. Their proposal, *Woven Together: A Celebration of Continuing Change*, was, in the words of the jury, "a dynamic and engaging design that provoked much discussion.... Part of this discussion involved a deep appreciation of the incorporation of traditional motifs and themes in the creation of a unique and contemporary artwork."[13] In an extended artists' statement, Susan and Thom elaborated on the central ideas of the piece, their use of traditional motifs, and the importance of colour.

> The cycles of life are often depicted in Salish art using circular forms. In this artwork, not only do these circles represent the "cycle of life" in many scenarios but they also, metaphorically, represent the wheels of cars and other forms of transportation in this day and age. Traditionally one of our main implements was used for weaving, the

Woven Together, 2016
Painted aluminum
Approx. 7.62 × 6 × .01 m

"spindle whorl," a circular disc used for hand spinning wool into yarn. Another implement, the "mat creaser" was used for weaving rush/cattail mats for temporary shelters and used within our longhouse. As well there was the famous stone hammer that was used when carving houseposts. These contemporary graphic implement images are subtly incorporated within this overall design... traditional iconic imagery that inspired the creation of this artwork.

We have remained very thoughtful of all the colour contrasts and how they come together in this design... colours joining, connecting and ever changing to make more than we can imagine. Colour plays a significant role in this proposed artwork... embodying cultures and different beliefs around the world....

The elements connecting in the centre of the artwork illustrate a unified community with common interests and unique differences... all coming together to complete the circle... the circle always growing vibrantly in new directions making Victoria a unique and original part of the Pacific Northwest Coast... The central circle (spindle whorl) in the centre of this artwork is made up of multiple eye motifs, which represents all of our cultural backgrounds. It also creates four butterfly images within it—in all four directions... butterflies representing the ability to accept change and symbolizing metamorphosis, balance and grace as well as symbolizing the beauty of nature. The number four is very important within First Nations culture as it is representative of the four winds, the four seasons, the four directions, the four elements, the four moons, the four peoples....

This artwork is solely our original artwork, a creation of a unique legacy left to us by our ancestors. This contemporary artwork, although based on traditional motifs and elements of our Salish Peoples, represents everyone, universally.

We are excited that this work reminds us of the thriving Coast Salish culture... and connects to all cultural backgrounds of the people who love and share this land.[14]

The final work involved cutting, priming, and three-stage pigment-coating over eighty pieces of half-inch aluminum in varying shapes, sizes, and colours. The pieces were then fit together and mounted on an armature attached to rails on the facade of the parkade. The ribbed concrete of the facade is visible in various points, presenting a lively, almost playful feeling.

The ambiguity of the design—some viewers may see a sort of elaborate floral blossom—is characteristic of many of Susan's compositions. Even though they are based on traditional forms, she welcomes viewers to find meanings of their own as they reflect on the art. Whatever the reaction, there can be little doubt that she and Thomas with this piece had established new directions for architectural art based on Salish culture and motifs.

Since Susan's artwork first appeared in Victoria, home of the Lkwungen, Xwsepsum, and W̱SÁNEĆ Coast Salish Peoples, the City of Victoria has made more visible efforts to honour the original occupants of the region, installing several spindle whorl sculptures by Lkwungen artist Butch Dick in 2008, and in 2018 adding Lkwungen place names to downtown signage.[15] Susan is no longer alone in her mission to establish a visual "Coast Salish footprint" in the lands around the Salish Sea.

Red Oak

LOCATION: various locations, Seattle, WA

This was the first commission that Susan received from public authorities in Seattle, and her first experience working with architects and engineers to produce designs to a rigorous set of specifications. She received the invitation to submit a proposal as part of a project to install new trees and tree grates above a transit tunnel being built in downtown Seattle.[16] At the time she was working mainly in silkscreen prints. As she later recalled, "Why they sent it to me, I don't know, because it was for U.S. artists. Never mind. I applied, drawing on the fact that I'm Coast Salish and that Coast Salish people also resided in the southern area of Washington State."[17]

In the catalogue for an exhibition in Zurich that Susan would participate in three years later, Dr. Peter R. Gerber of the Univeristy of Zurich noted the evolution of Susan's style that the grates represented:

> Susan is now producing detailed architectural plans of the grate designs. . . . In her circular motif, she incorporates in a very intricate pattern, the oak tree leaves, the acorns and some birds. We are very far from the weaver's spindle whorl concept. The media is different, the technique is different, but we can still decipher the typical sharply incised lines and stylized elements such as crescents, wedges and U-forms and most of all the spinning movement of the whole design. Even when transferring the Salish pattern to so different an object than a tree grate, the artist has succeeded in captivating and keeping alive the spirit of the Salish iconography.[18]

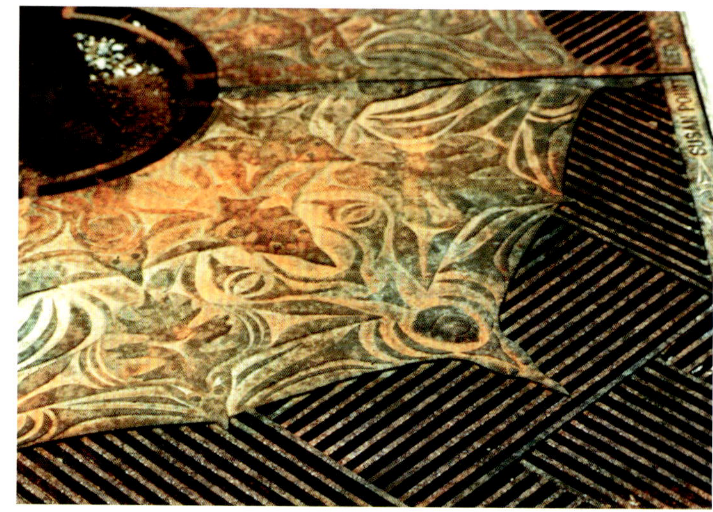

She created one segment of the four components out of various materials, from which a rubber mould was made, and then a local foundry cast each of the pieces in iron. The grates have gracefully endured the rigours of thirty years. They are not traditional Salish objects at all, but early examples of her ability to use Salish design elements in the service of urban life, to move Salishness in new directions. The project also helped her learn to work within exacting technical requirements, an important element in growing her reputation as an accomplished, creative artist working in a variety of mediums beyond the walls of galleries and private homes.

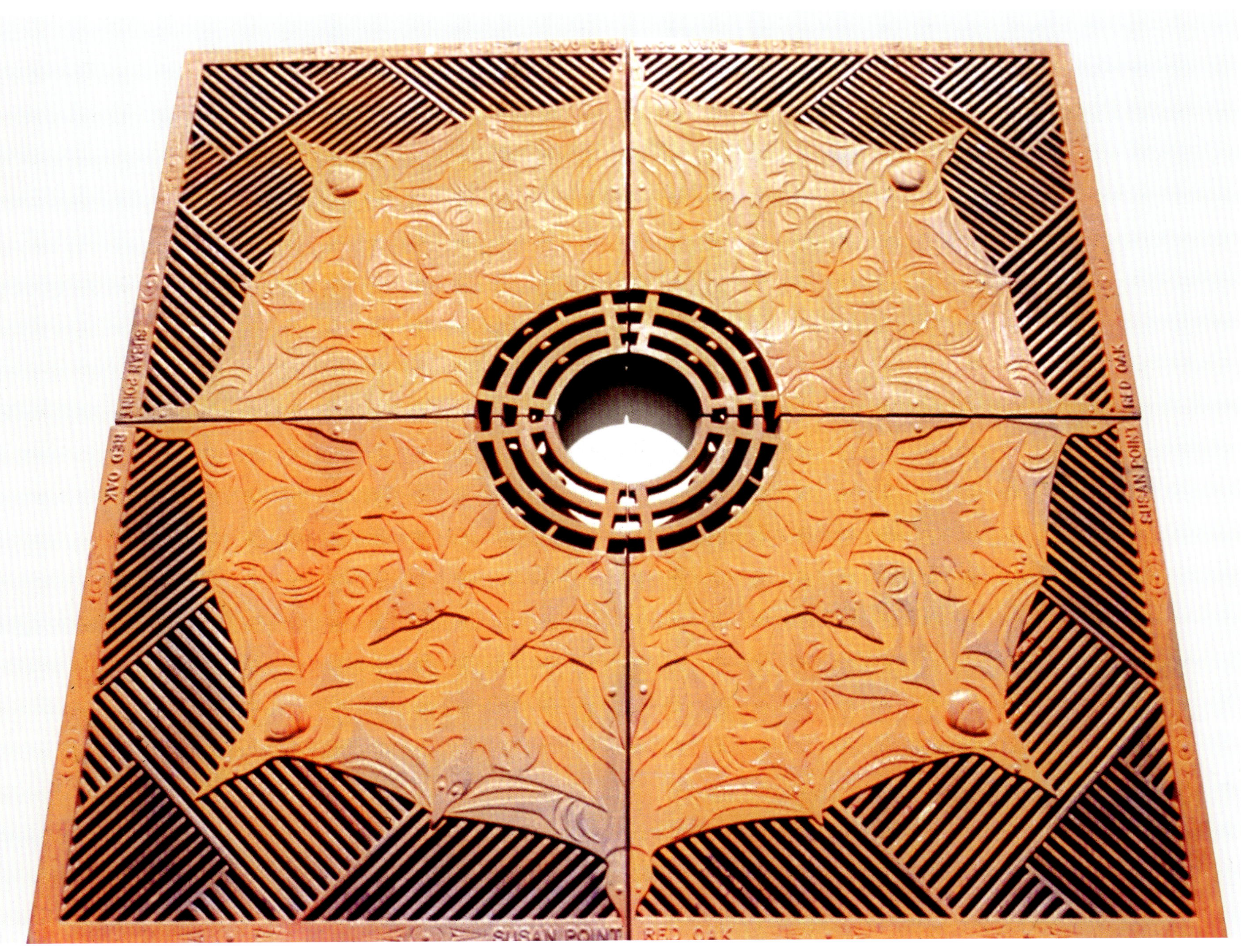

Red Oak, 1986
Cast iron
1.52 × 1.52 m

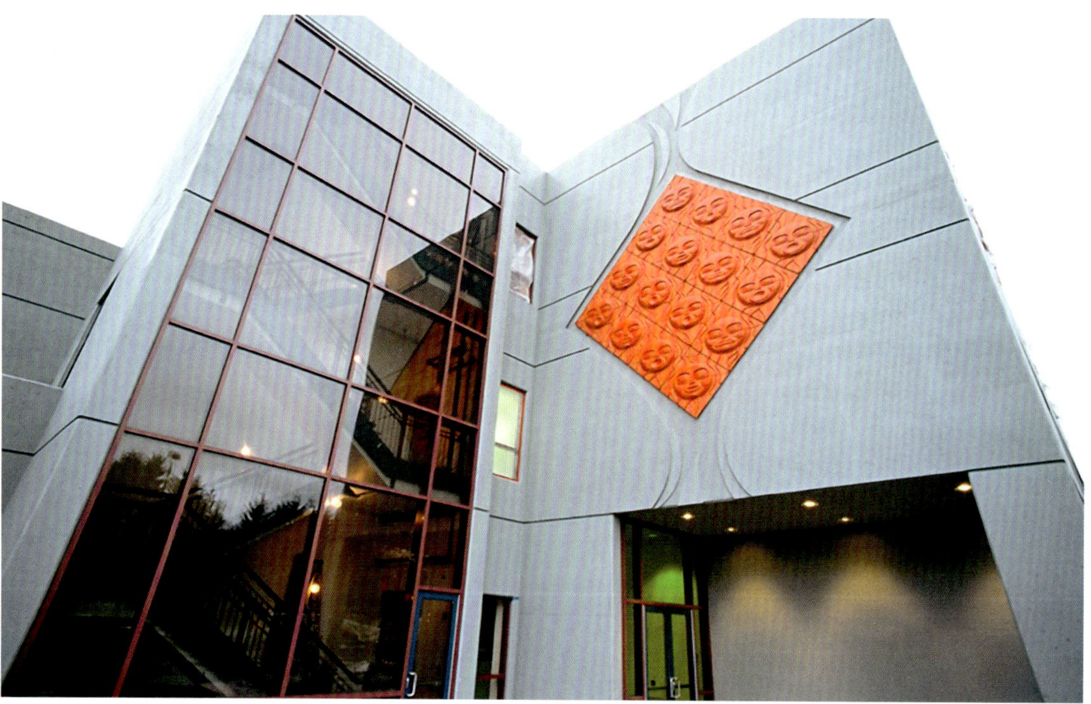

Four Corners

LOCATION: North Seattle College
9600 College Way N, Seattle, WA

This large-scale wall mural further develops, on a much larger scale and in a different material, an idea that Susan first explored in cast glass for a commission in Toronto (see page 213), while working within familiar environmental and cultural themes. The Coast Salish-style faces represent peoples of the past, present, and future: they honour both the diverse modern-day population of the Seattle metropolitan area and the dxʷdəwʔabš (Duwamish people), the original Salish inhabitants of what is now called Seattle. Above all, Susan wanted to celebrate the student body that arrives from the four corners of the earth.

As she always strives to do, Susan selected colouring and forms that refer to local topographic and cultural features. In this case, she learned that the college is close to Licton Springs—called Liq'tid (reddish mud) by the Duwamish, who long used the springs as a water source and place of healing. By colouring the Forton with red ochre and introducing graceful twists and turns of water forms around the design, Susan highlighted the strong human element in the design while linking the composition to important history from the site.

The elegant composition was complex to produce. *Four Corners* is based on four original faces (one appears in each corner of the work) that Susan hand-carved in detailed low-relief from laminated red cedar. She then carved eight triangular modules—the top and bottom halves of each of the four faces—and made polyurethane moulds of each, from which she then made plaster "mother moulds" to avoid distortion. From these, the final pieces were cast in Forton and pigmented with red ochre. The resulting thirty-two halves are arranged to create sixteen unique faces. Susan also designed a template that the architects and fabricators used to create curved lines recessed into the wall, so that water flows down, simulating the historic spring.

This "welcome wall," as Susan calls it, never fades into the background of the facade. It imparts a special character to this modern building, while gesturing both backward and forward in time.

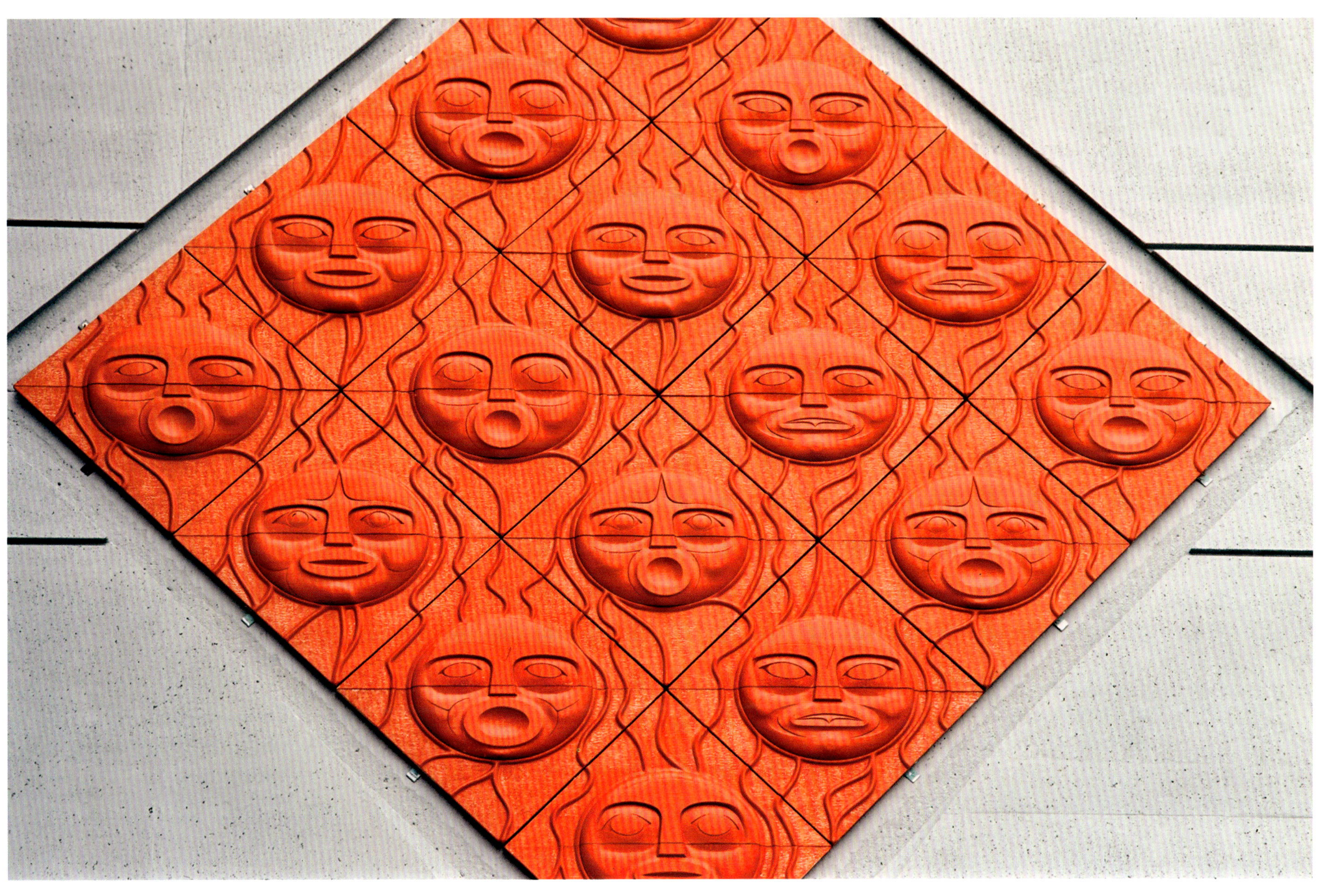

Four Corners, 1999
Pigmented Forton
6.1 × 6.1 × .15 m

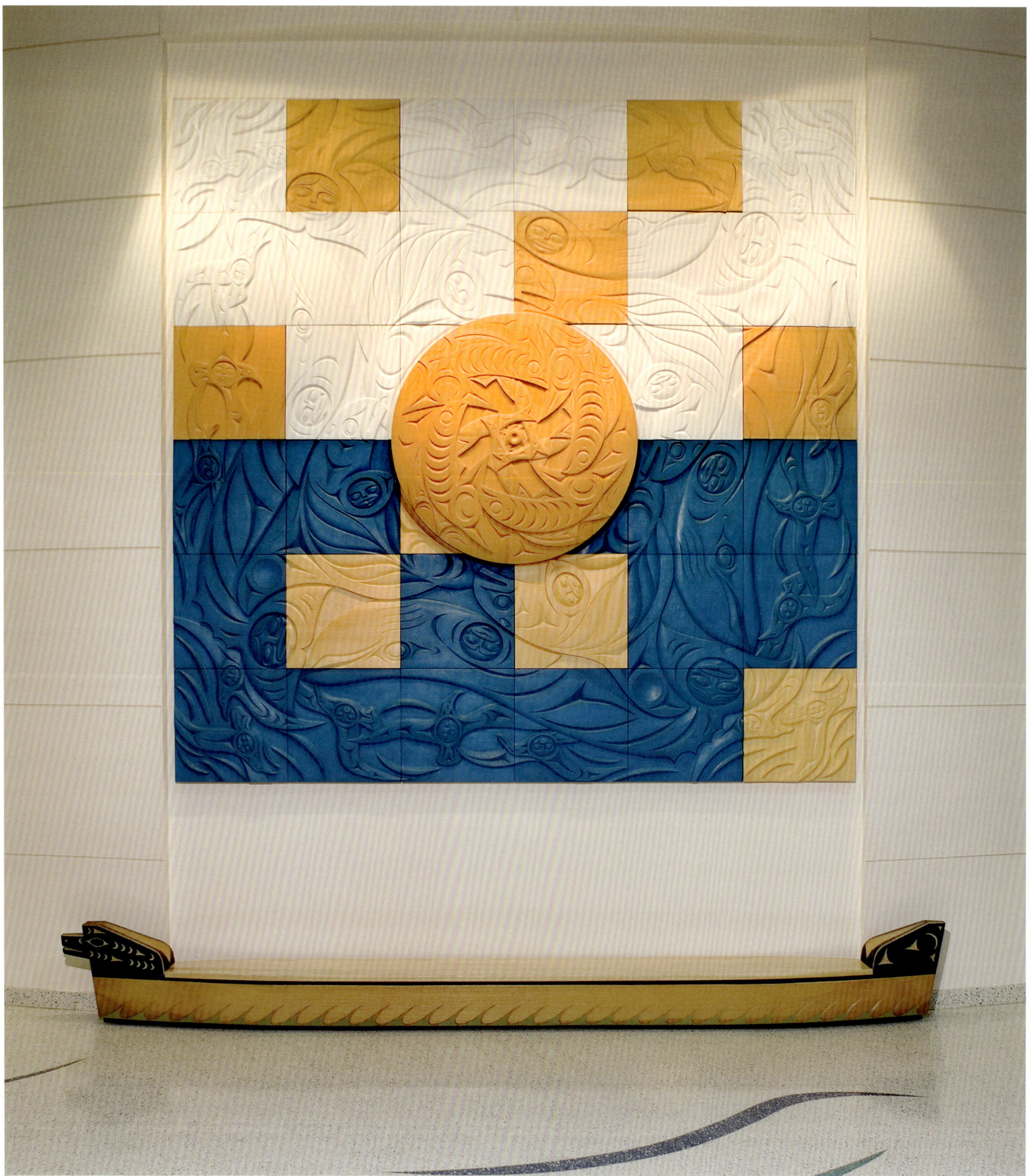

Continuing Cycle of Life, 2006
Yellow cedar, Forton
3.66 × 3.66 m

Continuing Cycle of Life

LOCATION: Seattle Children's Hospital
4800 Sand Point Way NE, Seattle, WA

Near the main public entrance of Seattle Children's is an atrium with two-storey-high walls, a perfect location for this striking mural of yellow cedar and coloured Forton. Susan explains that

> one of the things I tried to do was create an artwork that was pleasing and that everyone could interact with ... more so the children and their parents. I also wanted to make a piece that would inspire questions as to the content, the process and the mediums used. I feel that this artwork will be understood at a glance and is intriguing enough to invite the viewer to explore its finer details.
>
> At our initial meeting it was mentioned to me that if the artwork could distract a child or parent ... for even a moment ... it is worthwhile because it takes one's mind off the hospital or the surgery the child may be facing. I think this piece will hold their attention much longer. Even if one is rushing through I want that person to make a mental note to come back and have a closer look....
>
> I have always thought that my ancestral Salish art has a universal appeal to it. I feel Salish art is appealing because it is a grass roots visual language that can be easily read by anyone.[19]

In a separate statement, Susan described the content and meaning of the wall mural.

> The artwork focuses on an ocean theme, relating to the Pacific Northwest coast and its abundance of life and our connection to it. We are all part of the circle of life—that all life on earth depends on the sun's energy and that we are all connected. In the very centre of the design there are four salmon, four orca and then four grey whales. The number four is significant to the Salish peoples of the Pacific Northwest Coast in that four has many meanings. There are four faces, or four ages: the face of a child, the face of the adolescent, the face of the adult, the face of the elder. There are four directions or four winds, four seasons, four elements: fire, water, air, earth.... The coloured forton castings represent "sea" and "sky." With the addition of the yellow cedar carving representing land.[20]

She carved the work in several sections and then, with the help of Rosa Quintana and Mike Edwards, cast them in rubber moulds and then Forton.

The use of colour creates interest and underlines the main themes while focusing attention on the central whorl, which is of carved yellow cedar raised slightly above the background plane. The four large salmon are highlighted with deeply cut crescents; within these fish are four smaller fish in a square formation around the central spindle shaft. The four orcas lie outside the whorl, each with a small human face in the lower fin; and the four grey whales, large human faces in their bellies and tails, circle the orcas. At the edge of the mural are birds, again with human faces in their bodies, representing the sky element. The full Salish visual vocabulary of face spaces, crescents, wedges, and U-forms is used in every part of the design.

When the work was first installed it included a Salish-style wood canoe by Susan at the base, to serve as a bench, but the canoe was later moved elsewhere in the hospital. Fortunately, the mural remains in a waiting area, where children and their families have ample opportunity to appreciate the complexity of the art, and to try to follow the creatures as they move through their spaces.

Vision, 2010
Bronze
120.4 cm (diameter)

Vision

LOCATION: Mark McDermott Plaza
W Stevens Way NE, University of Washington, Seattle, WA

Vision is a memorial to Dr. Mark McDermott, a former physics professor at the University of Washington. His widow Lillian, also a professor of physics, commissioned Susan to create a permanent marker of his achievements, especially his pivotal role in overseeing the construction of the Physics/ Astronomy Building. The story of the medallion is a fine example of the care that Susan has taken to get to know clients so she can offer designs that blend her creativity with their interests.

Susan learned of the opportunity from Elizabeth Steinbrueck, owner of the Steinbrueck Native Gallery in Seattle. The McDermotts had long collected artworks by Indigenous Peoples and were clients of Steinbrueck, so in early 2008, when Lillian obtained permission to place an in-ground bronze monument in the plaza that already bore Mark McDermott's name, Steinbrueck wrote to Susan.

Lillian wished for the monument to take the form of a bronze spindle whorl with animal forms. Susan proposed carving a whorl design in yellow cedar to be cast in bronze, then refinishing the wood so it could become part of Lillian's collection, and invited Steinbrueck's and Lillian to visit her studio so she could understand more fully Lillian's vision for the whorl. Mark had been a passionate bird-watcher, so Lillian suggested an eagle to represent strength, a raven for wisdom, and three hummingbirds, one of Mark's favourite birds, to represent their three children. Susan proposed a design that incorporated the bird forms but kept the imagery simple, as Lillian wished, and preserved the fluidity of the overall design.

Susan revised the design after a second meeting with Lillian at her studio in April. She added part of a circle in the centre, beneath the beak of the p̓aq̓əs (eagle), which would have been occupied by the spindle. She softened the expression on the raven's face, and adjusted the styling of the hummingbirds to Lillian's liking. As Susan was well aware, since the piece would be set flush to the ground, it was also essential to design it so that water would flow off the piece and not pool on its surface.

The final design shows three hummingbirds toward the centre, framed by an eagle and a raven whose wings are strongly defined with Salish-style wedges. Susan explained to Lillian that

> I have used the traditional Salish wedge form to emphasize not only a burst of energy but also to represent enlightenment. As an example, Mark's work at the University will be a continuing legacy and the wedge shapes radiating outside the design, is for me, also representing young minds gathering knowledge and expanding beyond the university. For me this represents connecting generations and the cycle of life.[21]

In August 2009, Susan and her husband Jeff visited the site for the medallion and Lillian's home, where the wooden carving was to be housed. Lillian suggested naming the works *Vision*, both for her husband's vision for the building and Susan's vision for the artwork. The bronze medallion was officially installed on 21 May 2010, surrounded by a ring made in the physics department machine shop and inscribed "Mark N. McDermott Plaza Physics/ Astronomy Building."

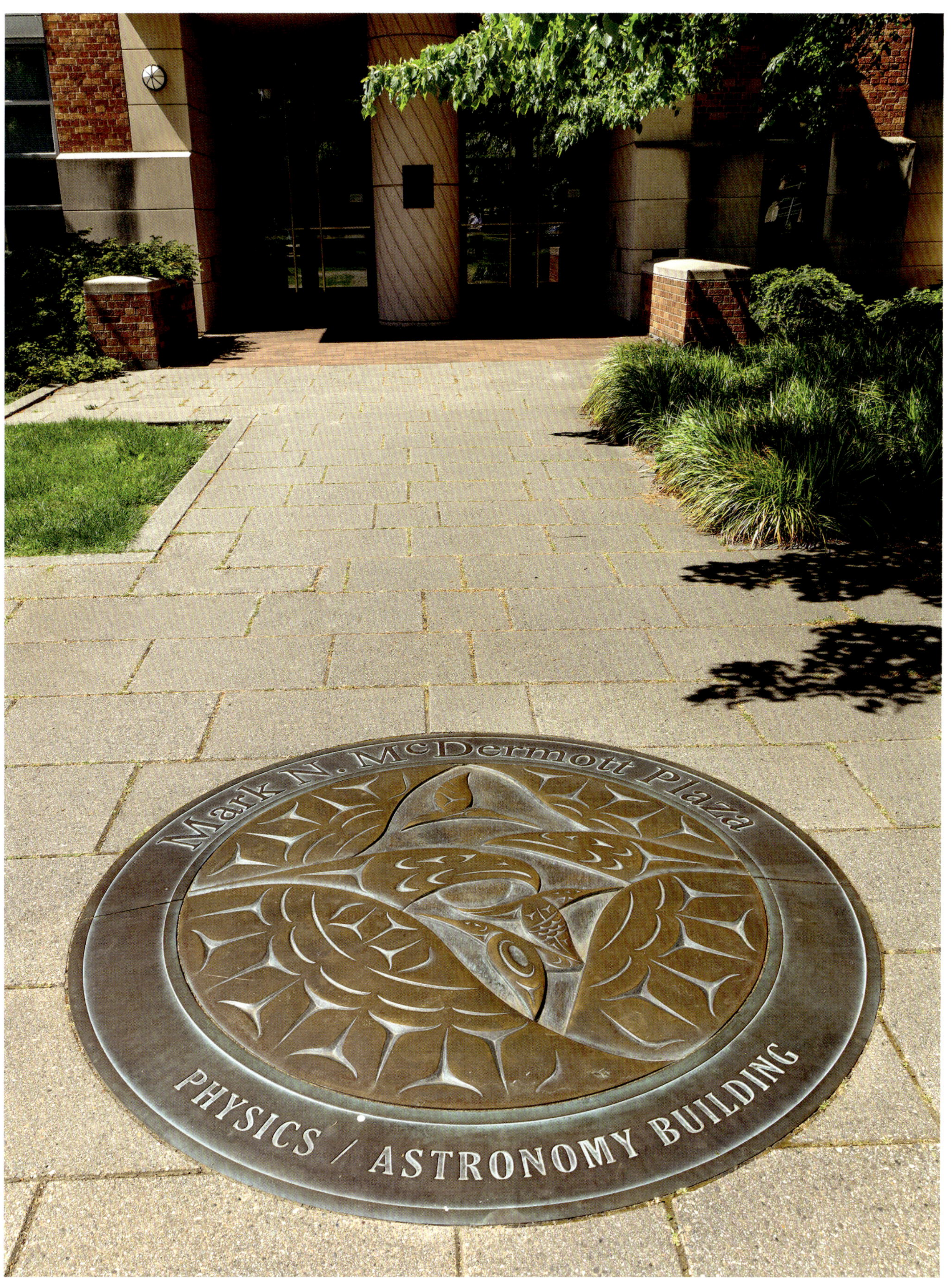
Mark N. McDermott Plaza
PHYSICS / ASTRONOMY BUILDING

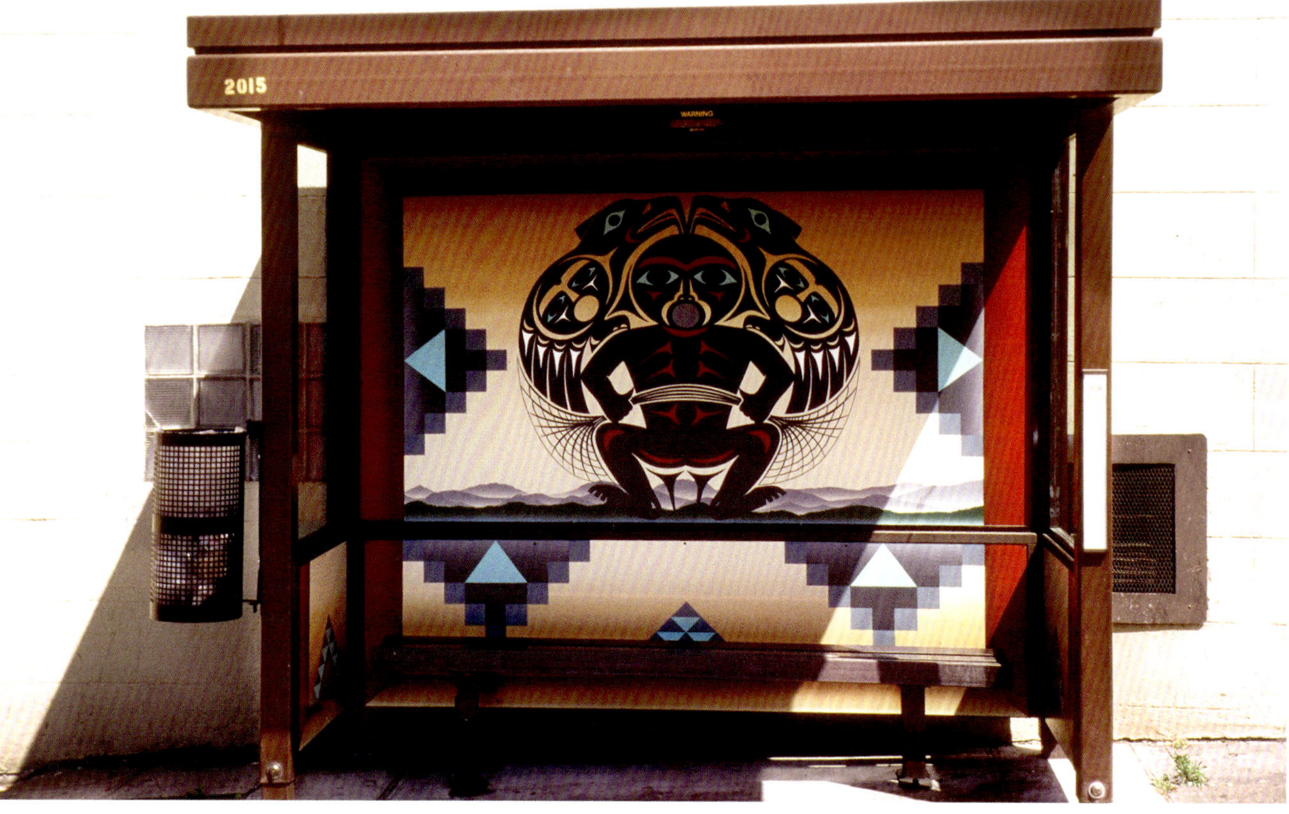

Aerial Hunter, 1993
Paint on plywood
2.44 x 2.44 m

Aerial Hunter

FORMER LOCATION: Denny Way at First Avenue N
Seattle, WA

Sadly, we can no longer appreciate this mural in person. The average life of bus shelter works in Seattle is only five to eight years, being subject to all the impacts of the outdoors as well as wood rot and graffiti. *Aerial Hunter* graced its location for a full twelve years, but eventually succumbed and was removed in about 2006. It is tempting to think that the imagery was so distinctive that those using the shelter respected it and tried to give it extra life.

The commission was awarded to Susan as one of three in 1993 in a program titled "Meeting of Cultures." The collaboration between King County's arts commission and transit agency was a "commemoration of the County's indigenous people" that asked each artist to create a mural for a significant Indigenous site, with themes to be drawn from local Indigenous knowledge.[22]

In her artist's statement Susan spoke about the traditional importance of the site, explaining that "Native Americans erected aerial nets for catching ducks. It is said that ducks which were 'started up' on Lake Union would always fly over the low place between Queen Anne Hill and the business district of Seattle."[23]

At the centre of the spindle whorl motif is a human hunter grasping a net, the form of the body emphasized by red wedges and crescents. Two sawbill ducks sit on his shoulders and the body of each duck contains a human face. Geometric weaving patterns are on either side of the hunter and a stylized evocation of the local landscape is at the base of the composition. As with so many of Susan's compositions, the profound links between humans and animals are celebrated in Salish form, in this case depicting an important food gathering activity for the Duwamish people of what became downtown Seattle.

The First People

LOCATION: Seattle Art Museum
1300 1st Ave, Seattle, WA

As the Seattle Art Museum approached its seventy-fifth anniversary, Dr. Barbara Brotherton, the museum's curator of Native American art, was eager to acquire artwork by Susan. Within a few weeks of Dr. Brotherton's inquiry in February of 2007, Susan sent a series of sketches to Seattle that outlined this striking sculpture in western red cedar and yellow cedar: eight Salish-style faces, four in light wood and four in darker wood, in a frame of curved, root-like lines that evoke trees and moving water.

In Susan's notes to Dr. Brotherton she revealed the themes and ideas expressed in the work. The use of cedar celebrates its status as the "Tree of Life," with the alternating colours of the wood referring to basket weaving. The faces, mouths open to symbolize Oral Traditions, are dramatized as People of the Cedar, people coming from all four corners of the earth, lines flowing around them to weave together past, present, and future generations.

> Although this artwork is relating to Salish, it can represent peoples of all cultures . . . any person of any cultural background can read their own story into the piece . . . [I am trying] to incorporate the subtleties into the faces as I do not want to offend anyone. . . . In my early stages, [I] appropriated use of Salish designs through ignorance, naivety and hugely because there was a lack of protocol because of our lost culture due to European contact. This art piece I am very fond of—totally within any protocol—it doesn't belong to anyone—solely original artwork but the product of the unique legacy left by my ancestors. This design represents everyone.[24]

Susan also felt that the people were coming from the heart of the earth, from grass roots—she referred to the root forms as the "bloodlines" of her people, as well as a "river rebraiding itself over time." The holes in the composition are for "airing out the piece."

In a later message to Barbara, Susan expanded on the roots of her Salish ideas.

> I have learned so many stories and legends from my elders by listening to the retelling of legends like the Northwind Fishing Weir, the Wolf people, the Great Flood, the Salmon people, the Whale people and family stories too. As well, I have been retold ancient knowledge about the natural wealth of the Northwest Coast.
>
> All of this rich history of my Salish people has been preserved through our oral tradition—a key part of our smokehouse ceremonies and tribal gatherings—continuing over time—connecting generations. Our unique heritage was a time honoured gift from our homelands. My ancestors were taught by the land, sea and sky. They listened to the wind and everything around them. . . .
>
> I feel strongly that this piece is special because it tells where all our stories come from—it doesn't depict a particular point in time—it doesn't represent one particular tribal legend. For me, it is the whole story of our original culture. A uniquely Salish vision![25]

With Susan's drawings and notes in hand, Dr. Brotherton was able to successfully pitch the opportunity to the museum's collections committee. She explained that, given the demand for her art, Susan mostly worked in less labour-intensive mediums; this was a rare chance to acquire a large

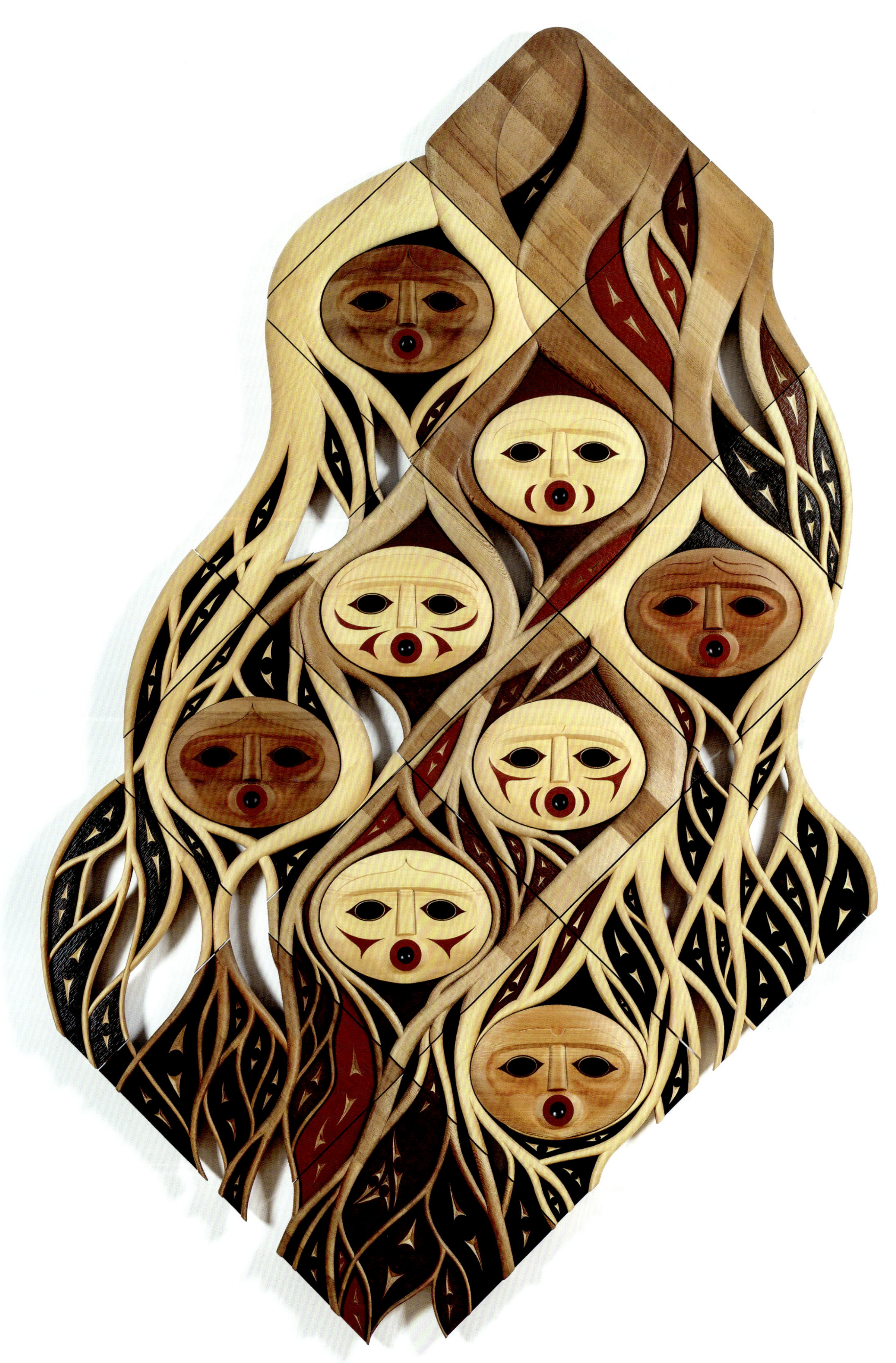

The First People, 2008
Western red cedar, yellow cedar
3.66 × 2.26 m

Shapers, 2002
Glass, carved western red cedar
Approx. 101 × 101 × 10 cm

work, hand-carved specifically for the museum, "that retains the ethos of ancient Coast Salish forms" yet is "vibrantly contemporary." The committee had initially sought Susan's *Northwind's Fishing Weir* (1997; see page 188), but as Dr. Brotherton explained, "Susan considers this piece to be perhaps her most important because it represents for her a profound synthesis of Salish ancestral teachings that, in spite of almost total cultural devastation, have managed to survive."[26] The committee wisely agreed to acquire *The First People*, and it is now on display as part of the museum's permanent collection.

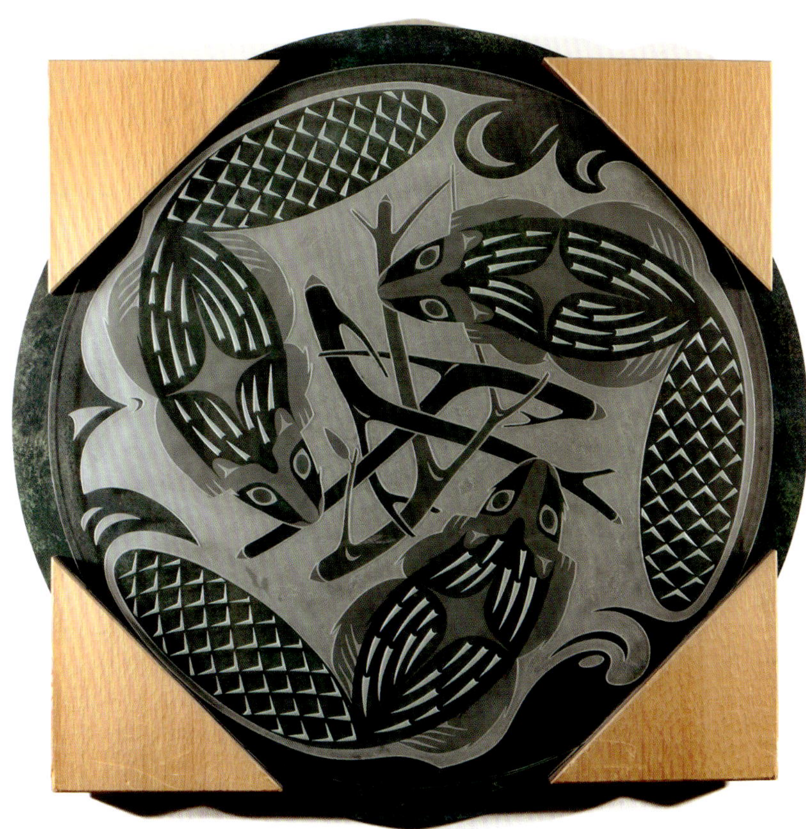

Shapers

LOCATION: Harborview Medical Center
325 9th Ave, Seattle, WA

In May 2001, 4Culture, King County's public art agency, offered Susan a commission for an artwork to join the Harborview Medical Center's Cultural Heritage Collection. She was invited to Seattle to see the spaces that might be available for installation; the work was to be located in the West Hospital, which was built in the 1990s and has more space and light than the East Hospital, built in 1931.

Susan considered offering an existing glass sculpture, but because of that work's large size and the fact that it needed to be free-standing, she decided to create a new work that could be wall-mounted. In her proposal she said, "the design I have chosen for this piece consists of beaver images, to represent the many people within the hospital, often in a hurry and always busy."[27]

Shapers is composed of two panes of glass secured by wood. The back piece is textured to give a water effect, and the front piece is carved with two beavers, their tails and backs accentuated with Salish-style wedges and crescents, "swimming" around a central element of interlocking branches. The art hangs in a long hall near the entrance of the West Hospital, labelled with a statement from Susan that explains the prevalance of Indigenous art from northern B.C. and describes her objective in all she creates: "to revive traditional Coast Salish art in an attempt to educate the public to the fact that there was, and still is, another art form indigenous to the central Pacific Northwest Coast."

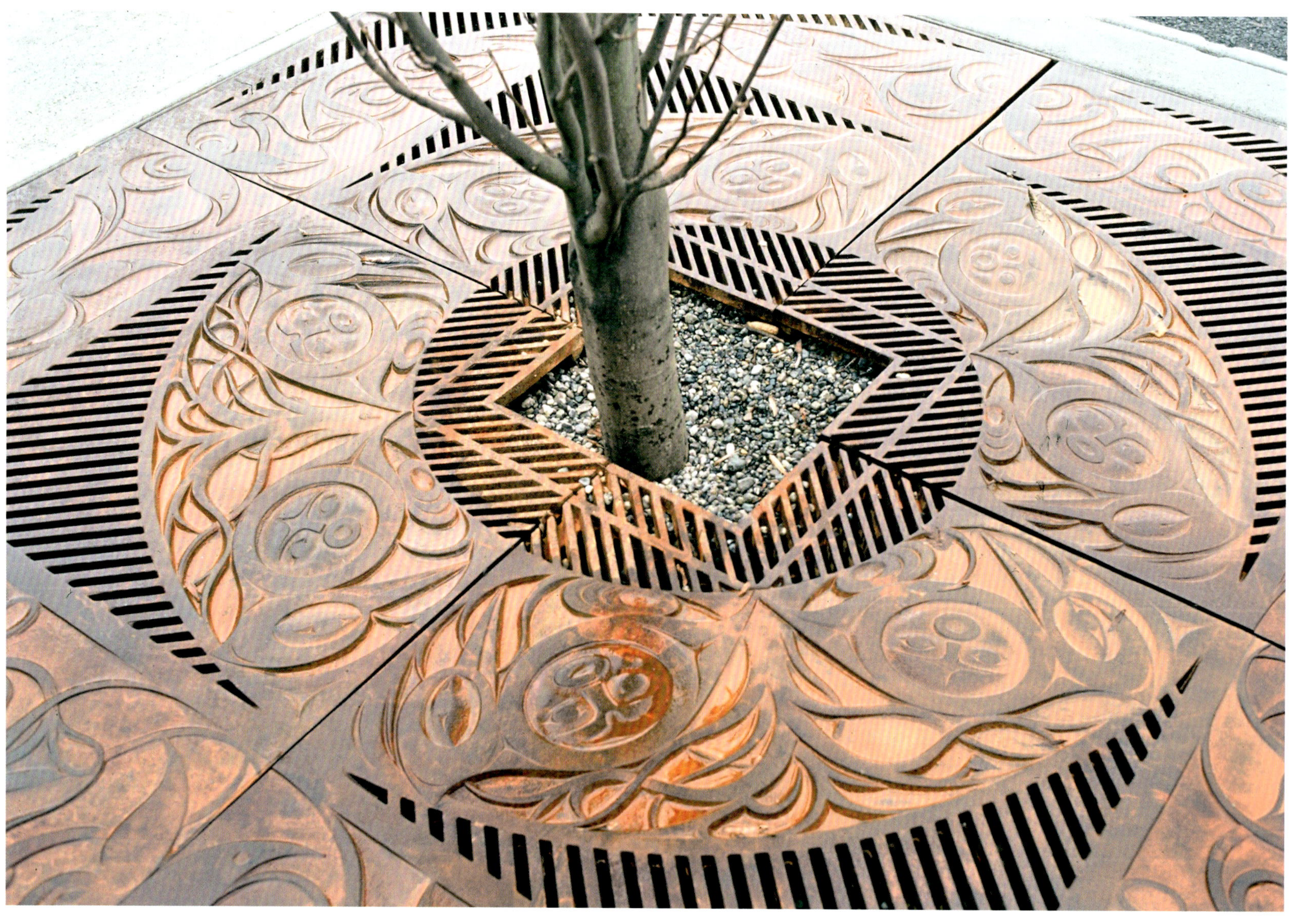

Written Into the Earth

LOCATION: CenturyLink Field
800 Occidental Ave S, Seattle, WA

The Washington State Public Stadium Authority issued a national call in 1998 for artists to develop new works for a football/soccer stadium that was being planned to replace the Kingdome. Of the 254 artists who responded, twenty-two were selected to develop specific proposals, of whom Susan was the only non-U.S. resident. A jury chose the final twelve artists, nine men and three women who were publicly announced in March 1999: eight from Seattle; one each from New Mexico, California, and Oregon; and Susan.

Her proposal included a series of tree grates and a sixteen-piece sand-cast bronze sculpture. In her proposal, Susan described the theme of the works.

> I wanted to give the eye, the mind, and the soul of the viewer a deep new experience of Salish splendor—tough, unyielding and everlasting—in a variety of mediums. Images speak to the eye and address the mind. Sometimes form alone can satisfy the eye but the mind can only be satisfied with meaning. Although my ancestors' earlier Salish world of reality stretches back nearly a hundred centuries, their names and most of their teachings are long forgotten

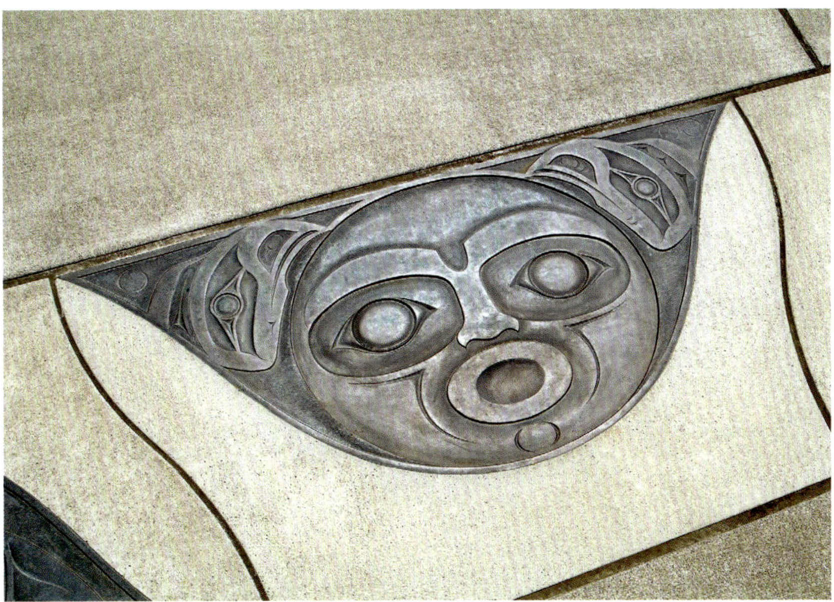

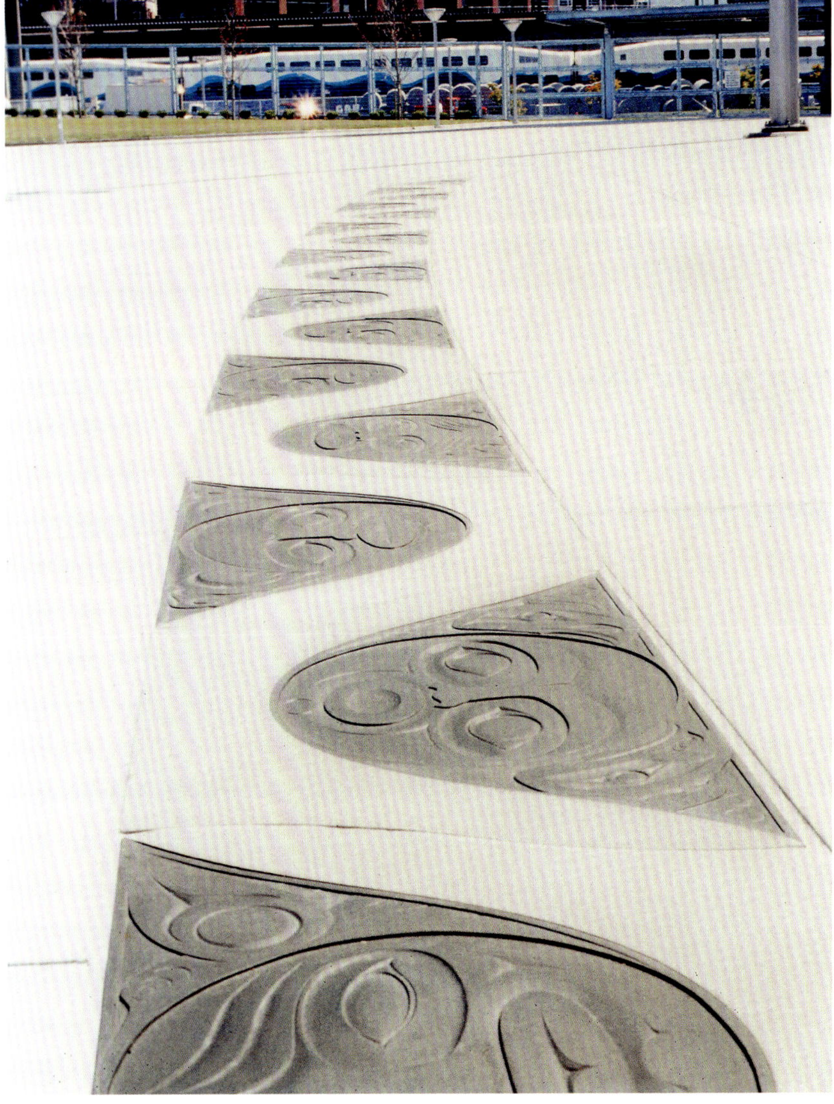

Written Into the Earth, 2002
Cast iron, sand-cast bronze
Circles in Time (iron grates):
122 × 122 cm or 122 × 183 cm (each)
Bronze sculptures: 64 × 147 cm (each);
64 cm × 208.5 m (total installation)

> but the shapes of a few of their thoughts have survived in stone artifacts, some still covered in the earth. While the public ventures around this beautiful open air stadium, I hope what they discover imprinted on the surface (land) will speak to their eye and their mind.[28]

Susan wanted the bronze sculptures, which feature four different faces symbolizing all the people of earth, to be placed in the northwest quadrant to welcome all people to the stadium and to the Pacific Northwest. The faces are in a style Susan had already made familiar: a full face with mouth open to honour the Oral Traditions of the Salish Peoples. Around the faces the sculptures also featured bird motifs

> to help illustrate the human spirit and our desire to reach higher. As well, birds relate to nature and the outdoors. Incorporated with the birds are different celestial bodies. With the hummingbird, the earth; with the Thunderbird, the stars; with the owl, the moon; and with the phoenix, the sun. The positive forms within this design create a negative space which all together represents water. This positive/negative form can be found carved decoratively into ladle handles, borders on bowls and woven into blankets.[29]

The four faces were each repeated four times and set into the pavement in a long, gentle arc that prominently greets stadium-goers in front of the great staircase at the north side.

For the ductile iron tree grates, Susan carved in cedar three original spindle whorl motifs, which she named *Circles in Time*. As she explained, "the three distinct patterns relate to the earth, the water and

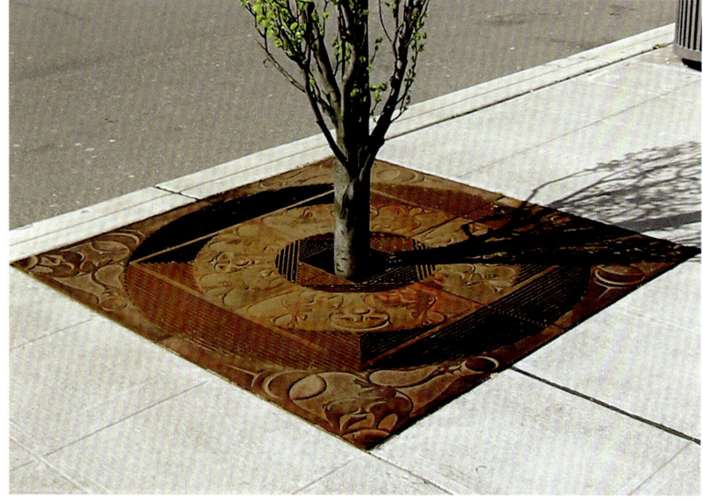

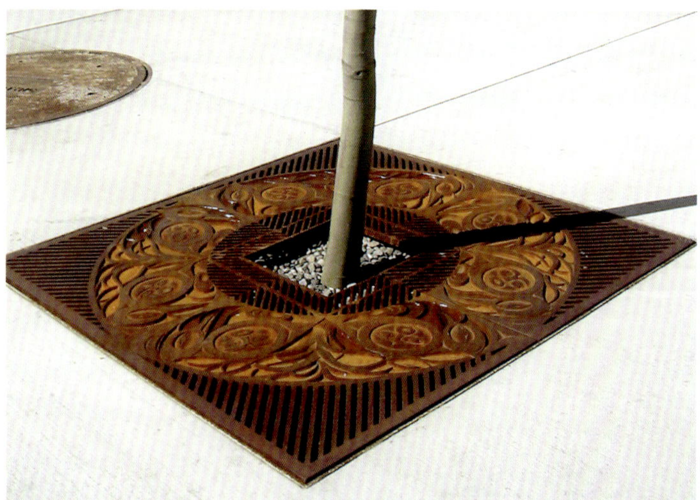

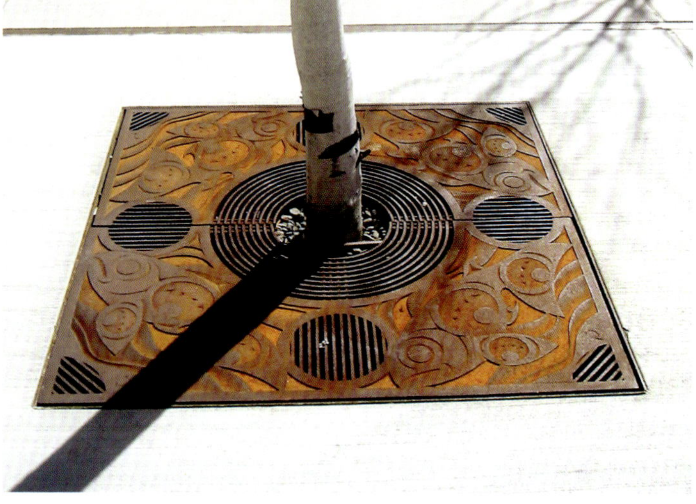

the air and with the inclusion of a human element, to the three surrounding communities adjacent to the Stadium [Pioneer Square, Chinatown, and the International District]. In these designs, earth is represented by the caribou, water by the salmon, and air by the woodpecker."[30]

Because the twenty-four grates needed to function in two different-sized openings, Susan designed different border treatments: in one instance, a woodpecker whorl design is surrounded by a square with a striking image of small birds, leaves, and vines in four semicircles. Tree and branch forms unite the various animals and human faces, all done in Susan's contemporary style using Salish forms.

The facility was opened in July 2002 as Seahawks Stadium, and the art installed that October. A stadium program guide says, "Point's work is intended to celebrate the rich visual expressions of Coast Salish culture at a time when many local native cultural traditions are being lost."[31] These works in metal are alive with creatures and human faces—as Susan hoped, there is much in this work for both the mind and the eye.

Written Into the Earth, 2002
Circles in Time: "Caribou" (top), "Hummingbird" (middle), "Salmon" (bottom)

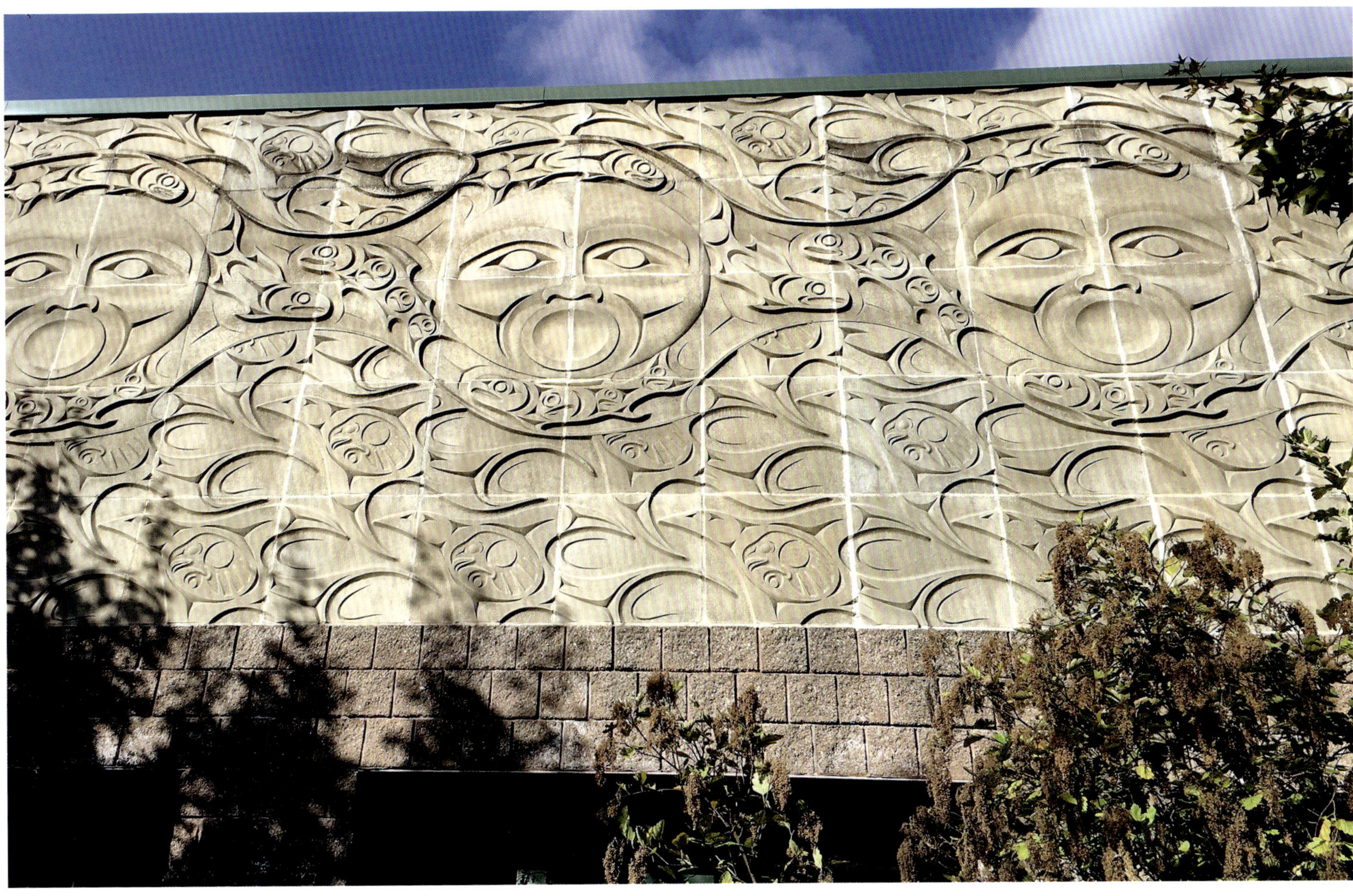

Water—The Essence of Life

LOCATION: West Seattle Pump Station
3051 Harbor Ave SW, Seattle, WA

King County's public art program, 4Culture, invited artists to propose artwork to be integrated into the new West Seattle Pump Station in 1993, just a few years after Susan developed her successful multi-unit carving and casting system for the House of héwhíwus in Sechelt (see page 117). This was to be a juried competition. The invitation outlined a four-phase project that offered enticing opportunities for design work, including the east facade of the pump station and two security gates.

In her application Susan said the theme of her work would be "New Beginnings," and the designs would feature "natural elements reflecting energy, water, and possibly wildlife but with the human spirit integrated so as to give the feeling of interconnection between all elements of life and Mother earth."[32] She described the production process and the basis for the imagery in her artist's statement.

> This original design was created using fourteen grids to create a large repeat wall mural. . . . In order to precast this imagery into concrete wall units, each of the fourteen grids, 2′ × 2′1″ in size, had to be hand carved out of laminated red cedar exposing the intricate and detailed low relief multi-level imagery. Each of the fourteen patterns were then rubber molded along with plaster mother molds in order for them to be precast into concrete wall units. The wall mural covers approximately 1000 square feet.
>
> In producing this design, I worked within

Water—The Essence of Life, 1995
Cast concrete, water-cut aluminum
Approx. 92.9 sq. m (mural);
165 cm (each whorl on gates; diameter); 60 × 57 cm (each element of gate posts and wall)

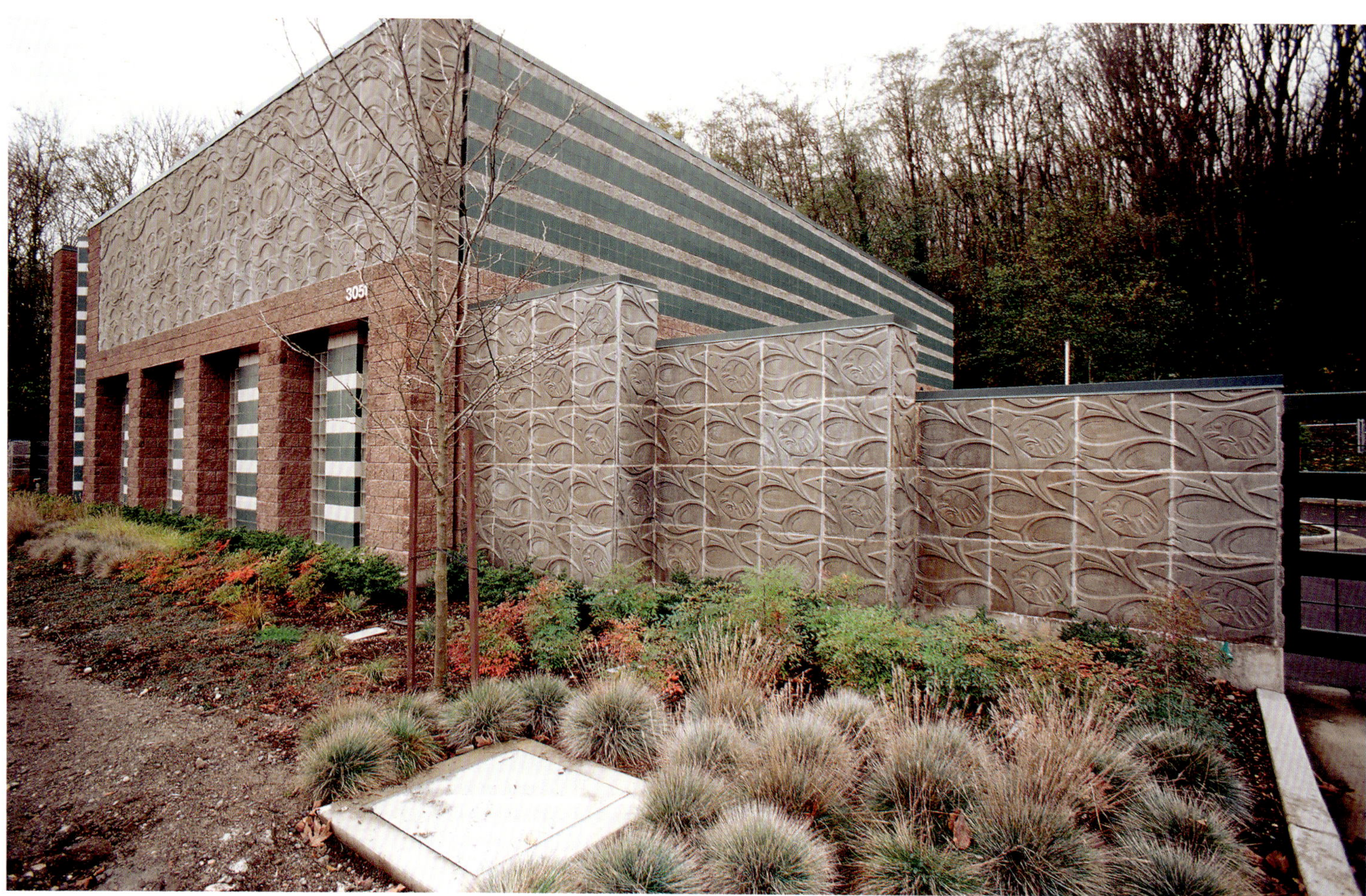

the Coast Salish art style which pays tribute to the aboriginal peoples that once lived in the Alki Point area. As this particular site is historically noted as a gathering site for the aboriginal peoples who once lived in this area when fishing was good, human faces and salmon were incorporated into this design; the human faces also representing the present day community who now live within this area. Within some of the salmon I incorporated eggs and within the birds I incorporated a baby bird which represents the continuing cycle of life and new beginnings or a renewal relating to an essential resource.

Also the imagery in this mural represents land, sea and sky by way of using animal motifs and a human face (in this case the human face represents the land and the salmon represents sea and the birds represent sky). As water is the function of this building, and because I feel water is the essence of all life and life basically entails land sea and sky, I felt it appropriate to use this imagery. As well, this design is also intended to show the integration between man and nature as they are all inter-connected in one way or another to show the unity of life. In the overall design I also tried to create a look of energy and fluidness.[33]

Fluidity is certainly a dominant impression produced by the mural. The concrete has stood up well, and more than a decade after installation the relief details are easy to appreciate. The whorl design

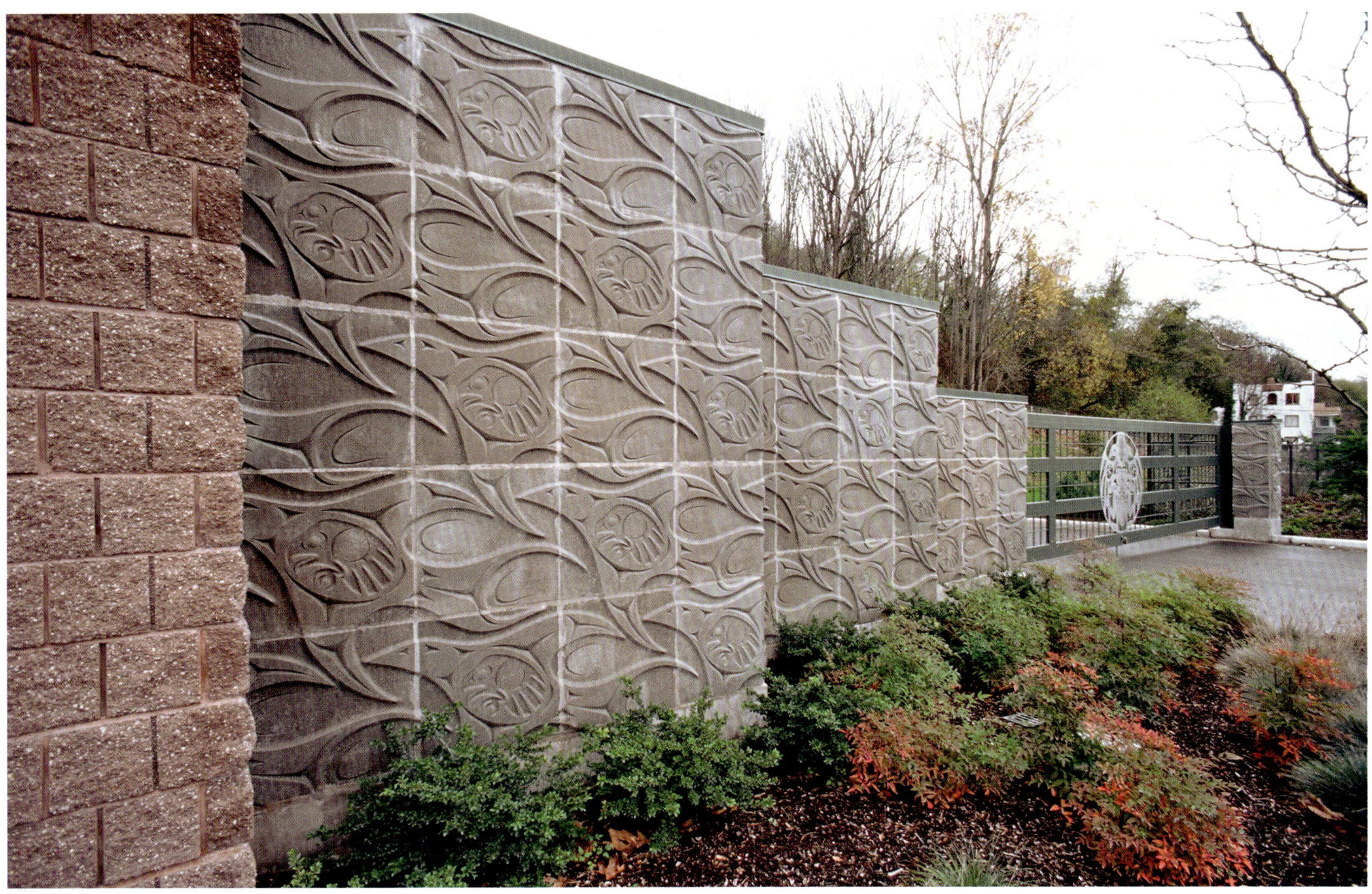

on the gates, based on a number of whorls that Susan saw in museums, also remains in fine form. The central figure is a human with hands raised in a welcome posture; on either side is a šxʷəxʷaʔas (Thunderbird). The laser-cut aluminum whorl stands out very well against the green of the gates.

As Susan hoped, the works are a fine tribute to the original inhabitants of Alki Point (originally known as sbaqWábaqs, "prairie point"), and a fresh and contemporary introduction to Salish forms on a big scale. Though trees have grown between the sidewalk and the pump station, it is worth taking a closer look—this is Susan's contemporary art in Salish style at its biggest and boldest.

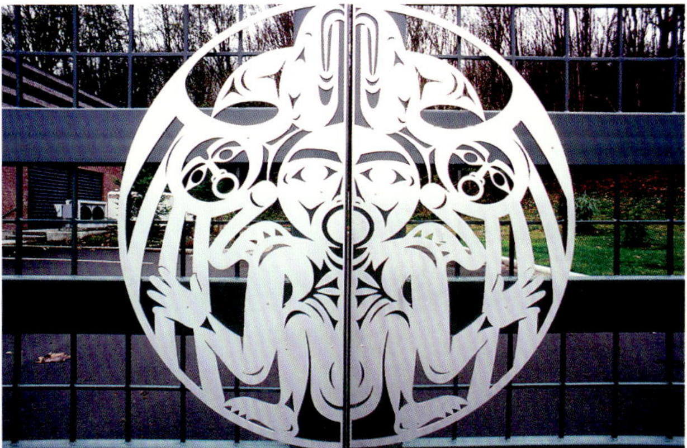

Water—The Essence of Life, 1995

▸ **Northwind's Fishing Weir, 1997**
"Northwind and Mountain Beaver Woman" (plank six)

OVERLEAF: **Northwind's Fishing Weir, 1997**
Carved and painted western red cedar, concrete
165 × 91.4 × 15.2 cm (each)

Northwind's Fishing Weir

LOCATION: Green River Trail
112th St off Pacific Hwy, Tukwila, WA

With their paddle-shaped mix of materials and the complex story they tell, these six planks are one of Susan's most unusual artworks. In 1991, 4Culture invited proposals for art that would retell the Duwamish story of Northwind's weir, and be located near the remains of a Duwamish weir on the Duwamish River south of Seattle. As the commission noted in the invitation, the Duwamish are the people of si'áb siʔał (Chief Seattle), and the people on whose lands the city of Seattle is located. Few examples of Duwamish art remained to be seen in their place of origin after the Point Elliott Treaty of 1855, when most of the artworks disappeared or were shipped away by collectors.

The commission wished to recognize the "rich, local heritage of the Duwamish people and their culture."[34] The invitation included the story of the Northwind Fishing Weir, as compiled by historian David Buerge, which tells of a war between the people of Northwind and the people of Southwind—who was married to Mountain Beaver Woman, the daughter of Northwind. The Northwind people killed all the people of Southwind except Southwind's mother, Sq'u'l'ats. Victorious, Northwind brought extreme cold to the land, and built a fish weir of ice across the river, preventing salmon from swimming upstream. After the war Sq'u'l'ats lived alone on a mountain with only cattails to burn for warmth, crying for her dead son and tormented by Ravens, who were slaves of Northwind. One day Stormwind, the son of Mountain Beaver Woman and Southwind, went hunting and came across Sq'u'l'ats, his grandmother. Together they decided to defeat Northwind. Sq'u'l'ats wove baskets to catch the rain, then released it into the river while Stormwind ripped up trees and threw them at the weir. It was destroyed (though the remains can still be seen at low tide) and Northwind fled into the mountains. He was allowed to return to the valley for a few months each year to visit Mountain Beaver Woman, which is why in the winter it is still cold.

After a jury process that lasted several years, Susan's proposal was chosen for the largest commission. Although this story has no equivalent among the Musqueam people, Susan felt it was rich with opportunities to design images using Salish art elements. She proposed telling the story using culture-specific shapes called "spirit planks," which "were used by shamans to visit the land beyond for the purpose of recovering souls. It is my intention to use the form for reviving the almost lost art form of the Duwamish and the retelling of the Northwind Fishing Weir story. Traditionally there are six spirit planks to a set. I am going to use these spirit planks as a 'story board.' Each story board will illustrate a key part of the... story."[35]

The planks would be carved in western red cedar and painted, inserted into concrete frames, then mounted on small concrete plinths and set along a path being built between Boeing lands and the river. Susan outlined the meaning of each of the planks as the viewer encounters them walking from north to south.

The first shows "Southwind at the top attached (married) to Mountain Beaver Woman below.... There are mountains in the background and two beavers circled around Mountain Beaver Woman's head facing her husband showing that he was her choice. This is because the legend reads two ways—one, that Mountain Beaver Woman is Northwind's daughter but the other saying that both Northwind and Southwind sought to marry her but Southwind was her choice."

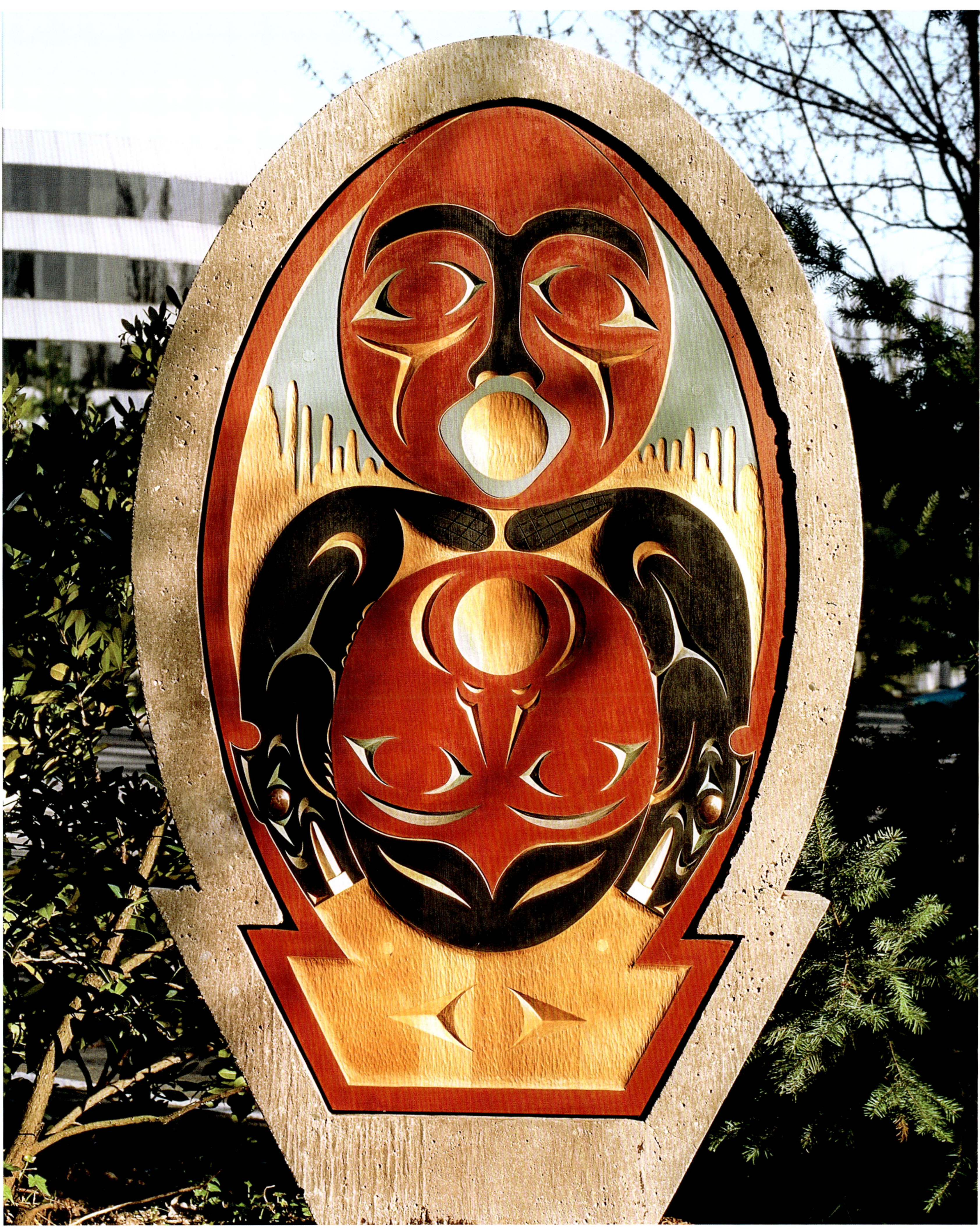

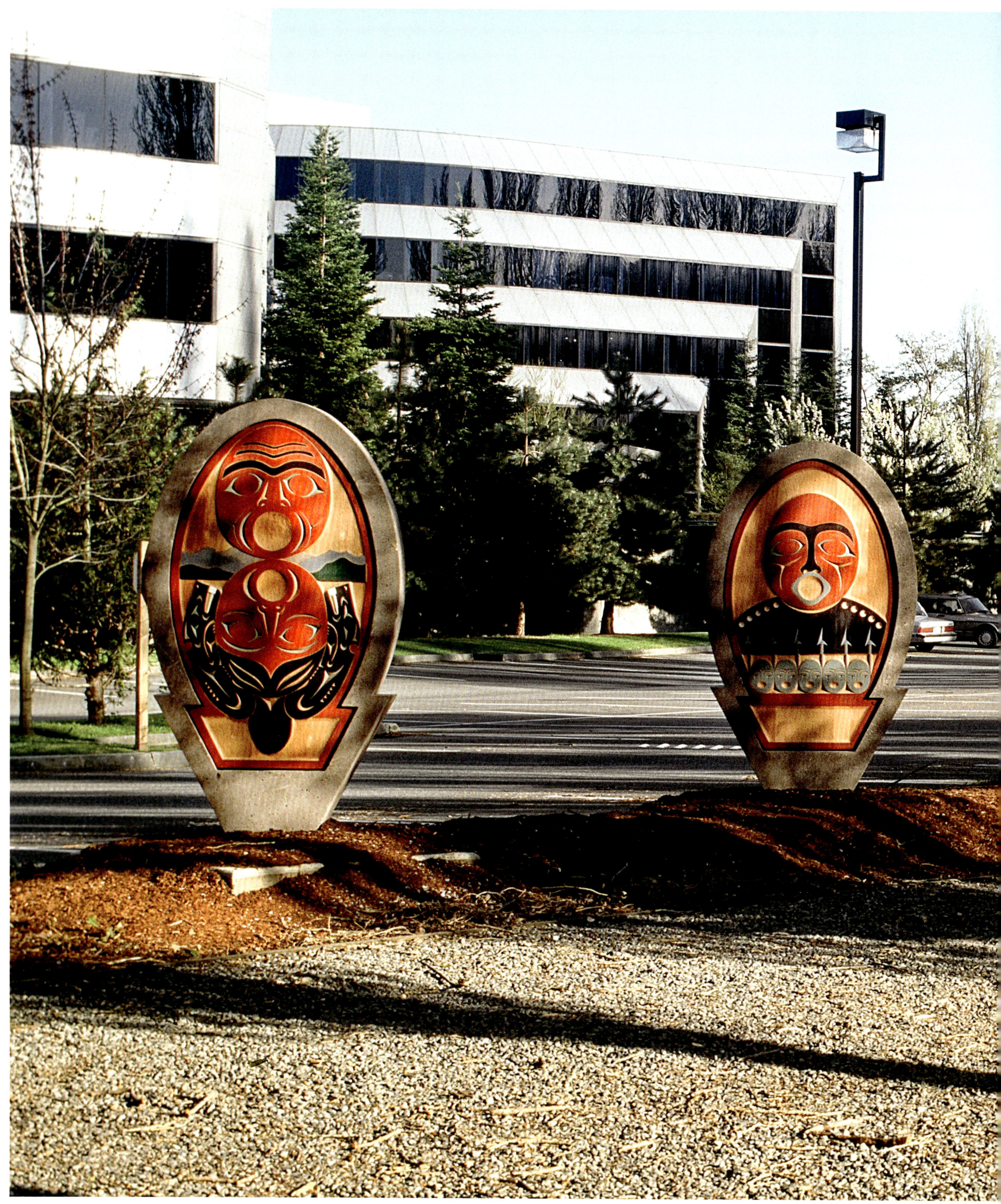

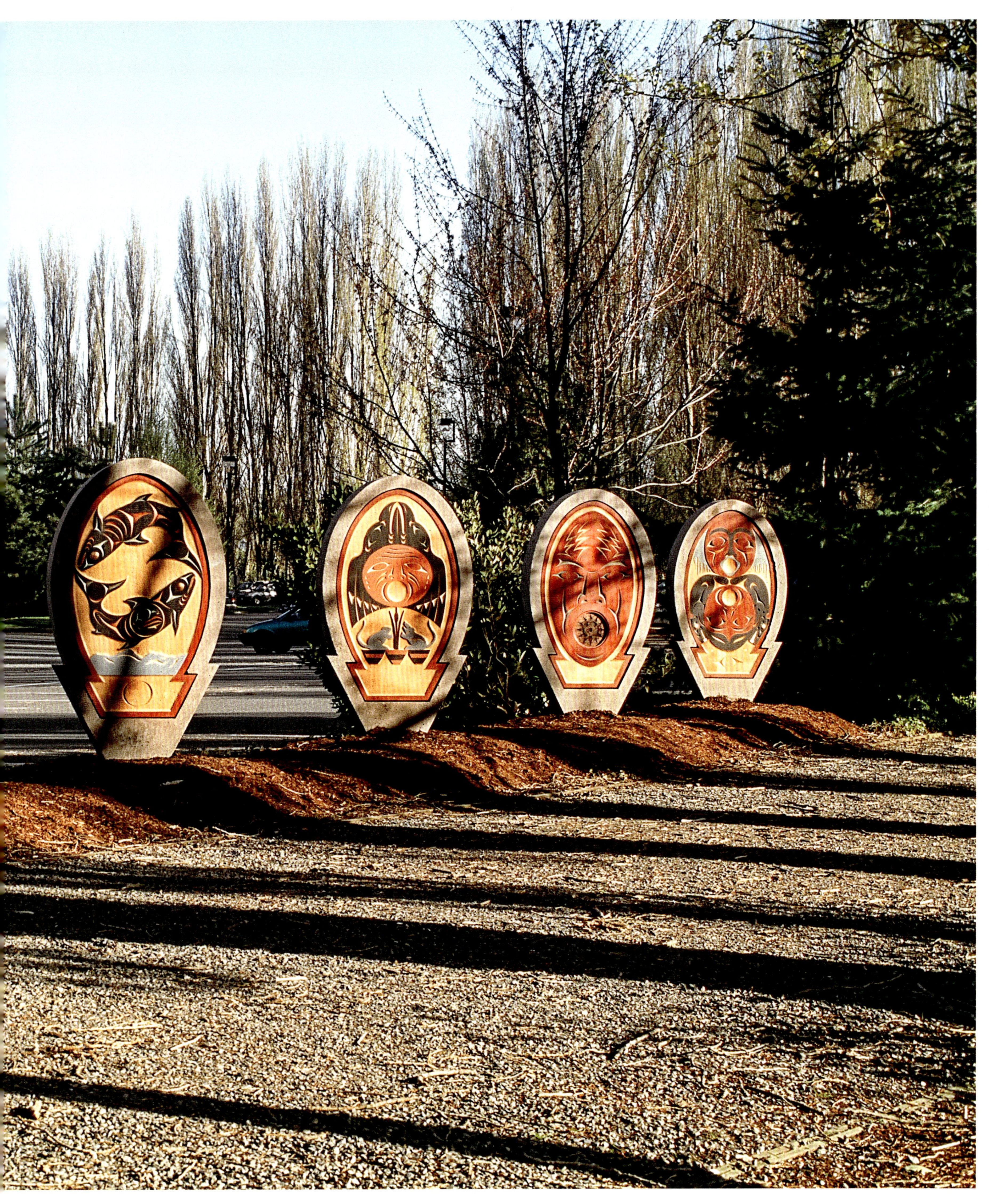

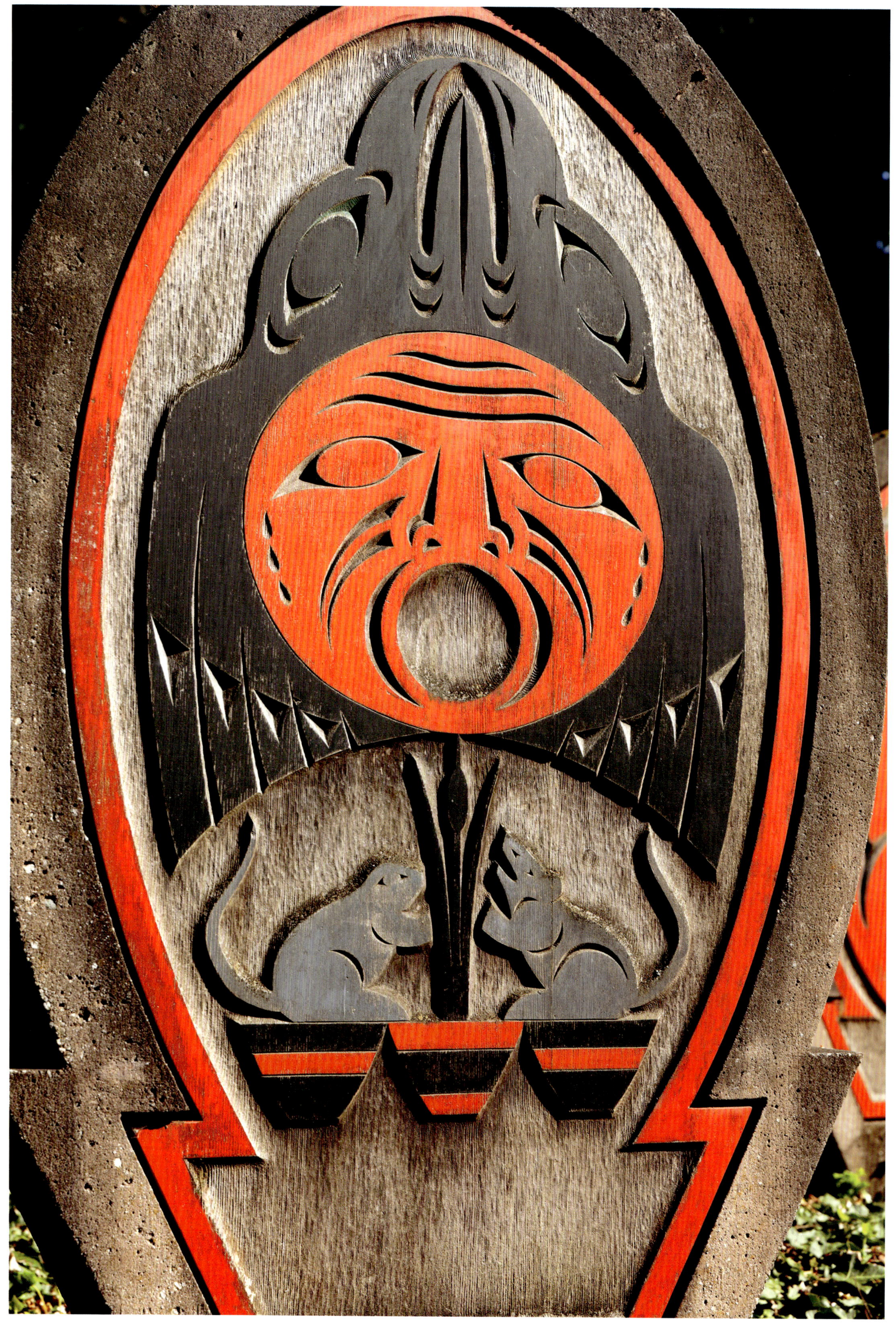

Northwind's Fishing Weir, 1997

"Sq'u'l'ats" (plank four)

"Stormwind" (plank five; detail)

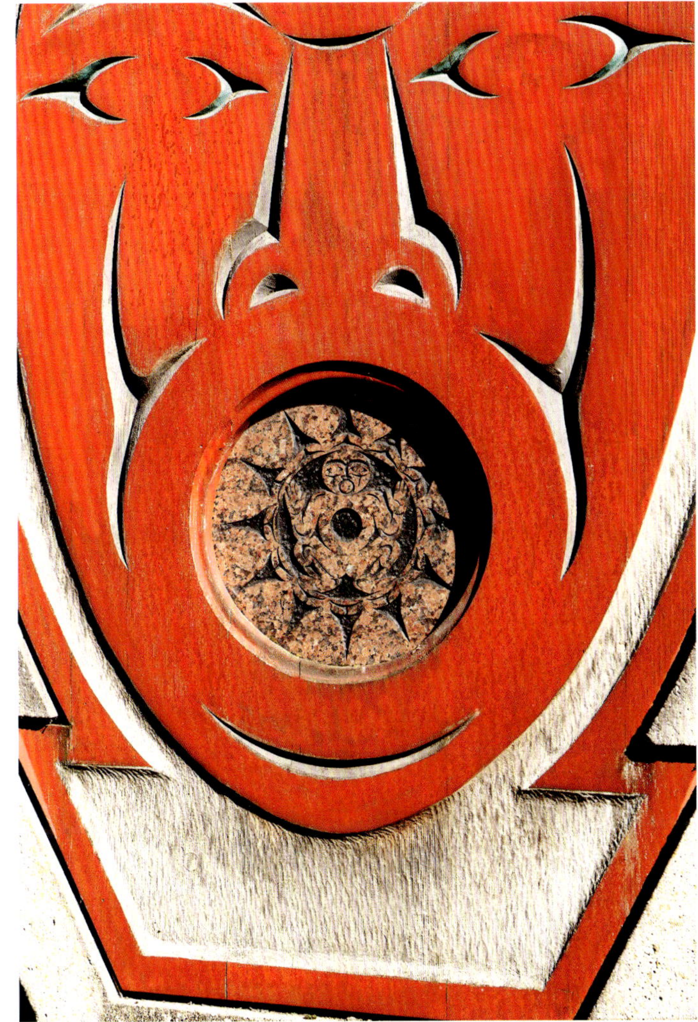

The next plank shows "Northwind and his warriors with spears. The crescent at the top is to symbolize the moon and the wedge shapes descending are to symbolize icicles. This is to emphasize his power." Next comes "the ice fish weir and two salmon blocked from getting upstream to spawn."

The fourth plank shows "Sq'u'l'ats, the mother of Southwind. The tears she has wept for her son are shown as well as some lines on her cheeks to emphasize the filth coming from the ravens above her head. The wings of these ravens form her hair with the small wedge shapes further emphasizing her filth. Her two servants shown down below, the rat and the mole, who are bringing her a cattail stalk to put on her fire. Below them are the baskets she had been weaving."

On the next plank is "a very angry Stormwind, son of Mountain Beaver Woman. On his forehead are lightning bolts to indicate his power. In his mouth is a scene of the battle showing the ice fish weir covered in trees blown down by Stormwind and the steady downpour created by his grandmother when she emptied her baskets of water, flooding the land."

The final plank features "Northwind at the top... with Mountain Beaver Woman below. This symbolizes his return every year to visit Mountain Beaver Woman. Around his head is the cold which he brings with him every winter season—this is symbolized by icicles. Again, around Mountain Beaver Woman's head are two beavers, facing down."[36]

It is a rich and complex story, one that has been told for thousands of years. Susan's visual representation is a departure from oral tradition, as Barbara Luecke, the project manager, observed in a thank-you note to Susan, but it "does more than honor the Northwind Legend. The presence of the story in art connects the site to something ancient and timeless... in an effort to renew the importance of the cultural contributions made by the First People in Puget Sound. Although native stories and artforms were once nearly wiped out, they have not been erased. Thanks to you, many new people will learn and remember some of the complex layers of the past which surround us."[37]

Woven to Place, 2011
Carved western red cedar and acrylic on canvas
5.79 × 2.74 × .05 m

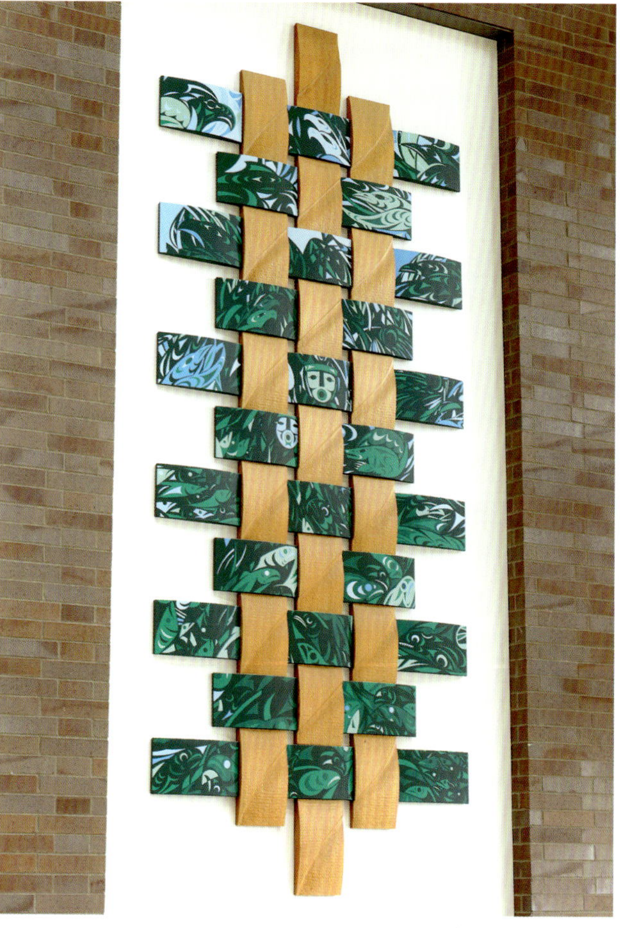

Woven to Place

LOCATION: Salish Hall
12401 SE 320th St, Green River Community College
Auburn, WA

A beautiful forested area forty kilometres south of Seattle is the setting for the main campus of Green River College. Near the centre of the campus is Salish Hall, a fitting place for a monumental work by Susan. *Woven to Place* is mounted in a recessed area on a high brick wall in the atrium, a space suffused with natural light. The setting is very contemporary, filled with steel columns and glass walls. The scale of the art and its specially designed location encourage viewers to spend at least a few moments admiring the composition.

It is an ingenious creation made of forty-seven pieces arranged to simulate a piece of Salish weaving; nineteen carved cedar rectangles form the vertical warp, and twenty-eight hand-painted polyester panels stretched over birchwood frames form the horizontal weft. When visitors move in close they can appreciate the gentle curves of the natural wood panels, the colour gradations from the deep green at the base to the light blue above, and the classic Salish forms in the paintings. And there is much to see, as Susan made clear in her proposal to the Washington State Arts Commission.

> I have based my artwork concept on the natural location of the college . . . the forest imagery is a visual metaphor, woven together through a series of gently shaped panels, mimicking the form of Salish basketry. The materials mesh an indigenous artistic medium (carved cedar) with a traditional fine art medium (paint on canvas), a visual expression of the connections between all forms of life. . . . The carved cedar panels tie the piece together, and root the artwork in a uniquely Northwest Coast Style . . .
>
> Carved imagery will include traditional Salish elements combined with deep relief scallops and contours. The flowing designs will incorporate subtle imagery intended to spark the imagination of viewers to complete the imagery themselves.
>
> The canvases have easily readable imagery relating to the land, the sea and the sky, illustrating the connections between all forms of life. The top section of the artwork will have eagles, ravens and thunderbirds. Towards the centre there will be animal and human elements, and at the bottom the imagery will include aquatic motifs like herring, salmon and whales."[38]

Woven to Place is a poem, in wood and painted canvas, about the importance of the earth and all who call it home. Humans appear but they are just one part of a much greater story. It is unforgettable.

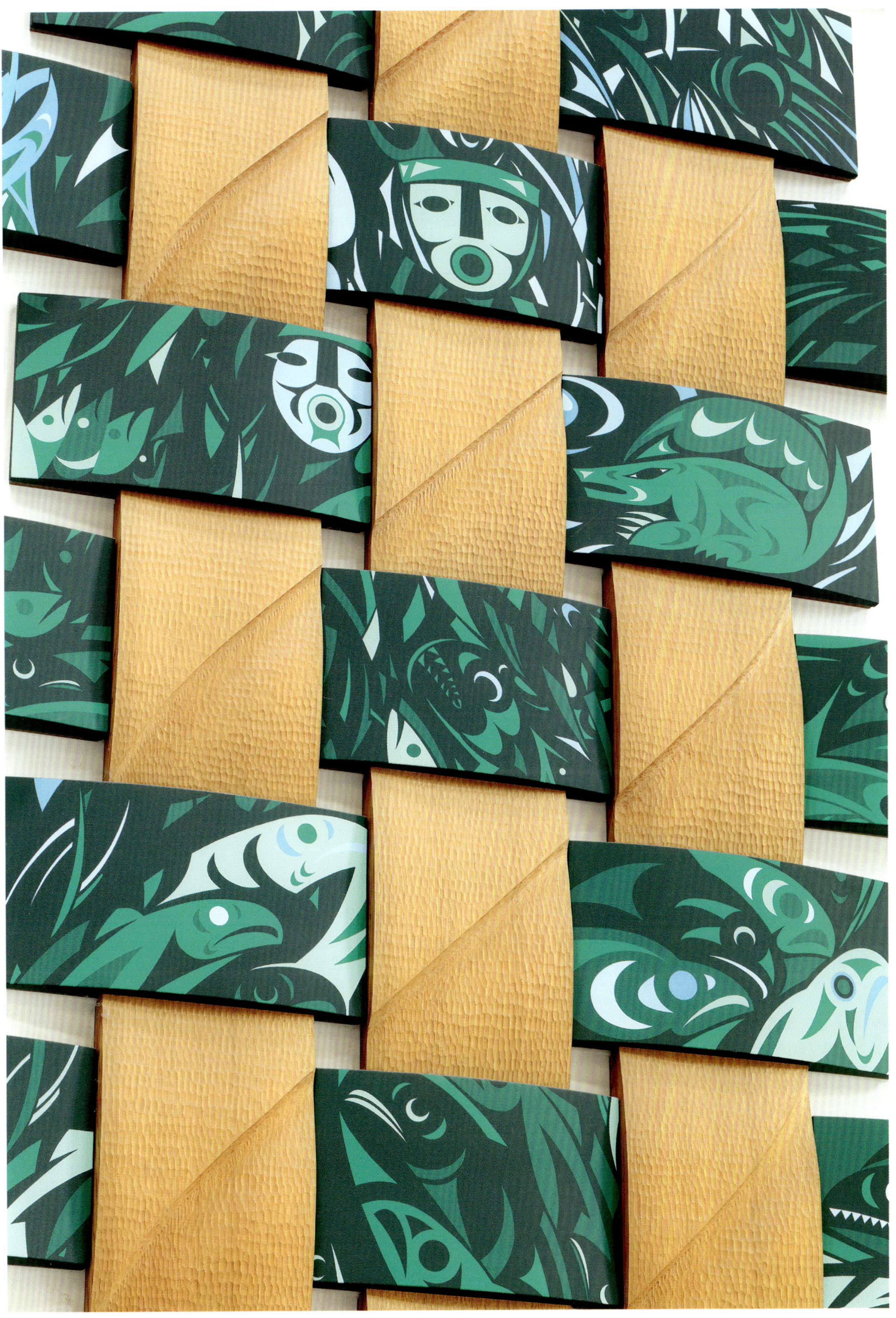

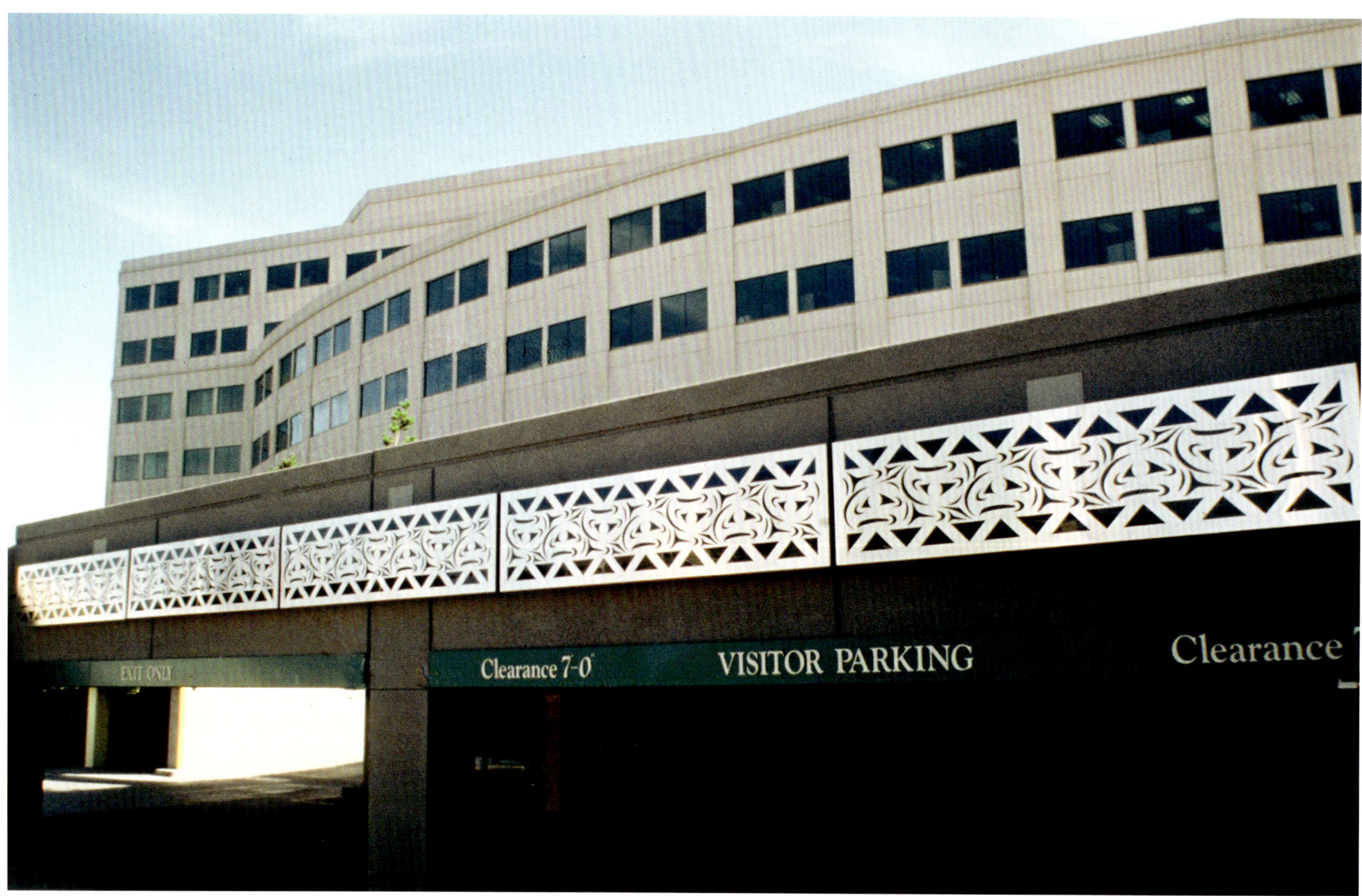

Sea to Sky

LOCATION: Natural Resources Building
1111 Washington SE, Olympia, WA

This ornamental feature for a parkade in downtown Olympia was the first of a long and successful series of works for the Washington State Arts Commission, also known as ArtsWA.[39] *Sea to Sky* is an early example of Susan's experimentation with materials like metals and glass, and was one of the works that helped her develop a foundation of skills working with and responding to the requirements set out by architects, engineers, and arts administrators. In an undated artist's statement, Susan describes her inspiration and the method of construction:

Within this particular design, part of the imagery was taken from traditional Nisqually basketry and bowl motifs—that being the triangular patterns running across the top and bottom of the design. These geometrical patterns represent mountains and valleys which in this case corresponds to forestry and agriculture; and the overlapping salmon heads in the center of the design corresponds to fisheries.

The material for this art mural consists of 14-gauge stained steel and plexiglass and was fabricated in five sections, each section being 10′3″ in life.... The design itself was fabricated from laser cut stainless steel and backed by

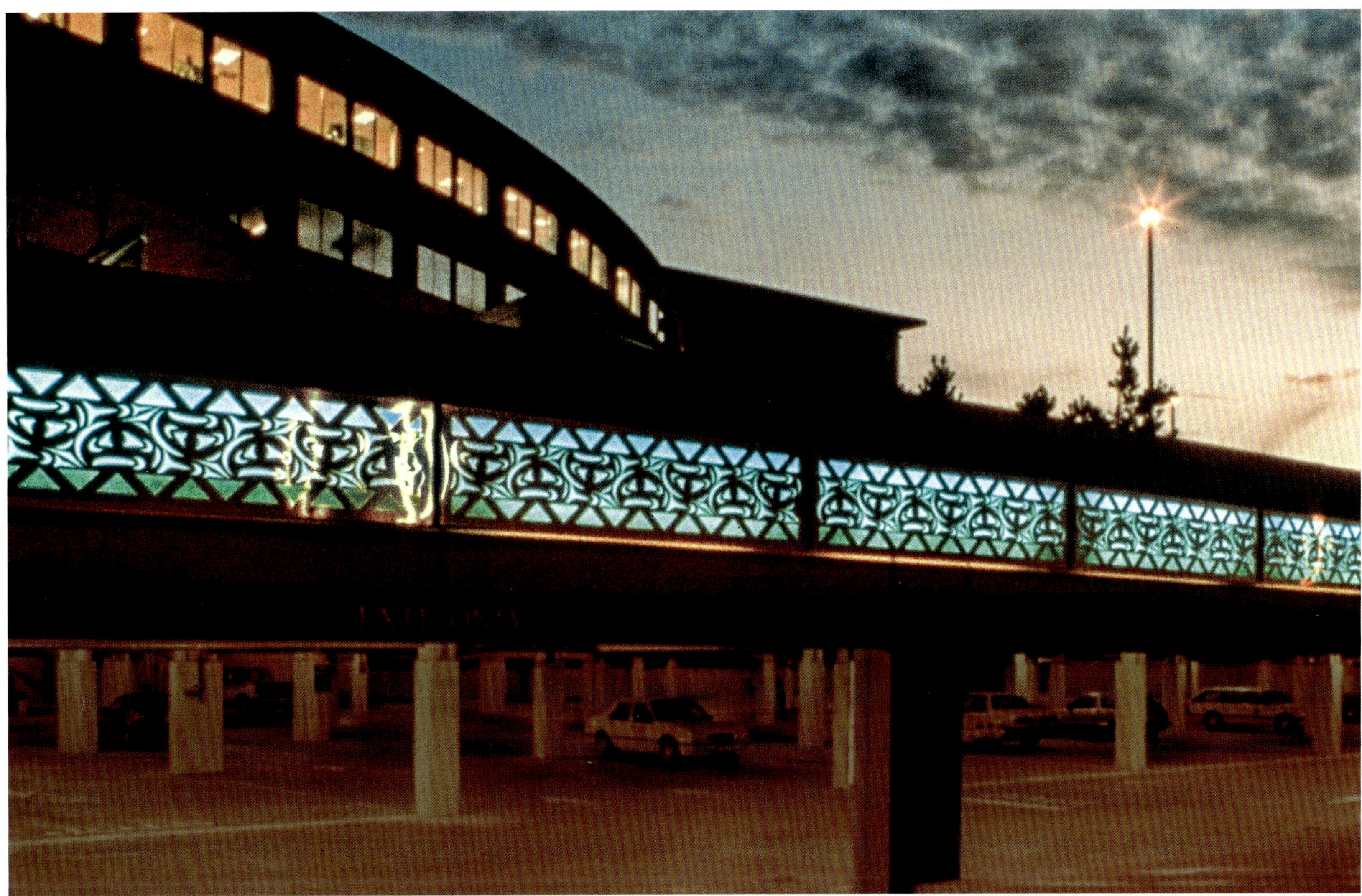

colored plexiglass (which was mounted flush to the back of the stainless steel surface). This art mural was also backlit with fluorescent lighting and set on a timer switch for evening viewing. In order that the florescent lights could be changed whenever necessary, hinges were mounted along the top of each section.[40]

Susan's reference to sq̓ʷali'abš (Nisqually) basketry and bowl motifs is a sign of her meticulousness in exploring local Salish elements for her artworks. She enjoys the ongoing challenge of learning how other Salish groups expressed themselves artistically so that her designs will never be unconnected with a site, but linked deeply to it through symbolism. Susan brings Salish motifs into the heart of the state's capital in a quiet but meaningful way, introducing ancient local culture to citizens in the present and future.

Sea to Sky, 1993
Stainless steel, coloured Plexiglas
.81 × 15.54 × .31 m

THE EVERGREEN STATE COLLEGE

The lushly forested campus of The Evergreen State College is just outside Olympia, Washington, at the south end of Puget Sound, one of the many bodies of water that comprise the Salish Sea. *Scinqua*, the first of two pieces there by Susan, was the result of a commission in 2005 from ArtsWA, the state's public art agency; it led directly to a residency that same year during which Susan produced the second, *Moon Journey*.

It was at Evergreen that she first met Bruce (subiya) Miller, a sqʷuqʷóbəš (Skokomish) Elder, teacher, and weaver, whom she would later describe as one of the three people (along with her mother and her uncle Dominic Point) that she thinks of as "larger than life," saying, "I know it's partly because of their teachings, 'oral teachings,' which is our Salish tradition."[41]

Moon Journey

LOCATION: The Evergreen State College
2700 Evergreen Pkwy NW, Olympia, WA

In 2005, The Evergreen State College invited Susan for a five-day artistic residency. At first she was hesitant because, as she stated in the course description, "I'm a visual artist rather than a lecturer or teacher." However, she continued, "I remembered a promise that I had made to my mentor—to pass on whatever I had learnt to other Salish artists." The response to *Scinqua* also played a large role. "It was a touching and humbling experience to discover that my artwork had reached others in ways I had never imagined, and this experience influenced my decision to become involved in [the residency]."

Susan's daughter Kelly joined her in Olympia and was an active participant in the workshop and the carving. Susan's plan for their short time with the students was to guide them in the creation of medallions in yellow cedar, approximately forty-six centimetres in diameter, that would be cast in bronze and placed around the grounds of the college. Seven young artists from various local Salish groups enrolled in the course. In her course description Susan said

> the goal in working with these Traditional designs is to create a series of artworks that pay tribute to our ancestors. These whorls are all graphic and floral in nature—like the petroglyphs or petrographs, which were the first Salish markers. Our ancestors drew inspiration from their environment and from nature, just as we do now.
>
> The spindle whorls seen in this documentation have lost their original stories and family ties; my hope is that we can use them as an inspiration and a guide, linking them to our own artistic style as we work. There is much to be learned from studying Traditional artefacts; they teach us to understand the key elements of the Salish art form, and provide a vocabulary from which we can expand and develop a personal style.

To ensure the students' work left a permanent legacy, Susan approached Jeff White of the Tacoma

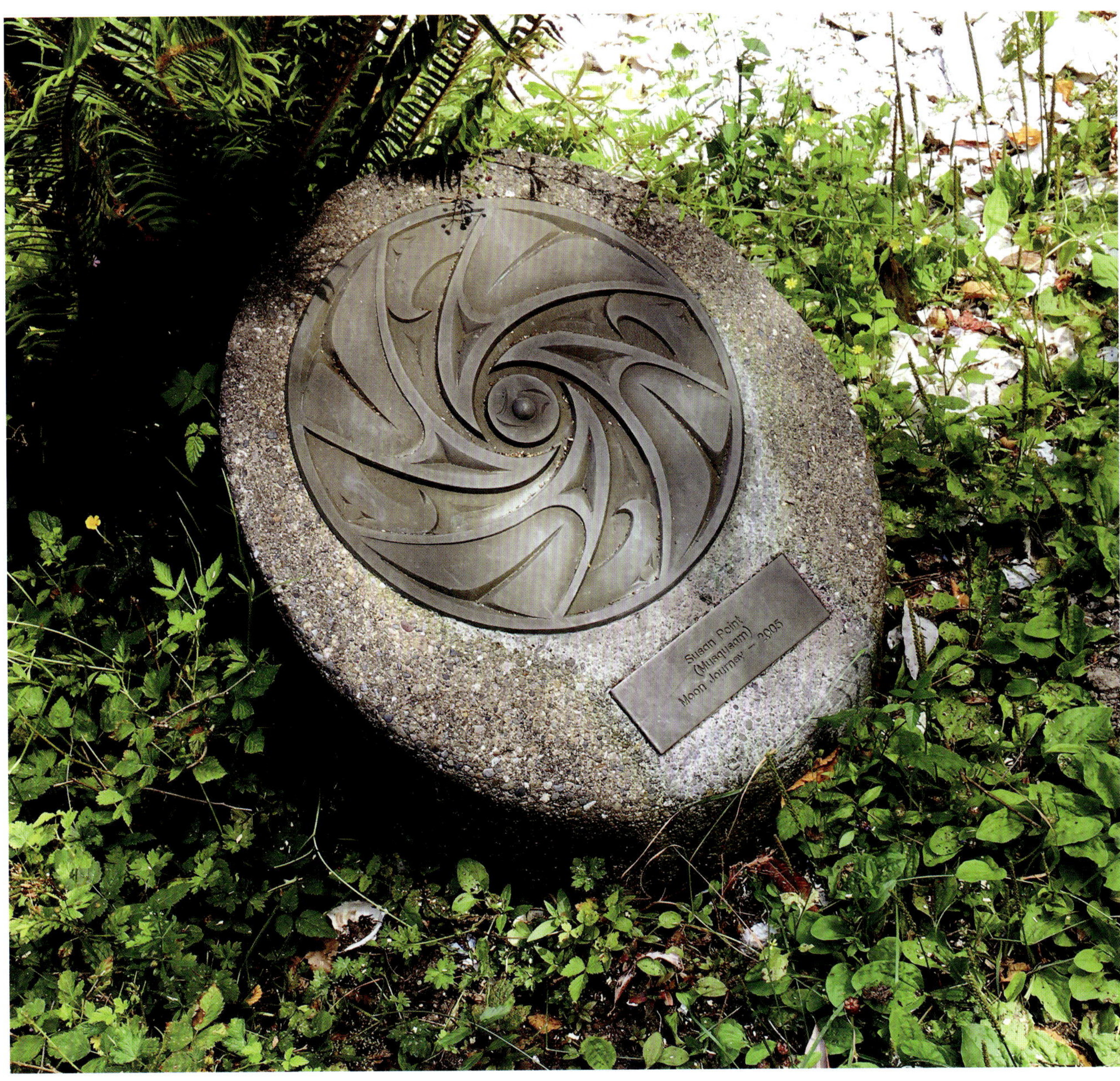

firm Urban Accessories, whom she had come to know and admire during production of the tree grates from *Written Into the Earth* (2002; see page 182). Jeff agreed to donate much of the cost of casting the whorls in bronze, and the work was completed by July 2007.

The whorls of the seven students, as well as Susan's, are set as guideposts on a path to the main entrance of s'gʷi gʷi ʔ altxʷ (House of Welcome). *Moon Journey* is modelled on a serigraph that Susan designed and printed in 1997, and shows four eagle wings (or perhaps orca fins) interspersed with eagle heads or waves and arranged around a moon. It is the last whorl on the path, nearest the entrance.

Moon Journey, 2005
Cast bronze
44 cm (diameter)

Scinqua, 2005
Carved western red cedar, glass, copper
3.05 × 3.05 × .2 m

Scinqua

LOCATION: The Evergreen State College
2700 Evergreen Pkwy NW, Olympia, WA

Upon entering the Daniel J. Evans Library you will find your gaze drawn to the north wall, the permanent home of Susan's beautiful spindle whorl *Scinqua*. The work celebrates the ongoing presence of the local Salish Peoples of the southern reaches of Puget Sound through the depiction, in Susan's words, of

> two human faces calling upon a higher source... and, at the same time, offering a gift of gratitude for the power he has brought to the people of the water... offering food for the Thunderbird. These faces have a lot of different interpretations. They can represent both native and non-native peoples coming together or represent peoples of the water coming together (encompassing the three sub cultures... the river people, the lake people, the ocean people).
>
> On the outside of the red cedar whorl, there are seven glass salmon with human forms incorporated within (3 male and 4 female) which represent the native peoples of the 7 inlets of this area as well as our native peoples in the surrounding area.[42]

The name *Scinqua* refers to the two-headed serpent that curves tightly around the human faces, who are offering it as gift to the Thunderbird. In her proposal Susan noted that during a 2002 residency at the Pilchuck Glass School in Stanwood, Washington, she had learned a number of glassworking techniques and was eager to try them in shaping the salmon and human figures. One of the delights of this artwork is its accessibility, which allows close study of the details of those figures. The college community greeted this magnificent whorl with enthusiasm, especially the representatives of the various local First Nations, who gather regularly in the campus Longhouse, s'gʷi gʷi ʔ altxʷ (House of Welcome).

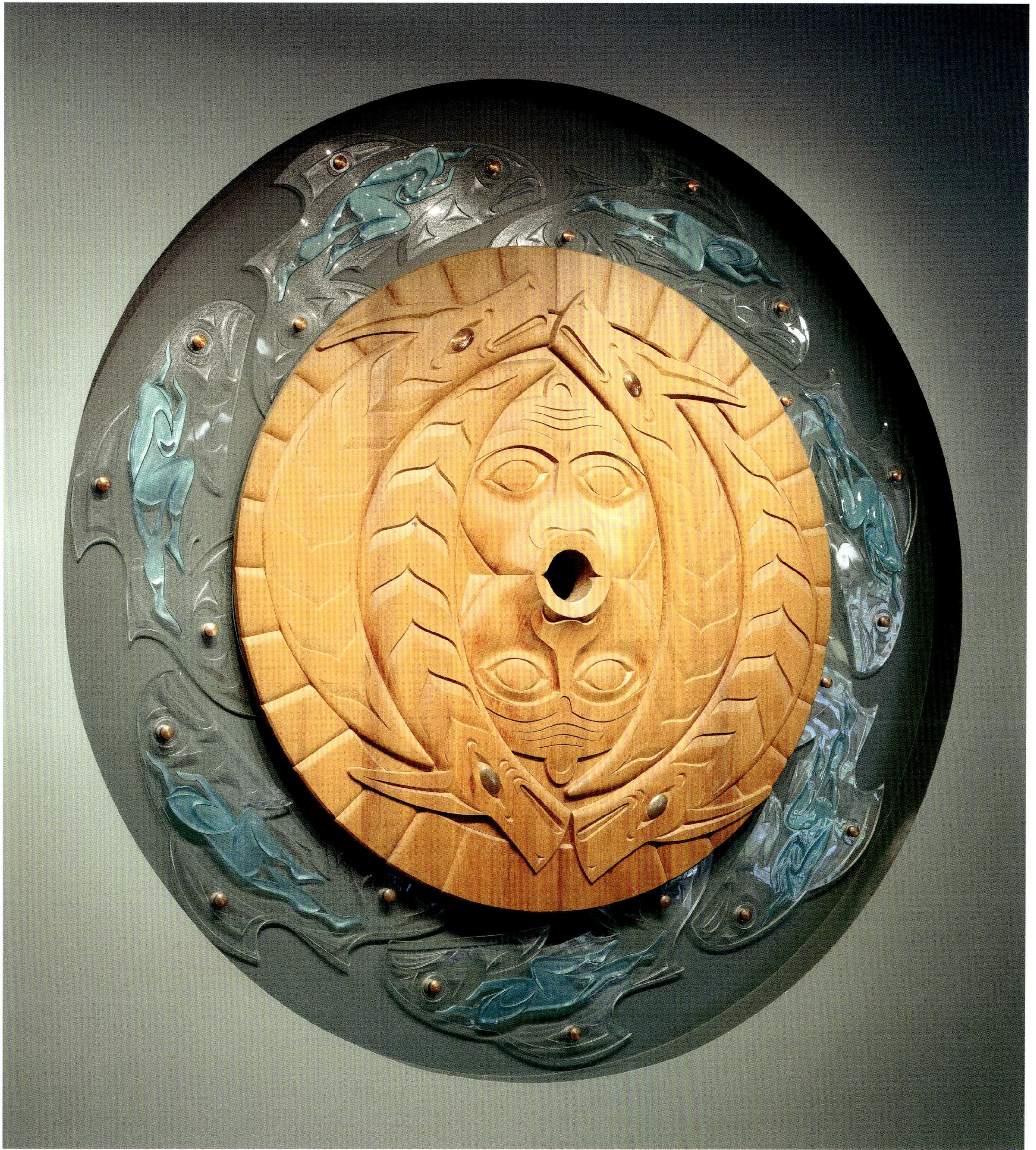

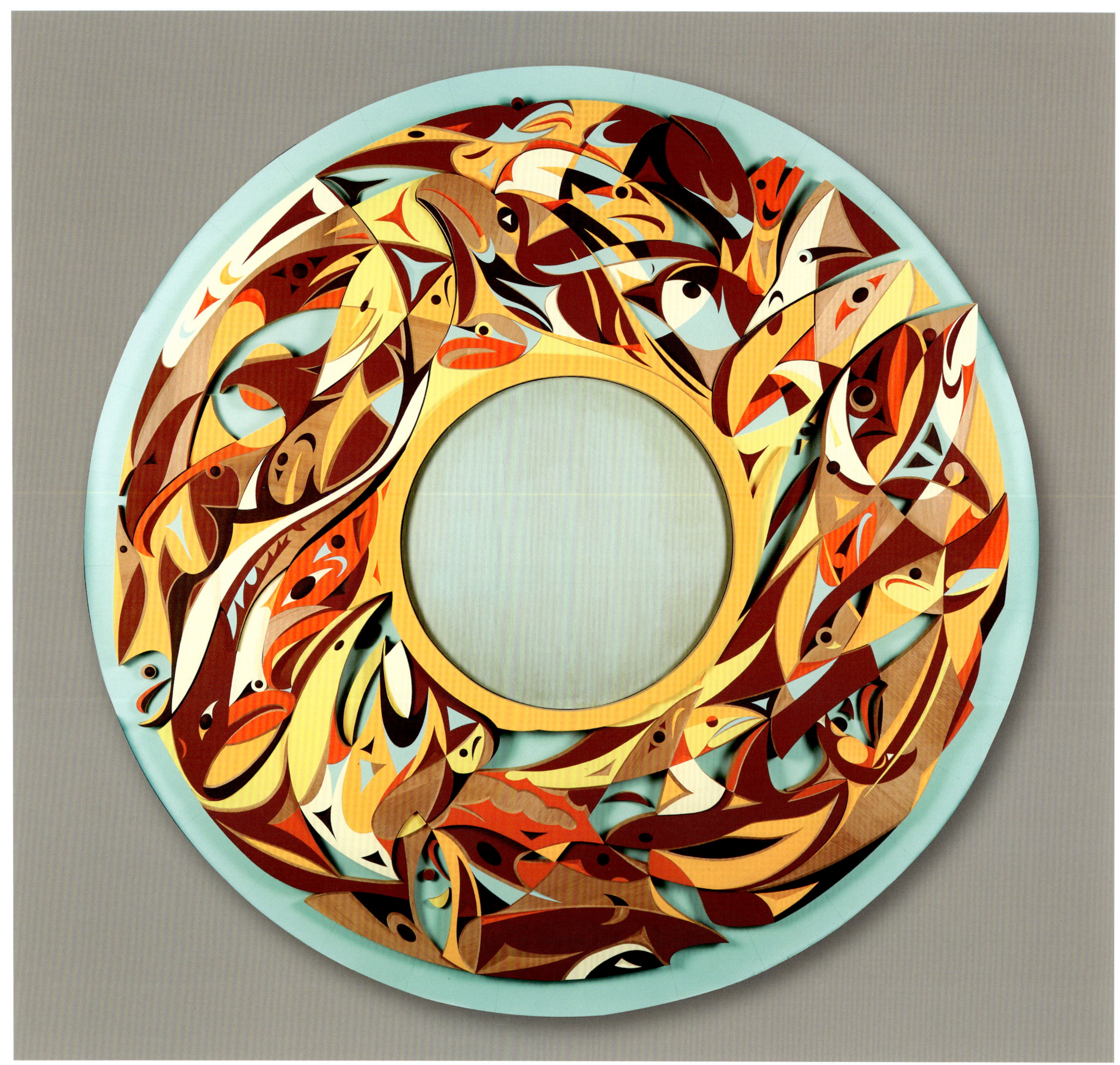

Beyond the Edge, 2015
Painted western red cedar
1.83 × 1.83 × .08 m

Beyond the Edge

LOCATION: Portland Art Museum
1219 SW Park Ave, Portland, OR

As Susan's reputation grew steadily and spread far beyond Salish territories, more art museums were eager to acquire artwork by her, including the Portland Art Museum (PAM), about five hundred kilometres south of the Musqueam settlement.

In February 2014, Dr. Deana Dartt, the curator of Native American Art, invited Susan to submit a proposal for an artwork that was moveable (as the museum's pieces routinely rotate or go out on loan) and would complement and bridge the old and the new, such as Susan's *On the Edge* (2000), a spindle whorl in carved glass, stainless steel, and Texada marble. The new work was to incorporate ideas of resilience, interaction, and independence, and confluences of ideas, cultures, and art forms.

This gave Susan lots of creative room to manoeuvre. She sent her proposal on 15 July, emphasizing that she had "something great in mind, something that would charm the donors." Her proposed design was scalable to whatever size the museum preferred, but she envisaged it approximately 183 centimetres in diameter and three centimetres thick. The design consisted of integrated and overlapping figures, with each distinct shape to be painted a different colour, "which essentially makes the artwork act as a puzzle, pieced together. It is a story about west coast life."[43]

The museum commissioned the piece on 2 September 2014 and it was delivered one year later. Each piece was carved separately and fitted to its neighbour. They form a grand sweep of Salish forms and colour: salmon and other fish; eagles, ravens and other birds, all curving gracefully around a central void. Susan's signature style draws the viewer in to discover just how many separate living forms are brought into one rich visual statement.

Following exhibition at PAM, *Beyond the Edge* was loaned to the Vancouver Art Gallery for its exhibition *Susan Point: Spindle Whorl* from February to May 2017. The label in that exhibition revealed that Susan had been inspired by comments from a prominent Canadian environmentalist.

> *Beyond the Edge* and *The Edge* [2009; a print] evolved from the same thumbnail sketch. Dr. David Suzuki, a Canadian scientist and activist, often makes reference to human beings affecting the *thin blue line*, which inspired me to create these images.
>
> Beyond the edge of the earth's rocky crust there is a *thin blue line* separating life on earth from the infinite blackness of space. This is our atmosphere... just a few kilometres of water vapour and other gaseous molecules. Within the zone of our thin biosphere, life moves and evolves. We humans are part of a web of interconnections closely linked to one another. All of our behaviours, whether biological, cultural or economic in nature, are activities within a larger ecosystem; we humans are not independent. In a very short time we have transformed from small societies living within nature, to handling small pockets of wilderness within our expanding human landscape. Every aspect, particularly living beings on earth, is being impacted with our actions... we each hold the world in our hands.[44]

This beautiful composition summarizes, in Salish forms, some of Susan's central beliefs about the interconnectedness of all life, and her personal observations about changes to the natural world that have occurred in her own lifetime: the silencing of the frogs, and the disappearance of edible and medicinal plants that her mother showed her as a girl.

Intersection of Enlightenment

LOCATION: Eastern Washington University
526 5th St, Cheney, WA

After the Washington State Arts Commission invited Susan in 2000 to create a piece for Eastern Washington University, she visited the campus with her husband, Jeff Cannell. On a tour of the university museum's collections, several historic belongings caught Susan's attention—especially the cornhusk bags, local Interior Salish examples of the traditional weaving style of the Indigenous Peoples of the Northwest Plateau (historically called the Plateau Indians, the term refers to the many Peoples who live in an area stretching from central B.C. to northern California, and as far east as Montana). These were made using cornhusks, roots, hemp, cherry and cedar bark, and other fibres.

Not surprisingly, these objects particularly interested Susan because of the long history of weaving among the Musqueam and other Coast Salish Peoples and her own personal collection of reed baskets made by several generations of the women in her family. She was impressed not only with the skill of the cornhusk bag weavers but equally by the geometric designs on the baskets.

Following the site visit, Susan received background information from the university on the local spoqin (Spokan) people, which deeply influenced her design. In her proposal she recognized that officials at the university preferred that wood be the principle material; noted that an eagle sculpture would eventually be placed somewhere on the school grounds; and observed that since this was Salish territory, "the artwork should remain sensitive to the original first peoples of this area. In other words, the artwork should not have a northwest coast look but rather a reflection of this area's specific art."[45] She also felt the work should relate to the programs on offer at the renovated Monroe Hall facility (which the work would be located in front of), which included Women's Studies, African American Studies, and Chicano and Chicana Studies. Finally, she was taken by the peaceful nature of the local landscape of rolling hills.

Susan's final proposal was inspired in part by the cornhusk bags, but more broadly by the great weaving tradition and art among the Plateau Salish of the area, as she observed in her proposal.

> Symbolically, baskets gain their strength from the fibers that come from different directions, not unlike the strength of a campus where students arrive from different corners of the earth. Baskets are also supple, flexible, and eager to adapt to the load they carry at any given time.
>
> In this idea I would like to incorporate a woven design into the landscape, incorporating imagery from the baskets found in this area—the stylized human form. Through this large-scale weaving sculpture, I want to show how lives intersect and are woven together and how every person, unique in their own sense, is a vital part of a whole that forms a society in which we live....
>
> ...Inspired from a human motif found on a local basket, I created several variations for this sculpture. Although ancient in origin, these motifs have a very contemporary look as well. This type of imagery has also been seen on petroglyphs found in the neighbouring

Columbia region, evidence that no culture lives in isolation, we are all affected by those around us.... These human forms symbolically represent all the men and women from the four corners of the earth coming together and also represents the different groups within this new facility of Eastern Washington University.

...The imagery on these basketry components can also reflect not only the human form but also motifs relating to other important aspects of life in this area (i.e. native plants and/or animals such as salmon, bird images) thus showing the integration of man and environment as well.[46]

The sculpture is made up of twenty-four separately carved pieces of western red cedar. Nine of the pieces are plain but curved at the edge to simulate where strands of weaving would flow over and under one another. The pieces nearest the edge of the sculpture are carved more deeply, at a steeper angle, to represent the edge of a basket. Many of the pieces are carved with human forms in low relief, while others carry an image of a sməyəθ (deer), a salmon, or a bird styled in what Susan referred to as a rock art form. Ten years after she started working in wood, it is interesting to see how creatively Susan used the material, and how carefully she consulted local traditions to honour a group of Salish cousins east of the Cascade Mountains.

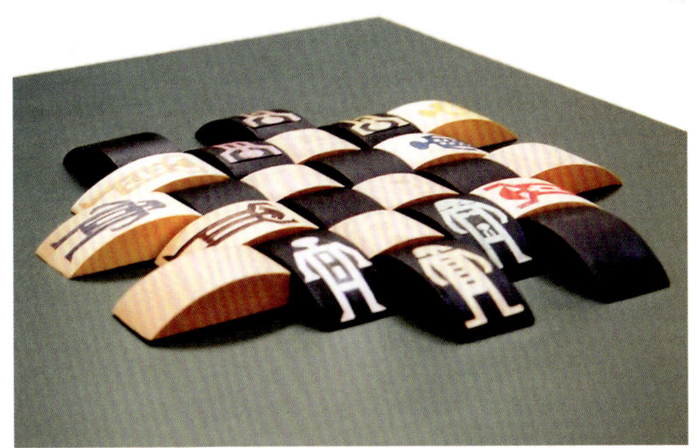

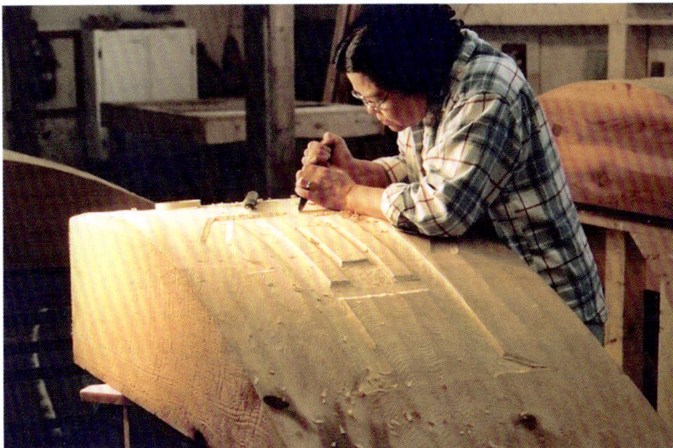

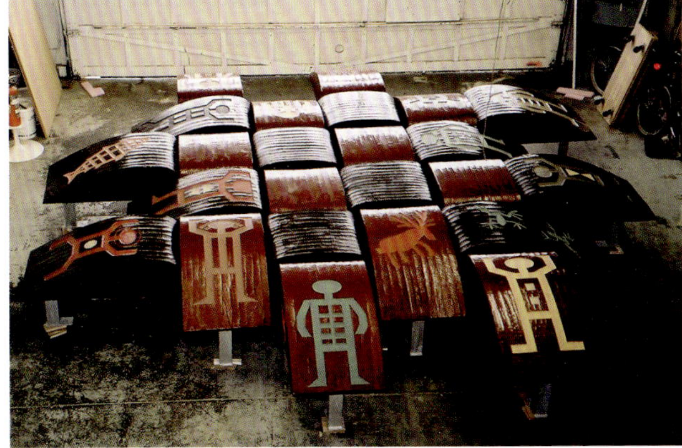

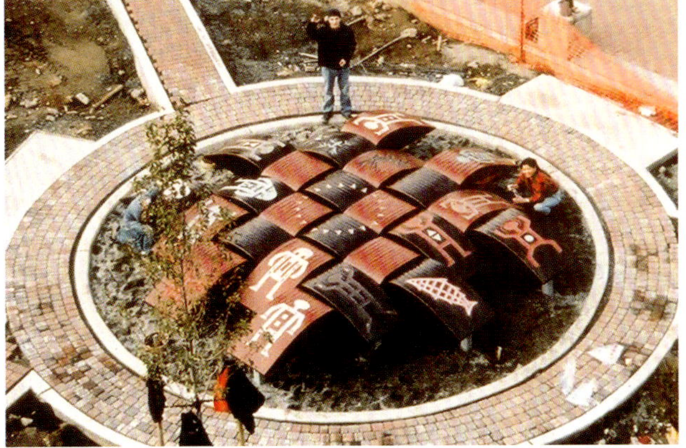

Intersection of Enlightenment, 2001
Carved and painted western red cedar, galvanized steel
.51 × 6.1 × 6.1 m

Susan first created a model (top), then carved each element at her Coast Salish Arts studio (second from top). The completed artwork (third from top) was installed in 2001 (bottom).

Slahal, 1988
Acrylic on canvas
1.83 × 1.83 m

Slahal

LOCATION: BC Lottery Corporation
74 West Seymour Street, Kamloops, BC

The British Columbia Lottery Corporation commissioned this dramatic rendition of some of the key elements of the story of sləhel̓ (Slahal), sometimes known as the bone game or stick game, an ancient game still popular among Salish Peoples on both sides of the international border.

Susan has arranged the four bone pieces and the sticks, including the "king" stick, within the body and wings of a Thunderbird. The wings of the Thunderbird open up symmetrically to contain seven of the sticks, and the king stick terminates in a Thunderbird head. Part of the beauty of the design comes from the repeated wedge elements on the wings, which give the whole piece a strong sense of outward movement.

Oral Traditions suggest that the game originally arose many ages ago, when there was competition between humans and animals to determine who would be food. Even though humans eventually prevailed, Indigenous Peoples never lost their respect for the creatures that gave them sustenance. Eventually the game evolved as a way of solving disputes without resorting to war. It also became popular as a gambling game.

This is one of Susan's earliest public works, which introduced her Coast Salish style to people in the territory of the Tk'emlups te Secwepemc, an Interior Salish First Nation. The composition speaks to the responsibility that humans have as stewards of the environment, the importance of learning from Elders, and the importance of life knowledge learned and relearned orally, in this case through a game that brings laughter and social opportunities.

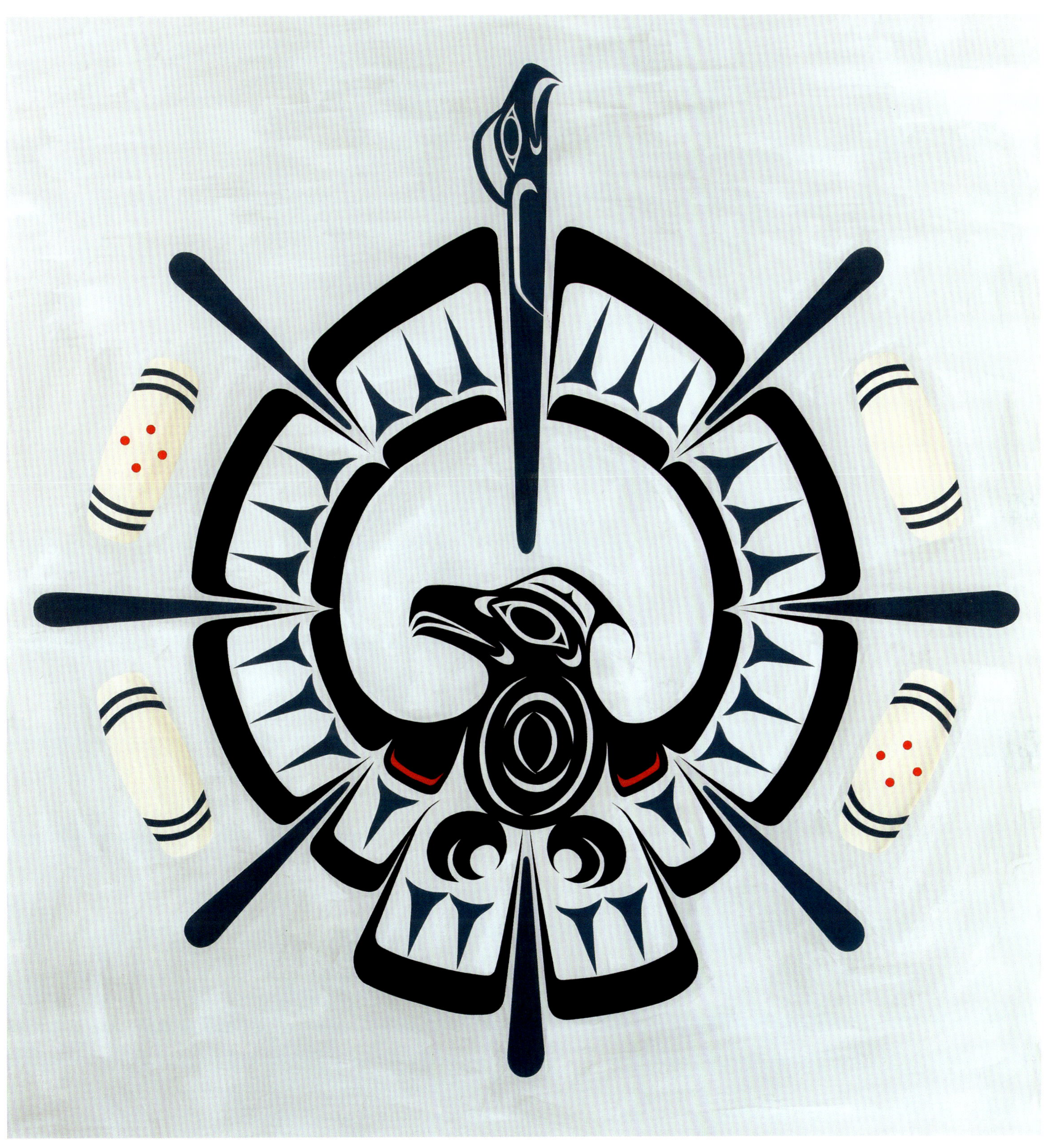

Part Four

Turtle Island and Beyond

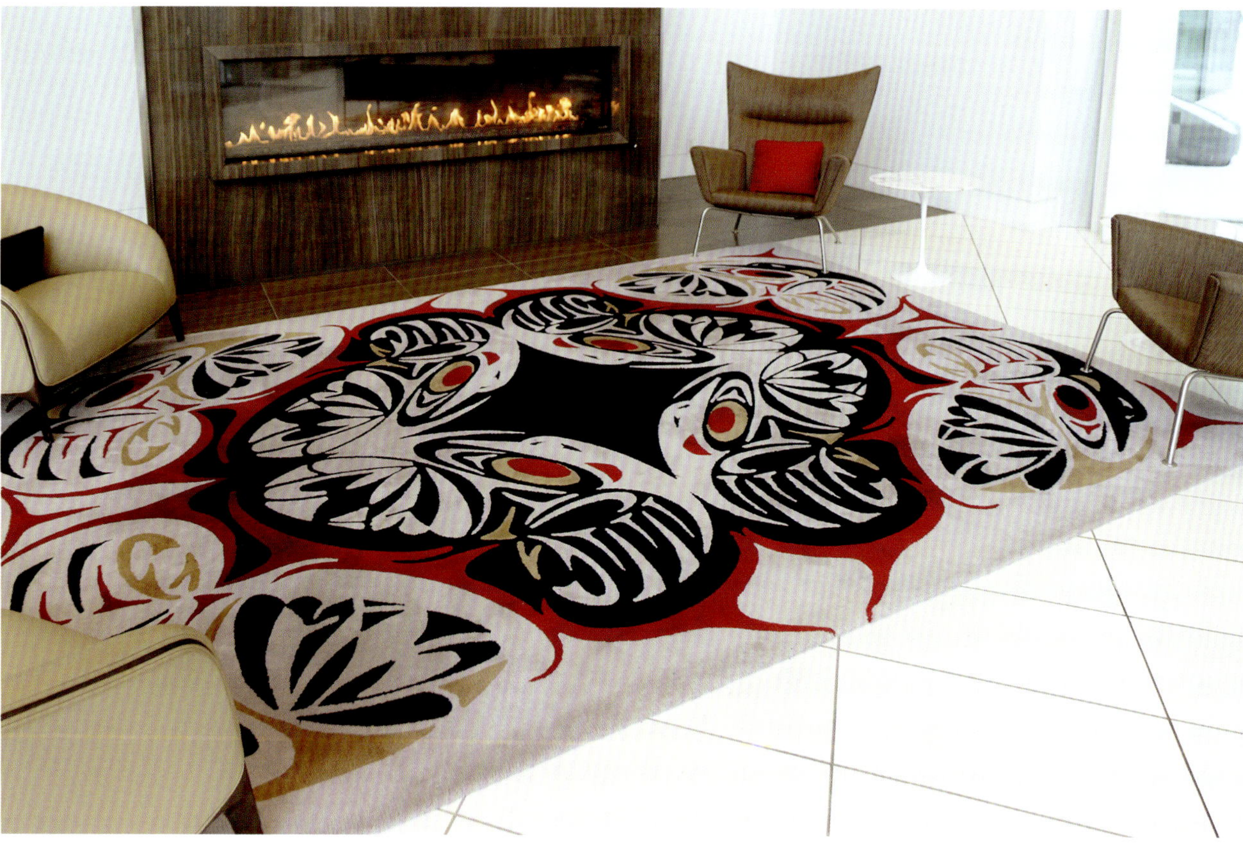

Goose *and* Hummingbird, 2014
Wool
2.44 × 3.66 m (Goose);
3.35 × 4.88 m
(Hummingbird)

Goose *and* Hummingbird

LOCATION: Imperial Oil
505 Quarry Park Blvd, Calgary, AB

Having firmly established herself among the most esteemed and sought-after artists in the country, Susan fields requests from organizations far outside Coast Salish territory. Among the artworks in this final part are three major commissions that enabled Susan to explore new materials and resulted in works that are important in understanding her evolution as an artist. However, since they are housed in corporate settings, they are not readily accessible to the public in the way that most other work in this volume is.

Nearly forty years into her career she can still be driven by the opportunity to work in new mediums, and for new audiences. These carpets are located in Moh'kinsstis (Calgary), traditional territory of the Niitsitapi (Blackfoot), as well as home to Métis Nation of Alberta, Region III, and the people of the Treaty 7 region including the Siksika, the Piikani, the Kainai, the Tsuut'ina, and the Stoney Nakoda First Nations. The larger of the two carpets shows several groups of three tiṅ (hummingbirds), in traditional black, white, and red, on a gold background that anchors the composition. The design is very fluid and at first glance seems almost abstract, until you search for the birds, captured in flight, their bodies and wings curving around one another in an arrangement that also evokes butterfly wings. The bodies of the birds are defined by wedges and crescents, the latter of which also compose the frame. The frame is made of Salish-style crescents that create an effect that could almost be described as a Salish rococo.

Goose uses the same colour palette but on a white background. In the central section is a white ʔeχeʔ (goose), filled with wedges and V-shapes, repeated four times, the heads of the geese arched toward each other to leave a black lozenge at the heart of the design. A space filled with Salish forms, symbolizing a butterfly wing or perhaps a flower, completes the design, which is repeated in each corner. Both carpets were woven from Susan's designs by Masland Carpets in Saraland, Alabama, with 100 percent natural New Zealand wool.

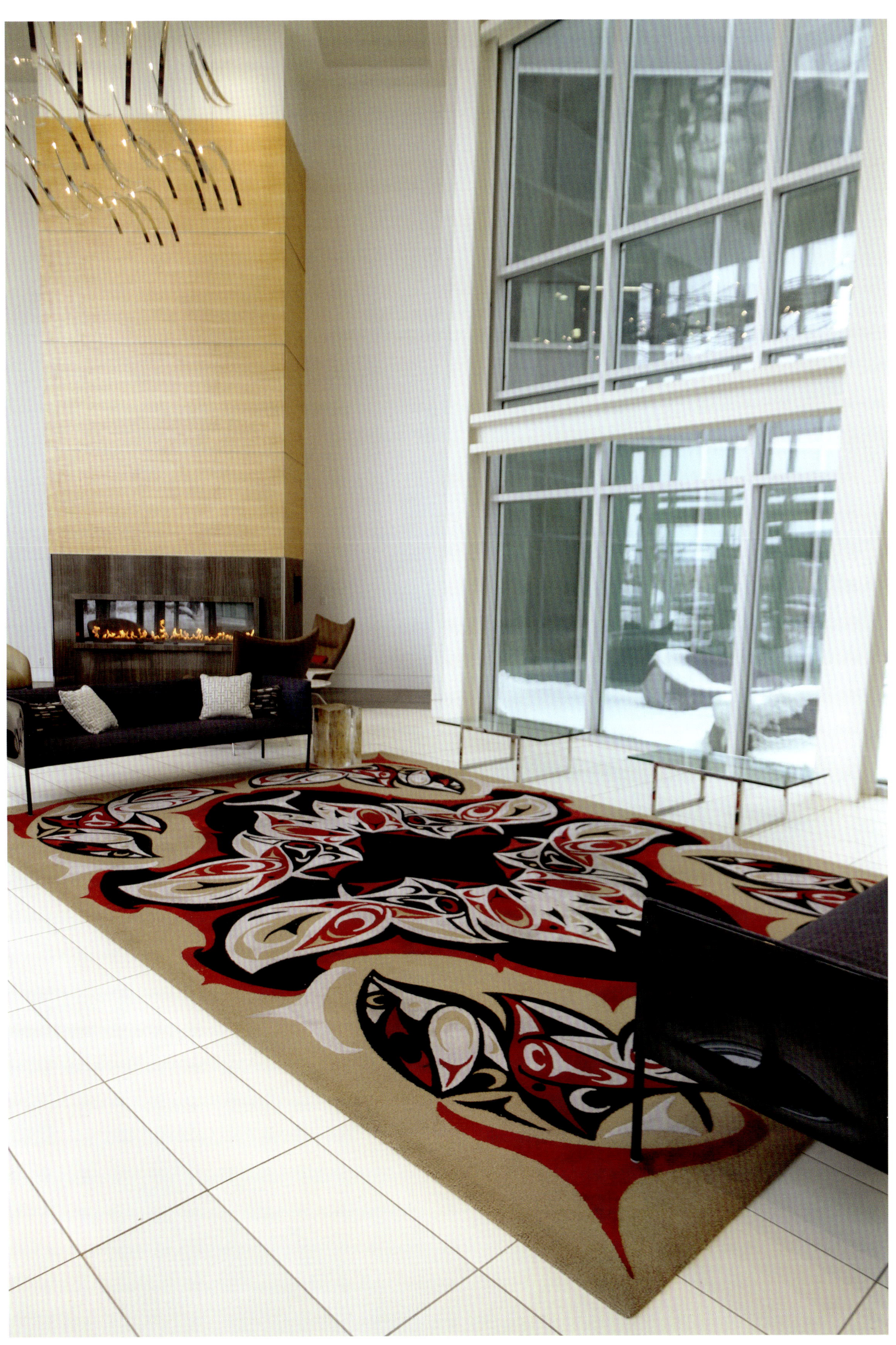

Affection, 2016
Aluminum, concrete
46 × 76 × 203 cm

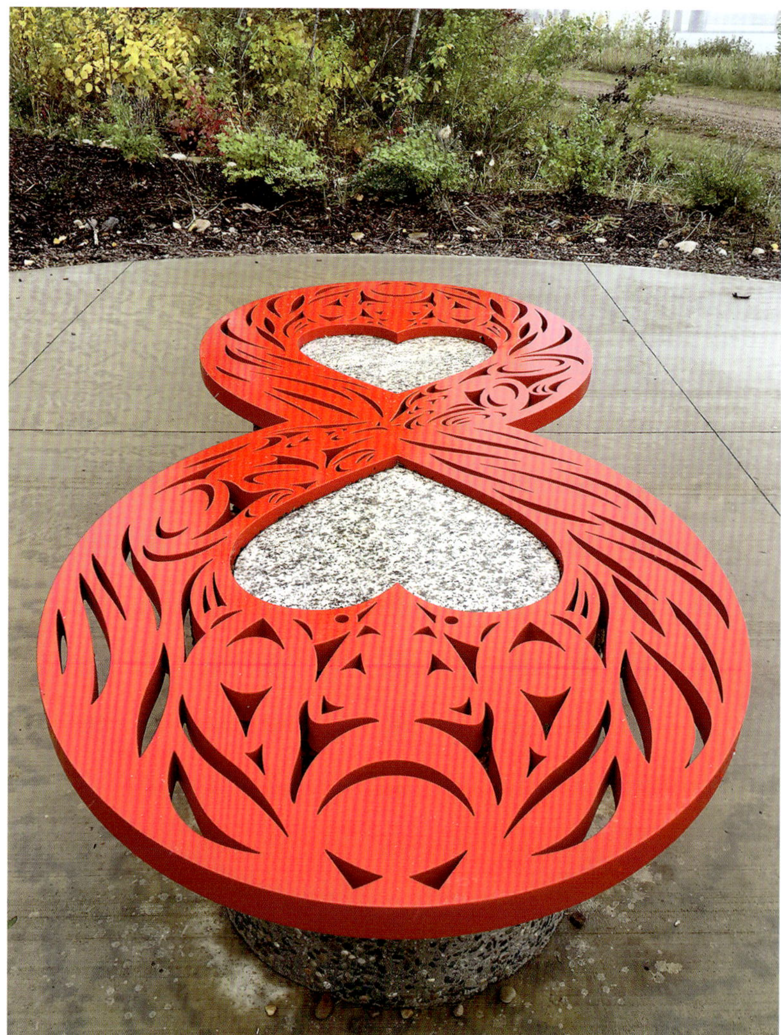

Affection

LOCATION: MacDonald Island Park
1 MacDonald Dr, Fort McMurray, AB

Susan's most northerly piece of public art is on an island at the confluence of the Athabasca and Clearwater Rivers, part of an interpretative trail in the boreal forest that was developed by the Regional Recreation Corporation of Wood Buffalo. The area is in Treaty 6 territory, the traditional unceded territory of the Plains Cree, Woodland Cree, Beaver Cree, Saulteaux, Niitsitapi (Blackfoot), Métis, and Nakota Sioux Peoples. In 2014, Susan was selected as one of the artists invited to create a unique artwork in one of seven locations on the trail. The trail and the artworks were officially open in late September 2016.

Affection combines the functionality and durability of a contemporary material with a timeless theme, expressed in memorable forms. The design is developed around a version of the infinity symbol, the centres forming two hearts. In the design proposal Susan explains the symbols and meaning of the piece.

> *Affection* is a sculptural and functional combination of bas relief pierced from solid... aluminum that is powder pigmented red....
>
> Love is all around us. We learn it from nature as children; it is a celebrated emotion on mother-earth and will continue infinitely into the future.
>
> It is this impassioned idea of Love being infinite that I have balanced by artwork in pairs on the infinity insignia.
>
> I have modified the classic figure 8 insignia in this case to include two distinct hearts. The hearts are a pair of earthen coloured concrete pedestals creating a functional sculpture that seats two, a Love seat.
>
> The Love seat attracts the notion of sharing and my contemporary designs based on traditional elements are tranquil and easy to relate to.
>
> Love is represented by pairs, shown in my design with pairs of bird motifs & wolves, all linked together with a braided rope. Birds are often related with the joys and highs of affection, while wolves are revered for their loyalty within family. The bird motifs in my design not only create the distinct hearts but are all linked together with a braided rope. The wolves are looking on each other and are about to embrace.[1]

This example of Susan's Coast Salish imprint lives in a different kind of forest by inland waters, offering walkers an intriguing point of departure for reflecting on universal truths.

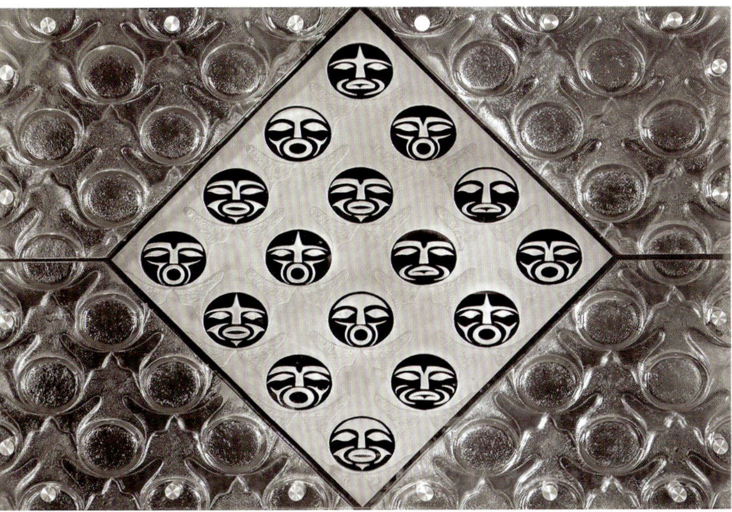

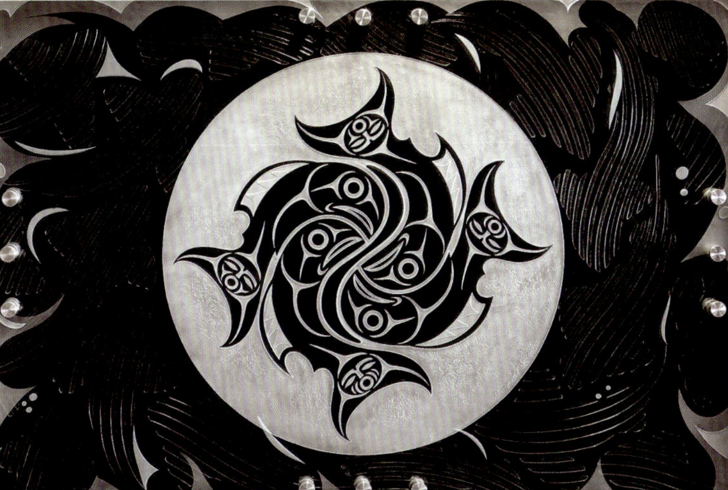

Freedom, 1997
Carved and kiln-cast glass
111.8 × 162.6 cm

Continuing Life-Cycle, 1997
Carved and kiln-cast glass
111.8 × 162.6 cm

ROGERS PARK

Early in Susan's career, as her work became better known and she added three-dimensional art in various mediums to her growing body of prints, she gained more champions and patrons. One of the earliest and most important was Bud Mintz, owner of Potlatch Arts in Vancouver; another was Fraser Clark, who learned of and acquired Susan's work through Mintz, and eventually formed a relationship directly with the artist.

Clark established Bay of Spirits Gallery in Toronto and it soon became an important Indigenous gallery, especially for art from the Pacific Northwest of Canada. In 1996 and 1997 he was involved in making the film *In the Hands of the Raven*, which was built around interviews with leading Northwest Coast First Nations artists including Robert Davidson, Don Yeomans, and Susan Point.

Clark was particularly devoted to matching great art with potential buyers, and used his "show gallery" to attract major corporate clients.[2] This led to Sprint Canada and Nortel offering major commissions to Susan, all in glass—three for Sprint Canada and a fourth, *Salmon Waterfall*, for Nortel. In 2005 Rogers Communications bought Nortel's Brampton headquarters, located on the traditional unceded territory of the Mississaugas of the New Credit First Nation, and then purchased Sprint Canada the next year, thereby acquiring all four of these major works by Susan.

Freedom

LOCATION: Rogers Park
8200 Dixie Rd, Brampton, ON

Communication is the central theme of this mural composed of two slabs of glass. The back slab is deeply carved and textured, and the front panel, as Susan notes, "is a more subtle continuation of the main image using kiln cast glass technique."[3]

The central diamond shape is much lighter than the surrounding glass, so that the sixteen faces stand out sharply. Susan developed this design so that the faces do not repeat: there are four original faces, one in each corner, which have been halved and rejoined to make sixteen different images to symbolize the interconnectedness of all the peoples of the earth. The birds in the background represent freedom.

Continuing Life-Cycle

LOCATION: Rogers Park
8200 Dixie Rd, Brampton, ON

A second glass wall mural combines sce:ɬtən (salmon) and human forms. Like its sister mural it has two slabs, with the front panel deeply carved and textured. Four salmon, their tails containing human faces, swirl around the centre of the front panel. Human faces are designed into the tails of each fish. The salmon symbolize the cycle of life and the four seasons; the human faces represent people from the four corners of the earth. Outside the main circle is a "subtle school of salmon," which "represents continuing communications."[4]

Generations, 1997
Glass, stainless steel
243.8 × 83.8 cm

Generations

LOCATION: Rogers Park
8200 Dixie Rd, Brampton, ON

The largest of the Sprint Canada commissions arranged by Fraser Clark is *Generations*, a glass and stainless steel representation of a traditional Coast Salish housepost. Susan chose glass to match the contemporary style of the boardroom in which this piece, *Freedom*, and *Continuing Life-Cycle* were originally located. As she explained at the time, the figures in *Generations* depict "four traditional human heads, four bears . . . and rock art," derived from drawings that date back over ten thousand years. "The human heads are meant to represent story-telling by all ethnic groups from generation to generation. The rock art represents documentation and communication of our history as well as experiences in the history of those generations. The bears represent the lands; and also represent the great hunter known for strength, power and human-like qualities."[5] The label that accompanies the piece further elaborates, explaining that the symbols for the four elements—sɬeq̓ʷəm (air), həy̓qʷ (fire), qaʔ (water), and təməxʷ (earth)—are shown, and that "the dominant human faces represent an oral tradition of story-telling and passing on of clan rites and privilege."

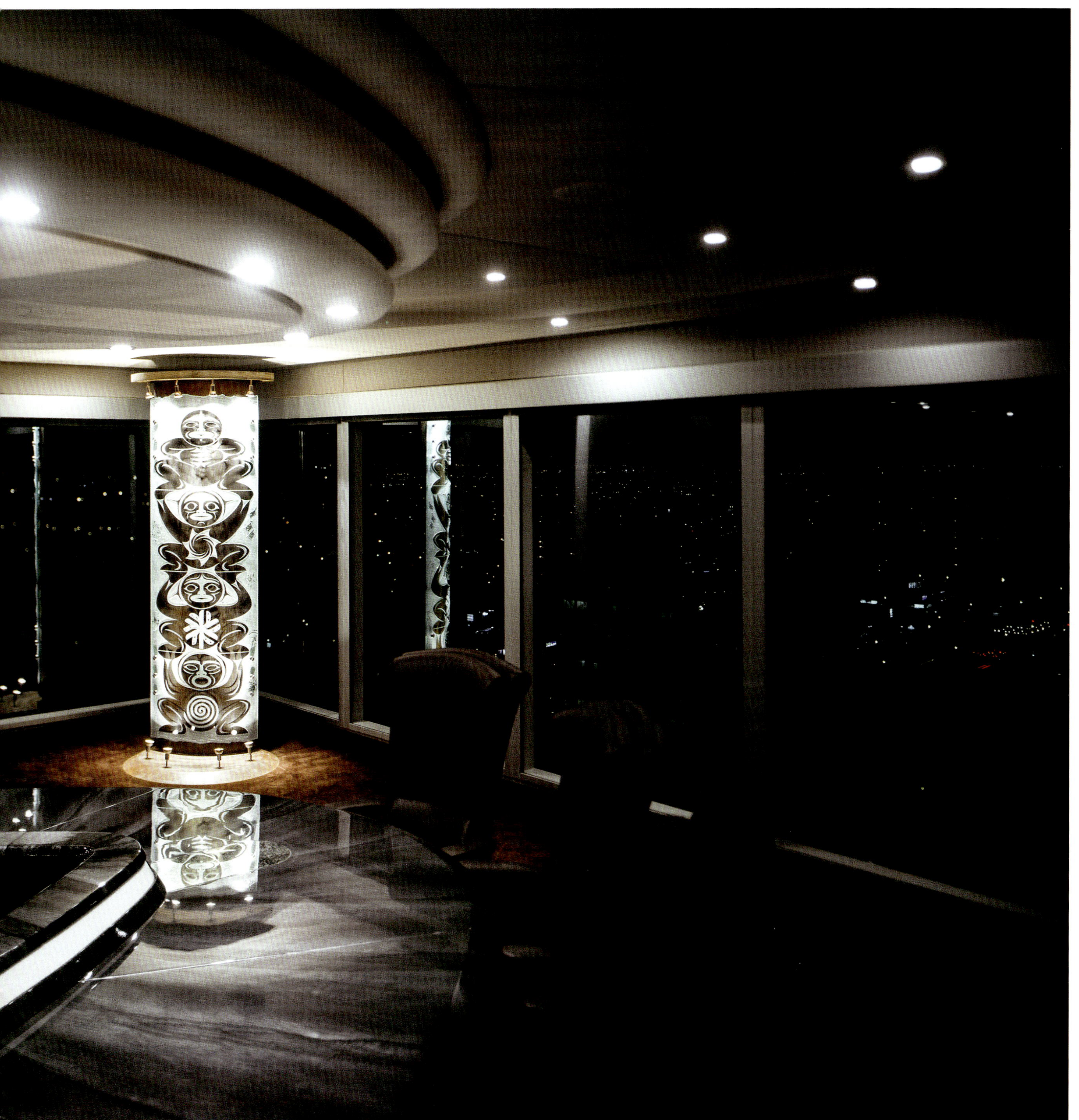

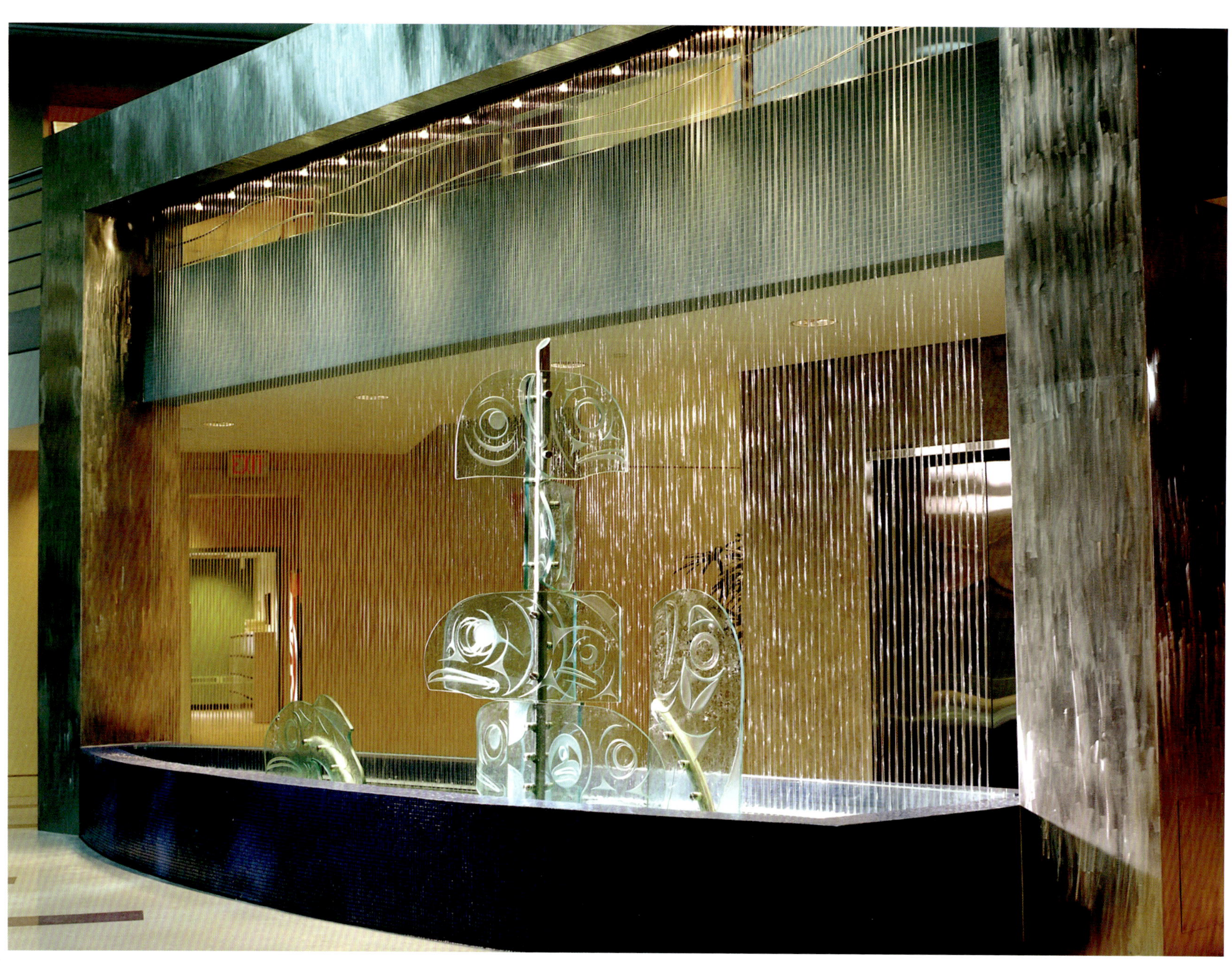
EXIT

Salmon Waterfall, 1998
Glass, stainless steel
Approx. 4.57 × 6.86 × 1.65 m

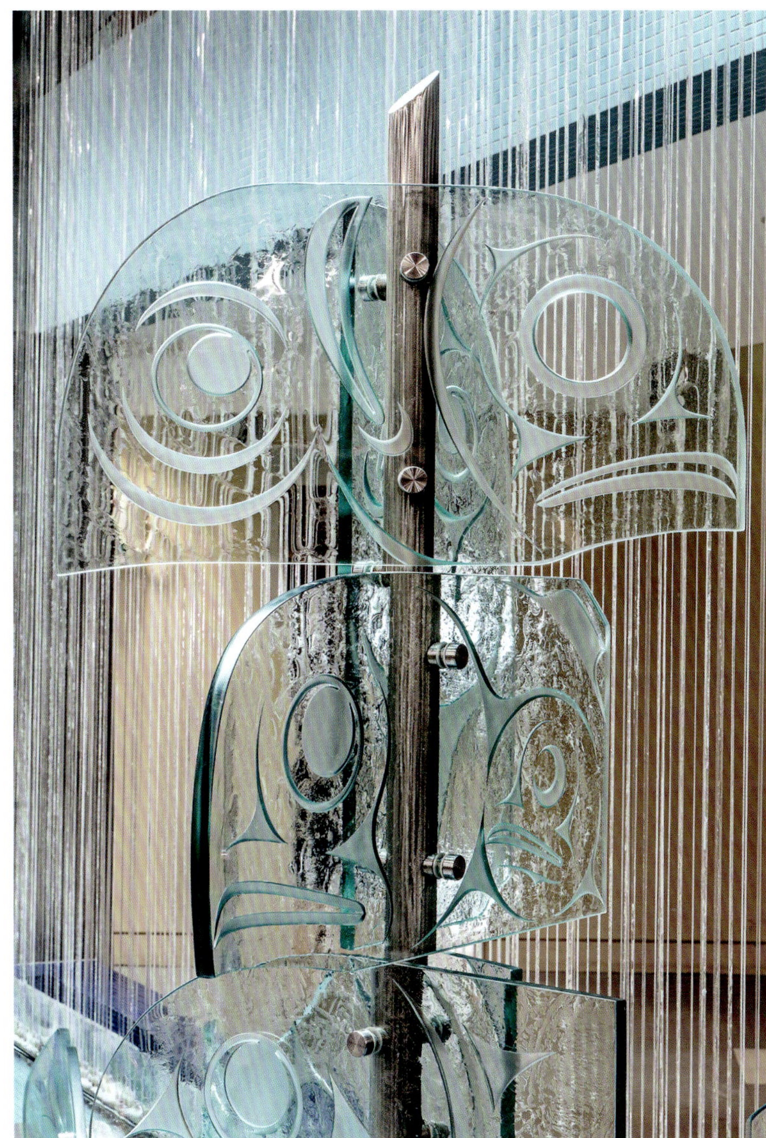

Salmon Waterfall

LOCATION: Rogers Park
8200 Dixie Rd, Brampton, ON

The last of Susan's telecom commissions is made of nine cast-glass salmon heads affixed to stainless-steel supports in a shallow pool. The salmon are variations of engraved-wood designs that Susan had seen in several museum collections, displaying quintessentially Salish eye shapes, mouth forms, and highlights of wedges and crescents. The clean and simple lines of the terminations are very modern, however, to match the bright metal supports. The work speaks to corporate workers in the twenty-first century about the importance of the natural world, and our dependence on creatures living beyond walls for both food and refreshment of the spirit.

These four works arranged by Fraser Clark solidified Susan's reputation as a creator of glass artworks that, while honouring Salish traditions and incorporating traditional Salish art elements, could come to life in non-traditional mediums to suit modern spaces. They offer further proof that stories arising from Oral Traditions can be reshaped to new settings and given fresh meaning without sacrificing any of the essential messages: respect for the land and its creatures, the interdependence of humans with other life, and the ongoing need for communication between peoples.

Ongoing Journey, 2006
Carved and painted red cedar
305 × 61 × 7.2 cm (each)

Ongoing Journey

LOCATION: 180 Queen Street West
Toronto, ON

As the twentieth century turned into the twenty-first, Susan was commissioned to create a number of important works in Toronto, on the traditional territory of the Mississaugas of the New Credit First Nation, the Haudenosaunee, and the Huron-Wendat, and the home to many diverse Indigenous Peoples. The most recent of these commissions came her way thanks to Karen Mills, a public art consultant specializing in partnering First Nations artists with corporate patrons. Early in 2005, Mills contacted Susan to share a city-approved public art opportunity that was part of a major office tower development in the heart of Toronto, just west of the Georgian-era Osgoode Hall. Federal court offices and Health Canada were to be the major tenants in the building. The announcement that Mills sent to Susan noted that "among the important issues to be addressed by the Federal Courts will be land claims laid by Native groups. The Owner is interested in offering public art opportunities to aboriginal artists."

Proposals were adjudicated by a committee that included an architectural historian, three artists (one of whom was Charles Pachter), a First Nations ethnologist from the Canadian Museum of Civilization (since renamed the Canadian Museum of History), and representatives of the owner (GWL Realty Advisors, a subsidiary of Great West Life) and the Canada Council for the Arts.

Susan's initial proposal was for a series of four Salish houseposts, carved in the round if siting allowed, which would provide an interactive experience and welcome visitors to the building. The theme of four "would be incorporated into the artwork for these panels, relating to all native peoples in the four corners of the country."[6]

The housepost idea did not make it through the committee, but Susan's second idea did. This proposal was still built around the concept of welcome, but dramatized the idea through four large paddles, each carved and painted on both sides, which would be set in a row in the atrium. The rebirth of canoe making and racing among the Musqueam and other Salish groups in Susan's own lifetime gave her fresh images from which to draw inspiration. She says that "as a teenager, I remember canoe races at Stanley Park. Our Musqueam canoe, named the 'Seven Sisters,' was carved from one of the 7 cedars that blew down in Stanley Park. That canoe was carved by my uncle Dominic Point."[7] Susan outlined her new idea for the committee in late November.

> The idea really focuses on the theme of welcome, and of the multiple journeys intertwined in the history of Canada (the journeys of First Nations Peoples and European settlers, all of whom used the rivers as highways).
>
> It would also represent all the journeys undertaken by all those involved in treaty and land claim negotiations, reflecting the fact that the building will in part be used for the Law Courts.
>
> The paddles would rest on their bases, pointing upwards in a traditional native symbol of welcome. The position is a salute of peace or a sign for parley—paddles were held point up as canoes approached shoreline settlements and camps.[8]

As each side of each of the paddles is unique, Susan was able to use a range of design approaches to feature many forms and Salish elements. The paddles are mounted at ninety degrees to the low wall north of them, as Susan requested, to enable the easy viewing of each of the eight sides.

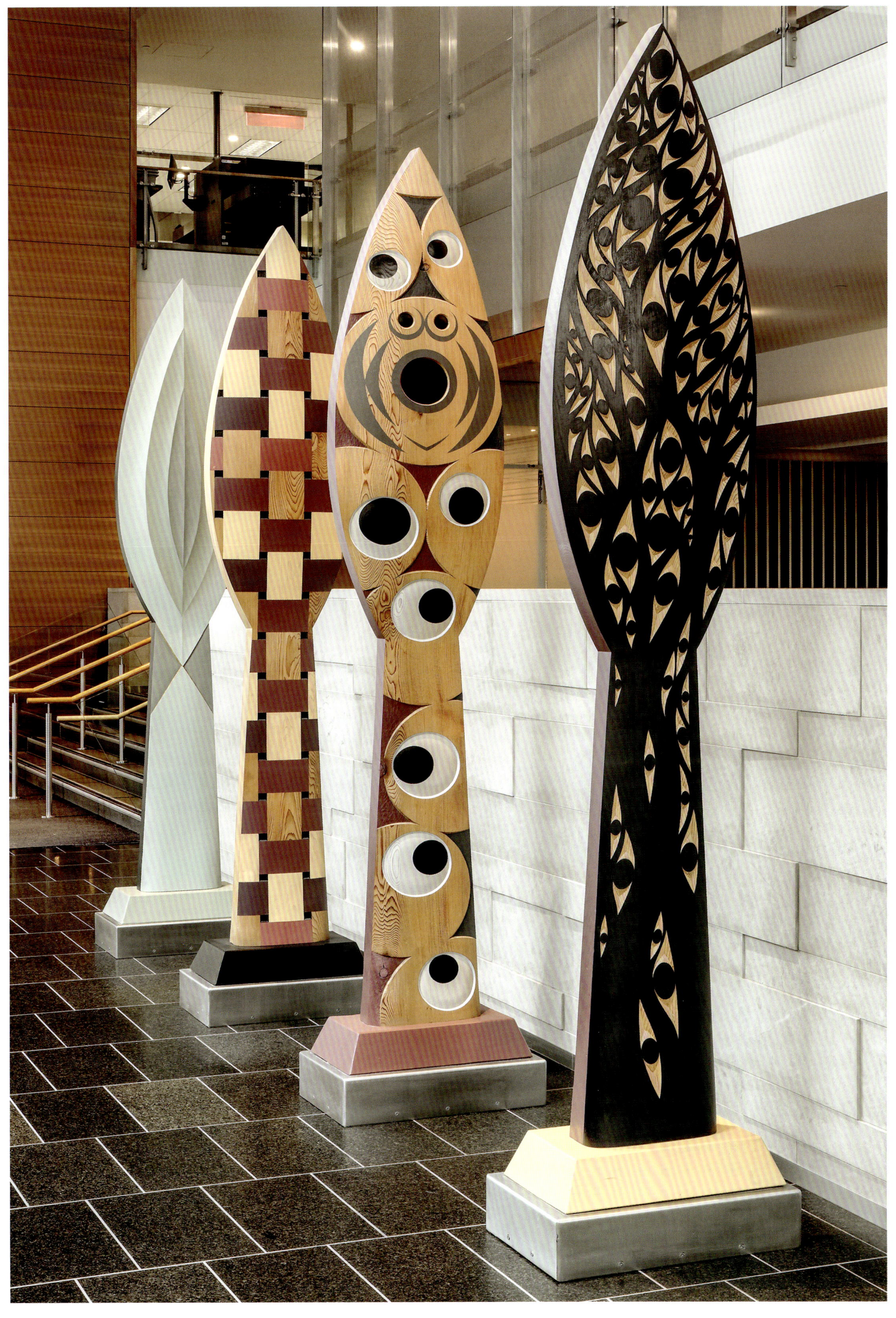

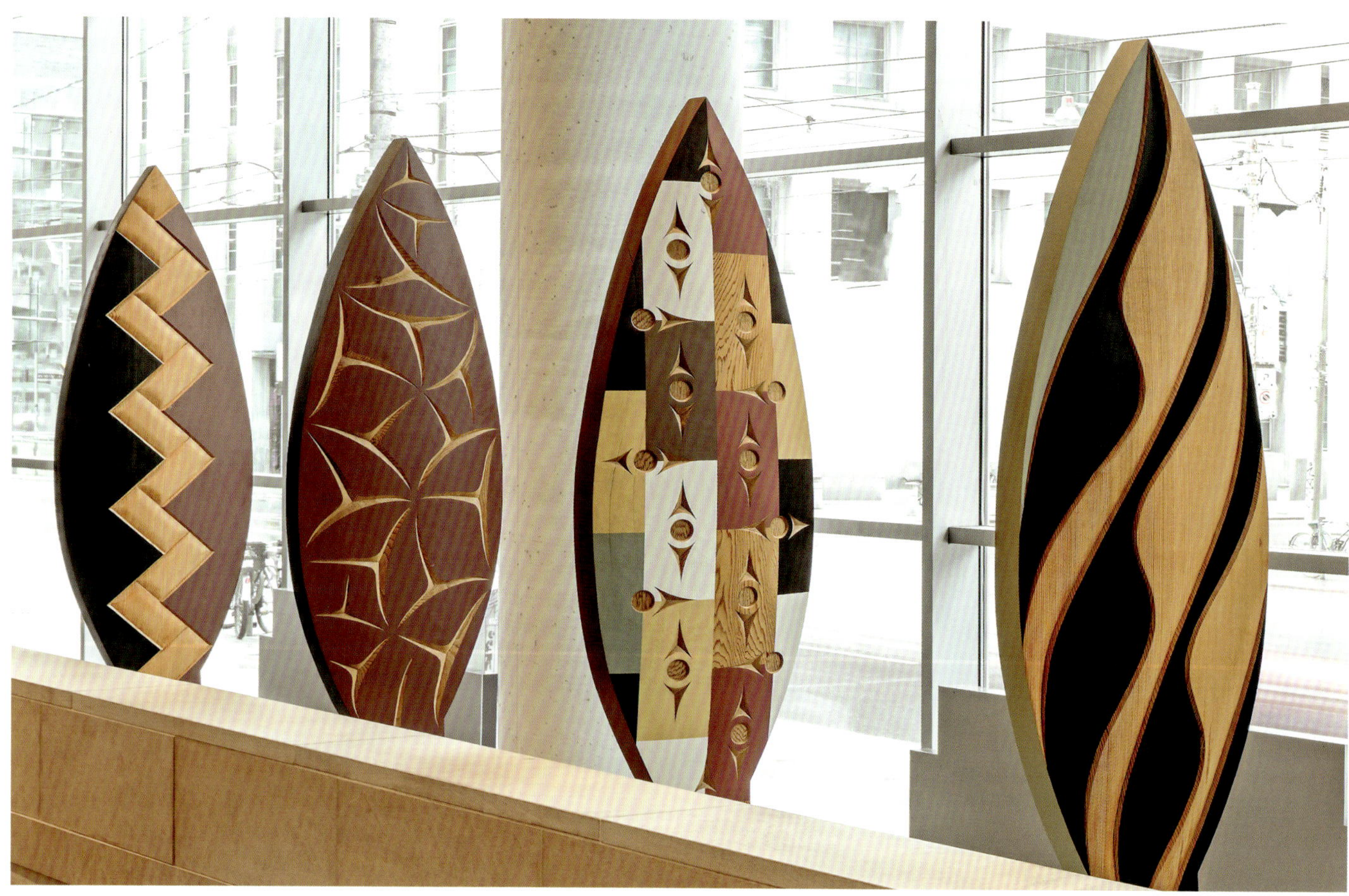

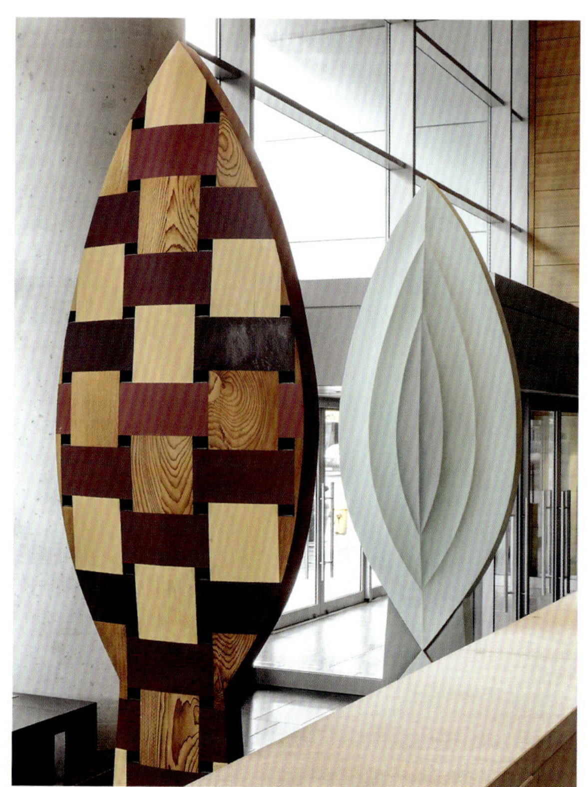

Susan's family and several other artists helped her to shape each paddle and carve and paint the surfaces, most of which are lightly incised with a palette of sage green, staľəẁ (Fraser River) green, yellow, ochre, brick red, and black. One of the sides shows faces, one with a large open mouth to represent the concepts of parley and discussion. Another shows branches with highly stylized seeds or leaves, referring to the plant life along the riverways. Another combines rectangles in a pattern echoing traditional Salish weaving. Many of the designs are geometric and abstract, but the multiplication of wedge forms and ovals or circles bracketed by wedges and crescents clearly arises from Salish experience and art.

Table of Reconciliation, 2007
Carved and painted western red cedar
61 × 162.6 cm

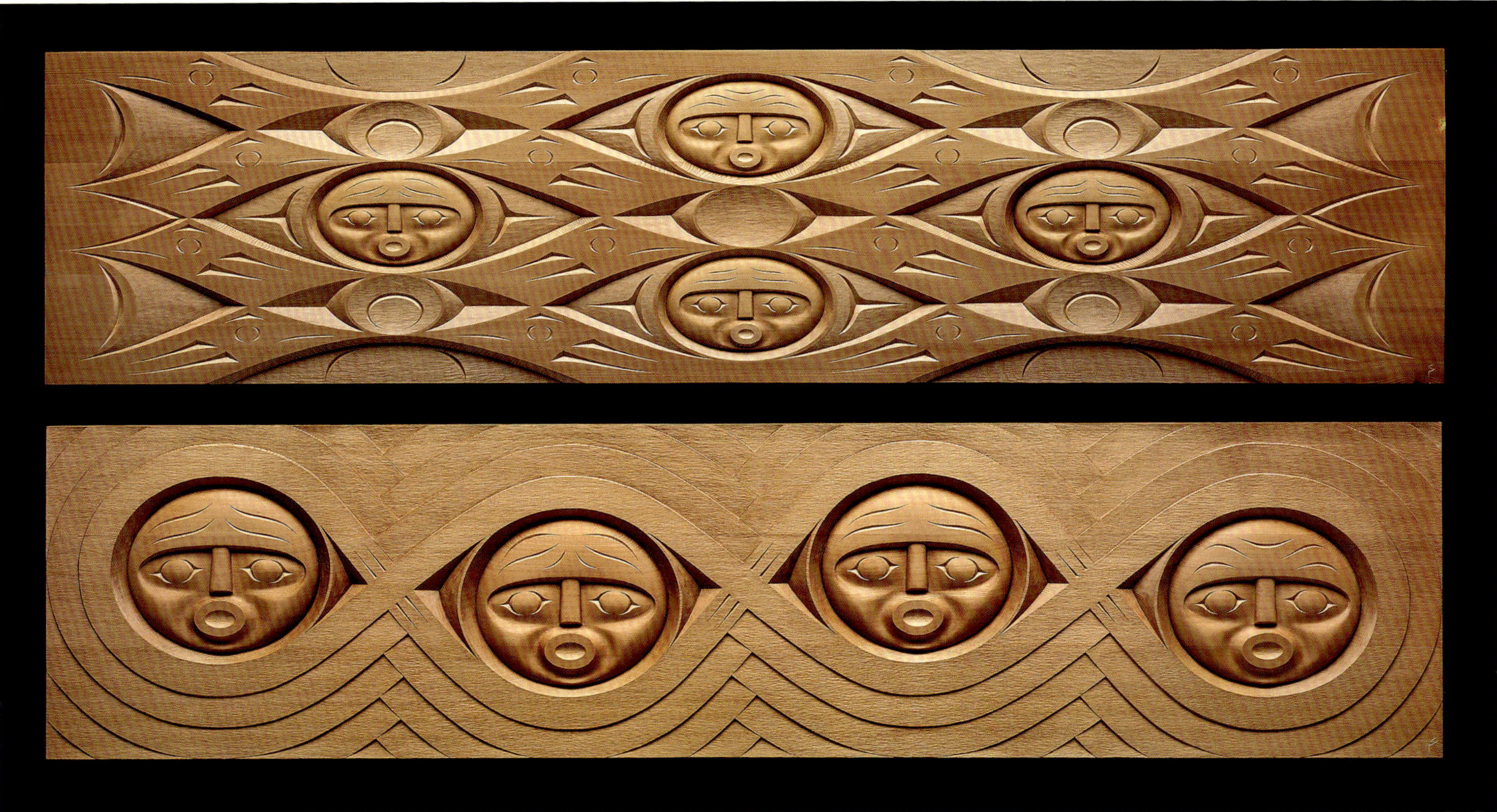

Table of Reconciliation

LOCATION: United Church of Canada
73 Queen's Park Cr E, Toronto, ON

On 2 February 2007, Susan received a message from Reverend Douglas Throop, the United Church of Canada chaplain at Simon Fraser University and minister of Ellesmere United Church in Burnaby. His congregation was looking to commission a carver for a communion table in their new church at SFU, "hopefully from one of the three nations that have an ancestral claim to Burnaby Mountain," and he had learned of Susan from a Mrs. Sparrow when he met with Dionne Paul at the House of héwhíwus in Sechelt a few months earlier.[9] His message made it clear that the table would be symbolically important to him and the congregation.

> Last year was the 20th anniversary of the United Church's Apology to 1st Nations Peoples. I was formerly the United Church minister with the KanienKehaka of Kahnawake, Quebec. I was hoping that the communion table would

> not only speak of the work towards reconciliation—to me a symbol of what happens when Christians gather for the feast at Christ's table—but of the places where the stories of both our ancestors embrace each other. Again this is a "wish-list" with the table to arise from the inspiration of the carver—I'm a painter so I know of freedom of expression.[10]

Susan finished carving two panels for the table in August of 2007. The front panel features four faces deeply cut into the red cedar, framed in a weave of narrow bands that mimic the tight weave of classic Salish mats, hangings, and robes. The four faces symbolize the four peoples, the four sacred directions, the four seasons, the four elements, and perhaps also for some in the congregation, the four gospels. The back panel repeats the motif of the four faces, but they are smaller and framed in a weave of fish and bird designs using deep V-cut crescents. The imagery is intended to remind churchgoers of shared beliefs about the sacredness of all creations in the web of life.

Congregants celebrated the table at the opening service of their new church, in the Cornerstone building at SFU, on 9 September 2007. The congregation soon joined with another church in North Burnaby, however, and the table was no longer needed. Fortunately, they offered it to the national headquarters of the United Church in Toronto, where it was re-dedicated on 17 September 2014.

Reverend Throop, now a minister in Port Hope, about one hundred kilometres east of Toronto, attended the ceremony and spoke to the origins and meaning of Susan's work.

> We wanted a table that spoke of reconciliation, a table that spoke of where do the traditions of Christianity and the traditions of the Coast peoples embrace each other... Susan Point, a very famous Coast artist, created this for us. The four faces are held together in a basket which is our mother the earth, a basket where all creation is woven together. This is carved of living cedar and therefore has life.... The congregation was overwhelmed when the panels were finally displayed. It was a tremendous joy to see this great work of art that had been more than their expectations. To live with it in the time that we did on Burnaby Mountain was a great joy. We hope that those who come to this space for worship listen carefully to what this table is saying to them.[11]

Some in the congregation that commissioned this art may have known that Susan suffered, as did so many of her generation, by being taken from her home and family to a residential school. She laments the loss of her birth language and the loss of knowledge from her parents and Elders about the traditional Musqueam ways of living and thinking about the world. But through her art she shows a vision of an ancient way of life, reborn to exemplify the idea that all people are joined together in creation.

NATIONAL GALLERY OF CANADA

The collection of the National Gallery of Canada, which is located on the traditional unceded territory of the Algonquin Anishnaabeg people, includes twenty-seven works by Susan. All but one were donated by George and Christiane Smyth, and all are prints except for *The Circle Within* and *Salish Weave*, the piece that lent its name to the Smyths' extensive collection of Coast Salish art [see p. 131]. The Victoria couple consider themselves "activist collectors" who work hard to promote local artists, often commissioning works directly from artists and frequently lending or donating works to institutions including the University of Victoria, the Museum of Anthropology, Simon Fraser University, and Stanford University in an effort to spread knowledge and understanding of Coast Salish art. The Smyths donated *The Circle Within* and *Salish Weave* to the National Gallery in 2016, along with fifteen prints by Susan.

Salish Weave

LOCATION: National Gallery of Canada
380 Sussex Dr, Ottawa, ON

This is Susan at her creative best. For this elegant geometric composition carved in low relief with various birds and salmon, Susan combined the two types of cedar traditionally used by the Salish Peoples. *Salish Weave* has all the hallmarks of her mature work: beautifully carved pieces fitted precisely together, and perfectly controlled lines using classic Salish elements of crescents and wedges. It is a tribute not only to the creatures it depicts, but to the heritage of weaving in her own family and among the many Salish Peoples.

It seems fitting that the Smyths would name their collection for this piece. It is contemporary art rooted in ancestral forms, and a work that provokes a strong response. We admire the matching of colour and texture, and the intricate weaving together of the nine different sections, each telling a part of a Salish story.

The Circle Within

LOCATION: National Gallery of Canada
380 Sussex Dr, Ottawa, ON

Salmon are the stars of this striking artwork. Inevitably the viewer's gaze is drawn to the yellow cedar in the heart of the design, which shows eight salmon composed of classic Salish elements, with a deep wedge behind the head and wedges or crescents around the eyes. Eight polymer squares surround the centre, identical to it except for the circular elements in the centres. The contrast of the yellow cedar and the polymer emphasizes the central square and echoes the title. The careful geometry of the design comes alive as the eye follows the lines of the nine circles. Using a traditional salmon theme that is prevalent in her work, Susan achieves a brilliant synthesis of content, form, and traditional and synthetic materials.

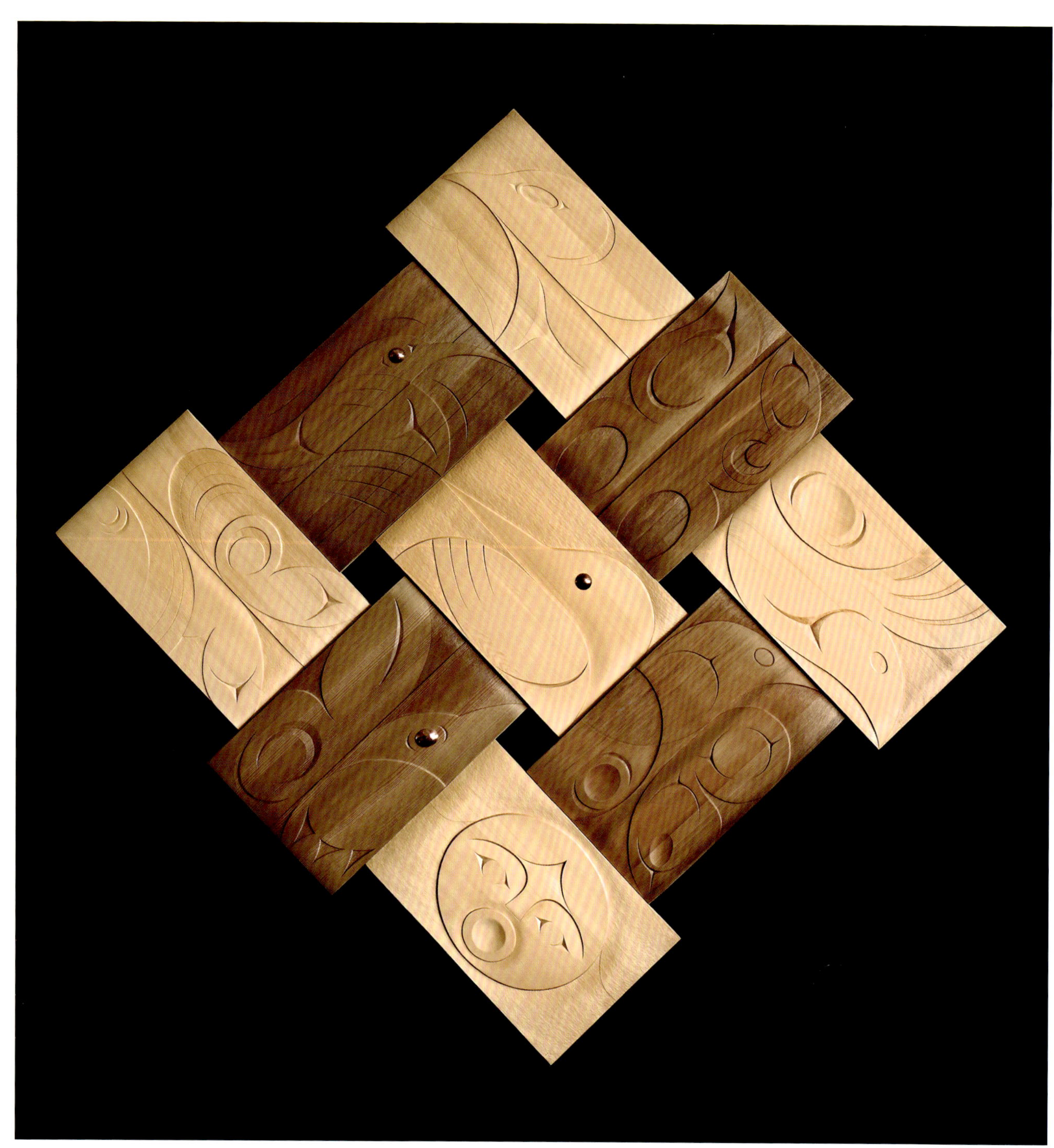

Salish Weave, 2003
Carved yellow cedar and
western red cedar with
copper features
1.62 x 1.63 x .06 m

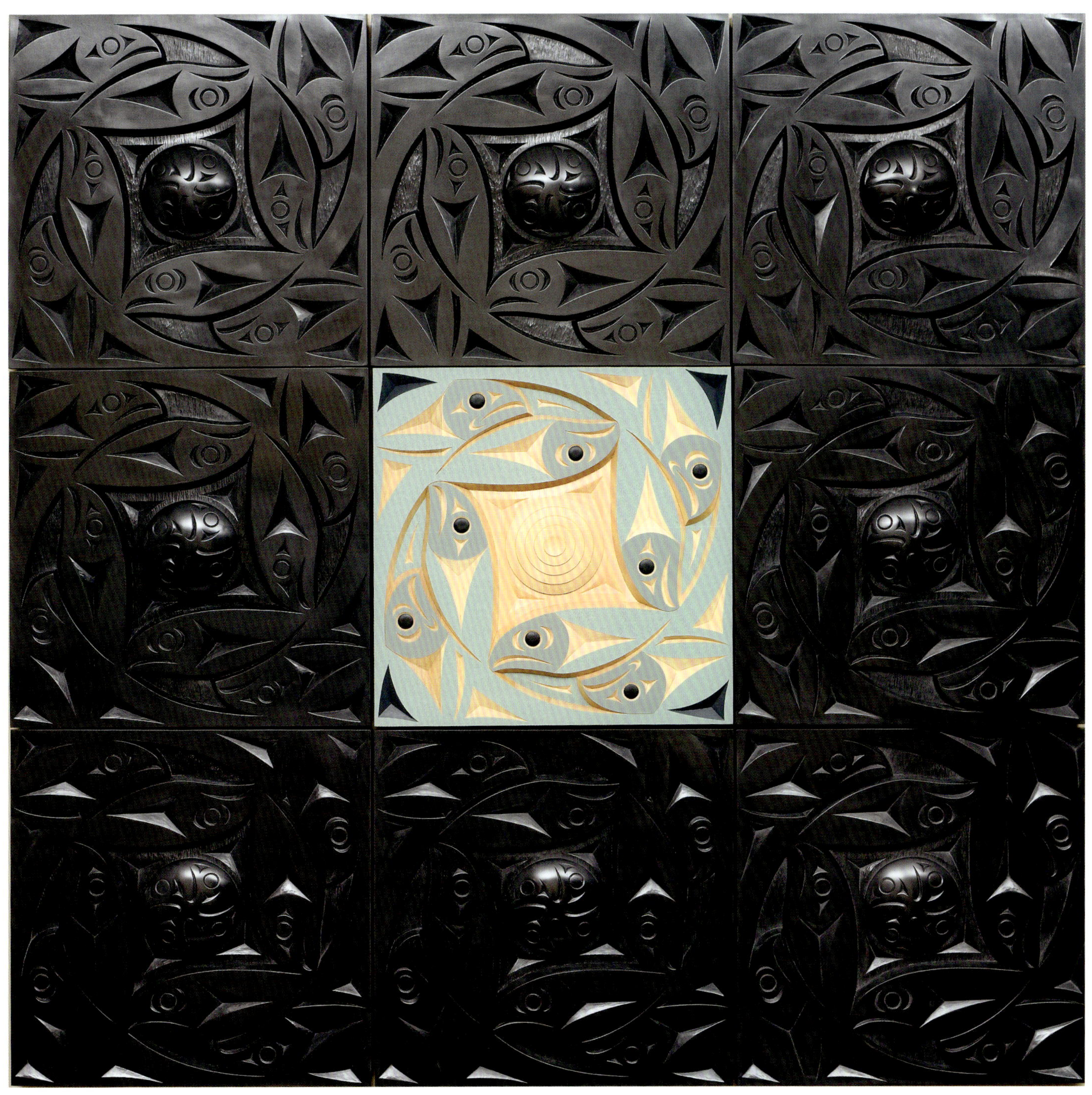

The Circle Within, 2007
Painted bronze polymer and
yellow cedar
1.37 × 137 × .05 m

Butterfly Grid, 2016
Forton
207 × 154 × 6 cm

Butterfly Grid

LOCATION: Indigenous and Northern Affairs Canada
10 Rue Wellington, Gatineau, QC

This dramatic composition was displayed in the exhibition *Susan Point: Spindle Whorl* at the Vancouver Art Gallery in the spring of 2017. The large scale, the unrelenting whiteness so uncharacteristic of Susan's work, and the adjacent photo of the Sechelt Indian Residential School ensured that few visitors passed it without stopping.

Susan is a survivor of the Sechelt residential school, also known as St. Augustine's Indian Residential School. Canada's residential school system caused tens of thousands of First Nations children to be taken from their families and sent to schools run by Christian churches, in an effort to assimilate them into mainstream society. An estimated six thousand children died in the schools. The experience was so painful for Susan, as for so many, that it is still difficult for her to speak about this time, even within her own family. She has tried to address the experience and what she lost through her work. Art inspired by traumatic experiences can help the artist but it can also invite the viewer to confront historical events, perhaps for the first time. Many Canadians are finally beginning to understand the horror of the residential schools and the magnitude of what these First Nations children endured, and lost.

In the exhibition catalogue Susan describes the imagery depicted on the cross, and the tragic inspiration for the work.

> This original work is impossible for me to title as it, unfortunately, represents the disconnection from the wisdom and teachings I lost as a young child, as well as our Hunquemi'nem language.
>
> The beautiful imagery within each grid is made up of butterfly wings overlapping each other in a circular format like that of a spindle whorl ... that represents the cycle of life and the close connection of my people upon this land.
>
> On the wings of the butterflies are designs, in my contemporary art style, depicting salmon, eagles and ravens ... Coast Salish imagery that was taken from me as a child ... traditional imagery created in various forms by my ancestral artisans.
>
> The edges of this piece are fragments of butterfly wings ... metaphorically clipped from the First Nations children who were taken from their families and put into residential schools as I and my siblings were.
>
> This piece is a symbol of power for those of us who had strength and resilience and survived the residential school system.[12]

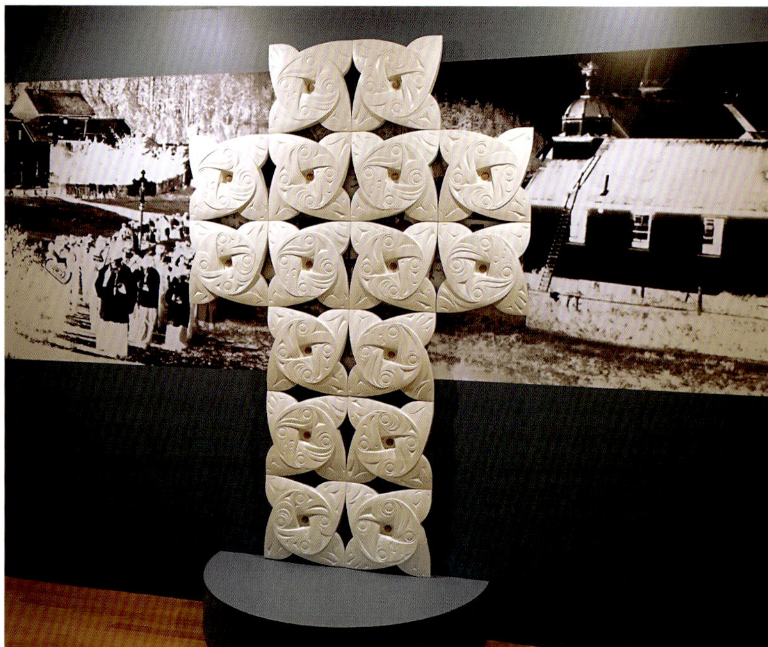

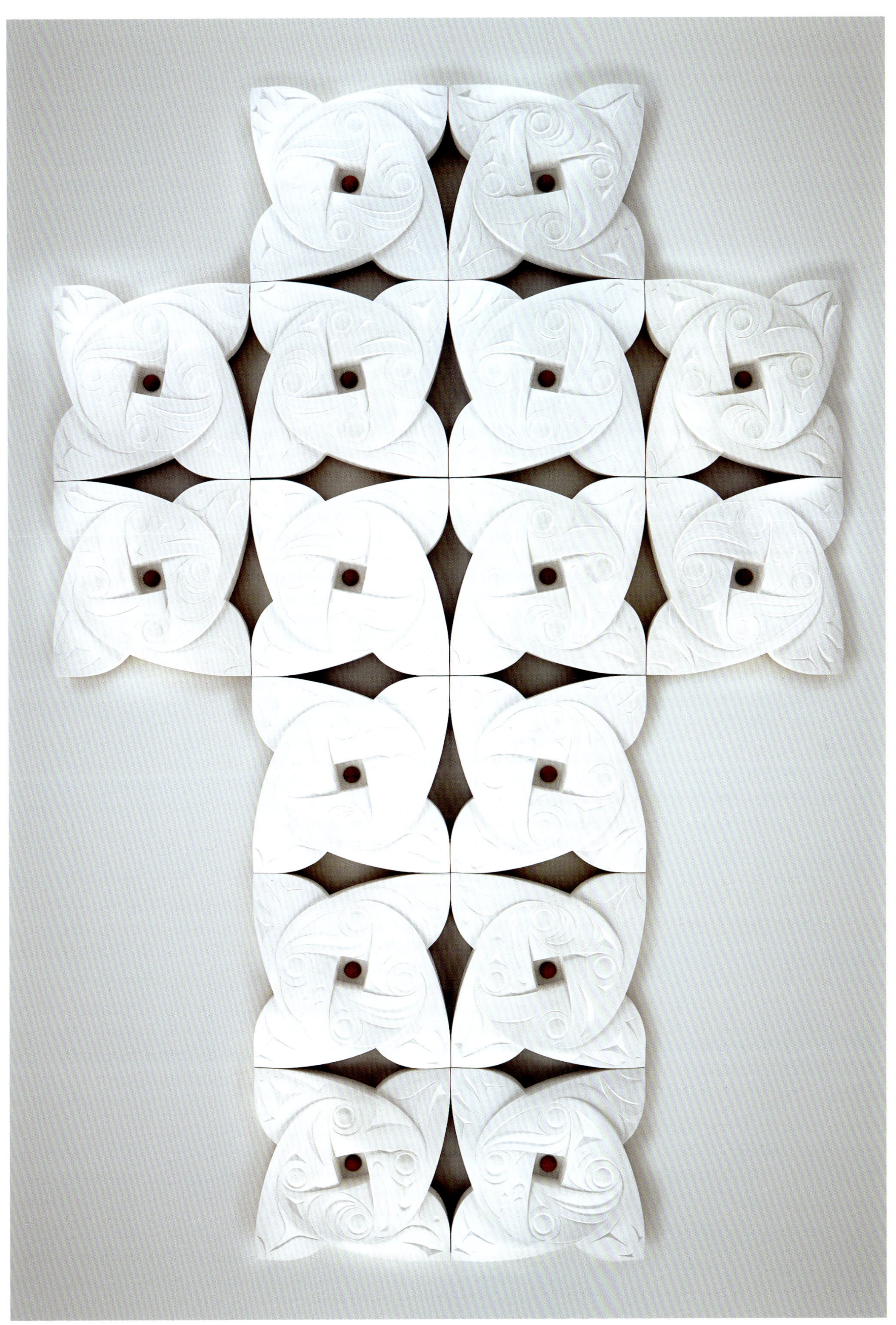

The Beaver and the Mink, 2004
Carved and painted western red cedar
with copper features
1.90 x 1.22 x 2.29 m

The Beaver and the Mink

LOCATION: National Museum of the American Indian
4th St SW & Independence Ave SW, Washington, DC

A panel of Canadian Indigenous-art professionals chose this sculpture by Susan as a gift from Canada to honour the opening of the National Museum of the American Indian at the Smithsonian Institution in Washington, D.C. in 2004. The Minister of Foreign Affairs, the Honourable Pierre Pettigrew, presented the work. In a press release he said he was "delighted and proud" to present the work on behalf of all Canadians, and described it as "contemporary yet deeply traditional."[13]

The work is inspired by the Coast Salish Traditional Story of the Beaver and the Mink, which provides a deeply satisfying explanation of how the rivers came to be filled with salmon. As told by Musqueam Elders, the story is as follows.

> *Beaver and the Mink—A Tale of the Salmon Families from the People of the Grass*
>
> Once there were no salmon in any of the rivers. The salmon who now swim so abundantly, evolved from humans who lived in a village along the river. The sockeye [sθəqəy̓], coho [kʷəxʷəθ], humpback [hu:ṅ], spring [st̓ᶿaqʷəy̓] and dog salmon [k̓ʷal̓əxʷ], all began as these human families, each living in their own longhouse in the village.
>
> One day, the Beaver and his friend the Mink decided to paddle to the village to see how the Salmon People lived. As they watched they noticed a baby sleeping in a swing by the longhouse belonging to the Sockeye family. Mischievous, Beaver and Mink decided to take the baby to make the salmon people follow. The two friends paddled upstream as fast as they could, tearing small pieces of clothing off the baby to leave in the water as a trail. At the head of the river they safely left the sleeping baby floating in the water.
>
> Back in the village a search was launched with all the salmon families except for the Humpback family, who said they would begin their search the next day, helping out. The rest of the salmon people swam up the river following the trail of the Sockeye baby's clothing. Exhausted after swimming against the current and through the rapids, they found the Sockeye baby still asleep, floating in the river. It was at that point that the Salmon families decided to make the river their home.
>
> Each year they still return up river to spawn, although the Humpbacks return every other year, because they began their search on the next day.[14]

Susan's large and complex composition is set on a curved base that represents a canoe. The negative spaces between the figures increase the dramatic, three-dimensional quality. One side of the whorl is carved with four stylized Salish salmon swimming out from a small face, representing the core of the story. The other side shows a large human face with copper discs for eyes and a fin on the forehead to symbolize the link between humans and salmon; together, the two sides also represent the five species of salmon. The beaver and the mink appear twice on each side.

In a statement, Susan said that "in creating my art, I feel a need to continually express my cultural background and beliefs yet, at the same time, my work continues to evolve with changes within and outside of my community."[15] This sculpture brings an ancient story firmly into the twenty-first century.

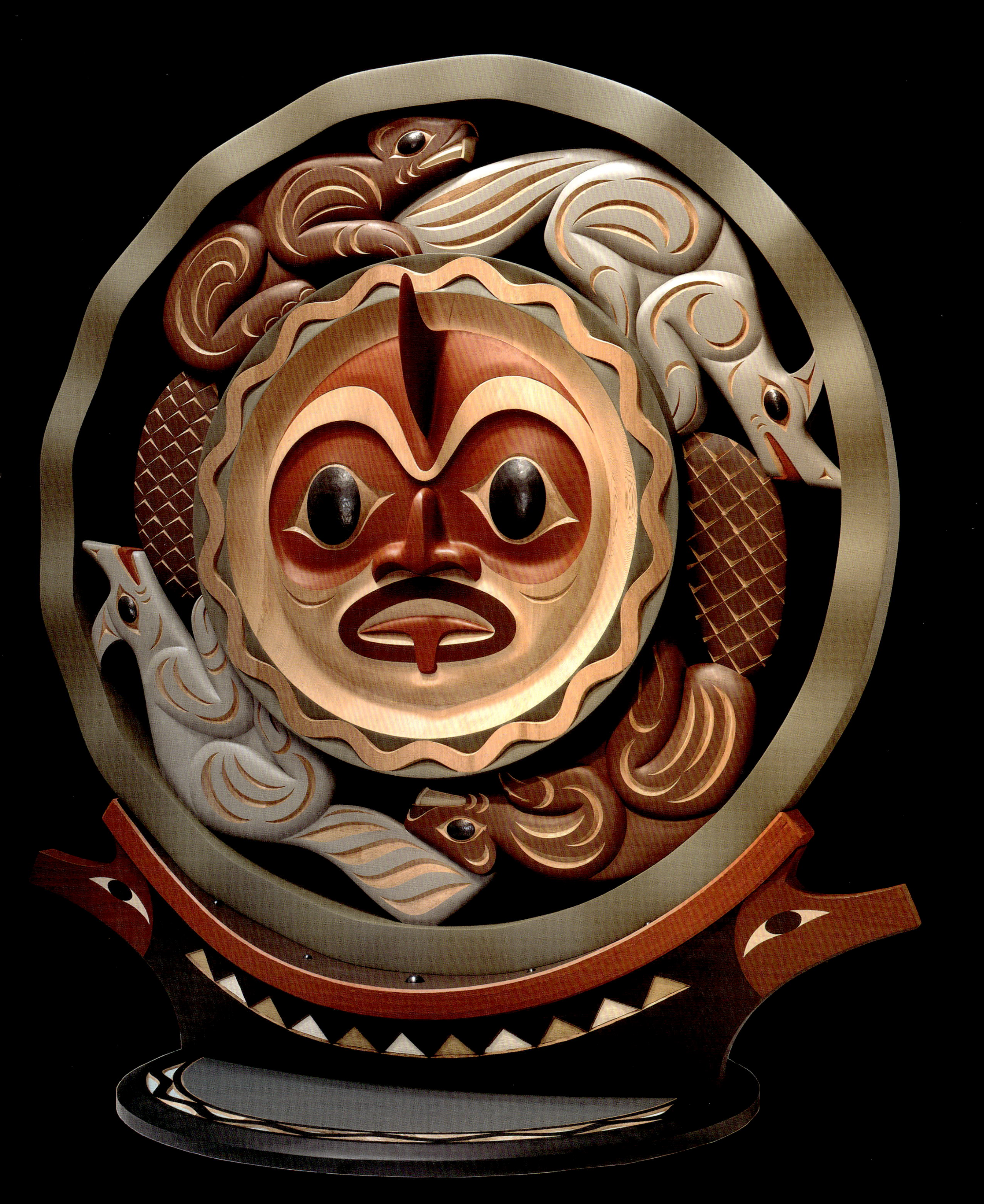

The Beaver and the Mink, 2004

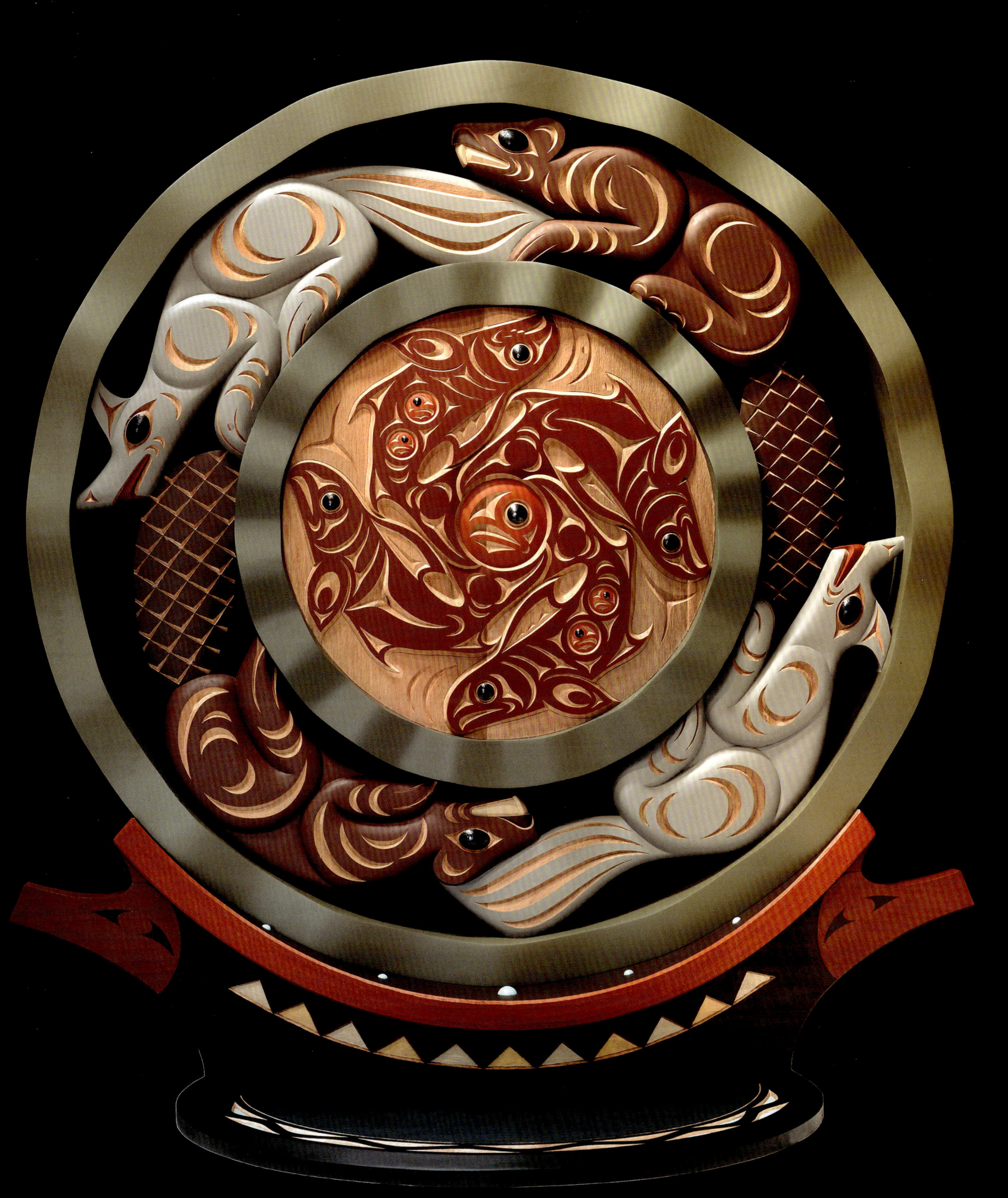

Salmon Spawning Run, 2012
Carved and painted western red cedar
2.13 × 1.98 m

Salmon Spawning Run

LOCATION: Mint Museum Uptown
500 South Tryon Street, Charlotte, NC

An exciting sign of the growth of Susan's international reputation came in 2008, when she was contacted by one of the curators of the Mint Museum in Charlotte, North Carolina. To celebrate its October 2010 move to a new facility called Mint Museum Uptown, a project called *Ten Ten Ten* was designed to "invigorate the new permanent collection galleries," in the words of curator Annie Carlano, by inviting "ten of the world's most innovative artists" to create works specifically for an entryway and nine galleries in the museum.[16] Susan was the only Canadian and the only Indigenous artist among an intriguing mix of women and men from the U.S., Japan, Israel, Ireland, the Netherlands, and Iceland.

As she explained in the video she produced to accompany her work, Susan chose to work in wood to honour the life cycle of the salmon, a species that her people have long called "The Giver of Life." The work itself is built around a spindle whorl containing two salmon, a female and a male, balanced on opposite sides of the whorl. Eggs of varying sizes are carved in circles in the belly of the female, and the belly of the male is defined by wedges. The eyes of both fish are emphasized with wedges and crescents. The whorl is surrounded by forty-four salmon eggs showing fry in different stages of development; the number and scale dramatize the fecund nature of the spawning salmon.

The work is a Salish sculpture and an appeal to work together to help the salmon survive into the future, as Susan explains in the video.

> My art is in honour of our last remaining spawning wild salmon.... One by one our streams are being lost.... Salmon navigating these streams face all kinds of abuse... after years of freedom and struggle in the open seas this is not what they deserve while returning to their rocky stream beds where their odyssey began.... This windfall and old-growth cedar spindle whorl is a tribute to the salmon and all waterways. I believe the appeal is universal because many people in many regions can understand the story. Children of the future can look back and see that we were all conscious of what was happening whether we were helpless or not.
>
> My artwork is done in my Coast Salish native art style. It has been hand carved and hand painted using subtle but bright colours of the salmon. West Coast native images are more than stylized symbols. Each character has its own face and history. Our people believe that salmon is the giver of life. As indicators of wealth and the cycle of life, salmon in pairs are good luck.... I have incorporated salmon eggs in various stages of development around the outside of the whorl symbolizing the protection they need to continue.

North Carolina is far from the Musqueam home settlement by the Salish Sea in many ways, but it is encouraging to think that Susan's story told with Salish forms can have significance for people everywhere. With this commission she joins artists from around the world, exploring the dimensions of their art and their roots in a dramatically contemporary building.

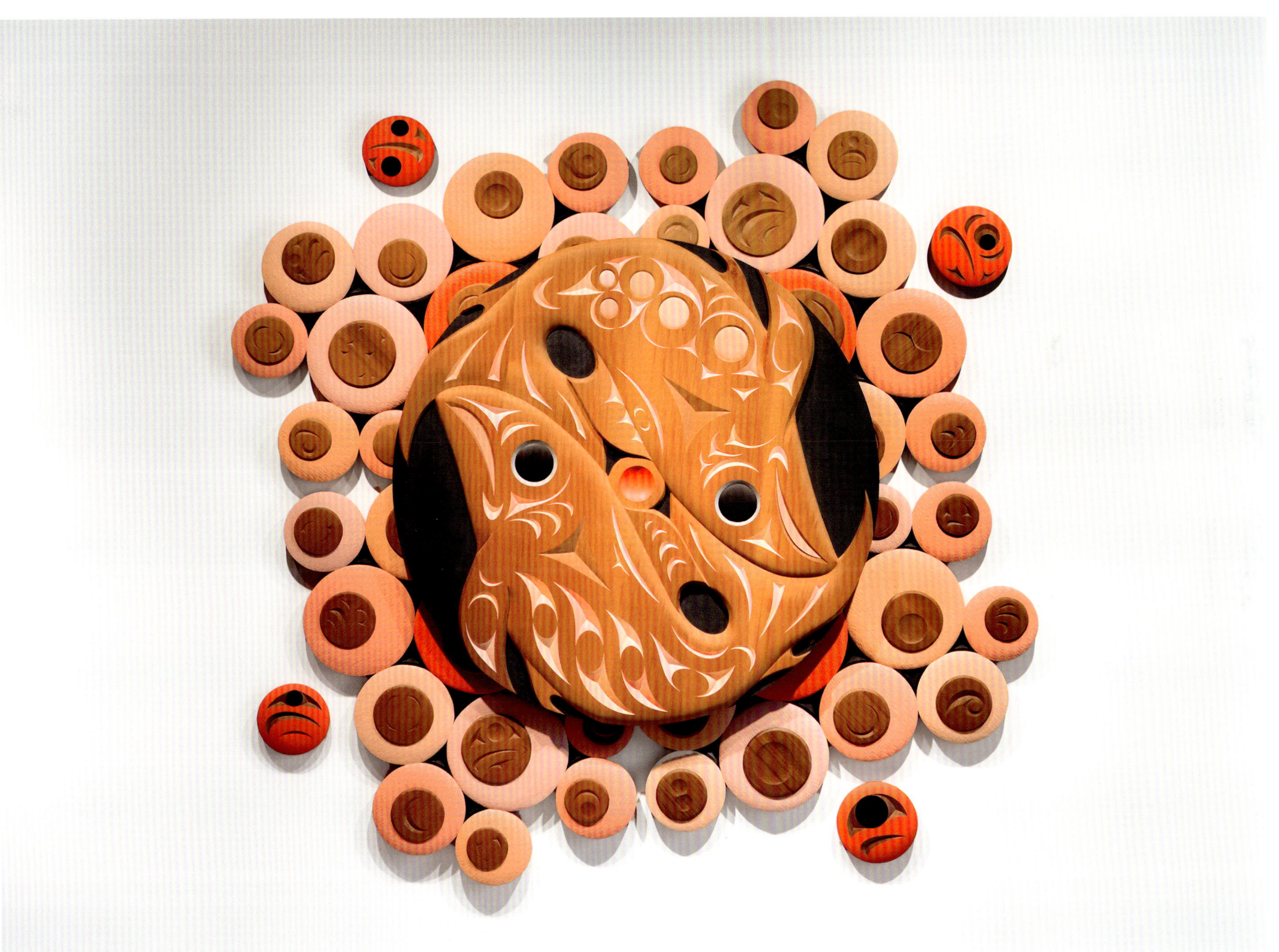

Eagle, 1988
Gold
5.5 × 8.2 × 2.6 cm

Salmon, 1988
Silver
5.7 × 6.8 × 5.0 cm

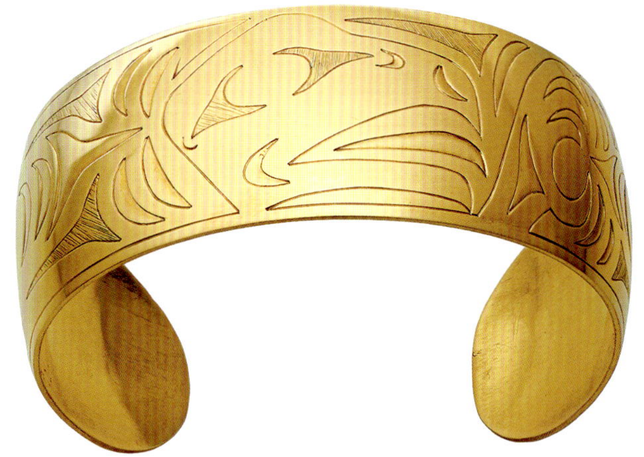

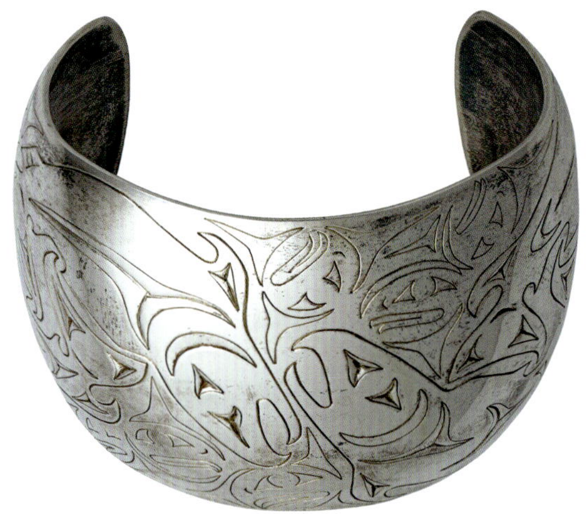

Salmon Run, Eagle, Salmon

LOCATION: Ethnographic Museum of the University of Zurich
Pelikanstrasse 40, 8001 Zurich, Switzerland

The public art pieces that are held at the greatest distance from the Musqueam settlement are in Zurich, and were acquired by the Ethnographic Museum during the first decade of Susan's career as an artist, when there was still resistance in the local Vancouver art market to the results of her ongoing study of early Salish work.

Her art came to the attention of Dr. Peter Gerber, curator of ethnology at the Ethnographic Museum, when he was working on a book with photographer Maximilien Bruggmann about First Nations Peoples of the Northwest Coast. Encouraged by several colleagues in Switzerland, in the spring of 1988 Dr. Gerber curated an exhibition of the work of three artists: Susan Point, Joe David, and Lawrence Paul Yuxweluptun, "representatives of the middle and younger generation of Native artists in Canada," as he described them in the catalogue.[17]

Susan and her husband Jeff visited Zurich before the exhibition opened. Susan brought prints, and *Salmon Run*, which she had recently completed. While in Zurich she finished the silver bracelet that is shown here. The exhibition, from 10 May to 20 August 1989, marked the first public showing of her work in Europe.

These works mark a transition period in her career; she created only a limited number of paintings and pieces of jewellery before moving on to prints, wood carvings, and works in glass and metal. The three pieces shown here are part of a collection of forty-five pieces by Susan held at the museum (the remainder are prints) that all show clearly how eager Susan was to incorporate what she had learned about the Salish aesthetic into her own personal style. A number of salmon are engraved into the curve of the silver bracelet in a design featuring crescents and wedges, some quite deeply incised into the metal. In the gold bracelet she uses an eagle motif, a simpler design than in the silver, but again with crescents and wedges to define the various parts of the bird.

The painting is derived from a box in the collection of the Museum of Anthropology at UBC. The colour gradients on the salmon heads, whose eyes are framed by narrow crescents or wedges, foreshadow the experiments with colour that Susan would use skillfully in various mediums over the next thirty years. The old Salish piece that inspired this painting is reborn in Susan's work, which honours the past and tells of the story of the salmon run in a new medium that at times seems almost whimsical.

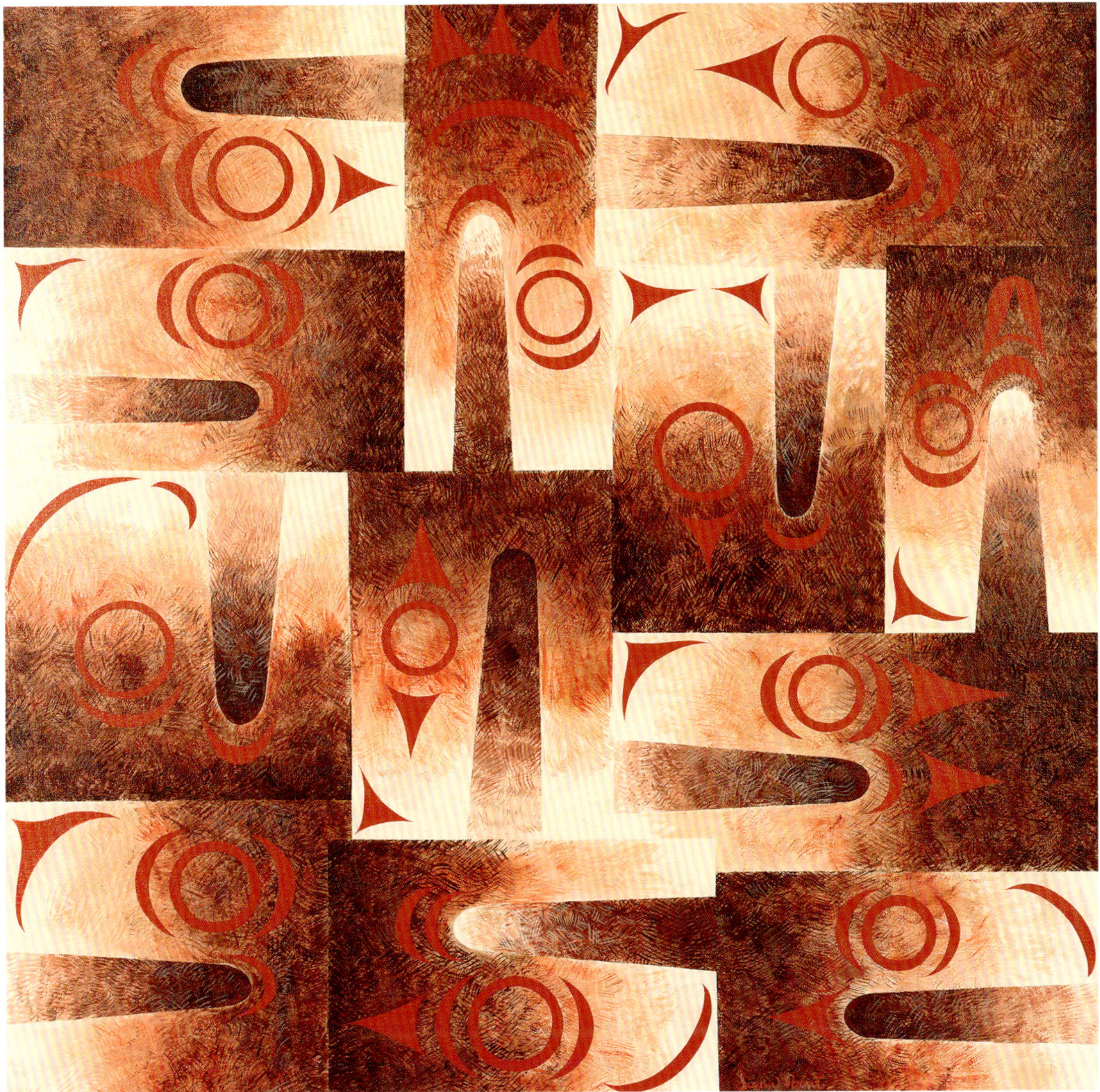

In the Zurich catalogue entry for this painting, Susan says, "this painting . . . was inspired by a traditional wood panel carving. As I like to experiment with different brush techniques and play with colour, I found that in doing this particular painting it was a nice opportunity express myself spontaneously without knowing what the exact end result would be."[18]

At a time when many local collectors in the Vancouver area were still equating Northwest Coast Indigenous art with northern styles, the curators in Zurich, a continent and an ocean away, were giving Susan's work an important vote of confidence. Within two years Susan would complete her first monumental architectural facades in shíshálh (sxəxeʔɬ; Sechelt), and soon after that, begin doing large-scale carvings in wood. From her decorations for St. Paul's Church to her *Salish Girl* for UBC's *Reconciliation Pole*, she has created an extraordinarily rich body of work in various themes, mediums, and locations. We can only hope there are many more to come.

Salmon Run, 1988
Acrylic on canvas
92 × 91 cm

Acknowledgements

MY FIRST THANKS must go to Susan Point herself. No working artist, wife, mother, and grandmother could have been more generous with her time and her support of this project. We spent hundreds of hours in interviews over many years as we reviewed the individual artworks that are the core of the book. She has spent many more hours in the last two years searching through her studio archives for background material. Her son Thomas Cannell has been a great help in these searches, as has her daughter Kelly Cannell, both of them artists also, trained in part by their mother's instruction and example. Susan's husband, Jeff Cannell, also made important contributions in recalling significant details of particular commissions and vignettes of some milestones in Susan's career.

Next, I am deeply indebted to my wife, Alison. She has endured the agonies of my writing, turning my drafts into proper typescript which I have been able to share with Susan as the project gained momentum. Alison has been an organizer, format artist, photographer, traveller, and a huge support to me. Her skills, combined with Susan's interest and support, are the two leading reasons why this book has come to life.

Another essential factor has been the wonderful response from various donors. David McLean, his wife Brenda, and their family have generously agreed to be the project's lead sponsor. Through his foundation, Michael Audain, a longtime admirer of Susan's work, was an early supporter, as was Dr. Brandt C. Louie, through London Drugs. I am also indebted to well-known supporters of the arts such as Dr. Joesph Segal and his wife Rosalie, Dr. Yosef Wosk, and Mrs. Fei Wong. I owe special thanks to a great friend in Toronto, Roger Lindsay, who was instrumental in a successful application to the W. Garfield Weston Foundation. A highlight of contacts made in 2017 was to meet the creators of the most important collection of contemporary Salish art in Canada, if not the world, Christiane and George Smyth of Victoria. This meeting led to an important gift made by them through their Foundation. Individuals touched in special ways by one or another works of Susan's, also came forward. Notable among this group was Martha Lou Henley, daughter of Jean Southam, the donor of the marvellous stained glass window in Christ Church Cathedral. Beyond these donors were friends from youth and from my working life in Vancouver, Victoria Huntington and Doreen Braverman. As the manuscript neared completion, the first donor from Washington State appeared: Urban Accessories of Tacoma, whose Vice-President, Jeff Wright, is a great admirer of Susan's work. Jeff explained that he knew of no other artist who could carve with the care and precision necessary to produce a taper good enough to guarantee the best result of a cast in iron or other metals.

The donors' response is, I believe, a strong indication of the high regard so many in our city and beyond have for Susan's work. This feeling is shared by those friends and colleagues who gave me introductions and support in my search for donors. These included Scott McIntyre, Canadian publishing legend, who was also instrumental in steering me toward the company that accepted the publishing project, Figure 1 Publishing in Vancouver. Other assistance came from Jane Hungerford; Michael Francis, former chair of the board of governors at Simon Fraser University; Dean Peter Elliott of Christ Church Cathedral; Don Evans in North Vancouver; and the Hon. Janet Austin, Lieutenant Governor of B.C. I am deeply grateful for their help.

Susan's art, and Coast Salish art more widely, has been studied and written about for several decades. In this regard, I am especially grateful to Dr. Anthony Shelton, Director of the Museum of Anthropology at UBC, for agreeing that this book could become part of an ongoing series of books issued by the museum and for authorizing a partnership with Figure 1 Publishing to that end. It was a great pleasure to have the opportunity to speak with Dr. Michael Kew, noted anthropologist and scholar in this field. He and his wife welcomed me to their home and he gave important hours of interview time, speaking about the nature of Salish art and culture and his long acquaintance with Susan and her family. Other scholars and curators assisted me along the way, and I would especially like to acknowledge conversations with Bill McLennan, Curator and photographer at the Museum of Anthropology, and Dr. Barbara Brotherton, Curator of Native American Art at the Seattle Art Museum, who, assisted by her colleague Dr. Jay Miller, gave invaluable help in providing and confirming the correct names of various Coast Salish Peoples in what is now Washington State. Dr. Karen Duffek, Curator of Contemporary Visual Arts and Pacific Northwest at the Museum of Anthropology, UBC, provided excellent information on correct naming of certain First Nations on the B.C. Coast.

Like many who deal with art in public places from many locations, I have received wonderful help from a large number of people: curators, facilities managers, museum administrative staff, public sector employees at various levels of government, and professionals in various fields. Among these are Kris Andersen, Ministry of Tourism, Arts and Culture, Victoria, B.C.; Elizabeth Ball, Councillor, City of Vancouver; Rita Beiks, former Curator, Art Program, Vancouver International Airport, and her assistant Cynthia McCreery; Cynthia Bowles, Ministry of Indigenous Relations and Reconciliation, Victoria, B.C.; Lee Brooks, Arctic Raven Gallery, Friday Harbor, WA; Leslie Cone and Rebecca Elliott at the Mint Museum in Charlotte, North Carolina; Anne Crouchley, Portland Art Museum; Dale Cummings, King County Transit; Kevin Gibbs and Katrina Petryk, Indigenous Art Centre, Ministry of Indigenous and Northern Affairs Canada in Ottawa; Alyssa Goad, Coast Mental Health; Simi Heer, Laurel Kennedy, Rob Rothwell, and Clint Senior for the Vancouver Police Department; Greg Hill, at the National Gallery of Canada; Deprise Hotton, Ana Maria Mendez and Theresa Wells, Regional Recreation Corporation of Wood Buffalo, Fort McMurray, Alberta; Jordan Howland, with King County 4Culture in Seattle; Mary Jo Hughes, Emerald Johnstone-Bedell, and Caroline Riedel, University of Victoria Legacy Art Collection; Dave Johnson, Tukwila, Washington Parks; Verna Kirkness, former

Director, UBC First Nations House of Learning; Amanda Knowles and Kelda Martensen at North Seattle College; Evan Koch and Lisa Reitzes, Seattle Children's Hospital; Dony Le Donne at Rogers Communications in Toronto; Dr. Lillian McDermott at the University of Washington and Elizabeth Steinbreuck of the Steinbreuck Galley in Seattle; Ashley Mead at the Seattle Art Museum; Anne Murray, Vice-President Marketing at the Vancouver International Airport; Connie Pavone and Marnie Rice, Mayor's Office, City of Vancouver; Deborah Proby, Raven's Cry Theatre; Sarra Scherb, Stonington Gallery; Robin Silvester, Port of Vancouver; Nathan Sowry at the National Museum of the American Indian in Washington, D.C.; Rev. D. Throop, Port Hope, Ontario; Christine Wasiak, First Nations House of Learning, UBC; and Jenny Wyma, Coordinator, Imperial Oil in Calgary.

During the course of research I was privileged to be able to meet several of the artists who played important roles as Susan's teachers, and fellow artists who supported her in the development of her composition. Notable among these meetings were interviews held with John Livingston at his Victoria studio and Rosa Quintana at her studio in Agassiz. Rosa and her husband, Mike, were the artists who cast a number of Susan's earlier large-scale pieces. I was also able to speak with Peter Braune, Master Printmaker on Granville Island; Jeff White at Urban Accessories in Tacoma; and Yves Trudeau of Studio One Glass Art in Burnaby.

Susan's warm personality, her creativity, and her legendary strong work ethic impressed many whose own work brought them into contact with her. Several of these individuals gave me invaluable help via recollections of their interactions with her, particularly Bryan Newson, former Director of the Public Art Program for the City of Vancouver; Andy Croft of PCI Developments, builders of the Marine Gateway project; and Don Vaughan, whose landmark urban study for the Triangle West neighbourhood at Coal Harbour led to one of Susan's earliest public art commissions for the City of Vancouver.

I particularly want to thank Chris Labonté, President of Figure 1 Publishing, and all the members of the creative team, whose professionalism has ensured that this book is a beautiful and important addition to the corpus of Canadian art publications. It has been a pleasure to work with Michael Leyne, Lara Smith, Naomi MacDougall, and Jessica Sullivan.

In closing I want to mention several others who offered help, advice, and support: Richard Berthelsen, Senior Project Manager, Strategic Protocol and External Relations, City of Toronto; Dr. Daniel R. Birch; Dr. John Blatherwick; Jennifer Borland, City of North Vancouver; Daphne Bramham, journalist with Postmedia; Joanne Chan at London Drugs; Evangeline Englezos at Vancouver Fraser Port Authority; Darin Geunette, Manager of Public Affairs at BC Ferries; Anne Giardini, Chancellor of Simon Fraser University; Laura Grabhorn, Assistant Director, Longhouse Education and Cultural Center at The Evergreen State College; Don Rose, former Chair of the Board of TransLink; Dr. Samy Khalid; Martin Segger, former Director of the Maltwood Gallery at the University of Victoria; Chantal Shah at the Audain Foundation; Tom Teranishi, recipient of a Courage to Come Back Award; Hilary-Morgan Watt, a distant cousin who is a curator in Washington, D.C.; Ann West, formerly of the Canada Council programs, who believes strongly that Canada needs more books on its visual artists; Gary Wyatt of the Spirit Wrestler Gallery in Vancouver; and, last but not least, our son Michael, who gave vital technical consultation along the way, and our daughter Catherine, for her hospitality and assistance with accessing several of Susan's artworks in Seattle.

Pronunciation Guide

Reproduced with permission of the Musqueam Indian Band Language Department.

hən̓q̓əmin̓əm̓ has thirty-six consonants, twenty-two of which are not found in English. Some—like t̓ᶿ—are very special sounds, as they appear in only a handful of languages around the world. Since the majority of hən̓q̓əmin̓əm̓ sounds are not found in English, the English alphabet (orthography) is not an adequate or straightforward system for writing hən̓q̓əmin̓əm̓ words. So instead, we use a number of symbols from the North American Phonetic Alphabet (NAPA), which is based on the principle that each sound is represented by a single distinct symbol. This is a significant advantage for learning how to read, as the hən̓q̓əmin̓əm̓ alphabet creates consistency of interpretation and predictability of pronunciation. Though some of these letters may appear foreign at first, a symbol like the schwa (ə) represents a very common vowel sound in English and is found in the pronunciation guides of most English dictionaries. Other symbols—like θ or š—are used in the alphabets of many other Native languages of North America, as well as in several languages of Europe and elsewhere around the world.

The following is a brief Pronunciation Guide to the hən̓q̓əmin̓əm̓ orthography.

You'll note that upper case (capital) letters are not used in the hən̓q̓əmin̓əm̓ orthographic system, even at the beginning of a sentence.

VOWELS

i = the i in "pizza"

e = the e in "bet"

a = the a in "father"

u = the u in "flute"

ə = the u in "but"

Sometimes vowels will be followed by a colon ":". This means the vowel is lengthened.

CONSONANTS

Some sounds that are pronounced the same in both hən̓q̓əmin̓əm̓ and English are:
h, k, l, m, n, p, s, t, w, y.

Other consonants include:

c = "ts" sound as in "cats"

č = "ch" sound as in "cheese"

ɬ = Place your tongue as though you were going to pronounce an "l" sound and then simply blow a steady stream of air past the sides of your tongue. (This is called a lateral fricative.)

ƛ̓ = This sound starts like a t̓ (see below) and then releases into the ɬ sound described above.

q = Similar to "k" only with your tongue pulled farther back to stop the air flow at the uvula.

š = "sh" sound as in "shirt"

θ = "th" sound as in "think." (This symbol, from the Greek alphabet, is called theta.)

t̓^{θ} = This sound starts like a t̓ (see below) and then releases into the theta θ sound.

x = Sounds like the "h" in "huge."

χ = This is a uvular fricative: a slightly raspy sound made at the back of the mouth.

ʔ = The "interruption" that you hear in the middle of the expression "uh-oh." (This symbol is called a glottal stop.)

What does that little comma above or beside a letter mean?
Some hən̓q̓əmin̓əm̓ consonants, such as c̓, k̓, ƛ̓, p̓, q̓, or t̓, are categorized as glottalized or ejective stops. They are distinguished from their non-glottalized counterparts (c, k, etc.) by an audible popping sound upon their release.

l, m, n, w, and y represent the group of consonants known as resonants, characterized as such because of the reverberating or "resonant" quality of their sound. Their glottalized counterparts—l̓, m̓, n̓, w̓, and y̓, like the glottalized stops, are also represented with an apostrophe. Glottalized resonants are pronounced with a creaky sound quality (called laryngealization).

What does that little "w" (ʷ) next to a letter mean?
The little ʷ next to a letter means that the particular sound is made with your lips rounded. So the hən̓q̓əmin̓əm̓ word kʷe:l, to hide, sounds very similar to the English word "quell."

Notes

INTRODUCTION

1 Susan A. Point, interview by author, 9 April 2010, Coast Salish Arts, Vancouver, BC.

2 Ibid.

3 Susan A. Point, interview by author, 23 November 2010, Coast Salish Arts, Vancouver, BC.

4 Susan A. Point, email message to author, 21 March 2018.

5 Ibid.

6 Ibid.

PART ONE: CLOSE TO XʷMƏΘKʷƏY̓ƏM (MUSQUEAM)

1 Verna J. Kirkness and Jo-Ann Archibald, *The First Nations Longhouse: Our Home Away from Home* (Vancouver: First Nations House of Learning, 2001), 29.

2 Bill McLennan, interview by author, 2 June 2017, UBC Museum of Anthropology, Vancouver.

3 Susan A. Point, "Coast Salish Housepost," statement by Susan A. Point, n.d., Archives of Coast Salish Arts.

4 Wayne Suttles, "Productivity and its Constraints: A Coast Salish Case," in *Coast Salish Essays* (Vancouver: Talonbooks, 1987), 103–04.

5 J.E. Michael Kew, *Sculpture and Engraving of the Central Coast Salish Indians*, UBC Museum of Anthropology, Museum Note No. 9 (Vancouver: UBC Museum of Anthropology, 1980), 1.

6 Ibid., 3, 4.

7 Karen Duffek, *New Visions: Serigraphs by Susan A. Point, Coast Salish Artist*, UBC Museum of Anthropology, Museum Note No. 15 (Vancouver: UBC Museum of Anthropology, 1986), 1.

8 Ibid.

9 Duffek, *New Visions*, 2–3.

10 Kirkness and Archibald, *The First Nations Longhouse*, 46.

11 Susan A. Point, email message to author, 21 March 2018. The exhibition was *Salish Images: Northwest Coast Artists Tribute to Salish Art*, January 28–February 9, 1986; the Museum Note was Duffek, *New Visions*.

12 J.E. Michael Kew, *Sculpture and Engraving of the Central Coast Salish Indians*, UBC Museum of Anthropology, Museum Note No. 9 (Vancouver: UBC Museum of Anthropology, 1980), 4.

13 Susan A. Point, "Welcome Figure," artist's statement, ca. 1997, Archives of Coast Salish Arts.

14 Susan A. Point, "Musqueam Houseposts," artist's statement, ca. 1997, Archives of Coast Salish Arts.

15 Susan A. Point, interview by author, 7 September 2017, Coast Salish Arts, Vancouver, BC.

16 UBC Museum of Anthropology, "Call for Proposals for Musqueam Art Commission," MOA leaflet, July 2006.

17 Susan A. Point, email to Jennifer Webb, 18 January 2010.

18 James Hart, email message to Susan A. Point, 3 November 2016.

19 Amanda Siebert, "Haida Master Carver Jim Hart Tells the Story of Indian Residential Schools in Reconciliation Totem Pole," *Georgia Straight*, 31 March 2017.

20 Susan A. Point, email message to author, 21 March 2018.

21 Mary Stewart, email message to Susan A. Point, 26 January 2007.

22 Nancy Southam, *The Tree of Life Stained Glass Windows*, pamphlet issued by Christ Church Cathedral, ca. 2009, 2.

23 Dean Peter Elliott, quoted in John Mackie, "Tree of Life to Light Up the Entrance at Christ Church Cathedral," *Vancouver Sun*, 21 March 2009.

24 Southam, *The Tree of Life*, 3.

25 Susan A. Point, letter to Dean Elliott, 16 October 2006, Coast Salish Art Archives.

26 Ibid.

27 Mackie, "Tree of Life."

28 Robert D. Watt, "Unveiling of Tree of Life Window," typescript of remarks given at unveiling of *The Tree of Life*, 5 April 2009, personal archives.

29 Vancouver Convention Centre Expansion Project (VCCEP), "Call to Coast Salish Artists," request for proposals, June 2008.

30 Susan A. Point, "Letter of Interest," response to VCCEP request for proposals, ca. June 2008, Archives of Coast Salish Arts.

31 Ibid.

32 Susan A. Point, speaking in Vancouver Convention Centre, digital video *Human Spirit by Susan Point*, 6 July 2010, https://www.youtube.com/watch?v=LSMuryAAYvc.

33 Ibid.

34 Susan A. Point, email messsage to Rand MacKenzie at the Vancouver Convention Centre, 30 April 2009.

35 "First Nations Art and Totem Poles: 'People Amongst the People' Coast Salish gateways," City of Vancouver website, n.d., http://vancouver.ca/parks-recreation-culture/totems-and-first-nations-art.aspx (17 July 2018).

36 Susan A. Point, email message to author, 21 March 2018.

37 Matt Hern, *Common Ground in a Liquid City: Essays in Defense of an Urban Future* (Oakland: AK Press, 2010), 31.
38 Susan A. Point, "People Amongst the People; Three Portals for Stanley Park," proposal for artwork, ca. 2005, Archives of Coast Salish Arts.
39 Point, "People Amongst the People," proposal.
40 Susan A. Point, "People Amongst the People," artist's statement, ca. 2005, Archives of Coast Salish Arts.
41 Susan A. Point, email message to author, 21 March 2018.
42 Ibid.
43 Point, "People Amongst the People," artist's statement.
44 Point, "People Amongst the People," proposal.
45 Ibid.
46 Ibid.
47 Ibid.
48 Ibid.
49 Ibid.
50 Ibid.
51 Ibid.
52 Ibid.
53 Ibid.
54 Susan A. Point, email message to author, 21 March 2018.
55 City of Vancouver Public Art Program, "Put a Lid On It: Art Underfoot Competition," request for proposals, 2004.
56 Kelly Cannell and Susan A. Point, "Art Underfoot Competition Proposal for the City of Vancouver," 3 May 2004, Archives of Coast Salish Arts.
57 Susan A. Point, email message to author, 21 March 2018.
58 John Pigeon, "Logo Ties Various Groups," 24 *Hours*, 22 June 2006.
59 Rob Rothwell, "Beyond the Call," *Blue Line*, January 2015.
60 Susan A. Point as told to Vesta Giles, "New Works," in Michael Kew, Peter Macnair, and Bill McLennan, *Susan Point: Coast Salish Artist*, ed. Gary Wyatt (Vancouver: Douglas & McIntyre, 2000), 46.
61 Ibid.
62 Coast Foundation Society call for artists, deadline date 8 February 1999.
63 notes from Susan A. Point to Sharlene at the Coast Foundation Society office, 11 April 2001, Archives of Coast Salish Arts
64 Susan A. Point as told to Vesta Giles, "New Works," in Kew, Macnair, and McLennan, *Susan Point: Coast Salish Artist*, 49.
65 Susan A. Point, "The River—Giver of Life," artist's statement presented to Langara Student Union, ca. 1998, Archives of Coast Salish Arts.
66 Susan A. Point, "The River—Giver of Life," proposal to the Langara College Student Union officers, ca. 1998, Archives of Coast Salish Arts.
67 Susan A. Point, "Salish Gifts," proposal to Marine Gateway Public Art Program, September 2013, Archives of Coast Salish Arts.
68 Ibid.
69 Ibid.
70 Ibid.
71 Ibid.
72 Ibid.
73 Ibid.
74 Ibid.
75 Ibid.
76 Susan A. Point, "Fusion," artist's statement, n.d., Archives of Coast Salish Arts.
77 Ibid.
78 Susan A. Point, email message to author, 21 March 2018.
79 Susan A. Point, "Land Sea and Sky," artist's statement, ca. 1993, Archives of Coast Salish Arts.
80 Susan A. Point, email message to author, 21 March 2018.
81 Susan A. Point, "Flight," artist's statement, ca. 1996, Archives of Coast Salish Arts.
82 Susan A. Point, fax message to Frank O'Neill, 24 May 1997.
83 Susan A. Point, "Musqueam Welcome Figures," artist's statement, ca. 1996, Archives of Coast Salish Arts.
84 Susan A. Point, remarks at the opening of the Musqueam Welcome Area, YVR Airport, 20 April 1996, Archives of Coast Salish Arts.
85 Susan A. Point, letter to Frank O'Neill, 12 August 1997, Archives of Coast Salish Arts.
86 Susan A. Point, proposed text for labelling *Cedar Connection*, ca. 2009, Archives of Coast Salish Arts.

PART TWO: FROM SHÍSHÁLH TO SEMIAHMOO

1 Susan A. Point, "Spawning Salmon," description of artwork, n.d., Archives of Coast Salish Arts.
2 Susan Point described this work in a statement about the 1991 commissions received from the Sechelt First Nation: Archives of Coast Salish Arts, undated.
3 *A Timeless Circle*, 2016 (video). Produced by Buzzworks Creative for the Resort Municipality of Whistler, funded by Resort Municipality Initiative Funds, Province of British Columbia.
4 Yvonne Schmidt, quoted in Thomas A. Lascelles, "Appendix A: The Save St. Paul's Indian Church Society Report," in *Mission on the Inlet: St. Paul's Indian Catholic Church, North Vancouver, B.C., 1863-1984* (Vancouver: St. Paul's Province, Order of the Oblates of Mary Immaculate Place, 1984), 51.
5 Percy Paull, quoted in Lascelles, "Indian Art Work Report," in *Mission on the Inlet*, 53–54.
6 Susan A. Point, "Story of Life," concept proposal, April 2013, Archives of Coast Salish Arts.
7 Ibid.
8 Ibid.

9 Susan A. Point, "Salish Wolf," artist's statement, ca. 2001, Archives of Coast Salish Arts.

10 "imesh Mobile App," Simon Fraser University: Bill Reid Centre website, n.d., https://www.sfu.ca/brc/imeshMobileApp.html (18 July 2018).

11 Christiane Smyth, email message to author, 6 January 2018.

12 Hugh Ker, email message to Susan A. Point and Jeff Cannell, 17 November 2003, Archives of Coast Salish Arts.

13 Susan A. Point, "River—Giver of Life," leaflet produced by Weatherhaven Limited, 2006, Archives of Coast Salish Arts.

14 Ibid.

15 Susan A. Point, interview by author, 1 June 2017, Coast Salish Arts, Vancouver, BC.

16 Susan A. Point, "Water Guardians," proposal to Surrey Public Art Selection Committee, ca. 2015, Archives of Coast Salish Arts.

17 Susan A. Point, quoted in "Frogs," City of Surrey website, n.d., https://www.surrey.ca/culture-recreation/18450.aspx (1 December 2017).

18 Susan A. Point, letter to Robert Davidson, ca. 1998, Archives of Coast Salish Arts.

19 Urban Art Management, "Request for Expressions of Interest & Statement of Qualifications For Coast Salish Artists, River Green, Hillsboro Investments Limited," March 2010.

20 Susan A. Point and Thomas Cannell, artists' statement, in Urban Art Management, "Final Report: River Green *Fishtrap Way*," February 2014.

21 Ibid.

22 Ibid.

23 Jane Fernyhough, "Staff Report," in Malcolm D. Brodie, "Report to City Council: Richmond Oval Buttress Runnels—Artist Design," 18 July 2006, https://www.richmond.ca/__shared/assets/071706_ovalitem214411.pdf.

24 "Public Art Project Request for Expression of Interest and Qualifications," n.d., ca. early 2006, Attachment 1 in Brodie, "Report to City Council."

25 Susan A. Point, "Richmond Oval—Description of Artwork," 4 July 2006, Attachment 4 in Brodie, "Report to city Council."

26 Susan A. Point, email message to author, 21 March 2018.

27 Adele Weder, "Oars to the Ground," *Canadian Architect* 54, no. 2 (2009): 20.

PART THREE: SALISH LANDS

1 Bill McLennan, "Contemporary Architectural Carvings," in Kew, Macnair, and McLennan, *Susan Point: Coast Salish Artist*, 97.

2 Ibid., 98.

3 Lee Brooks, email message to Susan A. Point, 3 March 2004.

4 Richard Walker, "Traditional Coast Salish House Posts Call Attention to Rich Tribal History," *Indian Country Today*, 13 February 2003, https://indiancountrymedianetwork.com/news/traditional-coast-salish-house-posts-call-attention-to-rich-tribal-history/.

5 Richard Walker, "Dream is Still Alive," *Journal of the San Juan Islands*, 26 February 2003.

6 Richard Walker, "250 Attend Posts Dedication," *Journal of the San Juan Islands*, 26 May 2004.

7 Kim Lunman, "Victoria Eccentric Bestows Millions," *Globe and Mail*, 5 July 2001.

8 Susan A. Point, email message to author, 21 March 2018.

9 "The Wolf People," n.d., ca. 1993, Archives of Coast Salish Arts.

10 Susan A. Point, remarks made at unveiling ceremony for *Kneeling Stool*, University of Victoria, Victoria, BC, 27 October 1993.

11 Susan A. Point, letter to David Titterton, 22 October 1998.

12 City of Victoria, "Public Art for Johnson Street Parkade," request for proposals, 2014, Archives of Coast Salish Arts.

13 Jury for Johnson Street Parkade public art project, quoted in Nichola Reddington, City of Victoria, email message to Susan A. Point, 6 May 2015.

14 Susan A. Point and Thomas Cannell, "Woven Together," artists'statement, ca. June 2015, Archives of Coast Salish Arts.

15 Jeff Bell, "Use of Lekwungen Place Names on New Signs 'Meaningful': First Nations," *Times Colonist*, 21 March 2018; "Signs of Lekwungen," City of Victoria website, http://www.victoria.ca/EN/main/residents/culture/public-art/signs-of-lekwungen.html (18 July 2018).

16 Bruce Ellison, "Tree Grate Criteria 60% Design Review," memo from technical arts coordinator for City of Seattle, 5 December 1986, Archives of Coast Salish Arts.

17 Quoted in Katherine Martin, ed., *Women of Spirit: Stories of Courage from the Women Who Lived Them* (Novato, CA: New World Library, 2001), 217.

18 Peter R. Gerber and Vanina Katz-Lahaigue, *Susan A. Point, Joe David, Lawrence Paul: Indianische Künstler der Westküste Canada/Native Artists from the Northwest Coast* (Zurich: Völkerkundemuseum der Universität Zürich, 1989), 73.

19 Susan A. Point, "Art Commission Proposal: The Ambulatory Care Building Children's Hospital & Regional Medical Center," submitted to the Seattle Children's Hospital, ca. 2003.

20 Susan A. Point, "Continuing Cycle of Life," artist's statement, ca. 2004, Archives of Seattle Children's Hospital.

21 Susan A. Point, email message to Lillian McDermott, 28 February 2008.

22 City of Seattle, "Windows to the Past," public art documentation, ca. 1993, Archives of King County Metro Transport.

23 Susan A. Point, "Windows to the Past."

24 Susan A. Point, "Seattle Art Museum Notes: Story/Metaphors for Artwork," ca. 2007, Archives of Coast Salish Arts.
25 Susan A. Point, email message to Barbara Brotherton, 22 February 2007.
26 Barbara Brotherton, "The First People: Project Rendering and Project Description," 1 March 2007, Archives of Coast Salish Arts.
27 Susan A. Point, letter to Ann Friedman, 30 July 2001.
28 Susan A. Point, "Written Into the Earth," proposal, n.d., ca. 199, Archives of Coast Salish Arts.
29 Ibid.
30 Ibid.
31 Seahawks Stadium and Exhibition Center, "Stadium Art Program Guide," n.d., ca. 2002.
32 Susan A. Point, application to "Call for an Artist to Integrate Artwork into the Design of a New West Seattle Pump Station," ca. 1994, Archives of 4Culture and King County Public Art Collection.
33 Ibid.
34 "Northwind's Fishing Weir: A Retelling of Native Truths," call for proposals, Archives of 4Culture and the King County Public Art Collection, 1991.
35 Susan A. Point, "Northwind's Fishing Weir Proposal," ca. 1997, Archives of 4Culture and King County Public Art Collection.
36 Ibid.
37 Barbara Luecke, letter to Susan A. Point, 1 May 1997, Archives of 4Culture and King County Public Art Collection.
38 Susan A. Point, "Green River College: A Public Art Project: Final Proposal," n.d., ca. May 2010, Archives of Coast Salish Arts.
39 Others include Four Corners, 1999 (see page 172); Intersection of Enlightenment, 2001 (see page 204); Scinqua, 2005 (see page 200); and Woven to Place, 2011 (see page 194).
40 Susan A. Point, description of *Sea to Sky*, undated, ca. 1993.
41 Susan A. Point, email to Barbara Brotherton, 22 February 2007.
42 Susan A. Point, "Scinqua," artist's statement, n.d., ca. 2004, Archives of Coast Salish Arts.
43 Susan A. Point, letter to Dr. Deanna Dartt, 15 July 2014, Archives of Coast Salish Arts.
44 Susan A. Point, in *Susan Point: Spindle Whorl*, edited by Grant Arnold and Ian Thom (Vancouver: Vancouver Art Gallery; London: Black Dog, 2017), 114.
45 Susan A. Point, "Proposal to Eastern Washington University," n.d., ca. 2001, Archives of Coast Salish Arts.
46 Ibid.

PART FOUR: TURTLE ISLAND AND BEYOND

1 Susan A. Point, "Affection Design Proposal," n.d., ca. 2016, Archives of Coast Salish Arts.
2 Fraser Clark, in discussion with author, 6 September 2017.
3 Susan A. Point, "Freedom," description of artwork, n.d., ca. 1998, Archives of Coast Salish Arts.
4 Ibid.
5 Susan A. Point, "Generations," description of artwork, n.d., ca. 1998, Archives of Coast Salish Arts.
6 Susan A. Point, "Public Art Proposal to GWL Realty Advisors," 19 March 2005, Archives of Coast Salish Arts.
7 Susan A. Point, email message to author, 21 March 2018.
8 Susan A. Point, "Ongoing Journey," description sent to the committee, November 2005.
9 Rev. Douglas Throop, email message to Susan A. Point, 2 February 2007.
10 Ibid.
11 Rev. Douglas Throop, speaking in "Tree of Life Communion Table," digital video, recorded 17 September 2014, published by United Church of Canada, 8 March 2017, https://www.youtube.com/watch?v=BvkxWHhPxcA&feature=youtube.
12 Susan A. Point, quoted in *Susan Point: Spindle Whorl*, edited by Grant Arnold and Ian Thom (Vancouver: Vancouver Art Gallery; London: Black Dog, 2017), 130.
13 Embassy of Canada, "Canada Presents Major Art Work to Smithsonian," press release, 15 September 2004.
14 "Beaver and the Mink – A Tale of the Salmon Families from the People of the Grass," n.d., ca. 2004, Archives of Coast Salish Arts.
15 Embassy of Canada, "Canada Presents."
16 A. Carlano, director of Mint Museum, email message to Susan A. Point, 2 January 2009.
17 Peter R. Gerber and Vanina Katz-Lahaigue, *Susan A. Point, Joe David, Lawrence Paul: Indianische Künstler der Westküste Canada / Native Artists from the Northwest Coast* (Zurich: Völkerkundemuseum der Universität Zürich, 1989), 5.
18 Ibid., 94.

Bibliography

Arnold, Grant and Ian Thom, eds. *Susan Point: Spindle Whorl.* Vancouver: Vancouver Art Gallery; London: Black Dog, 2017. Published in conjunction with an exhibition of the same title, organized by and presented at the Vancouver Art Gallery, 18 February–28 May 2017.

Brotherton, Barbara, ed. *S'abadeb—The Gifts: Pacific Coast Salish Art and Artists.* Vancouver: Douglas & McIntyre, 2008. Published in conjunction with an exhibition of the same title, organized by the Seattle Art Museum and presented at the Seattle Art Museum, 24 October 2008–11 January 2009; the Heard Museum, 21 February–16 August 2009; and the Royal British Columbia Museum, 20 November 2009–8 March 2010.

Croes, Dale, Susan Point, and Gary Wyatt. *Susan Point: Works on Paper.* Vancouver: Figure 1, 2014.

Duffek, Karen. *New Visions: Serigraphs by Susan A. Point, Coast Salish Artist.* UBC Museum of Anthropology, Museum Note No. 15. Vancouver: UBC Museum of Anthropology, 1986.

Gerber, Peter R. and Vanina Katz-Lahaigue. *Susan A. Point, Joe David, Lawrence Paul: Indianische Künstler der Westküste Canada / Native Artists from the Northwest Coast.* Zurich: Völkerkundemuseum der Universität Zürich, 1989.

Jensen, Vickie. *The Totem Poles of Stanley Park.* Vancouver: Westcoast Words, 2004.

Kew, J.E. Michael. *Sculpture and Engraving of the Central Coast Salish Indians.* UBC Museum of Anthropology, Museum Note No. 9. Vancouver: UBC Museum of Anthropology, 1980.

Kew, Michael, Peter Macnair, and Bill McLennan. *Susan Point: Coast Salish Artist.* Edited by Gary Wyatt. Vancouver: Douglas & McIntyre; Spirit Wrestler Gallery, 2000.

Kirkness, Verna J. and Jo-ann Archibald. *The First Nations Longhouse: Our Home Away from Home.* Vancouver: First Nations House of Learning, 2001.

Kuckkahn, Tina, ed. *Cultural Luminaries: Illuminating the Past, Lighting the Way to the Future.* Olympia, WA: House of Welcome Publishing, 2006.

Laurence, Robin. *A Sense of Place: Art at Vancouver International Airport.* Vancouver: Figure 1, 2015.

Suttles, Wayne. *Coast Salish Essays.* Vancouver: Talonbooks, 1987.

———. *Katzie Ethnographic Notes.* Edited by Wilson Duff. Anthropology In British Columbia Memoir No. 2. Victoria: British Columbia Provincial Museum, 1955. [Issued with Dr. Diamond Jenness's *The Faith of a Coast Salish Indian*, a previously unpublished manuscript, which Dr. Suttles modified and supplemented in discussions with the son of Dr. Jenness's informant.]

Wilson, Jordan. qeqən / House Posts: *A Walking Tour of Musqueam House Posts at UBC.* Vancouver: Belkin Art Gallery and UBC, 2018.

Image Credits and Permissions

Credits listed by photographer

Jeff Cannell, courtesy of Archives of Coast Salish Arts: 12, 15, 23, 31, 35, 38, 56, 65, 78 (left), 86–87, 99–101, 110, 144, 158, 163, 166, 170, 171, 182, 185–87, 205
Thomas Cannell, courtesy of Archives of Coast Salish Arts: 139, 148
Fraser Clark: 214–16
Toni Hafkenscheid: 213, 217–20
Janet Dwyer Photography, courtesy of Salish Weave Collection: 224, 225
Michael Leyne: 116
Naomi MacDougall: 78 (right)
Ana Maria Mendez: 212
Bob Mathison, courtesy of Archives of Coast Salish Arts: 164, 165, 172
Bud Mintz: 21
Kenji Nagai: 18, 40–55, 59, 60, 62, 76–77, 80 (right), 81, 83, 84, 88–91, 96, 102–07, 108–09, 112, 120, 121 (left), 122–28, 132 (bottom), 134–36, 138, 141, 142, 145–47, 150–52, 155 (bottom), 177, 181, 192–95, 201, 207, 229, 231
Kenji Nagai, courtesy of Archives of Coast Salish Arts: 9, 61, 66–74, 221, 154, 155 (top)
Unknown photographer, courtesy of Archives of Coast Salish Arts: 16, 22, 32, 37, 39, 63, 108, 118, 119, 121 (right), 153, 167, 173, 183, 189–91, 196, 197
Alison Watt: 92–94, 132 (top), 133, 168, 199, 226
Jeff White, Urban Accessories, Tacoma, WA: 184
Jennifer Wyma, Imperial Oil: 210, 211
Mike Zens, courtesy of Archives of Coast Salish Arts: 174

Permissions and sources listed by page number

19 (left) Courtesy of North Vancouver Museum & Archives.
19 (right) © City of North Vancouver, courtesy of City of North Vancouver.
26 (left) © Her Majesty The Queen in Right of Canada represented by the Canadian Heraldic Authority, 1999-2000. Reproduced with permission of the Office of the Secretary to the Governor General, 2018.
26 (right) Photo of Peter Liljedahl's Governor General's Academic Medal by Justin Carmichael, SFU.
80 (left) Courtesy of Vancouver Police Department
82 Courtesy of Stonington Gallery.
130–31 Vancouver Fraser Port Authority [awaiting conf on both]
137 SFU Art Collection. Gift of Salish Weave Collection of George and Christiane Smyth. Photo by Dale Northey.
161 Courtesy of University of Victoria Legacy Art Galleries.
178 Courtesy of King County Metro Transit Archives.
180 Seattle Art Museum, 2008.31. Margaret E. Fuller Purchase Fund, in honour of the 75th Anniversary of the Seattle Art Museum. Photo by Susan Cole.
202 Portland Art Museum, Portland, Oregon. Museum purchase: Helen and Franklin Drake and Elizabeth Cole Butler Auction Proceeds.
227 Collection of Indigenous and Northern Affairs Canada / Collection des affaires autochtones et du Nord Canada. Photo by Lawrence Cook.
233 Project Ten Ten Ten commission. Museum Purchase: Funds provided by Fleur Bresler, Libba and Mike Gaither, Laura and Mike Grace, Betsy and Brian Wilder, Amy and Alfred Dawson, Aida and Greg Saul, Missy Luczak Smith and Doug Smith, Beth and Drew Quartapella, and Kim Blanding. 2012.107. Collection of The Mint Museum, Charlotte, North Carolina. Art © Susan Point 2012.
234 © Ethnographic Museum at the University of Zurich. Inv.-No. 20816 (top), 20817 (bottom) / Photos: Kathrin Leuenberger.
235 © Ethnographic Museum at the University of Zurich. Inv.-No. 20821 / Photo: Kathrin Leuenberger.

About the Contributors

SUSAN A. POINT, OC, DFA, DLITT, RCA, is a descendant of the Musqueam, Coast Salish Peoples; she is the daughter of Edna Grant and Anthony Point. Susan Point inherited the beliefs of her culture and the ancestral traditions of her people from her mother, Edna, who learned from her mother, Mary Charlie-Grant. Point's distinctive style has led the resurgence of Coast Salish art. She draws creativity from the stories of her ancestors and continually innovates with non-traditional materials and techniques, thereby inspiring a new generation of artists.

Point is most proud to be an Officer of the Order of Canada, and has been presented with the Queen Elizabeth II Diamond Jubilee Medal for her contributions to Canada. She has been recognized with an Indspire Achievement Award, a YWCA Woman of Distinction Award, a B.C. Creative Achievement Award and Lifetime Achievement Award, and a lifetime appointment to the Royal Canadian Academy of Arts, and was named to the *Vancouver Sun*'s 2010 "B.C.'s Top 100 Influential Women" list and the City of Vancouver's 2012 "Remarkable Women" list. Point has honorary doctorates from the University of Victoria, Simon Fraser University, the University of British Columbia, and Emily Carr University of Art and Design. In 2016, Point became a member of the City of Vancouver's Civic Merit Award, and in 2018 she was awarded the Audain Prize for Lifetime Achievement in the Arts, and named Ambassador of the Arts by the Metchosin International Summer School of the Arts.

ROBERT D. WATT, MA, AIH, LVO studied at UBC and Carleton University before working in the Public Archives of Canada, Capilano College, and as the City Archivist for the City of Vancouver. In 1973 he joined the Centennial Museum (now known as the Museum of Vancouver) as the Curator of History. While at the museum Watt developed a deep and enduring interest in the art and cultures of the Indigenous Peoples of the West Coast. In 1977 he worked with Bill Reid on the creation of the Jubilee Goldsmith's Workshop for young Indigenous artists. This interest led to Watt's introduction to the earliest stages of Susan Point's art. He was appointed Director of the Museum in 1980.

In 1988, Watt was appointed the first Chief Herald of Canada. He oversaw the creation of a contemporary and Canadian system of heraldic identification before his retirement in 2007, when then–Governor General Michaëlle Jean appointed him Rideau Herald Emeritus. From 2009 to 2012 he served as Citizenship Judge in the Vancouver office of Citizenship and Immigration Canada.

Watt has received many honours and awards, including the 125th Canadian Confederation Medal and the Queen's Golden and Diamond Jubilee medals. In 2008 he was invested into the Royal Victorian Order by Prince Charles at Buckingham Palace. Currently, Watt serves as President of l'Académie international d'héraldique and Honorary Colonel of the 12th Vancouver Field Ambulance. He lives in North Vancouver with his wife, Alison Jean Watt.

MICHAEL KEW I was born in Quesnel, B.C. in 1932. My ancestors had arrived there in search of gold. I attended all twelve grades of school in one building, graduating in 1949 in a class of twelve students. After graduating from UBC with a BA in anthropology I served for three years as assistant to Wilson Duff at what is now called the Royal B.C. Museum in Victoria, then studied among Métis, Cree, and Chipewyan Peoples in northern Saskatchewan. With a federal grant I did a doctoral degree in anthropology at the University of Washington, supervised by Dr. Simon Ottenberg. I then taught at UBC until my retirement in 1997.

However, my knowledge of anthropology really began when I married Della Charles of Musqueam and became another in-married member of that hәn̓q̓әmin̓әm̓ Salish community. For my small understanding of their way of life, I am immeasurably indebted to my late wife, her kin, and all the Musqueam people and their interconnected villages, who have so kindly shared their knowledge with me. It has been immensely rewarding, as an "uncle" and anthropologist, to watch Susan build upon her family's teachings to take the rich traditions of her cultural heritage into new domains.